Praise for *My Secret Brexit Diary*

'If the treaties are the legal texts of the Brexit talks then this is the human version, revealing a Michel Barnier who is much warmer and far less diplomatic than his public persona. It's a masterclass in how the EU operates, and a rare glimpse into the tensions on their side.'
– Adam Fleming, Chief Political Correspondent, BBC News

'For historians writing about the UK's long and painful exit from the European Union, Michel Barnier's account is essential reading. For anyone interested in Brexit, it offers a valuable guide to the EU's negotiating strategy and the people who shaped it.'
– Jennifer Rankin, Brussels Correspondent, *The Guardian*

'This is a political thriller: 500 pages of twists and turns, advances and setbacks, taking place behind the scenes in an altogether extraordinary negotiation.'
– Nicolas Demorand, *France Inter*

'The former European chief negotiator has delivered his Brexit novel: a unique experience of four and a half years recounted day by day, in the theatre of the powerful with its noble aims and petty squabbles, its backtracking and its bluffs, its laughter and its tears, including very personal ones. And it's absolutely riveting.'
– Mathieu Laine, *Les Échos*

'How did the European Union deal with the challenge of losing a leading member state? In this unique insider's account, the EU's chief negotiator reflects on the Brexit process, how it unfolded and how he managed the EU's approach to the talks. Required reading for everyone interested in figuring out what happened and why.'
– Anand Menon, King's College, London

'This book is required reading for anyone seriously interested in the exhausting saga of the Brexit negotiations, and it is good to have an English edition of what is undoubtedly an important historical document.'
– Robert Tombs, University of Cambridge

My Secret Brexit Diary

Barnier

MY SECRET
BREXIT DIARY

A Glorious Illusion

Translated by Robin Mackay

polity

Originally published in French as *La Grande Illusion. Journal secret du Brexit (2016–2020)*
© Éditions GALLIMARD, Paris, 2021

This English edition © Polity Press, 2021

Illustration 12 source: Ingram Pinn, 2018, 'Taking Back Control', *Financial Times* /
FT.com. 27 July 2018. Used under licence from the *Financial Times*. All Rights Reserved.

Polity Press
65 Bridge Street
Cambridge CB2 1UR, UK

Polity Press
101 Station Landing
Suite 300
Medford, MA 02155, USA

ISBN-13: 978-1-5095-5086-9 (hardback)

A catalogue record for this book is available from the British Library.

Library of Congress Control Number: 2021943873

Typeset in 11.5 on 14pt Adobe Garamond
by Fakenham Prepress Solutions, Fakenham, Norfolk NR21 8NL
Printed in Great Britain by CPI Group (UK) Ltd, Croydon

The publisher has used its best endeavours to ensure that the URLs for external websites
referred to in this book are correct and active at the time of going to press. However, the
publisher has no responsibility for the websites and can make no guarantee that a site will
remain live or that the content is or will remain appropriate.

Every effort has been made to trace all copyright holders, but if any have been overlooked
the publisher will be pleased to include any necessary credits in any subsequent reprint or
edition.

For further information on Polity, visit our website:
politybooks.com

To Oriana and Theodore, both born during this long negotiation, who kindly shared their grandfather with the British

Beat at this gate that let thy folly in,
And thy dear judgement out!

Shakespeare, *King Lear*

La Grande Illusion is a wonderful film by Jean Renoir, released in 1937. It is also the title of an essay by Norman Angell (*The Great Illusion: A Study of the Relation of Military Power in Nations to their Economic and Social Advantage*), published in 1910, in which the English author argued that, given the economic and financial bonds uniting the European nations with one another, war had become an impossibility. Although this prediction turned out to be wrong, in his book Angell clearly shows that war is a process of mutual depletion in which there is no winner.

Contents

Illustrations

1. The first lie of the Brexit campaign: in May 2016, Boris Johnson alleges that the £350 million per week relinquished by Brussels would be used to fund the NHS instead. © Darren Staples/Reuters
2. A hateful conflation from Nigel Farage in June 2016, which intentionally misattributes the cause of the flow of Middle Eastern refugees to freedom of movement within the EU. © Daniel Leal-Olivas/Stringer/Getty Images
3. Thyborøn, Denmark, 21 April 2017, a trip out to sea in minus 22 degrees Celsius, to listen to fishermen who work in British waters. © Henning Bagger/Denmark OUT/AFP/Getty Images
4. 12 May 2017, on the yellow line that divides Northern Ireland and the Republic of Ireland, or the 'invisible border' between the EU and the UK. © Michel Barnier
5. With Brian Burgess, an Irish farmer, and his 'European cows', several metres from the Northern Irish border. © Michel Barnier
6. Patrick Blower, *Telegraph*, 19 June 2017. © Garland/Telegraph Media Group Limited 2021
7. My two deputies, Sabine Weyand and Stéphanie Riso, and I received David Davis, Tim Barrow and Olly Robbins on 17 July 2017 – they had left their papers behind! © Thierry Charlier/Reuters
8. At Berlaymont, seat of the European Commission, a convivial moment on my birthday with my whole team, 9 January 2018. © Michel Barnier
9. In May 2018, at the Derry/Londonderry Guildhall. A spontaneous discussion with Northern Irish school pupils. © Michel Barnier
10. For four years, we visited a new capital city each week in order to meet their nation's government, the national parliament, trade unions or businesses. Here we are in Lisbon with Prime Minister Antonio Costa, 26 May 2018. © Michel Barnier
11. A frank and direct discussion with the Hungarian Prime Minister

Viktor Orbán in his office in Parliament in Budapest, 4 June 2018. When it comes to Brexit, he always supported the EU. © Government of Hungary. Photographer: Balázs Szecsődi.

12. Ingram Pinn, *Financial Times*, 27 July 2018. © Financial Times

13. Christian Adams, *Evening Standard*, 4 March 2019. © Christian Adams/Evening Standard

14. Jean-Claude Juncker and I meet Theresa May in Strasbourg. Demanding negotiations don't preclude courteous manners! © Alex Kraus/Bloomberg/Getty Images

15. Meeting of the Brexit Steering Group at the European Parliament, chaired by the Belgian Prime Minister Guy Verhofstadt. European unity is founded on transparency and trust. © EU/Étienne Ansotte, 2019

16. Teatime! The role of Leo Varadkar, the Irish Taoiseach, was decisive throughout the negotiations. Photo taken 8 April 2019 in Dublin. © Charles McQuillan/Stringer/Getty Images

17. No one, not even Nigel Farage, ever convinced me of the added value of Brexit. Here we are in Strasbourg at the European Parliament, where we had many tussles during the plenary session. © EU/Étienne Ansotte, 2019

18. Andy Davey, *Evening Standard*, 16 September 2019. © Andy Davey/Evening Standard

19. 17 October 2019, in the early hours. After three years of effort, we had reached an agreement with Boris Johnson and his negotiator Stephen Barclay on the UK's exit from the EU. © EU/Jacqueline Jacquemart, 2019

20. During this long journey, I felt the need to return to Savoie, my 'homeland' and the place where my roots lie. © Michel Barnier

21. 28 January 2020, with my two new deputies, Clara Martínez Alberola and Paulina Dejmek Hack. The task force takes up anew the reins of negotiation over our future relationship. © Michel Barnier

22. At the Élysée with Emmanuel Macron on 31 January 2020, the day of the UK's exit from the EU. © Ludovic Marin/AFP/Getty Images

23. Patrick Blower, *Telegraph*, 3 March 2020. © Garland/Telegraph Media Group Limited 2021

24. In Brussels on 29 June 2020. One of the official negotiation sessions

between the British and the Europeans. © John Thys/AP/SIPA/ Getty Images

25. Peter Brookes, *The Times*, 18 September 2020. © The Times/News Licensing

26. In Berlin on 12 October 2020, with Chancellor Angela Merkel. We were both environment ministers for our respective countries in 1994. In her words: 'Europe's future is more important than Brexit.' © Bundesregierung/Steffen Kugler

27. In London, 27 October 2020. En route between our hotel and the conference centre where the negotiations were taking place; remaining anonymous was not easy. © Michel Barnier

28. In the basement of the conference centre in London, in the room we were assigned by the British. Our teams worked here, night and day, for weeks. © Michel Barnier

29. 10 December 2020, fifteen days away from a deal which at that point still seemed unlikely. PM Boris Johnson and David Frost were in Brussels for a business dinner with the President of the European Commission, Ursula von der Leyen. © EU/Etienne Ansotte, 2020

30. In the late hours of 23 December 2020, my adviser Matthieu Hébert and I prepare the speech for my last press conference. © Michel Barnier

31. Elena Mongiorgi, *Lacrima Europa*, January 2020. © Elena Mongiorgi

The Main Players

For the UK

David Cameron – Prime Minister from May 2010 to July 2016. In January 2013 he committed himself to holding a referendum on his country's membership of the EU.

Theresa May – Prime Minister from July 2016 to July 2019. It was under her leadership that the majority of the UK's negotiations on the country's withdrawal from the EU and the framework for a future relationship were conducted. However, the Withdrawal Agreement reached with her on 14 November 2018 was never ratified by the House of Commons.

Boris Johnson – Leading figure in the Brexit campaign and Prime Minister of the UK since July 2019. It was under his leadership that the final version of the Withdrawal Agreement and the Trade and Cooperation Agreement on the future relationship between the EU and the UK were agreed upon.

David Davis – Secretary of State for Exiting the European Union from July 2016 to July 2018. The first of four successive negotiators on the UK side. Resigned on 8 July 2018.

Dominic Raab – Secretary of State for Exiting the European Union from July to November 2018. The second UK Brexit negotiator. Resigned on 15 November 2018.

Steve Barclay – Secretary of State for Exiting the European Union from November 2018 to January 2020. The third UK Brexit negotiator. His post was abolished on 31 January 2020 when the UK left the EU.

Olly Robbins – Europe Adviser to Prime Minister Theresa May. The UK's permanent negotiator and the EU team's principal interlocutor throughout the negotiations on the UK's withdrawal until Boris Johnson took over in July 2019.

David Frost – Europe Adviser to Prime Minister Boris Johnson, succeeding Olly Robbins in the role. On 31 January 2020, the day the

UK left the EU, he was appointed head of the newly formed Task Force Europe, leading the UK's negotiating team during discussions on the future relationship.

Michael Gove – Leading figure in the Brexit campaign and minister of state in Boris Johnson's government, responsible for the implementation of the Withdrawal Agreement and the Protocol on Ireland and Northern Ireland.

Dominic Cummings – Leave campaigner and supporter of hard Brexit. Chief adviser to Boris Johnson when he took office as Prime Minister. Left Downing Street abruptly on 13 November 2020.

Tim Barrow – The UK's Permanent Representative to the EU, part of the British negotiating team for four years.

For the EU

Jean-Claude Juncker – President of the European Commission from November 2014 to November 2019. It was under the authority of this Luxembourgish politician that the Withdrawal Agreement and the Political Declaration setting out the framework for the future relationship between the UK and the EU were negotiated.

Ursula von der Leyen – President of the European Commission since December 2019, of German nationality. It was under her authority that the Trade and Cooperation Agreement with the UK was negotiated.

Donald Tusk – President of the European Council from December 2014 to November 2019, a Polish national. Led many of the discussions on Brexit between the EU's other twenty-seven heads of state or government.

Charles Michel – President of the European Council since December 2019, a Belgian national. Presided over discussions between the twenty-seven heads of state or government on the future relationship between the UK and the EU.

Martin Schulz, **Antonio Tajani**, and **David Sassoli** – Successive presidents of the European Parliament from 2014 to 2021.

Guy Verhofstadt – Belgian MEP. Followed the negotiations closely on behalf of the European Parliament as chairman of the Brexit Steering Group.

Martin Selmayr – Senior European civil servant, of German nationality.

Followed the negotiations with the UK very closely as Head of Cabinet to Jean-Claude Juncker and subsequently as Secretary-General of the European Commission until August 2019.

David McAllister – MEP, of German nationality. Chaired the European Parliament's UK Coordination Group during the second round of negotiations.

Sabine Weyand – Senior European civil servant, of German nationality. Deputy Chief Negotiator for Brexit until May 2019, when she became Director-General for Trade at the European Commission.

Stéphanie Riso – Senior European civil servant, of French nationality. Director of the task force in charge of negotiations until September 2019, when she became Deputy Head of Cabinet to European Commission President Ursula von der Leyen.

Clara Martínez Alberola – Senior European civil servant, of Spanish nationality. Became EU Deputy Chief Negotiator for Brexit in January 2020. Previously Head of Cabinet to European Commission President Jean-Claude Juncker.

Paulina Dejmek Hack – Senior EU official, of dual Swedish and Czech nationality. Became director of the negotiating task force in 2019. Previously an adviser in the cabinet of European Commission President Jean-Claude Juncker.

Maroš Šefčovič – Slovak Vice-President of the European Commission. Responsible for the implementation of the Withdrawal Agreement and the Protocol on Ireland and Northern Ireland.

A Warning

'I don't like this Michel Barnier.' So, that's settled then!

In a lengthy profile published by *Le Monde* in 2018, the great British photojournalist Sir Donald McCullin explains why he voted for Brexit.* The child of a poor family, born in London's Finsbury Park, in March 2017 McCullin was awarded a knighthood. 'We didn't join Europe to be strangulated, to have our sovereignty destroyed… We joined the EU for economic reasons, and for defence and security, not to be told by Brussels what I'm allowed to put in my bin.'

This fear of having pedantic regulations imposed by Brussels, regarding environmental standards for example, is nothing new. Already in 1987, Gordon Cartwright, a character from the novel *The Commissioner*, gin and tonic in hand, proclaimed: '[W]e have to clip the wings of those bureaucrats in Brussels. Clip their wings, keep them under control, don't you agree? Fair trade and competition is one thing, but bloody-minded interference is something else altogether.'

The author of this novel, published by Arrow, is a certain … Stanley Johnson, who worked at the European Commission during the 1980s, and expressed in his book the exasperation created at the time by regulatory zeal and the desire of certain Brussels technocrats to take everything in hand and fix it all perfectly.

I took the time to read Johnson's book as part of my 'research' into the reasons that drove his son Boris, along with 17,410,742 other British citizens, to vote to leave the European Union.

So can we explain the vote as a rejection of a Europe that meddles in waste sorting and imposes too many environmental constraints 'from above'?

Quite apart from the fact that the Europe of today is far more pragmatic and efficient than that of the 1980s, there are obviously other reasons, some of which are specific to the United Kingdom.

* *Le Monde*, 17 August 2018, 'Sir Donald McCullin en son pays'.

First of all, the feeling, to quote Sir Donald again, that 'continental Europe is another world, of which England is not a part'. Europe is too different from the UK. This island country, facing out toward the 'open sea', draws from its glorious past the idea that it is better to stand alone.

And then there are other reasons related to the British political system, which is strongly bipartisan, preventing the concerns of many political groups and citizens from being properly represented in the capital. It is quite natural, then, that they should see a referendum or a European Election as an opportunity to express themselves.

Finally, the UK is home to a tabloid empire that makes it its daily business to denigrate the EU with simplistic arguments and false stories. The 2016 referendum campaign was fuelled by these caricatures and untruths. For example, as soon as the result was declared, the Leave campaign acknowledged that leaving the EU would not in fact enable £350 million a week to flow back into the NHS, the UK's health system, as promised on their famous red bus. Similarly, the image of UKIP leader Nigel Farage posing in front of a billboard depicting crowds of migrants from Syria and elsewhere on the march deserves to be remembered as the apex of cynicism and a clouding of the issues, calling to mind the outrageous propaganda caricatures of another era.

But let's face it, such shortcomings in the public debate on Europe are not the preserve of the British alone. There are also far too many EU politicians who keep a low profile, are ashamed of Europe, make no attempt to explain anything, and fail to take responsibility. I have long been convinced that it is the silence, the arrogance and the remoteness of European elites that fuels fear and encourages demagogy.

And then there is a final, even more serious reason, which is at work in all our countries, and certainly in many regions of France. It is the feeling that Europe, its governments and its institutions, are out of touch with the legitimate concerns of the people; discontent with a Europe that does nothing to protect against the excesses of globalization, a Europe that has for too long advocated deregulation and ultra-liberalism, with insufficient regard for the social and environmental consequences.

The financial crisis of 2008 very nearly brought it all down. The crisis was the result of a caricature of liberalism and a notion of 'pure' or 'perfect' competition to which first London, and then Europe, had ended up conforming. It wrenched open great fault lines of poverty, exclusion and despair, which also go some way towards explaining the anti-European sentiment found in the UK and elsewhere.

This anger is also being expressed against a Europe that has not been able to control its external borders or convincingly demonstrate its solidarity. A Europe that has not been able to protect its industry, nor anticipate the digital revolution that is now intruding upon all aspects of our lives. A Europe seen as overly complex and insufficiently democratic. And above all, to put it bluntly, a Europe that no longer offers any promise of progress or any hope of a better future for all.

What was, and remains, the raison d'être of the European project? Since the 1950s, Europe has above all stood for the choice to face up to the great changes afoot in the world and to come to terms with them rather than just passively suffering them. To be the actor of its own destiny rather than a spectator. To assert a shared sovereignty, in an era when the nation alone is no longer enough. And finally, to pool resources on a continental scale in order to yield common benefits and to pursue projects that are larger than any one country.

The ECSC, the European Coal and Steel Community, formally established in 1951 in the wake of a war that left our continent in ruins, initiated the industrial reconstruction of Europe and, through this 'de facto solidarity', promoted a lasting peace between our nations.

The CAP, the Common Agricultural Policy, launched in 1962, enabled us to regain our collective food sovereignty and to preserve the diversity of territories, traceability and product quality.

The cohesion policy, developed from 1988 onwards under the impetus of Jacques Delors, has enabled the most disadvantaged regions progressively to catch up as our Union has expanded.

The transition from a set of national markets to a single market, in 1993, promoted the development of our companies, in particular SMEs and MSBs, while offering consumers more choice.

And since 1999, the single currency has facilitated trade between the countries that adopted it and shielded us from exchange rate risk. As is too often forgotten, the euro is also an instrument of emancipation, protecting us from American monetary hegemony. During the recent crises – the sovereign debt crisis, and then the current health crisis – it is the euro and the European Central Bank's monetary policy that have saved us from the precipice.

All these shared benefits are something to be proud of! And we can also be proud of the fact that we have reinforced and shared them over time, especially since 1 May 2004, when Poland and nine other countries joined the EU in that great moment of reunification of the European continent. In fifteen years, we have welcomed – and it was no easy task! – more than a hundred million new European citizens who left poverty and dictatorship for the promise of shared progress. What other group of nations, what other continent, has achieved so much collectively? None.

But, for the past fifteen years at least, Europe has failed to mobilize Europeans around collective projects that respond to the great transformations afoot in the world. Transformations in the face of which our nations, alone, can do little: climate change and pandemic, industrial and technological change, the challenges of migration and of the invisible powers of financial markets and terrorism, the unilateralist temptation in the US, the rise of China and the influence of Russia.

If we really want to take on these challenges, then we must rediscover the ambition that first led to the construction of Europe, and begin building new common goods for the twenty-seven member countries. To be fair, the Commission has embarked upon some valuable initiatives in recent years. For the protection of our environment via the European Green Deal, for an industrial policy fit for the challenges of digital technology, artificial intelligence and sustainable energy, for a genuine European defence force, and for control of our external borders. And for continued control, via supervision, regulation and greater transparency, of the power of the financial markets and the new giants of the digital economy. We owe all of this to the generations to come. What we ourselves do not do for Europe, no one else will do for us.

Some time ago, on a train, I met Mark, a British professor who works in Amsterdam on European space policy. He summed up his misgivings about Brexit in a single sentence, eight words full of dreams and regrets: 'Only together can we explore the Solar System.'

What is true for the Solar System is also true for other challenges. In the coming world, a world of increasingly powerful and uprooted continent-states and multinationals, no country in the European Union, whether the smallest or the largest, stands the slightest chance of safeguarding its sovereignty without combining it with that of its neighbours.

It is our duty to be clearsighted about this. Today, in the twenty-first century, where do the risks of servitude lie and how can we protect ourselves from them? The great illusion consists in the idea that we can face alone the often brutal transformations our world is going through. That we can stand alone against new political, economic and financial giants. And in believing in the promise of solitary identities and sovereignties, rather than in solidarity.

On the other hand, though, we can never meet these challenges if the European Union insists on conducting its business from Brussels, at odds with the identities and the sovereignty of the peoples that make it up.

We are not a European people. We do not want to be a European nation. Right now, we are twenty-seven separate populations, speaking twenty-four official languages. We are twenty-seven nations and we have twenty-seven states, each of which holds on to its differences, its traditions, and its culture.

People have their reasons, no doubt. And the feelings they express must be listened to and respected. I have never confused popular sentiment with populism.

I understand and I share every person's special attachment to their country, to their homeland. But this rootedness can and must go hand-in-hand with a commitment to Europe.

Throughout my life I have had a certain idea of Europe. This idea has never replaced or weakened my pride in being French, or diminished the strength of my patriotism. 'A patriot and a European' – this is the best summary of my political position and my fundamental convictions.

We all have our regrets and our dreams. What I am certain of is that every citizen is needed. Each and every one of us has a role to play in maintaining the European dream alongside our national dream.

At the end of this long negotiation, it was this same message I chose to convey when, at the beginning of 2021, I was invited to speak by European Movement Ireland: '*Ní neart go cur le chéile.*'*

The European Union will never be a panacea for all ills. It cannot

---

* In Gaelic: 'No strength without unity.'

and must not be. Indeed, it is quite right for it to take a back seat when the burden of its standards threatens to stifle local initiative or inflame national resentments.

But by working together at all levels, we can build a Europe that protects and inspires us. A Europe that Europeans will not want to leave. A Europe that allows us once more to be stronger together in the world. We have to approach this world with our eyes open, without nostalgia for past glories. It is a world which will only become safer if it becomes fairer.

It's very late in the day. But it's not too late.

My vote is cast!

A referendum was being held – a different referendum – and this was my very first vote as a young French citizen… Early in the morning of 23 April 1972, in a town hall in Val des Roses, Albertville, a place so familiar to me.

Once a church, the hall had now been claimed for more republican purposes: it frequently hosted public meetings and, on election days, this was where the polling station was set up.

On that particular day, the question submitted to the French people by President of the Republic Georges Pompidou was a simple one: 'Do you agree with the new opportunities opening up in Europe, the draft law submitted to the French people by the President of the Republic, and authorizing the ratification of the Treaty concerning the accession of the United Kingdom, Denmark, Ireland and Norway to the European Communities?'

For the Gaullist party, the answer to this question was not so obvious. Some years earlier, in 1963 and then again in 1967, General de Gaulle had vetoed the accession of the United Kingdom. But times had changed and so had the French president, and a young Gaullist activist like myself had no qualms about answering 'yes' to the question.

Moreover, this was the first time citizens of my country had been directly consulted on the European project. I remember well how the question divided socialist leaders, and in particular how Georges Pompidou, who had established a constructive relationship with Edward Heath, the British Prime Minister at the time, was able to use the referendum as a way to gracefully move on from his illustrious predecessor's double veto.

I have never regretted the vote I cast that day.

Origins of the Referendum

Wednesday, 23 January 2013. David Cameron, aged 46, had been the UK's Conservative Prime Minister since 2010. His party had formed the country's first post-war coalition government together with the Liberal Democrats. Their policy of austerity, implemented with great zeal, had succeeded in easing pressure on public finances. Growth was gradually returning. But the government now found itself faced with the rise of the anti-immigration and Eurosceptic UK Independence Party (UKIP).

It was on this day, in a speech given at the financial news agency Bloomberg, that the Prime Minister chose to talk about his country's future within the European Union. He began by recalling the very particular position of the British within the Union:

> We have the character of an island nation: independent, outspoken, passionate in defending our sovereignty.
>
> We can no more change that British sensibility than we can drain the English Channel.
>
> And because of that sensibility, we come to the European Union with a frame of mind that is more practical than emotional.
>
> For us, the European Union is a means to an end – prosperity, stability, the anchor of freedom and democracy both within Europe and beyond her shores – not an end in itself.*

Cameron went on to enumerate three major challenges facing the EU: the Eurozone crisis, the competitiveness challenge and the gap between the EU and its citizens. 'If we don't address these challenges', he warned, 'the danger is that Europe will fail and the British people will drift towards the exit.'

* https://www.gov.uk/government/speeches/eu-speech-at-bloomberg.

The Prime Minister maintained that he did not want this to happen, and set out the way forward for a competitive, flexible and fair Europe in which power would flow back to member states and the Union would be accountable to the people. He then proposed a referendum on his country's membership of the Union – to be held not immediately, but once an attempt had been made to reset the relationship with a 'new settlement' between the EU and the UK.

Much has been written about the timing of and the reasons behind this announcement, which helped reassure voters who may have been tempted by Nigel Farage's UKIP, thus putting David Cameron on track for a second term in office, which he would go on to win in 2015.

In any case, with David Cameron re-elected as Prime Minister, the European Commission wasted no time in setting up its first task force, under the supervision of British Director-General Jonathan Faull, to deal with 'strategic issues related to the UK referendum'.

On 19 February 2016, discussions with the UK brought to fruition Cameron's 'new settlement', addressing the concerns he had expressed three years earlier, in particular by acknowledging that the UK would not be bound by the objective of an 'ever closer union among the peoples of Europe'.

On the subject of the free movement of persons, the UK gained the right to limit access to social benefits for newly arrived workers from other member states for up to four years. It also gained the option to index child benefit for parents working in the UK, but whose children have remained in their country of origin, to the standard of living in their country of origin.

We all know what came next. These measures, aside from being questionable from the point of view of social justice, would not prevent the British from deciding, after all, to leave the European Union.

DIARY

2016

Friday, 24 June 2016: A rude awakening

This early summer morning began with a rude awakening for all Europeans. We went to our beds last night certain that the British had voted to remain in the European Union. All initial commentaries suggested this was the case. Even Nigel Farage, one of the most ardent Leave campaigners, seemed to have conceded defeat.

Now, this morning, everyone is stunned. The precise counting of votes is finished. Fifty-two per cent of the British public who voted have chosen to leave the EU!

It's an earthquake. For the first time, an EU country has decided to leave.

By chance, I have an appointment this morning with François Hollande at the Élysée Palace. He is as shocked as I am. A profound geopolitical change is imminent in Europe. For the French President as for the German Chancellor – for all of us – this is a wake-up call, a collective failure from which we must try to draw some lessons.

Sunday, 26 June 2016: Three British divides

Now that the shock has subsided, the analysis begins.

In reality, Thursday's vote reveals a threefold divide within British society.

First of all, a geographical divide. England and Wales may have voted to leave the EU, but the Remain camp accounted for 62 per cent of voters in Greater London and Scotland, and 56 per cent in Northern Ireland. Poring over this map of a 'Disunited Kingdom', I also note with interest the position of the great industrial working-class cities affected by the decline of industry, whose Leave vote can in part be understood as a rejection of the Prime Minister's austerity policy.

Second, a very clear social divide between graduates and well-off workers, who voted to remain in the Union, and the working poor and the unemployed, many of whom voted Leave as a symbol of their rejection of a Europe they associate with globalization, and in particular with the arrival of workers from Eastern Europe, who they accuse of stealing jobs and driving down wages.

Finally, there is also a generational divide behind this result, a divide between young people, who see their future as being within the EU – more than 70 per cent of 18–24-year-olds voted to remain – and older people, the majority of whom voted to leave. In this generational battle, the older cohort had a significant weapon at its disposal: participation. In all, 83 per cent of over-65s cast their vote, compared with only one in three young people.

Thursday, 7 July 2016: On the plane with Jean-Claude Juncker

Jean-Claude Juncker lands in Warsaw this afternoon to participate in the NATO summit and to sign a cooperation protocol between the EU and the North Atlantic Alliance alongside Donald Tusk, President of the European Council.

For the past ten months, at the Commission President's request, I have been his special adviser on defence and security policy. These are issues that have always been of interest to me; indeed, in 2002 I chaired the European Convention's Working Group on Defence. My group's suggestions at the time for strengthening defence cooperation within the EU have now been incorporated into the Treaty. It's all in there: a stronger role for the High Representative for Foreign Affairs and Security Policy, a European Defence Agency, the solidarity clause and the possibility for a group of countries to set out as 'pathfinders' by way of 'structured cooperation'.

Aside from my interest in the subject, Jean-Claude Juncker's proposal that I should work alongside him was rather touching since, only two years earlier at the EPP [European People's Party] congress, we had competed as nominees to become the centre-right European election candidate and, ultimately, to stand for President of the European Commission. He won, with the decisive support of the CDU/CSU [German Christian Democratic Union/Christian Social Union parliamentary party]. I lost, but honourably so, having received a respectable 40 per cent of the votes cast.

So here I am on this sunny afternoon, on the plane to Warsaw with the President of the Commission. He has kindly invited me to join him tomorrow for a private meeting with President Obama and several members of his cabinet.

Suddenly, President Juncker turns to me, gestures to his young diplomatic adviser Richard Szostak not to listen, and says: 'Michel, I have a sensitive matter to discuss with you. Would you consider returning to the Commission in a permanent position, to lead negotiations with the United Kingdom following its decision to leave the European Union?' Naturally, I am taken aback by the question. To tell the truth, the day after the British Brexit vote, my mind had been more on how I could make myself useful in my own country, during what looked likely to be both a historic and a perilous period.

For fifteen years now, at various times and in various different capacities, I have had to deal with the major issues that will lie at the heart of the Brexit negotiations: first as Commissioner for Regional Policy and Constitutional Affairs from 1999 to 2004, then a little later in 2008 as President of the European Agricultural and Fisheries Council – but above all from 2010 to 2014 as European Commissioner for Internal Market and Services.

My answer to Jean-Claude Juncker is therefore unhesitating and positive. 'I have to check how the idea will go down in certain quarters', he adds with a smile. 'Don't mention anything, we'll talk again soon…'

That evening, we have a beer together in the hotel restaurant while watching the European Cup semi-final between France and Germany. France wins 2–0. What a day!

Wednesday, 13 July 2016: Enter Theresa May

Following a fortnight of political upheaval, Theresa May enters 10 Downing Street as David Cameron's successor. The daughter of a vicar, like Angela Merkel she has the reputation of being a tenacious and determined woman. Equipped with experience gained as Home Secretary in David Cameron's government, Mrs May is, after Margaret Thatcher, the UK's second female Prime Minister. Like the 'Iron Lady', as a minister she had no qualms about taking very tough positions, openly admitting that she wanted to create a 'hostile environment' to discourage illegal immigration, for instance. She also advocated the UK's withdrawal from the European Convention on Human Rights. During the referendum campaign she paid lip service to Remain, while leaving room for ambiguity. The new Prime Minister now says that she intends to 'make a success of Brexit'. She declares herself in favour of a clean break: 'There must be no attempts to remain inside the EU, no attempts to rejoin it through the back door, and no second referendum.'

The government is expanded with the introduction of a new portfolio: Secretary of State for Exiting the European Union. The position is given to David Davis, a staunch Conservative whom I know, as he was my counterpart as Minister of State for Europe between 1995 and 1997. At the time, we were both members of the Westendorp Group responsible for drafting the Treaty of Amsterdam. There is a larger-than-life side to David, a heartiness even – a sign of great self-confidence. Since working together, he has become a staunch Eurosceptic and an advocate of a 'hard' Brexit. It seems this will be a hard-fought game.

Theresa May appears to be well aware of the challenge that lies ahead: '[O]ur country needs strong, proven leadership – to steer us through this period of economic and political uncertainty, and to negotiate the best possible terms as we leave the European Union.' 'We will forge a bold new positive role for ourselves in the world.'

Wednesday, 27 July 2016: Provocation?

At the most recent meeting of the College of European Commissioners, before the August break, Jean-Claude Juncker proposed my nomination. In the twenty days since then, there have been no leaks. President Juncker has secured the support of Angela Merkel, François Hollande and Donald Tusk. In a press release today, the European Commission finally announces the name of its 'Chief Negotiator' in the discussions that must follow with the United Kingdom.

The President carefully clarifies a few points regarding internal organization: 'Michel will have access to all Commission resources necessary to perform his tasks. He will report directly to me, and I will invite him to brief the College on a regular basis so as to keep my team abreast of the negotiations. I am sure that he will live up to this new challenge and help us to develop a new partnership with the United Kingdom after it has left the European Union.'

The announcement is widely reported in the media. The Commission has thrown its support behind a man of politics, a former European Commissioner, and has stated its intention to stand alongside him and play its part. And, of course, to work with the member states of the Union and the Council, on the one hand, and the European Parliament, on the other.

On the other side of the Channel, the news is greeted with great surprise. And, as always, the tabloids and the conservative media, which had already dubbed me 'the most dangerous man in Europe' when I was appointed as Commissioner for Financial Regulation, are having a field day. Even the *Independent* opines that 'Mr Barnier's appointment looks like a provocative act by Jean-Claude Juncker'.

Monday, 8 August 2016: First names

From the terrace of a Sicilian villa where I am spending a few days' holiday with my wife Isabelle and a few friends, I begin to put together my team.

I need one or two competent deputies who command respect in all departments of the Commission. My former Head of Cabinet Olivier Guersent recommends a young French woman, Stéphanie Riso, an economist who has worked in several Commissioners' cabinets on monetary and budgetary issues. I call her and she gives me an agreement in principle. She is a lively and direct woman who doesn't mince her words, and who will be particularly useful in helping me negotiate the explosive issue of the financial settlement with the British.

I have no intention of putting together an entirely French team, of course. We will meet on 31 August in Brussels to get organized. Georg Riekeles, whom I called during the summer, will also join us. Georg is as loyal as they come, and I had immediately asked him to accompany me in this new project.

Wednesday, 31 August 2016: Trio

Stéphanie, Georg and I prepare for my scheduled meeting later this afternoon with Jean-Claude Juncker's Head of Cabinet, Martin Selmayr. It's clear what is required here: we must be as proactive as possible, otherwise the structure and personnel of my team will end up being imposed 'from above'.

First priority: to appoint my deputy. We draw up a shortlist, at the top of which is a senior European civil servant of German nationality, well known and well respected, a former adviser to Pascal Lamy, and with whom I worked a great deal during my first term as a Commissioner from 1999 to 2004: Sabine Weyand. Sabine has recently been appointed Deputy Director-General for Trade.

At 5.30pm I head up to 'the thirteenth', the presidential floor of the Berlaymont building, to meet with Martin Selmayr. With me I have a few initial slides outlining the major issues of the negotiations, the mandate of the task force and its structure. The meeting is brisk and straightforward. I make a point of mentioning Sabine's name in connection with the post of deputy. Mr Selmayr's response is unhesitating: 'Good thinking. But she won't be coming. She's too useful where she is.'

In spite of this refusal, I call Sabine in the evening and she tells me that, naturally, she is attracted by the unusual prospect of the Brexit assignment. I inform her of Martin Selmayr's reservations and ask her to make good use of her network. I will have Mr Selmayr on the line several times over the next few days, and finally, at the beginning of September, he will agree to let me recruit this brilliant woman, as adept politically as she is technically.

Thus a trio is swiftly formed at the head of my team. I will have alongside me these two strong women, not at all alike, with different but complementary personalities and convictions, both of whom command great respect. Sabine will be my deputy and Stéphanie will be our Director of Strategy, in charge of legal and budgetary affairs and relations with other institutions and with the European Parliament. The immediate signal sent both within and outside the Commission will be that a professional and highly competent team is in place here.

Sunday, 2 October 2016: Birmingham – Theresa May in the spotlight

It's all happening!

The day after I took office, Theresa May speaks at the Conservative Party conference in Birmingham, unveiling some of her strategy and offering pledges to the most hard-line Brexit supporters.

The Prime Minister emphasizes her vision for the future relationship between the EU and the UK, calling for a free trade agreement with sector-specific provisions. This strategy may help the UK to keep open lines of communication with British citizens who have expressed their desire for the UK to regain full sovereignty over future legislation, to have powers to limit immigration, and to form new trade alliances.

As far as the EU is concerned, it would allow the integrity of the internal market and the four fundamental freedoms associated with it to be respected, while maintaining trade relations and close cooperation in certain sectors.

But let's not be naive: this negotiation cannot end up providing à la carte access to the internal market without any of the associated obligations, particularly in terms of the free movement of persons. On this we shall be vigilant!

Finally, the Prime Minister makes an important announcement: she clarifies that the UK will activate Article 50 of the Treaty of Lisbon before the end of March 2017, thereby triggering the two-year process of withdrawal of a member state from the European Union: 'There was a good reason why I said – immediately after the referendum – that we should not invoke Article 50 before the end of this year. That decision means we have the time to develop our negotiating strategy.'

As the President of the European Council Donald Tusk remarks in the aftermath of May's speech, this announcement does indeed bring 'welcome clarity on the start of Brexit talks'.

Monday, 3 October 2016: Getting started

Task Force 50 is open for business.*

For the moment, we are a small team.

Sabine Weyand, Stéphanie Riso and I have each chosen an assistant to help us with all the preparation, organization and planning.

At my side is Barthélemy Piche, a young elected representative from Savoie, who up until now has worked as a parliamentary assistant in the Senate. Justyna Lasik, a young and extremely dynamic and efficient

---

* So called in reference to Article 50 of the Treaty on European Union, which provides for the withdrawal of a member state.

Polish woman who successfully participated in the trade negotiations with Japan, will assist Sabine Weyand, while Stéphanie Riso will be joined by Marco Abate, who also has a great deal of experience, a good sense of humour – and a talent for telling anecdotes, which is no bad thing.

Of course, the indispensable Isabelle Misrachi will join us to strengthen our team. She has been with me since 1999, when I became European Commissioner for Regional Policy. Alternately assistant and head of my secretariat, she has amply proved her extraordinary tenacity, determination and organizational skills.

Georg Riekeles will be in charge of relations with the twenty-seven EU countries and the European Parliament, in his capacity as diplomatic adviser. Georg and I have been working together for almost fifteen years. In 2004 he was an international student at Sciences Po in Paris, and approached me at the end of a conference on European defence. He joined my team at the Quai d'Orsay as a young policy officer. He is Norwegian, and therefore a native of a country that is not a member of the EU. I have full confidence in him: ever creative and curious about people and ideas, this Nordic man, married to a Mediterranean, brings a different perspective and knows the UK well, having studied there as well as in Paris.

Finally, the Director-General of Human Resources, Irene Souka, recommended that I choose a young Belgian woman, Claire Saelens, as my secretary; we immediately struck up a good rapport.

Thanks to the efficiency of the technical services team, by pushing some parts of the Directorate-General for Communication and the Secretariat-General down the corridor, and in some cases even into a different building – for which I was truly sorry – we have come to occupy half of the fifth floor of the Berlaymont building, headquarters of the European Commission.

The open-plan office, with movable partitions, makes for a rather noisy environment. My office is the standard size of a general manager's office. Straight away, I bring in a large oval glass table, which is to be my main tool for the upcoming negotiations. And above all, I hang on the wall a number of photos that are important to me and that immediately create a more familiar atmosphere.

A prized photo of Albertville on 17 October 1986, the day when we were chosen by the International Olympic Committee to host the 1992

Winter Olympics – a beautiful image of young Savoyards carrying their flag aloft, excited at the prospect of the Games to come.

A portrait of Nelson Mandela, on the occasion of our brief meeting on the tenth anniversary of the end of apartheid. And a photograph of the Polish Pope John Paul II, receiving myself, together with Jean-Claude Killy, for a private audience.

Above my head, I place a poster that was given to me long ago by one of the leaders of Poland's Solidarity (Solidarność) movement, Bronisław Geremek. To me this poster is symbolic of the whole European project, an enterprise of reclaimed freedom and reunification.

In this office I bring together for the first time our small team, which is set to expand very quickly. We need to recruit experts to cover every one of the numerous and complex objects of negotiation. Stéphanie, Sabine and I draw up an initial organization chart. For the Commission, this will be both a unique and a complex negotiation. Many are keen to be a part of it, and I am sure we will have no difficulty in putting together the best possible team.

However, from the outset I point out – and will repeat to every new team member – that we must be 'amicable pros'. Making sure we are professional and competent is the least we can do to honour such a historic and serious task. But being amicable is also key to increasing our collective efficiency: amicable within the team, amicable with the other Commission departments, and amicable with the outside world. I am reminded of Georges Pompidou's insistence that no political team can do without 'a collective morale to guide their actions'.

Tuesday, 4 October 2016: The Hague

This morning we take a train from Brussels to The Hague – a stopping service that allows plenty of time for a four-way conversation between myself, Sabine, Stéphanie and Georg. It marks the beginning of our travels through the EU countries, the first stop on our grand tour of European capitals.

I am surprised at the length of the journey. If we want to make good on our mission, we may have to think about taking trains that don't stop at every single station… But it must be admitted that, in just a few days and nights, and with little in the way of resources, the team has managed to put together an exceptional programme. The mission of this small 'commando' unit is to travel through the twenty-seven countries of the Union over a period of a few weeks, establishing personal contacts with ministers and prime ministers so as to find out where each of them draws their red lines and, in broad terms, to construct our own line of negotiation on the basis of four first principles that I will, from now on, recite to each of my interlocutors.

The journey at least gives me time to refine the messages to be conveyed to the Netherlands' Prime Minister Mark Rutte.

First, there can be no negotiations until we receive notification from the British government. In the Council, the twenty-seven member states have been very clear on this point.

Second, we will only succeed in this negotiation by building and maintaining very strong unity between the twenty-seven member states.

Third, no EU country should find itself in a position where it is has less say than a country outside the Union.

And finally, no country outside the Union should be given a veto on, or even the right to intervene in, the decision-making process of the twenty-seven.

These are the key points to which we will hold fast throughout our work, and which are the conditions for its success.

Mark Rutte is very direct and friendly. I am impressed by the way he delegates and manages his cabinet, the key members of which he has brought together for the occasion. He and his ministers express full support for our team and he tells me that, for him, the interests and unity of the twenty-seven member states will be paramount throughout the negotiations, despite his country's strong relationship with the UK.

Wednesday, 5 October 2016: Bucharest

From The Hague we head straight for Bucharest. In the Romanian capital I meet my friend Dacian Cioloş, now Prime Minister of this great country, set to become the sixth largest economy in the EU once the UK has left.

A longstanding relationship has bound us together since the time when, as a young civil servant in the Romanian Ministry of Agriculture, Dacian was in charge of monitoring the decentralized development cooperation project in the Argeş region, which I had launched in 1996 as President of the General Council of Savoie.

In 2007, we both ended up, as agriculture ministers for our respective countries, tasked with securing a reform of the Common Agricultural Policy which would only be concluded in the early hours of a lengthy night of negotiations which the British were trying their best to derail.

Naturally, after this I closely followed Dacian's candidacy for the post of European Commissioner, and his eventual appointment to the strategic post of agriculture.

Throughout those five years in the Barroso II Commission, our friendship and solidarity remained unwavering. As it did when I, along with Antonio Tajani and others, needed the support of the College to pass regulatory texts that offended the liberal or ultra-liberal sensibilities of certain colleagues and senior officials – which was the case with my proposal to establish access for all to a basic bank account in every country. And indeed, when he himself came up against the same ideological resistance to his 2010 proposal for a mechanism to enable farmers to finally come together to negotiate their prices with industrialists!

Mr Cioloş has invited us to dinner at a Romanian government residence, a former *dacha* away from the city centre. The 'technical' ministers he has gathered around him are politically astute and have good instincts.

The Romanian Minister of Labour, Dragoş Pîslaru, tells me: 'We will be stronger in this negotiation if we're really united. And this unity, this coherence, cannot be cemented by reactions or defensiveness *alone*. The twenty-seven must stand together, with a positive and proactive agenda, moving forward together and regaining the confidence of our citizens.' At the end of these initial visits, the key elements we need for our negotiations are already falling into place.

Thursday, 6 October 2016: 'Our enemy is the Commission'

'We have allies among the twenty-seven, and we must make use of them. Our enemy is the Commission, which wants to be forgiven for making Cameron lose. Many of the twenty-seven need us.'

I am told that these remarks, which have been reported to me, were made yesterday in private before a group of businessmen in London by UK Trade Minister Liam Fox. This Scottish MP, a former defence minister for David Cameron and a former candidate for the Conservative leadership, losing to Theresa May, is obviously at the forefront when it comes to imagining the future of trade relations between the UK and the EU. But first of all, Brexit must be achieved, and he is in favour of a fast-track agenda. That, however, is no reason to propagate such untruths.

So it was the Commission that lost David Cameron the election? This is to pass over in silence, just a little too quickly, the 'new settlement' agreed with him at the European Council on 18–19 February 2016, in the midst of the migrant crisis – a settlement that further strengthened the UK's special status within the Union. In the end it wasn't enough to prevent Brexit, but not for lack of trying...

It is also to forget that, if all European leaders voluntarily kept silent throughout the referendum campaign, they did so at the express request of the British Prime Minister. According to him, any intervention by 'Brussels technocrats' or foreign leaders would have been immediately exploited by the 'Brexiteers'...

In any case, Liam Fox's statement only strengthens my determination: we must secure and consolidate the unity of the twenty-seven as rapidly as possible.

Friday, 7 October 2016: Notre Europe

The foundation created by Jacques Delors celebrates its twentieth anniversary today! And so it is time for us to speak about 'Notre Europe' – an institute chaired by my friend Enrico Letta, former Prime Minister of Italy, and managed with great determination by a young Savoyard, Yves Bertoncini.

In his speech, Jean-Claude Juncker acknowledges that 'the European Union must be ambitious on big projects and more modest on small matters'. Which is another way of saying that the lessons of Brexit are not just there for British citizens to draw from. And to be sure, Europe and Brussels have produced too many laws and regulations over the past thirty years, constraining citizens, consumers and businesses, and placing onerous obligations on their daily lives.

Yesterday, President François Hollande had also referred to the British decision, but in a rather more prickly tone: 'There must be a threat, there must be a risk, and there must be a price' for leaving the EU, he warned.

That same evening, in Savoie, in the pretty village of Domessin where my assistant Barthélemy is a town councillor, I honour a very old promise made to the mayor Gilbert Guigue to lead a public debate on Europe. The room is packed: three hundred people have sacrificed their evening to discuss Europe – and they say that no one is interested! I will most definitely make sure to take the time to talk with citizens, however heavy the workload of my new mission.

Saturday, 8 October 2016: Theresa May among her own

In Birmingham, Conservative party officials are meeting, as they do every year at this time. Naturally, this year's conference is particularly focused on Brexit, with party leaders set to discuss the reasons why their fellow citizens voted Leave. In her speech, Theresa May asserts her desire to build a 'Global Britain' following Brexit, and to forge a new role for the UK on the world stage.

There is a not insignificant element of ideology and nostalgia for an exalted past in her proclamations, as in those of other party officials. For example, describing to party activists the bright future he predicts for the country when it leaves the EU, David Davis declared that, by leaving Europe, the UK would achieve flexibility at a time when adaptation is crucial. He claimed that the UK had already created a language and a legal system for the whole world and that, in order to grow, the country would soon embrace the whole world, and trade with the whole planet.

One of the reasons for the Leave vote was a rejection of the free movement of persons. But British politicians pretend they don't know that it was the UK itself which, at the time of EU enlargement, chose not to activate the clause that would have allowed limits to be imposed upon the free movement of workers from the new member countries.

Another reason, as correctly identified by Theresa May, was a yearning for protection: as she says, 'the referendum was not just a vote to withdraw from the EU. [...] It was about a sense – deep, profound and, let's face it, often justified – that many people have today, that the world works well for a privileged few, but not for them.'

The Prime Minister is quite right to raise this point. But in the face of globalization, in the face of great continental states such as China and the US, can a single country – even the UK – really be better placed to protect its citizens than twenty-eight countries acting as one? Isn't it better to stick together, in solidarity, rather than go it alone?

Monday, 10 October 2016: Warsaw

Our fourth capital in ten days. It's raining in Warsaw, but it doesn't make much difference to us!

The new Polish government is led by Jarosław Kaczyński's PiS ('Law and Justice') party. Here the language about Brussels is much the same as in London, as is the distrust. What these leaders are after is more an international syndicate than a political community.

London is not mistaken in looking to Warsaw for support from within the EU itself. I am told that the new British ambassador is on a mission over here.

This distrust of the Commission extends to the details of our own organization: the Minister of Foreign Affairs Witold Waszczykowski protests that the team, which is still in the process of being set up, does not yet include any Poles. Even when I cite the name of one of the first officials to join our team, who *is* Polish, a close adviser to my deputy Sabine Weyland, the minister replies, 'She's an international civil servant, she's not Polish. What we need is a less cosmopolitan approach to negotiation.'

I have to repeat forcefully, twice over, to him: 'I will be negotiating on your behalf, trust me!'

This trust certainly doesn't come easily – but I feel confident that it can be won from these ministers whose sovereigntism reminds me so much of what I hear in France. My conversations with Deputy Prime Minister Mateusz Morawiecki and Minister of European Affairs Konrad Szymański are, however, far more constructive.

Monday, 17 October 2016: The financial settlement

Back in Brussels, one thing is clear: the issue of the financial settlement will be a major point of contention with the British, but will also be a question of unity among the twenty-seven. None of the five Prime Ministers with whom I have already met wants to pay one euro more or receive one euro less on account of Brexit.

I discuss this subject today with the group of Directors-General, some of the most experienced men and women in the Commission, who are supporting me in this negotiation. And I am almost physically reassured to be able to share my thoughts with them, to provoke reactions and to hear their opinions.

On budgetary matters our position is clear. Thanks to Philippe Bertrand, the 'mad scientist' of the European budget, a photographer and aviator in his spare time, we have a method and, on the basis of the Union's accounts, we know exactly what the British owe us. What was decided with twenty-eight members must be paid as if there were twenty-eight.

Preliminary estimates indicate that if the UK were to settle its accounts with the EU on 1 April 2019, the gross liability would be €50–60 billion. Of course, this would need to be balanced against the sums owed to the UK, in particular in respect of the Common Agricultural Policy and structural funds.

Within the framework of the financial settlement, there is another €10–15 billion that could come into play in the future if certain guarantees given by the UK along with other European countries, for example with regard to European aid to Ukraine, were to be called upon. This is what we call 'potential liability'.

Finally, since the financial settlement with the UK will have to be global, we are working on other commitments that fall outside the European budget, such as those made by the European Investment Bank.

Even if we present only logical and rational arguments, I suspect that talks on these budgetary issues, to be dealt with at the very beginning of negotiations, will be arduous.

One important variable here will be the date of the UK's exit: the later the exit date, the lower the amount due on exit, since the UK will already have paid a significant proportion of the total as a member state.

Obviously, beyond the question of the financial settlement, the UK's departure will result in an overall reduction in the European budget. This may present an opportunity to review the structure of the budget and start from scratch, directing it more towards innovation and the political priorities of the Europe of tomorrow. It could also be an opportunity to reopen the important issue of the financing of the budget itself, something that Mario Monti is now looking into at the request of Jean-Claude Juncker.

On the revenue side, this will also be the moment to put an end to the UK rebate, which Margaret Thatcher negotiated at the Fontainebleau summit in 1984, and to discuss the 'rebates on the rebate' that have been negotiated over the years by other net contributors to the European budget, such as the Netherlands, Germany, Austria and Sweden. 'I want my money back', said Thatcher back in 1984. Today the tables are turned, but this famous phrase only serves to remind me that financial negotiations with London are never a straightforward affair.

Wednesday, 19 October 2016: Ljubljana

Our little team, professional as ever, arrives in Slovenia in good spirits. Leaving Ljubljana airport I have a strange impression of déjà vu: the nearby mountains and the neatly arranged houses along the roads in these villages remind me of Savoie.

Prime Minister Miro Cerar assures us that his country has no specific concerns about Brexit, and expresses his confidence in us: 'We'll be with you!'

Before meeting the Prime Minister, we share a meal with State Secretary for Foreign Affairs Sanja Štiglic, who welcomes us into a cottage on the edge of a large lake. It is cold and sunny. A wood fire crackles in the fireplace. It's a moment of great warmth, and I pick up the thread of a longstanding relationship with this country, the first to emerge from the former Yugoslavia.

It was back in 1993, when I was the newly appointed Minister of the Environment in Édouard Balladur's government, that I was charged with re-establishing dialogue and trust in the Upper Bearn region, which was in revolt against the state and its authoritarian creation of 'bear reserves'. Apart from a few ecologists with support back in Paris, and the militant ecologist Éric Petetin, all the elected Pyrenean representatives, hunters and shepherds were at the time united in their resistance against the capital. Through visits, listening and dialogue, we managed to restore calm, and the Upper Bearn Heritage Institution was created.

Hunters and shepherds, reassured of their importance and now listened to and respected, accepted the reintroduction of a few bears, re-establishing a chain of biodiversity in the French Pyrenees that was about to become extinct. And that is how the bears of Slovenia – whose habitat is most similar to those of the Pyrenees – entered the EU in 1994, ten years before the rest of their country.

Wednesday, 26 October 2016: Zagreb

We arrive this morning in Zagreb, where I am pleased to meet the young Prime Minister, Andrej Plenković, whose new government looks set to make a positive contribution to the agenda of the twenty-seven.

As far as Brexit is concerned, the Prime Minister is engaged and attentive, particularly as regards the question relating to the mobility of citizens, an issue in which his country has a very particular interest. Croatia was the last country to join the European Union, on 1 January 2013, and is still in a transition period during which free movement of citizens is not complete. The Prime Minister therefore asks whether Croatians who wish to do so will benefit from free movement to the UK prior to its withdrawal.

Another concern is, of course, the desire to preserve the funding for the cohesion policy planned for the current budget period (2014–20). As Mr Plenković rightly says, reducing the differences in living standards between Europeans is a concern that lies at the heart of the Union's project.

Strolling through the streets of the old town after this meeting, we pass a baroque building that houses The Museum of Broken Relationships. With goodwill, even after a painful break-up, it is sometimes possible to build a solid and harmonious relationship.

Friday, 11 November 2016: Focus on strategy

Upon our return from Austria, after a long week during which I also visited Denmark and Slovakia, Sabine, Stéphanie and I are working together with Jean-Claude Juncker's staff. For the first time I will be presenting a negotiation strategy to the President of the Commission.

First, there are a few issues in the Article 50 negotiation upon which agreement is essential, including the financial settlement that the UK must reach in order to settle accounts with the EU, and the need to agree upon the acquired rights of EU citizens living in the UK and UK citizens living in the EU. We also need to work on border issues, particularly in Ireland, and find a way to satisfy all aspects of the commitments of the Good Friday (Belfast) Agreement, signed on 10 April 1998 to end the Troubles that had torn Northern Ireland apart for more than thirty years. These three issues will have to be addressed in the first phase.

Second, Article 50 provides that, in stipulating the terms of withdrawal, the exit agreement should take account of the future relationship with the remaining countries. In doing so, the existing models – Norway, Switzerland, Canada and others – cannot be used as a reference, contrary to what is already being suggested in some quarters, because they concern countries that are far less economically integrated with the EU than the UK is. Any future agreement with the UK will therefore need to be far more thorough in establishing a 'level playing field', particularly with regard to competition rules and jurisdictional authority.

Third, once the shape of the new relationship has been established, it will be possible to start thinking about a time-limited transition period, the aim of which will be to make the move to this new relationship as smooth as possible. The transition will need to be heavily supervised and will probably require continuation of some of the *acquis communautaire*, in particular the regulatory framework of the internal market, i.e. standards, norms, the various supervisory authorities and, necessarily, the authority of the EU Court of Justice. Legally, the establishment of such a transition period must form part of the exit agreement.

Finally, just as important as the substantive issues is the organization of the negotiations. A few days earlier, Georg brought to my attention an article written by Andrew Duff, a former British MEP and a great connoisseur of EU arcana. Duff points out that the European Councils are likely to be crucial points in the negotiations. And he is quite right! Controlling the timeline, setting the tempo, is key. We will structure the negotiations according to our own calendar.

Monday, 21 November 2016: Raising a glass of Prosecco to Boris

Sabine Weyand, Stefaan De Rynck and I have just met Italian Prime Minister Matteo Renzi's sherpa at the Chigi Palace. It's late, but many are still out on the sumptuous streets of Rome around the Farnese Palace.

I got to know Stefaan De Rynck in 1999 when he became my spokesman at the Commission for Institutional Reform. I have always found it reassuring to turn to the wise and subtle analyses of this Flemish Belgian. He is now in charge of communication and relations with think-tanks in my team, and closely follows the public debate in the UK.

A few days ago, the British Foreign Secretary Boris Johnson got involved in a nasty dispute with the Italian Minister for Economic Development Carlo Calenda, and ended up threatening to stop buying Prosecco.

And so we decide to have a glass of Prosecco on the terrace; the moment is immortalized in Stefaan's tweet, which will be reported throughout the British press… Protectionism is not the right attitude, nor the right message to be sending!

Wednesday, 30 November 2016: Facing the press

For the first time since I took office, this morning I am speaking to the press, having been invited by Jean-Claude Juncker to present the progress of our work to the College of Commissioners.

The Berlaymont press room is packed. Journalists have come from all over Europe, some from further afield. There is a burst of flash photography. The Greek spokesman for the Commission, Margaritis Schinas, hands over to me. I choose to open this first briefing in English.

I admit that I still have some progress to make in this language. I did have a good teacher, though: on one occasion I received a sort of personal English lesson from the Queen of England herself! It was Tuesday, 6 April 2004 and Prime Minister Jean-Pierre Raffarin was hosting a lunch in honour of Her Majesty Queen Elizabeth, who had come to Paris to mark the centenary of the Entente Cordiale.

As Foreign Secretary, I had the honour of being seated to the right of the Queen, who speaks impeccable French. As I had to go straight after lunch to the National Assembly to discuss current affairs, my intention was to give a special greeting to a delegation from the House of Lords and the House of Commons who would be attending the session for a while from the gallery.

'Ma'am, may I ask, how you would say in English *"Vive l'Entente cordiale"*?'

'You would say "Long live the Entente Cordiale"', the Queen immediately replied.

With this very special lesson in English under my belt, I repeated the phrase a few minutes later before the Chamber, looking out at the British MPs – somewhat to the surprise of some French MPs and journalists, many of whom thought that I had made a mistake and that the correct phrase should have been 'Long *life to* the Entente Cordiale'.

This episode was even reported in the humour magazine *Le Canard enchaîné*, which mistakenly mocked the foreign minister for his poor English.

But I never could have dreamt of having such an eminent teacher…

This meeting with journalists is an important moment, an opportunity to set the record straight, given the amount of 'fake news' that Brexit is provoking.

Today's speech gives me the opportunity to let everyone know my state of mind: neither aggression, nor naivety, nor revenge. I want to remain calm in all circumstances. And Georg has devised a nice phrase that will do the rounds of the news channels: 'Keep calm and negotiate.' A nice invitation to the negotiating table, and a little jab at the British… Stefaan De Rynck will later get a bright red mug made for me emblazoned with the slogan, which I will keep prominently on my desk.

This press conference is also an occasion for me to play teacher, explaining the difference between withdrawal – the terms of which must be set out within a two-year period – and our future relationship – which will no doubt take longer to negotiate.

Finally, I use it as an opportunity to draw attention to the countless consequences of Brexit: human, social, economic and financial, technical and legal. And to list the main issues that we will need to work on in the run-up to withdrawal: the rights of European citizens in the UK and of British citizens in the EU; settlement of the financial commitments made by the UK to the Union as a member state; and the future of the Union's new borders, particularly in Ireland.

I then head to the European Parliament to meet with the presidents of the political groups, after having spoken yesterday with President Martin Schulz and set out the inter-institutional working method I want to put in place. Schulz, always very European and direct, assured me of his trust. Around the table today I find other parliamentarians I have known for a long time: Guy Verhofstadt, Manfred Weber, Gianni Pittella, Philippe Lamberts, Gabriele Zimmer, Danuta Hübner…

They give me a warm and friendly welcome. They all know how much importance I attach to the work of the European Parliament, having always been convinced, in all my previous roles, that it has a crucial part to play in the balance of the institutions.

This is all the more true in the context of these negotiations, since it will be up to the European Parliament to ratify the Withdrawal Agreement. We are all fully aware of the political balance that must be maintained, and we agree to meet regularly to collaborate on refining the positions that it will be my job to put forward and defend.

Thursday, 22 December 2016: Grounded planes?

The Directorate-General for Transport sends me a memo on the impact of Brexit upon the various sectors it covers, should we fail to reach a deal with the UK.

The observations are extremely worrying, particularly as far as the aviation sector is concerned. In this domain the memo predicts an immediate and serious deterioration in traffic between the UK and the Continent; from a legal point of view, the absence of an agreement would be tantamount to a return to the pre-1992 situation when there were only bilateral agreements between the UK and individual member states.

The ability that a British company such as EasyJet enjoys under current EU rules to charter flights between France and Germany, for example, would end overnight. The entire aviation safety regime in force in the UK – currently maintained by the European Union Aviation Safety Agency – would also be called into question. Once again, I am reminded of the incredible complexity of the agreement we have to negotiate and the multiplicity of subjects it covers.

2017

Tuesday, 17 January 2017: Lancaster House – Theresa May shows her hand

Arriving in Strasbourg at midday, my team and I shut ourselves away to listen to Theresa May's speech at Lancaster House. Standing behind a lectern bearing the words 'Global Britain', the Prime Minister begins her address in a resolutely optimistic tone, praising the merits of a United Kingdom at the forefront of tomorrow's world, of a 'great, global trading nation that is respected around the world and strong, confident and united at home'.

I can't help but notice the paradox when she claims that the referendum vote 'was not a decision to turn inwards' but 'the moment we chose to build a truly "Global Britain"'.

However, it is not this optimistic – and somewhat debatable – message that really catches my attention, but three sentences that suggest to me that the content of this speech is far more significant than what has been said thus far:

> Not partial membership of the European Union, associate membership of the European Union, or anything that leaves us half-in, half-out. We do not seek to adopt a model already enjoyed by other countries. We do not seek to hold on to bits of membership as we leave.

In fact, Mrs May is about to do nothing less than set out her red lines in their entirety, even though we have not yet opened negotiations. And she does so in surprisingly specific terms: the UK will 'bring an end to the jurisdiction of the European Court of Justice', she says; and will end the free movement of people so as to 'get control of the number of people coming to Britain from the EU'; 'we do not seek membership of the Single Market'; 'I do not want Britain to be part of the Common

Commercial Policy and I do not want us to be bound by the Common External Tariff.' I am astounded by the sheer number of doors she is closing here, one after the other, by enumerating all of these points...

Have the consequences of each of these decisions been fully thought through, assessed and discussed? Does she realize that, in doing this, she is excluding almost all the models of cooperation we have managed to construct up until now with our partners, even the closest among them? Can we be sure that the referendum vote gave the British government *carte blanche* for such a total break?

In fact, for her to say all this amounts to writing off not only membership of the European Economic Area – of which Norway, Iceland and Liechtenstein are members – but also the kind of partnership we have with Turkey, which has a customs union agreement with the EU...

Even the positive notes in the speech seem to confirm this observation. Apart from some important and welcome assurances – on the transposition of existing European standards, the preservation of the rights of European citizens within the United Kingdom, the maintenance of the Common Travel Area with Ireland, and the UK's willingness to cooperate on matters of defence and security – Mrs May sets out without the slightest ambiguity her major objective: to negotiate a free trade agreement with the European Union. In other words, the kind of agreement we have with important but distant partners such as Canada and South Korea...

Admittedly, a few phrases lead me to suspect that the British negotiators are going to ask for more than this, since there is explicit mention of taking in 'elements of current single market arrangements in certain areas – on the export of cars and lorries for example, or the freedom to provide financial services across national borders'. But how could one possibly imagine that the EU would agree to such demands, clearly designed to benefit the City in return for concessions to German exporters?

I am equally sceptical of the targets Mrs May sets out for the process to come: 'I want us to have reached an agreement about our future partnership by the time the two-year Article 50 process has concluded.' Apart from the fact that this ignores the very letter of Article 50 itself, which states that the Withdrawal Agreement must set out the framework for our future relationship, it seems to me rather ambitious, to say the least, to imagine that in two years we will be able to undo a forty-four-year-long relationship, while simultaneously piecing together all the various elements of our future relationship, given that it took us no fewer than seven years of intense work to negotiate a simple free trade agreement with Canada...

I am astonished at the way the Prime Minister has just put all her cards on the table.

Thursday, 19 January 2017: Paris, National Assembly

After an initial whistle-stop tour of EU capitals to establish contact and lay the foundations for these negotiations, at the start of this year I begin a second tour of the twenty-seven countries, which should enable me to go beyond the governments alone and meet with representatives of the political, economic and social sectors.

And today, for the first time as a negotiator, I am speaking before the French National Assembly's information commission on the consequences of the British referendum and the monitoring of negotiations.

This is also the occasion for a first trip as negotiator with Tristan Aureau. As a young *maître des requêtes* [Master of Requests] for the Council of State when I was there myself, he accompanied me on a commission to Washington with the World Bank. This precise and methodical official had very quickly let me know he was keen to join me in Brussels on the Brexit project.

Having long been a parliamentarian myself, I am well aware of the important role played by national parliaments in public debate. I also have in mind the precedent of the free trade agreement between the EU and Canada, the CETA, ratification of which was jeopardized by the Walloon Parliament at the very end of the process. To avoid such pitfalls, the only solution, it seems to me, is to involve these parliaments as early as possible in the process.

Tuesday, 24 January 2017: UK Parliament

In the UK too, Parliament is important – and is determined to have its say.

In a long-awaited ruling, the British Supreme Court has ruled that the government must obtain the approval of Parliament before invoking Article 50 and launching negotiations to leave the European Union.

David Davis announced that a simple bill would be presented to Parliament in short order, so as to meet the deadline.

However, the Court has ruled that the government will not need to obtain the approval of the parliaments of Scotland, Wales and Northern Ireland, none of which will therefore be able to veto Brexit.

Thursday, 2 February 2017: White Paper

Our London representative informs me that the UK government's Article 50 invocation bill has just passed its second reading in Parliament with 498 votes in favour and 114 against. It is interesting to note that the against camp included forty-seven Labour MPs, along with fifty from the Scottish National Party, seven Liberal Democrats, one Green – and one Conservative, in the person of Kenneth Clarke, a former minister in the Thatcher, Major and Cameron governments, who remains true to his pro-European convictions and believes that the United Kingdom is 'embarking on a new unknown future' that is 'simply baffling to every friend of the British and of the United Kingdom throughout the world'.

Meanwhile, I am reading the White Paper just published by the British government. It is striking that its contents amount to little more than what was already said in Theresa May's Lancaster House speech.

I note that the government explicitly maintains its desire to leave the Single Market and foresees no role for the EU Court of Justice once the UK has left the EU. In his introduction to the document, David Davis adds that the government wants to withdraw from the Customs Union, stating that the UK will no longer be 'bound by the EU's Common External Tariff or participate in the Common Commercial Policy' – and yet the document promises a 'smooth, mutually beneficial exit'.

Despite the disarray of the last few weeks, if we are to take them at their word, the UK government's line seems clear enough.

Wednesday, 22 March 2017: European Committee of the Regions

For several weeks now, my team and I have been working on the speech I will give today to the European Committee of the Regions, made up of elected representatives at local and regional level from all twenty-eight member states.

Our aim is to set out our strategy publicly for the very first time, or, more precisely, to state what we believe to be the conditions for a successful negotiation.

In the course of our dialogues in Brussels and across the EU capitals, we have managed to identify three such conditions: maintaining unity among the twenty-seven, which will be achieved through public debate and transparency; removing uncertainty as quickly as possible for citizens, for the beneficiaries of the European budget, and at the Union's borders; and reaching agreement on the principles of an orderly withdrawal before we begin to discuss our future relationship.

I also aim to convey to the British government our desire to reach a deal, as calls for a 'no-deal' Brexit are increasingly rife in the British press.

In my speech, I set out a few examples of the consequences of a no-deal scenario: 'More than four million citizens – UK citizens in the EU and EU citizens in the UK – confronted with extreme uncertainty concerning their rights and their future; supply problems in the United Kingdom, disrupting value chains; the reintroduction of burdensome customs checks, inevitably slowing down trade and lengthening lorry queues in Dover; serious disruption in air traffic to and from the United Kingdom', etc.

Just as I am about to enter the Chamber, Tristan informs me that a terrorist attack is under way outside the British Parliament. The situation is still unclear: a car is said to have ploughed into the crowd, it seems that Parliament is locked down, and many people have already been injured...

I open my speech with some words of solidarity with the victims of the attack. The emotion is all the more palpable given that only this morning, all the staff of the European institutions had held a one-minute silence in memory of victims of the attacks perpetrated last year in Brussels. These atrocious deaths are a reminder that, beyond Brexit, we face common threats.

Wednesday, 29 March 2017: Notification

Ambassador Tim Barrow, Permanent Representative of the UK to the European Union, hand-delivers the long-awaited letter to Donald Tusk. Nine months after the referendum, Theresa May has today given notice of her country's wish to leave the European Union, triggering the two-year period under Article 50 of the Treaty on European Union during which we must find an agreement for the UK's orderly withdrawal and set out the framework for our future relationship. Negotiations can now begin.

Friday, 31 March 2017: Sadness and regret

As I do every week, I go over the weekly report sent to me by the Directorate-General for Communication, which surveys the reaction to Brexit among the twenty-seven member states.

Unsurprisingly, today they are all focused on Mrs May's letter of formal notice. Most heads of state or government have issued official responses. Their statements and communiqués are full of sadness and regret, as exemplified by those of the French, Belgian and Polish governments, which, while respecting the choice made by the British people, express their deep regret at the decision.

In parallel, there is an increasing number of calls for unity among the twenty-seven, whether from Slovenian Prime Minister Miro Cerar or Mariano Rajoy in Spain. Other governments, such as Denmark and the Netherlands, explicitly refer to the defence of their national interests.

In general, I am struck by a convergence of the prevailing tone. From Finland to Portugal, the priorities are the same. Everywhere there is talk of securing the rights of EU citizens living in the UK and of maintaining good relations with the UK in the future.

Behind the remarks of the various parties, I detect echoes of the discussions we have had thus far in each capital. The insistence of all upon the need to do things in the right order – ensuring an orderly withdrawal before discussing the future relationship – is symptomatic in this respect.

Tuesday, 4 April 2017: European Parliament resolution

The European Parliament has just sent me the draft resolution that will be put to the vote during the plenary session tomorrow in Strasbourg.

This nine-page text faithfully reflects the tone of the discussions I have been having for months with MEPs, and in particular with Guy Verhofstadt in his capacity as the European Parliament's Brexit Coordinator.

Over the last few months, the team has managed to develop a real rapport, free of all deference, with Guy Verhofstadt and the other members of this group. Verhofstadt, a cordial man, is a liberal and was Prime Minister of Belgium for nine years. Despite disappointments on the European front, he retains a certain utopianism and enthusiasm. He is a militant federalist, which I am not. But we share the same sense of urgency in regard to necessary reforms to the European project – and the idea that this project must be pursued with the citizens rather than without them. We also agree that unity is key in this negotiation.

There are other MEPs in this group, each with his or her own political affiliation and convictions, and each will follow the negotiations rigorously and attentively on behalf of the Parliament and the citizens of Europe. I am thinking of Elmar Brok, an MEP for thirty years and a pillar of the German CDU, who has negotiated several European treaties for the Parliament; Roberto Gualtieri, an Italian socialist, professor of history and chairman of the European Parliament's Committee on Economic Affairs, always attentive to details; Danuta Hübner, former European Commissioner for Regional Policy and member of the Polish Civic Platform; Philippe Lamberts, a tenacious and feisty Belgian MEP, co-chair of the Green Group; and Gabi Zimmer, a sincere and conscientious German MEP who chairs the United Left group in the Parliament.

This Brexit Steering Group also depends upon civil servants of the highest quality, brought together by the prescient Secretary-General of the European Parliament Klaus Welle, and led by his deputy Markus Winkler.

The European Parliament's text acknowledges receipt of the UK notice, sets out a number of general principles for the negotiations, and notes the importance of 'the Withdrawal Agreement and any possible transitional arrangement(s) entering into force well before the elections to the European Parliament of May 2019'.

The text defines clear positions on citizenship and the financial settlement in particular, marking out red lines that will serve me well when the time comes.

Wednesday, 5 April 2017: Farage in his element…

MEPs have turned up en masse for the plenary session. The seating arrangement is such that I find myself seated less than two metres away from Nigel Farage, former leader of UKIP, who sports an overjoyed expression and … Union Jack socks. The opportunity is too good to miss, and all the journalists present make sure to get multiple photos of our handshake – an expression of politeness rather than the sign of any views the two of us might have in common.

The speech that Parliament President Antonio Tajani has invited me to give following Jean-Claude Juncker's is kept deliberately brief and incisive. My aim is first and foremost to welcome the stance taken by the Parliament in its draft resolution, which, as I emphasize, is 'the first political position taken by a European institution in response to last week's letter', and will enable the European Parliament to 'set the tone' for the negotiations to come. I then recall the three conditions for the success of these negotiations, and again state that 'we do not seek to punish the UK'.

There follow a great many statements from all benches of the house, the vast majority deploring the British decision and calling for the defence of European interests. Nigel Farage, on the other hand, with his characteristic sense of proportion, describes the European Union as a 'mafia' and its members as 'gangsters' who have tried to take the UK hostage. All the members of his group, especially the British, have placed their country's flags on their desks, as if the juxtaposition of the national flag and the European flag were an abomination.

The resulting vote is clear: the resolution is adopted by 516 votes in favour and 133 against, with 50 abstentions.

Tuesday, 11 April 2017: Sherpas

This morning I meet with the sherpas of the twenty-seven heads of state or government, with a view to the forthcoming European Council of 29 April, which will have to adopt the guidelines that will provide my roadmap for the negotiations.

For weeks now, Sabine and a small team from the task force have been working very discreetly with the Council's General Secretariat to prepare the draft guidelines to be presented by President Donald Tusk. Today the sherpas are discussing them for the first time. I recognize most of them from having met them one by one over the past few weeks, in Brussels or during my tour of the capitals.

I use the meeting to reassure them that I wish to conduct these negotiations in a fully transparent manner. I am aware that some are reluctant to take such an unprecedented approach, but I am now convinced that this is the best way to meet the expectations of citizens while countering the risk of any leaks.

I receive a warm welcome. It seems to me that we have succeeded, through our efforts over the last few months, in forging a stronger unity than expected.

Wednesday, 12 April 2017: Tensions over Gibraltar

'The devil is in the detail.' In this case, it is in Gibraltar, where no one had really looked closely enough at the consequences of Brexit. But speaking on Sky News this morning, Michael Howard, who has served in several Conservative governments, adopts a dramatic tone: 'Thirty-five years ago this week, another woman prime minister sent a task force halfway across the world to protect another small group of British people against another Spanish-speaking country. And I'm absolutely clear that our current woman prime minister will show the same resolve in relation to Gibraltar as her predecessor did.'

Brexit has rekindled tensions over Gibraltar, a six-kilometre-square territory that has been British since the Treaty of Utrecht in 1713, and 96 per cent of whose 33,000 inhabitants voted to remain in the EU.

The aim of course is to avoid the reinstatement of a physical border for the 12,000 people who travel between Spain and Gibraltar every day. But this negotiation also gives Spain a certain leverage. In Spanish public debate, some see Brexit as an opportunity to challenge British sovereignty over the Rock. Others don't go quite that far, but seek to settle a number of disputes that have been ongoing for forty years, in particular the question of the management of Gibraltar airport, and the problem of customs controls in a territory that boasts a highly advantageous tax system...

For the twenty-seven, the matter is quite clear: no agreement between the European Union and the United Kingdom can be implemented in Gibraltar without obtaining the green light from Madrid.

Tuesday, 18 April 2017: Chef's surprise...

A new twist in London! Theresa May, back from the Easter weekend, has decided to call an early general election, even though her mandate runs until 2020. She is taking this gamble in the hope of strengthening her rather slight parliamentary majority (330 Conservative MPs out of 650). The election date is set for 8 June. Her aim is to obtain a clear mandate from voters to ensure an orderly exit from the EU.

According to projections, the Conservatives can expect a comfortable majority of more than fifty seats. This would give us a British government with more room for manoeuvre, but also greater visibility and stability for the next five years, something that would objectively be useful for our negotiations. Some pollsters predict a majority in the Commons of at least 130 seats, double that obtained by Tony Blair in 2005.

If she succeeds, Theresa May 'could become the most powerful Prime Minister since the Second World War', writes the *Financial Times*.

But for the time being, the negotiations, which we had hoped to get started on, will now be postponed for at least two months. In spite of this, I sense that the members of the task force are still committed, and are determined to use this delay to build solid negotiating positions with the twenty-seven.

Wednesday, 26 April 2017: Dinner in London

This afternoon, Jean-Claude Juncker and I head to London for a working dinner with Theresa May and her team. Alongside us are Martin Selmayr, Head of Cabinet of the President of the Commission with his deputy Clara Martínez Alberola, my deputy Sabine Weyand and Jean-Claude Juncker's diplomatic adviser Richard Szostak.

On the British side I find David Davis. He hasn't changed a bit. Still the same boyish smile, always ready with a joke. It is clear, however, that we are not on the same page. And today his stance is in direct opposition to the negotiating strategy we have chosen, which is to settle the terms of separation first before considering what to do next. To Theresa May's right is the key man for this negotiation, her sherpa Olly Robbins, and Ambassador Tim Barrow, the UK's Permanent Representative to the EU.

During Jean-Claude Juncker's brief private meeting with Theresa May, we have an almost friendly conversation with David Davis. He reminds me that he is the only current minister who, as an MP, took Mrs May to court when she was Home Secretary to oppose government plans for internet surveillance. The case was eventually decided by the EU Court of Justice, which ruled in favour of Mr Davis, recognizing that a member state cannot force internet companies to retain emails on a general and indiscriminate basis. Theresa May doesn't hold a grudge, then – although I'm sure she doesn't forget either…

This is the first time I have met the British Prime Minister. She is a very direct woman, with conviction in what she says, and is keen to make her authority felt, as she has just demonstrated by calling an early election. She has great determination to see things through, at least enough to want to negotiate a Brexit that will limit the damage to the UK, since she is convinced that it will have a negative effect upon the nation. To tell the truth, my immediate impression is of a strong and elegant woman, but with a certain rigidity in her physical and mental attitude. As I greet her, I can't help but glance at her shoes – for weeks now, the women on my team have been telling me about her zebra and leopard print pumps. And as dinner begins, so as to avoid getting straight down to business, in an attempt to break the ice I mention a common passion, hiking in the mountains – she in the Swiss Alps, I in the French Alps.

The conversation, over a meal of duck breast, is cordial, and it seems to me that the chemistry is good and that we will be able to talk to each other, even at times when we shall have to trust in each other and work to find compromises. But this is only a first impression.

When it comes to the substance, Jean-Claude Juncker, frank as always, will make her aware of his concern at the distance between our positions and those of her government. We are on the eve of a negotiation that has not yet begun. Some distance is normal and quite legitimate. But in this case, the gap is quite wide.

The distance is particularly clear in regard to one of the points that we see as a priority in this negotiation: the financial accounts that must be settled, as in any separation. Around the table, David Davis refers to a House of Lords report which indicated that nothing obliged the UK to pay.

To be honest, my sense is that the British are talking amongst themselves, as they did throughout the referendum campaign, and that they are underestimating the legal complexity of this divorce and of many of its consequences.

Evidence of this lack of realism was provided just three days ago by Davis himself when, in a radio interview, he said that the European Medicine Agency and European Banking Authority may possibly remain based in London after Brexit, and that this would be a matter for negotiation with the Europeans. There is obviously nothing to negotiate here. The UK has chosen to leave the European Union and these European agencies will automatically leave the UK.

Saturday, 29 April 2017: Green light from the twenty-seven on the negotiation framework

The political life of the EU runs to the rhythm of the quarterly meetings of the heads of state or government at the European Council. Former Polish Prime Minister Donald Tusk chairs this Council, and Jean-Claude Juncker, President of the European Commission, is a member, as is the High Representative for Foreign Affairs Federica Mogherini.

The Council convening today is decisive for me and my team, as it is expected to adopt the guidelines that will provide a framework for the Brexit negotiations. These guidelines will set out the red lines for negotiations and the Union's political objectives. They have been drafted over the past few months by President Tusk's cabinet and the Council's task force, headed by the highly competent Belgian diplomat Didier Seeuws, in close and continual contact with my team.

All of this work is finally bearing fruit: the text proposed to the heads of state or government is adopted in a few minutes, in a rare demonstration of unity. I see this as the payoff for all the trips we made to the European capitals, all the meetings during which we refined our strategy, clarified our approach and enriched its content.

In substance, these guidelines formalize the fundamental principles that have emerged over the period since I took office, foremost among which are the maintenance of a balance between rights and obligations, preservation of the integrity of the Single Market, indivisibility of the four freedoms of movement of persons, goods, services and capital, and the decision-making autonomy of the Union. And also the fact that a non-EU country, which does not have to respect the same obligations as a member state, cannot enjoy the same rights and benefits as a member state.

They also restate the main tenets of our method: a single negotiation, conducted transparently, en bloc, with a unified position.

They go on to set out very clearly the sequence of the negotiations, which will be conducted in two phases: a first phase devoted to defining the principles of an orderly withdrawal by the UK, and a second phase during which will be specified the details of the withdrawal and, in parallel, the framework – that is to say, the general contours, not the precise nature – of our future relationship with the United Kingdom.

The guidelines adopted today therefore focus on the three main issues of withdrawal – citizens, budgets and borders – explicitly setting out our positions on each one, while saying little about our future relationship.

In relation to borders, it is stated that no free trade agreement can be equivalent to participation in the Single Market, or to parts of it, and that it must 'ensure a level playing field, notably in terms of competition and state aid, and in this regard encompass safeguards against unfair competitive advantages through, inter alia, tax, social, environmental and regulatory measures and practices'.

These, then, are the guidelines that we shall follow scrupulously over the coming months, even if the British try to make us deviate from them.

Sunday, 30 April 2017: Leaks

Thursday's dinner with Theresa May was helpful. What is less helpful is that one of the participants saw fit to recount the dinner in full ironic detail to a journalist from the *Frankfurter Allgemeine Zeitung* (*FAZ*) who, under the headline 'The disastrous Brexit dinner', refers to it as 'a train wreck'.

'I'm leaving Downing Street ten times more sceptical than before', President Juncker is said to have told Mrs May on his way out, according to *FAZ*. Many in Brussels are eyeing Martin Selmayr, who is suspected of pulling strings from the shadows, although he denies it. In any case, the leak was well calculated and has produced the desired results: the *Financial Times* writes that 'daggers are now drawn'.

President Juncker is quite rightly furious about the leak, which puts him at odds not only with the British Prime Minister but also with other European Prime Ministers who may now fear that private conversations with the Commission President will end up in the press.

Wednesday, 3 May 2017: Guidelines approved

This morning I present to the College of Commissioners the recommendations that my team has been preparing for many weeks. Once adopted by the College, these recommendations will be sent to the Council and, if adopted, will become my mandate as negotiator.

The document, which will be my roadmap, follows on directly from the European Council guidelines, merely clarifying the scope of each subject.

At the end of the College meeting I go to the press room. Every row is packed. My tone is serious. I begin by remarking that the British referendum has caused ten months of uncertainty:

> We need to remove that uncertainty. It is high time to start negotiating. As soon as the UK is ready to come to the table, we shall start negotiating. […] Some have created the illusion that Brexit would have no material impact on our lives, or that negotiations can be conducted quickly and painlessly. This is not the case.

Friday, 5 May 2017: Florence, Palazzo Vecchio

Yesterday evening, Jean-Claude Juncker and I took off from Brussels to fly to Florence, where the European University Institute is holding its annual conference on the state of the Union. I was invited to give a speech on the protection of the rights of citizens in the upcoming negotiations, in the beautiful Salone dei Cinquecento of the Palazzo Vecchio.

From day one, I have been certain that this is the issue that will receive most attention from citizens on both sides of the Channel, and rightly so.

Indeed, as I say at the outset, the free movement of persons is, in my view, one of the greatest advances we have made. It is a tangible proof of the political space we have created. Millions of Europeans experience it every day, travelling to another member state to work or live, sometimes for decades at a time.

Behind the discussion of rights, I always think of all the families whose lives would be quite different without the European Union, those families made up of citizens from different member states who have chosen to come together across national boundaries, and who represent the true face of European citizenship. I have prepared my speech with these citizens in mind, from whom I receive so many letters every day. Together with my team, in particular Stefaan De Rynck and Marie Simonsen, who are responsible for this issue, I have decided to use a number of examples just to remind everyone that we are talking about the fate of real individuals, not just abstract rights.

These are rights that more than three million EU citizens in the UK and more than one million UK citizens in the EU now enjoy. They have legitimate questions. We need to give them answers.

For example, what happens to Polish workers employed in the UK if they lose their job? Would they still be entitled to receive UK unemployment benefit for a few months, even if they return to Poland to look for work? This is what EU law now provides for.

What happens if a freelance photographer from Edinburgh who lives in Malaga goes bankrupt? Will she still have access to the same healthcare, under the same conditions, as a Spanish citizen? If she decides to return to work in her country of origin, can she expect her social security rights acquired in Spain to be taken into account by the UK?

The Withdrawal Agreement must provide clear and affirmative answers to these questions.

My aim is simple: to allow all those who have settled in the UK and Britons who have settled in an EU member state prior to the UK's withdrawal to continue to enjoy the rights they have enjoyed up until now, for the rest of their lives.

I know that this will be one of the most difficult points in the negotiations, because I know that the desire to end freedom of movement played a major role in the British referendum. But I also know that we will find a solution, because the stakes are so high that we cannot fail. Failure would be neither in our interest nor in that of the UK.

Sunday, 7 May 2017: A new President of the Republic

Ahead of the UK general election, it is the French who are voting today, to choose their President.

Even though he does not belong to the Gaullist party that got me involved in politics at the age of 14, in this second round of the presidential election I am giving my vote to Emmanuel Macron, who in the first round obtained just over 66 per cent of the votes, as opposed to Marine Le Pen who won just under 34 per cent.

Following the defeat of Geert Wilders by Mark Rutte in the Netherlands in March, this result was one more sign that citizens recognize themselves more in a positive and pro-European vision than in the rhetoric of populists. Perhaps these votes also reflect the effect of Brexit and the election of Donald Trump in the United States – the feeling that, in the face of these great upheavals, we are stronger together as twenty-seven.

One thing is certain: this young president, marching towards his destiny to the sound of the *Ode to Joy*, will follow negotiations with the United Kingdom very closely.

Thursday, 11 May 2017: Dublin to Dundalk

I meet this morning with the economic and trade union leaders of Ireland, for the first in a series of dialogues I am now conducting in every capital with employers and socio-professional and trade union leaders.

I then go straight to the Irish Parliament, the Oireachtas, to address both houses. A rare privilege: to date, only John F. Kennedy, Bill Clinton, Ronald Reagan, Helmut Kohl, François Mitterrand and Tony Blair have been invited to give such a speech. I am all the more humbled by this. But the invitation clearly demonstrates the gravity of the situation in which Brexit places Ireland, and the sensitivity of the debate for citizens of this country.

The atmosphere is formal, dignified and simple. I'm used to huge auditoriums, but this one is more intimate. The two speakers, side by side, are at the centre. The government, headed by the Prime Minister, the Taoiseach, my friend Enda Kenny, is on the right. Behind him are the elected members of his party, Fine Gael, and on the other side of the chamber are the opposition, notably Fianna Fáil and the Socialists. My podium is in the middle. Behind me, two metres away, sits Gerry Adams, President of Sinn Féin, who became an Irish MP in 2011.

My team, in particular Nina Obermaier, in charge of the Irish question, and Dan Ferrie, our young Irish press officer, has carefully weighed up every word of this speech, drafted by Matthieu Hébert.

Matthieu, a French EU official, has been working with me since 2011 and is a talented speechwriter. Often working behind the scenes, he crafts the messages that we put forward to explain the EU's positions and report on the negotiations. I trust him, and therefore have made him part of the very small inner circle with whom I discuss policy and strategy.

Together, we have chosen today's exceptional platform to explain what it means to be a member of the European Union, to describe some of the progress made, some of the ways the EU benefits the daily lives of citizens, consumers and businesses, and what is lost when a country leaves.

Naturally, I also want to reassure the Irish people as to the stability of their island and the continuation of the dialogue with Northern Ireland, a dialogue between Catholics and Protestants that has been so fragile since the tragic violence that was brought to an end barely twenty years ago.

In 2000, as the new European Commissioner responsible for the EU's regional policies, I inherited as part of my portfolio the management of PEACE, a small initiative to support peace and reconciliation in Northern Ireland, and many of my early contacts expressed their desire to see this programme developed further. I visited Belfast and had the chance to meet with two men who had won Nobel Prizes for their personal work for peace: the Catholic John Hume, then an MEP, and the Protestant David Trimble. Both of them, at different times and in different places on the same day, said the same thing to me, in the same words: 'What brought us to the table was not London, not Belfast, not Dublin, but Brussels and the PEACE programme.' So this is how we supported and developed a programme that supports dialogue and exchange between the two communities.

Obviously, while negotiations have not yet begun, I would never want to be responsible for undermining the peace process and the Good Friday (Belfast) Agreement. We will therefore have to find solutions for preserving the free movement of persons in Ireland, and also for allowing the free movement of goods, while devising some way of controlling physical flows of trade into the Single Market – and all of this without reinstating a hard border. I remind my interlocutors in Ireland of what they already know: in order to ensure the control of goods, we will need the cooperation of the British authorities.

I choose to spend a considerable part of the next day on the border itself, accompanied by European Commissioner for Agriculture Phil Hogan – 'Big Phil', as the Irish call him – and Mairead McGuinness, the highly respected Vice-President of the European Parliament.

On a little road in County Monaghan, the Republic of Ireland is separated from the UK and Northern Ireland by nothing more than a yellow line in the middle of the road. Here more than anywhere else it is clear that, since its inception, the EU has managed to knock down borders within its territory, building bridges while helping to destroy walls and barriers. It is this achievement that we need to preserve in Ireland, one way or another.

Of course, I promised myself that, during these negotiations, I would not yield to polemics and attacks from the British tabloids, that I would be careful with the words I use, and that I would focus on the facts, figures and legal bases – in short, that I would set aside feelings and emotion in favour of objectivity. But here in Ireland, where I am put in mind of Sorj Chalandon's powerful novel *Return to Killybegs*, it is difficult not to be touched by the sensitivities and emotions of those who speak to me, and the memories that remind me of tragedies past.

Monday, 22 May 2017: Official mandate

Another important day for my entire team – historic, even. Six months after I took office, on 1 October, the General Affairs Council, which brings together all the foreign affairs ministers of the twenty-seven, has officially and unanimously confirmed my position and my mandate. Paradoxically, however, it's a quiet day like any other. For me, this mandate is proof, if any were needed, of the importance of teamwork and trust between the EU institutions. In dialogue with the Council, but also with the European Parliament, the mandate has been improved and strengthened in several respects. On the financial settlement, for example, although our plan, prepared with the European Commission's Directorate-General for Budget, was based on an accounting approach taking into consideration everything up to the withdrawal date, the Council decided in the end to adopt a more political approach based on the UK's participation in all programmes funded from the 2014–20 budget plan.

As I tell my team, no one here can claim to be an expert on Brexit. Making a success of it is therefore a question of being methodical, and every link in the chain will count.

Wednesday, 24 May 2017: Battle of the flags

The task force is now dug in on the fifth floor of the Berlaymont building. Space is limited, however, and many team members have had to settle for sharing an open-plan space. We are protected by a glass door that can only be opened with a special badge and the fingerprint of a team member – for what it's worth…

Inside, the task force is buzzing like a hive, with its sixty employees from sixteen EU countries – the exception being the Norwegian Georg Riekeles. The team is quite young, which serves to average out the age of their captain! Most are European civil servants, highly motivated and competent. And Sabine, Stéphanie and I have succeeded in creating that 'collective morale to guide our actions', a common spirit to ensure that we are effective in our mission. In this team, everyone talks to everyone else, with exchanges often taking place in the corridors. The task force is developing a strong capacity for anticipation and swift reaction, which will be essential in these negotiations.

Symbolically, and to lend a little colour to the whitish-grey or greyish-white walls, I had asked Technical Services to provide us with twenty-eight national flags to welcome the many visitors from the member states who arrive every day, including the British. The answer was curt and immediate, and was confirmed by the Protocol Service: 'Out of the question. The only flags in Berlaymont are EU flags.' I had been unaware of this cast-iron law. But I insisted nonetheless – and I owe it to Jean-Claude Juncker's understanding that, his having mediated in my favour, from now on the main corridor of the task force will be adorned with every colour of the European Union and its twenty-eight flags—with the Union Jack right in front of my office. A united Europe, not a uniform one.

Monday, 29 May 2017: Malta

Back to Malta, where the Conference of Parliamentary Committees for Union Affairs (COSAC) is being held, bringing together representatives of the twenty-eight national parliaments of the European Union. It's an opportunity to emphasize the unprecedented transparency we want to aim for in these negotiations, which should enable national and, in some cases, regional parliaments to participate actively in the democratic debate around the process.

We then meet Prime Minister Joseph Muscat, whose country has held the presidency of the European Union since January. Mr Muscat therefore played an important role in the rapid and unanimous adoption by the twenty-seven of the mandate that will serve as my roadmap in these negotiations.

Malta has longstanding links with the UK, which inspired its common law legal system and the structure of its civil service. It also has strong economic links with the UK, particularly in the tourism sector – around 25 per cent of tourists who visit the island are British – and in financial services. Finally, many Maltese students train in the UK and are concerned about recognition of their qualifications.

It comes as no surprise, then, that business representatives here are calling for as smooth a Brexit as possible.

Tuesday, 30 May 2017: 759 agreements...

Today's *Financial Times* has done the maths. By leaving the EU, the UK will automatically be exiting from 759 different agreements signed by the EU on behalf of member states with 168 countries, all of which London will have to renegotiate if it wants to retain the benefits they confer. Of these agreements, 295 concern trade, 69 fisheries, 65 transport, 49 customs and 45 nuclear issues.

As journalist Paul McClean points out in his article, this will mean a great many negotiations being conducted in parallel, with very few experienced negotiators available. Specialists in Brussels have worked for years on these issues of European competence, negotiating with our international partners on behalf of a Union of 500 million inhabitants... London will have to start from scratch.

Sunday, 11 June 2017: A wager lost...

Theresa May's strategy has backfired. She called a general election to strengthen her majority and her position in the Brexit negotiations. What happened was the exact opposite. Instead of gaining fifty or even a hundred more seats as it had hoped, the Conservative Party lost thirteen. The Labour Party gained thirty, achieving its best result since 2001. The Liberal Democrats also made gains, UKIP was eliminated, and there is no longer a clear majority in the House of Commons. This is a real political shock for London. Some commentators, including the *Financial Times*, explain it partly as 'the revenge of the young and Remainers'.

Forty-eight hours later, Theresa May announced a deal with a dozen MPs from the Northern Ireland Democratic Unionist Party (DUP) that will enable her to achieve an absolute majority in the House. The DUP, founded in 1971, was headed for nearly forty years by Ian Paisley, a well-known Unionist leader. Arlene Foster, who was briefly First Minister of Northern Ireland, is now at the helm. The Unionist position is clear to all: they oppose anything that would remove Northern Ireland from the United Kingdom. What price will Theresa May have to pay for this alliance? And what are the consequences for negotiations on the sensitive issue of the border between Northern Ireland and Ireland?

On Twitter, I read that in Brussels there is rejoicing at Theresa May's defeat, that I'm about to take a four-week holiday, and that I'm handing out champagne to my team. Frankly, I think I'll keep the champagne on ice for now. In order to lead these negotiations and make them successful, we need a stable partner who knows what they want.

Monday, 12 June 2017: Talks on the talks

I am joined today by Olly Robbins, accompanied by his deputy, Kay Withers, and the British Ambassador in Brussels, Tim Barrow. For the first time we go into the details of how the rounds of negotiation should be organized. We want the sequencing of negotiations to begin, at least in principle, with those issues where the UK's decision to leave the Union causes the greatest uncertainty: citizens' rights, the financial settlement, and the border issue, particularly in Ireland.

On the British side, it is unclear whether the delegation will always be led by a politician or more often, for the meetings themselves, by Olly Robbins, who wrongly describes himself as a 'bureaucrat'. In reality, he knows the ins and outs of British politics as well as anyone, having worked with Tony Blair, Gordon Brown and David Cameron, whom he advised on security issues. Robbins is a great British civil servant, of which there are many – most of them educated at Oxford or Cambridge. Few, however, boast such a deep understanding of domestic security and intelligence issues. Robbins has a self-assurance that is undoubtedly partly due to his stature, but there is more to it than that. Over the course of several conversations, I come to understand that he is more aware than others of the consequences of Brexit, and wants to try to limit its negative effects.

For our part, we are ready to negotiate, but we want there to be an official and public start to the negotiations and we want to report to the press on each round. This is a method that goes against the grain and against tradition in London. It is not all that usual in Brussels either. But I am very keen on it. I prefer transparency to leaks. All documents relating to the negotiations will be posted on the Commission's website, which is a first. This is essential in order to build trust with the member states and to show that I am not favouring anyone or any country.

All in all, it is a good discussion, during which we also establish, in principle, that we will negotiate in Brussels on the Commission's premises and that official rounds will be conducted in French or English. In response to a question from Robbins, I say that I do not rule out going to London from time to time to move the negotiations forward.

Sunday, 18 June 2017: A breath of fresh air

A breath of fresh mountain air before setting out on the long road of negotiation. Whenever current events give me some pretext, I return home to Savoie. The weather is magnificent on this 18th day of June. My pretext this time is the second round of the French legislative elections, and nothing can prevent me from going to climb the mountains. As has become tradition, I leave this Sunday morning for the Lac du Lou, then continue on to the Lac de Pierre-Blanche in the Belleville valley. The weather is cool and fine and the flowers are numerous, as are the cries of the marmots. I return here to draw from my home, from my country, the energy and strength that this long hike will require.

Monday, 19 June 2017: The first session – at last!

The great march begins this Monday morning with the official opening of negotiations. At last! It is now almost a year since 52 per cent of British citizens who voted decided that their country should leave the European Union. It is three months since Theresa May confirmed this decision by triggering the famous Article 50. High time for negotiations to begin.

After the formal welcome and a firm handshake with David Davis for the cameras, we find ourselves on the seventh floor of the Berlaymont building in a somewhat dingy room. The shutters have been drawn because just across the street is the building that houses most of the press agencies. I'm all for transparency, but perhaps not to the extent of leaving the doors and windows wide open during these first moments of negotiation!

We confirm our agreement on the timetable for the negotiations, at a rate of one week per month, and on the organization of three working groups devoted to citizens' rights, the financial settlement and the many other issues linked to secession: Euratom, governance, the situation of goods placed on the European market prior to Brexit... We decide to entrust to our two principal collaborators, Sabine and Olly Robbins, the task of leading a political dialogue on the singular issue of Ireland – although in fact the British, who were so desperate to start these negotiations today, will have to accept its place in the sequencing. As the heads of state, the ministers and the European Parliament have requested, we must settle issues of separation first, before discussing our future relationship. At 12.30pm, David Davis and I meet in my office. He gives me a very moving book, *Regards vers l'Annapurna*, which documents the great adventure of Maurice Herzog and Louis Lachenal with beautiful photos. A nice personal touch, even if that 1950 attempt did not exactly end well… For my part, since I know David Davis also likes mountains, and is even a rock climber, I give him a hiking stick bought the day before in Saint-Martin-de-Belleville, engraved with a nice edelweiss.

At lunch, Jean-Claude Juncker comes to greet us. Another sign of his confidence, and proof, were it needed, that the European Commission is in step with us. During lunch I deliberately ask Davis: 'Can you confirm that the United Kingdom wants to leave the European Union and also wants to leave the Single Market and the Customs Union?' To this threefold question, his answer is a clear 'yes'. Apart from his concern to hold to the commitments of the referendum, is he fully aware of all the consequences of this triple withdrawal?

Another question is whether he really has a clear mandate to implement this form of 'hard Brexit'. Judging from the political debate in the UK – and even within the government itself, between Philip Hammond and Boris Johnson – I don't think he does. But today, that is the choice they are making. So we are going to implement it, even if some argue that the door should remain open for the UK to backpedal on its decision. This is what the new French President, Emmanuel Macron, has recently suggested, along with Sigmar Gabriel, the German Vice-Chancellor, and Wolfgang Schäuble, the German Federal Minister of Finance.

In the afternoon the working groups are set up, and we will meet again for the first week of real negotiations on 17 July.

As I go to report to the press, I find David Davis in a corner, somewhat disgruntled. He tells me that he has a problem with a passage in the text that I intend to deliver to the press, and which I had sent him as a courtesy. He agrees on the sequencing, but he asks me not to use this word. Since it's only a matter of terminology, I agree instead to call it a 'step-by-step' negotiation, while making it quite clear that we will not move on to the second step without having reached an agreement on the first one…

My team and I have discussed these joint press conferences at length, convinced that they are the best way to mark out the progress that needs to be made at each session. They seem to us far more effective than laborious press releases, preparation of which would use up all of our energy for little gain. I doubt, however, that our British partners will accept this principle in the long run.

In the Commission's press room, many journalists are gathered. Outside, on the esplanade, all the British television channels are preparing for live broadcasts.

I try to send them a positive message by describing this session as 'important' and 'useful', while recalling the main principles underlying the Union's position and insisting, once again, that our aim is to reach an agreement and that the no-deal scenario is not one that we want.

A journalist from the *Daily Telegraph* asks me rather vehemently if I am prepared to make any concessions in this negotiation. How can one ask such a question and expect a reply when the negotiations haven't even begun? Keeping my tone steady, I reply that it is the UK that is leaving the EU, not the other way round. Another journalist asks me bluntly if I think I will still have David Davis as my interlocutor in a few weeks' time. Deep down I am not sure, but I answer calmly that I am negotiating with David Davis today because he is the representative of the UK government, but that the UK government is and will remain my interlocutor.

Thursday, 22 June 2017: After-dinner conversation

As decided by Donald Tusk, with the agreement of Jean-Claude Juncker, I have been invited to join the heads of state or government, who have been meeting in Brussels since 5pm, at the end of their dinner. The affair is very precisely choreographed, and perhaps a little stiff. All twenty-eight of them are around the table, and Turkey and Russia are under discussion over dinner. Theresa May is scheduled to speak to explain the political situation in London in the wake of the general election debacle, and is of course expected to talk about Brexit and to present her upcoming proposals on citizens' rights.

This might have been an opportunity for Mrs May to open up some form of direct negotiation with her colleagues in the European Council. But she knows that this is not possible, and that from now on there can be only one channel of negotiation – which has been entrusted to me. And so, this evening after her presentation, none of the other twenty-seven heads of state or government makes a response, and Donald Tusk suspends the session to allow her to leave the dinner…

It is at this point that I am invited to join the gathering. At Mr Tusk's invitation, I summarize the first day of negotiations in a few words. My message is simple: as yet there is no progress on substantial matters. 'The clock is ticking', however: at the next round of negotiations in July, we will have to push for a 'moment of truth', particularly on budgetary matters.

The British strategy is clearly to leave the issue of citizens and the Irish question in the shadows and, as Ireland's Minister for European Affairs Dara Murphy told me, to use past debts to buy pieces of the internal market 'à la carte'. This strategy may be clever, but in my view it is potentially explosive. We must make the financial question less dramatic: accounts must be settled as quickly as possible in an objective manner, on incontestable legal grounds, so that we can move on to other things.

Discussion around the table ends up being rather intense. Jean-Claude Juncker reminds us that it is necessary to maintain a single line of negotiation throughout, and to avoid both parallel discussions and scattershot public statements. Emmanuel Macron is concerned about the future relationship with the UK and wants to open discussions with his colleagues on this subject at an early stage. Such a meeting is necessary, and I will make sure it happens. But it cannot disrupt the sequencing of the negotiations. At the end of the year we must be able to see 'sufficient progress' on the first, and arguably most unpleasant phase – the separation – before we begin discussions on our future relationship with the UK.

Friday, 23 June 2017: Europe is back

'Europe is back.' This is the conclusion drawn by all commentators in the wake of the European Council. Who could have imagined such a tone a few months ago? The media are full of praise for the unity of the Europeans, the revival of the Franco-German alliance, the 'Macron effect'! At the end of last year, all the talk was of the return of populism and the disintegration of the European project following the British withdrawal…

Today, along with François Arbault, in charge of the internal market for our team, I take a break to visit the Bourget Air Show. François, a former Commissioner, is another loyal team member, and I am happy finally to be able to make this trip with him, since, like me, he has an interest in space and defence. I have often had occasion to appreciate his staunchness and his fine sense of European public service.

It has always been my belief that European space policy is the best proof of what we can achieve together and of what we could not achieve alone. Why do we not hear more about the major consequences this European policy has for the daily lives of businesses and citizens? The Galileo programme, at first held at arm's length by my late lamented friend and colleague Loyola de Palacio, in the Prodi Commission, is responsible for the European satellites that today make it possible for us to no longer depend on the Americans for geolocation, navigation and time measurement services.

Tuesday, 27 June 2017: David Davis calling

David Davis wants to talk to me on the phone – presumably to get my reactions to a document published two days ago by the British government setting out its position on citizens' rights. There are some useful and important elements in this text, but it clearly falls short of what the twenty-seven, and indeed citizens throughout the EU, are looking for in terms of the reciprocity of rights, their extension to the families of the citizens concerned and, above all, the ongoing security of these rights, which the British want to guarantee only within the framework of British law.

He asks me how I see things on the Irish question, avoiding any reference to the third major issue in this negotiation, the financial settlement.

On two previous occasions I have emphasized the need for us to make parallel progress on all three issues, not just two, if we are to succeed in these negotiations: 'I'm worried, David, very worried. If we don't make progress on the financial issue and if you don't start discussing the substantive matters with us in July, there is a risk that I won't be able to see sufficient progress by October.'

'I hear what you're saying', he replies, without further comment.

Saturday, 1 July 2017: Tribute to Helmut Kohl

On Emmanuel Macron's request, I accompany him to Strasbourg to pay tribute to the late Helmut Kohl in the European Parliament.

Before the ceremony begins, I go to greet a somewhat solitary Theresa May. She greets me very cordially with a 'Hello Michel!' I reiterate my eagerness to reach an agreement with her, despite the time constraints and the discomfort of her political situation back in London.

It is a moving ceremony. Jean-Claude Juncker, who has been personally affected by the death of his friend Helmut Kohl, pays him a warm and fitting tribute. Bill Clinton's speech is also sincere and touching. Emmanuel Macron, who of course did not know Helmut Kohl, insists upon the lessons to be drawn for the future from the German chancellor's great commitment. In veiled terms, he criticizes Brussels, its excessive bureaucracy and its remoteness from citizens, offering this fine phrase: 'Any building loses its meaning, and even its beauty, if it is no longer inhabited.'

Kohl, whom I met a number of times as a minister and as a Commissioner, and who graciously granted me several interviews, was one of the few heads of state or government in the Union who always spoke of Europe in a human way, from the heart.

Indeed, Jean-Claude Juncker recalls having seen Kohl cry on 14 December 1997, the day on which the Accession Treaty for the ten countries of Central and Eastern Europe was launched, completing the 'reunification' of the European continent. I remember well the enthusiasm with which Kohl recalled a visit to Prague during this process, recalling the infectious joy of the Czech youths dancing on Charles Bridge.

In the course of the speeches I note a few nice phrases: 'He wanted a European Germany, not a German Europe'; 'He believed that in Europe, domination must never prevail over cooperation'; 'With Europe, we are part of something bigger than ourselves.' I can't help but glance regularly during these speeches at Theresa May, who must feel rather isolated amid the European chorus, especially when Bill Clinton sets out the reasons for Europeans to stand united.

Concluding the tributes, Angela Merkel says that Helmut Kohl 'changed the lives of millions of men and women', including her own, at the time of German reunification and the fall of the Berlin Wall.

We will always have that wonderful image of Helmut Kohl and François Mitterrand holding hands in Verdun. In my office at the Quai d'Orsay I had this photo on a table next to the one I still have at Berlaymont, of General de Gaulle welcoming Chancellor Adenauer with infinite respect on the steps of the Élysée Palace in 1963. As well as the one of Jacques Chirac embracing Gerhard Schröder in 2004 on the beach where the Normandy landings took place.

Monday, 3 July 2017: Fishing in troubled waters

Much ado about nothing, or a bad omen for the future?

The British government has announced with much commotion that the UK will leave the 1964 London Fisheries Convention in order to regain control of its territorial waters. For the time being, this changes nothing. Within the EU, non-discrimination rules allow all fishermen and all vessels flying the flag of a member state to fish in the waters of other member states, including their territorial waters. The London Convention, which the UK intends to leave, is therefore de facto dormant.

But of course this announcement also sets the tone for future British stances.

Wednesday, 5 July 2017: Tribute to Simone Veil

The flood of homages and articles following the death of Simone Veil is entirely deserved. To repeat Angela Merkel's words about Helmut Kohl, she changed the lives of millions of women.

In all her struggles, she was strong and splendid. Today, standing before her coffin draped with the tricolour flag in the middle of the Invalides courtyard, I remember every one of the precious moments I spent with her.

In March 1978, it was she who came especially to Ugine to preside over my last major rally in the legislative election, four days before the first round. At the time, she was Minister of Health and had courageously just voted for the law that would decriminalize abortion. There were a thousand people in the room. The hospital unions had been mobilized to 'welcome' her. She held her head high, she stood her ground, she was persuasive. I am quite sure that it is partly to her that I owe my election that day, at the age of 27, as deputy for Savoie.

Jean d'Ormesson, speaking on the radio, says of her that she was 'above it all'… All these tributes remind me of a point I had forgotten: it was at the age of 18, having just returned from Birkenau, forever affected by the death of her beloved mother in that camp, that Veil committed herself to the reconciliation of the French and the Germans, and to preventing any recurrence of those wars on European soil that Victor Hugo insisted were 'civil wars'.

Emmanuel Macron finds the right words, concluding his tribute simply with: 'I have decided, in agreement with her family, that Simone Veil will rest, along with her husband, in the Panthéon.'

Thursday, 6 July 2017: Zeebrugge

An intense day. This morning I take up an invitation from the Greek trade union leader George Dassis, who is President of the European Economic and Social Committee. He is a warm man, clearly on the Left, passionately European in outlook. I have long enjoyed a trusted relationship with him, and have chosen his platform to clarify a number of conditions and consequences of Brexit.

The room is packed, and I make use of this forum to alert economic and social actors to the need to prepare. Whatever the outcome of the negotiations, the UK's exit means that there will be changes. The UK has chosen to leave the Customs Union and the governance of the Single Market, the combination of which alone can guarantee 'frictionless' trade in goods between our states.

The internal market without the Customs Union – that is, the European Economic Area Agreement for Norway, Iceland and Liechtenstein – still involves a system of customs procedures and controls, among other things to ensure correct application of preferential rules of origin.

On the other hand, a customs union agreement without the internal market – such as the EU's arrangement with Turkey – does not allow for the free movement of goods either, since it also implies a regime of customs procedures and controls for checking compliance with European standards, among other things. Naturally, for economic and social actors alike, the consequences of the UK's exit would be much worse in the event of no deal. We are not in a classic negotiation situation here where no deal would mean a return to the status quo. In the case of Brexit, no deal would instead mean a return to the distant past, with our trade relationship with the UK being based upon the World Trade

Organisation regime, implying, for example, tariffs of almost 10 per cent on the import of motor vehicles.

Although leaving the Customs Union would, in any event, involve the introduction of border formalities, no deal would mean extremely onerous procedures and controls, with no exceptions, something that would be particularly damaging for companies working on 'just-in-time' principles. For a sports equipment or industrial parts manufacturer based in the UK that today can send products without delay to the single market, this would mean, in concrete terms, having to keep products in stock for three or four days instead of a few hours, along with having to invest in renting warehouses and incurring increased transport costs and heightened logistical risk. In reality, no deal would worsen the 'lose–lose' situation that is bound to result from Brexit. And the UK would have more to lose than its trading partners. And so I say quite clearly this morning that, to my eyes, there is no reasonable justification for a no-deal Brexit.

After the speech, more than thirty participants have questions to ask me. And, as usual, I try to answer each one of them.

The Economic and Social Committee is in fact the foremost site for public debate with European civil society. I absolutely want us to lead this public debate on Brexit rather than react to it, and in every one of my visits to the capitals I will continue to carry the discussion forward and encourage debate.

I would also like to give this negotiation a more human, more concrete dimension. Which is why I travel to Zeebrugge this afternoon at the invitation of Geert Bourgeois, Minister-President of the Flanders region, just as I visited the 'border' between Ireland and the United Kingdom a few weeks ago.

Flanders has major economic links with the UK. Trade between the two is equivalent to two-thirds of France's trade with the UK. And the port of Zeebrugge – whose professional representatives I meet with, and hear their clear and convincing arguments – is in fact the main European hub for distribution to Ireland and the United Kingdom.

A little further out, along the seafront, 17,000 Toyota vehicles are lined up in impeccable order, waiting to be transported to those two countries, having been manufactured either in Japan or in the factory at Valenciennes.

From March 2019, vehicles that leave for the UK will be being exported to a third country, not transferred, as they are today, to another part of the Single Market. It will take a great deal of creativity to avoid the burden of controls on standards, rules of origin and potential taxation.

Here my message once again consists in underlining the urgency to begin preparations right now: 'The real transition period began in March 2017 and runs until March 2019. That's where we are. Use it!'

Wednesday, 12 July 2017: No whistling, just the clock ticking

Another meeting this morning with the College of European Commissioners, where Jean-Claude Juncker gives me a warm welcome. With the help of some slides, I present the state of the negotiations, which are scheduled to start again next week. For six months now I have been in direct contact with each of the Commissioners, and my team maintains a relationship with each of their cabinets as well as with their Directorates-General. I have always believed that collegiality means something, and that every Commissioner brings their own particular value to this institution in which, collectively and collegially, they play a role that has never existed at European level, that of Prime Minister.

All of them are following the negotiations, and relate to them differently depending upon their character and interests: Frans Timmermans, a Dutch polyglot, who tells me that he was a student at St George's British International School in Rome and has a sentimental attachment to the UK; Valdis Dombrovskis, former Latvian Prime Minister, always straightforward and direct, with a particular focus on the financial services he is responsible for.

This morning, one of them, the German Günther Oettinger, is concerned that the negotiations, which are scheduled to take place one week each month, are moving too slowly. I am aware that this is the case. It takes so much time and energy to inform and canvass opinions from the twenty-seven member states, to enter into dialogue with the sherpas of each head of state or government, and to consult with the European Parliament before and after each round of negotiations. But Oettinger is quite right: the pace of negotiations ought to be accelerated – as long as both parties are at the table!

Returning from the College, before entering the press room where some two hundred journalists are waiting for me, I take a few moments to concentrate on the messages to be conveyed. As always, we try to stay one step ahead... How should we reply to Boris Johnson's little quip yesterday? In the middle of a House of Commons session, he said that if European leaders expected the UK to pay their 'exit tax', they could 'go whistle!'

With his keen sense of repartee, Georg suggests a response that is very much to the point: 'I don't hear any whistling, just the clock ticking.' The phrase is both striking and amusing. We work on it with Dan and Matthieu, who suggests that I leave a slightly theatrical pause between the two halves of the sentence. A few moments after the meeting ends, I enter the press room. And, as I have resolved always to do from now on, I speak soberly and sincerely. Everyone knows our initial positions, set out in the nine position papers that are now public and have been approved by the Commission and the member states. We are now waiting for the British to set out their position on all of these issues regarding the divorce.

Unsurprisingly, the question comes up: an Irish journalist asks me what my reaction was to Boris Johnson's little quip. My response comes back immediately: 'I am not hearing any whistling. Just the clock ticking.' It will make the rounds, and will certainly have helped to strengthen my bond with the press corps before the negotiations begin.

Thursday, 13 July 2017: Open day for the British

So begins a very British day. Nicola Sturgeon, First Minister of Scotland, has gone out of her way to be the first in line to visit my office. I had proposed that we meet for coffee at 9am, but her plane is late. She joins me at 9.45am, disrupting everything else on my schedule for the day.

She is a likeable woman who knows what she wants. And after the disappointment she suffered in the last general election, where her party lost twenty-one seats, what she wants now is a soft Brexit, with the UK – and therefore Scotland, where 62 per cent voted Remain – staying in the Single Market.

Later, in the afternoon, First Minister of Wales Carwyn Jones, the jovial and very direct Labour leader, brings me the same message from his country.

At lunchtime I am intrigued to meet Jeremy Corbyn, leader of the Labour Party. As we pose for the press, he is keen to offer me the gift of an Arsenal shirt – the football ground is in his constituency – with my name on it. A sporting gesture that is rather touching.

For my part, my assistant Barthélemy has unearthed an old promotional tourist poster for Savoie, dating from 1948 and distributed at the time by the SNCF. I know how passionate Mr Corbyn is about public rail services. This is an opportunity for me to let him know that my province has much to thank the British for, going back to the creation of the Méribel resort by the Scotsman Peter Lindsay in the interwar years.

Corbyn is flanked by the Shadow Secretary of State for Exiting the EU, Keir Starmer, the Shadow Home Secretary Diane Abbott, and his Director of Strategy and Communications, Seumas Milne.

During the meeting and the lunch I have organized for him, Mr Corbyn informs me about the political situation after the elections and the rather impressive result he achieved for his party, defying all predictions.

I am obviously looking at a man who thinks he's going to be Prime Minister soon and is preparing himself. Naturally, I tell him that I am not negotiating with him, or with Nicola Sturgeon of Scotland or with Carwyn Jones of Wales, but that I am keen to understand what is happening in the House of Commons. In the same spirit, he asks me to explain our positions.

I once again set out the conditions for success. The sequencing that we have imposed on negotiations, with the divorce itself coming before the future relationship, is ultimately helpful to the British side as it gives them time to choose the route they want to take.

However, like Boris Johnson, Corbyn remains stuck on the idea that the United Kingdom can have its cake and eat it too, as the British say. He confirms that his party has accepted the referendum result and intends to implement the exit from the EU. I tell him that he needs to be aware of the balance of rights and obligations attached to each model of cooperation with third countries. You cannot have the advantages of the Norwegian model without freedom of movement of persons, and with only the constraints of the Canadian model.

His team seems friendly, if rather more concerned with the technical aspects than he is. We are ready to provide the information they need.

Monday, 17 July 2017: Round two

The second round of negotiations begins, but not without long and sometimes complex preliminary discussions with the British.

My team was busy until late Friday evening working out the details of this round, the list of participants, and the subjects to be discussed. And yet up until just a few days ago, David Davis was reluctant to come to Brussels himself for the beginning of the week. I had to explain to him that his absence would pose a problem not so much for me as for him, giving an impression of nonchalance that he would no doubt have some trouble in explaining.

The truth is that, at the beginning of this negotiation, I am faced with a British team that works very differently from ours. On one hand, there is a minister officially in charge of Brexit who does not want to go into the details of the negotiations and considers that his responsibilities lie with the political debate and public explanation in his home country. On the other hand, the key man in the negotiations, Olly Robbins, the Prime Minister's sherpa, clearly has Theresa May's confidence but does not want to, and cannot, speak publicly.

I don't want to spend any longer discussing who will represent the UK in this negotiation. That is for them to decide. One of the conditions of the negotiation is that there should be stable, responsible, mandated and accountable negotiators on both sides of the table. On the European side, they are in place.

Today's meeting is about our agenda for the week. I restate to Mr Davis that we really need to make progress on all issues concurrently in order that I can, as hoped, propose to European leaders in October that we start negotiations on the framework for the future relationship in parallel with the divorce. I tell him once again that I will not take on the responsibility for that decision if we have made only superficial progress. I hope the message gets through.

Mr Davis informs me that the UK is preparing several white papers on this future relationship, presumably to pressure us and force us to move more quickly. He is mistaken. We have time on our side. I am quite sincere when I say that the sooner we talk about the future the better, but we can only open this discussion with any chance of success if we trust one another. And that trust requires the settling of accounts, the securing of citizens' rights, and dealing properly with the always unpleasant questions that a divorce brings with it.

There are six of us around the table. On our side, Sabine, Stéphanie and I each have a file in front of us. Strangely, the three British negotiators have come empty-handed. And the photo taken of this meeting, at their request, is already doing the rounds on social media. Alex Barker, the perceptive journalist of the *Financial Times*, posts it on Twitter with the caption: 'Ha! Very funny Michel. As if we would forget to bring our negotiating papers.'

Clearly, in this negotiation we will need to pay as much attention to the language of gestures as to that of words.

Tuesday, 18 July 2017: Money, money, money…

In Sabine's office this morning, Olly Robbins, along with his deputy Kay Withers and HM Treasury Director General for International and EU Affairs Mark Bowman, are providing an update on the second round of negotiations that has just begun. Stéphanie is there, still taken aback by the bilateral meeting she has just had with the UK side on the financial settlement.

'We can't go on like this', she tells the British. 'For three hours, I explained over and over again our positions and the financial commitments which, from our point of view, must be covered by the financial settlement. You asked a great many questions, and contested most of our demands. There has been far too much aggression, and on your side you have given us nothing. We can't move forward if you don't explain your position and the commitments you are willing to cover. It's not enough to just say that you will meet your commitments without saying which ones…'

Coming to welcome the British team, I reinforce what Stéphanie has said, and remind them that we want to make 'sufficient progress' on this issue as well as on all the others, in parallel: 'They are inseparable.'

At this stage, the British team have clearly been instructed not to engage in any discussion about the figures or any details of the financial commitments. I add, in a more personal tone: 'I can see how sensitive this subject is in the British debate, but you must accept that at some point the reality of your commitments will have to be made known. The later you leave that, the more difficult it will be for everyone. And we are not prepared to change the sequencing. The past is the past. It may be linked to the discussion on the transitional period, but the future is the future.'

In truth, I have great admiration for these dignified, competent and lucid senior British officials. I do not envy them the fact that they have to answer to a political class a part of which simply refuses to accept today the direct consequences of decisions and stances they took a year ago.

Thursday, 20 July 2017: At the Élysée Palace

The President of the Republic had offered me an hour's meeting at noon with our respective teams, but he is delayed by a meeting in his office with the European Trade Union Confederation and its General Secretary Luca Visentini.

In his absence, the meeting is opened by Alexis Kohler, the precise and direct Secretary-General. Finally, Emmanuel Macron joins us and, over the course of a few minutes, I recap the conditions for the success of these negotiations and, as a counterpoint, the risks of failure. At the end of this second round of negotiations with the British, no concrete progress has yet been made, which is actually rather worrying.

The President, who during the European Council dinner had expressed his interest in opening early discussions between Europeans on the future partnership with the UK, confirms that things must be done in the right order and that the questions of divorce should be settled first, the most sensitive of which is that of the financial commitments that we are asking the UK to make good on. 'If they don't pay', I tell the President, 'there would be two options: either projects would grind to a halt all over Europe, or France and a few other countries would have to pay the UK's share.'

The President's reply is immediate: 'We certainly don't want that!'

Ultimately, beyond the always unpleasant questions of separation, what interests Emmanuel Macron above all – and myself too – is the future relationship with the UK, but also the reform of Europe so that it offers better protection and acts more effectively.

In a one-to-one meeting at the end of the interview, I am able to confirm, as I have with each of the other twenty-six heads of state or government, that I can count on the new French president's confidence in me for this mission.

Today we established an essential and direct relationship between my team and his. I shall do the same with Prime Minister Édouard Philippe, who intelligently deals with each subject, one after the other, in a working atmosphere that is unfailingly cordial, which is always a plus.

Thursday, 10 August 2017: Cypriot imbroglio

At 10 Downing Street, during dinner with Theresa May and Jean-Claude Juncker, we are served, in addition to a duck leg confit, a green salad with halloumi. This is a cheese from the Greek part of Cyprus made of half goat's and half cow's milk, 55 per cent of which is exported to the UK – but this is far from being the only problem we need to solve in Cyprus!

A British colony since the end of the First World War, after numerous crises and upheavals, in 1959 the island of Cyprus found itself with a new constitution under the terms of which the UK, Greece and Turkey renounced their dominance. The British reserved sovereignty over two military bases, and in 1960 Cyprus became an independent Commonwealth Republic with a Greek Cypriot president, Archbishop Makários, and a Turkish Cypriot vice-president, Dr Fazıl Küçük.

Following the 1974 conflict, in 1976 the leader of the Turkish Cypriots Rauf Denktaş unilaterally proclaimed the creation of the Turkish federated state of Cyprus. Thus the establishment of two states saw the island divided, with the creation of a 'green line' and, along this line, a demilitarized zone controlled by the UN. In Nicosia, the capital of the two states, an actual wall separates Greek and Turkish Cypriots, with only a very few pedestrian and road crossings.

My visit to Cyprus in 2001, as Commissioner for Regional Policy, left me with some memories and a strong conviction on the issue. I asked to meet with young Cypriots from both communities. Their hope was to live together, to work together and, in some cases, to marry. To me, the wall seemed utterly incongruous and archaic!

As on each of my previous visits, I told myself that, once again, Europe was a new frontier, and that the prospect of joining it would bring a new perspective on religious, nationalist and cultural quarrels and differences by offering everyone a new horizon – as was the case for France and Germany.

Since then, the Republic of Cyprus, which covers the southern part, with 900,000 inhabitants, has joined the European Union. The Nicosia wall has been opened up. Trade has normalized, and the EU has always maintained the ambition for the whole island of Cyprus to become European, via the project of a 'bi-communal republic'.

At the time of writing, we are not quite there yet. Kofi Annan's plan was rejected on 24 April 2004 by a majority of Greek Cypriot citizens. It will take further efforts from the United Nations and the European Union – which has also been contributing since 2006 to a financial programme for reconciliation and economic development on the Turkish side – as well as from the political leaders of both communities.

The military bases of Akrotiri and Dhekelia have remained under British sovereignty. These bases now account for 3 per cent of the island's territory and have their own legal system inherited from the colonial period, distinct from those of the UK and Cyprus. Around these bases there are many villages and farmlands, which de facto find themselves in a territory that is under British sovereignty. English is the island's third language.

Today, the UK is on its way to leaving the EU, but wants to retain sovereignty over its two military bases. We, along with our teams, must find and propose solutions that allow us to respect the integrity and the regulations of the Single Market, of which Cyprus will remain a member after March 2019, while the British territory of these two bases will leave it.

Monday, 28 August 2017: No way!

David Davis returns to Brussels this morning for the third round. I welcome him ahead of a first working meeting between our two teams. Speaking to journalists, I reiterate my concern about the passing of time and the lack of progress. We need clear British positions in order for constructive negotiations to take place. The sooner we remove the ambiguity, the sooner we will be in a position to discuss the future relationship.

Around the table, Sabine insists on a major point for us: we will not allow the UK to 'cherry-pick' elements of the internal market, let alone give a third country influence or veto over our regulations. In particular, she cites the UK paper on the issue of 'goods placed on the market' in the UK or the EU before the Brexit date, but which would actually be sold after Brexit. The legal status of such goods must of course be guaranteed up until the end of their lifecycle. In their paper on the subject, the British take the opportunity to suggest a general equivalence of our standardization or certification systems for products on the internal market. For example, a car produced in Italy that obtains British certification after Brexit could be sold throughout the internal market without any further guarantee, since these British certification decisions, supposedly equivalent to ours, would not be subject to our legal regime.

To make myself clear on this point, I tell Mr Davis that this issue is non-negotiable: 'No way!' To which he replies, with a certain levity: 'In that case there will be no agreement.'

This example clearly shows that the strategy the British have promised to the business community is to get the best of both worlds. As Boris Johnson would say, to 'have their cake and eat it'!

Tuesday, 29 August 2017: Transition period? What transition period?

Jean-Claude Juncker met yesterday with the German Chancellor, who is very motivated by and engaged with European issues despite her current priority: the upcoming federal elections scheduled for 24 September. The President gave the Chancellor a memo I had prepared with my team on the state of the negotiations and on a possible landing zone for this first phase, if the British genuinely want to move forward.

I have always thought that the best we could possibly do in this Withdrawal Agreement would be to deal with the issues of separation, to settle the accounts, to establish a short transition period following exit and, finally, in October or November 2018, to set out in a political declaration the contours of the future relationship that we will negotiate during the transition.

As for the British, they have until recently laboured under the illusion that not just Brexit, but the future relationship and a free trade agreement could all be negotiated in less than two years. They have now realized that this is both technically and legally impossible. And the time is undoubtedly approaching when we shall have to enter into further discussions on the transition period, both to avoid the cliff edge and to reassure the business community and allow ourselves time for the second phase of negotiations on our future relationship.

This transition period could consist of an extension of the Single Market for a year and a half after Brexit. It could include the maintenance of all the advantages of the Single Market and the Customs Union, but also certain European policies, notably on aviation, fisheries and agriculture, and obviously satisfaction of the corresponding obligations.

Such an extension would see us through to the end of the 2014–20 budget period, and should be an acceptable way for the UK government to pay what it owes for that period. This proposal is undoubtedly a generous one. In my view, though, it is both simple and logical, and in our mutual interest, if the British take advantage of it.

Wednesday, 30 August 2017: 'Cornering Barnier'

On Monday evening, David Davis met privately at the British Embassy with some of the journalists and commentators who have been following Brexit. A note in a sealed envelope is delivered to me. I don't know where it comes from, so I accept it with some caution. It purports to reveal the kind of language used at this event.

Some of it is not surprising: 'Not committing to pay anything until we know the shape of our future relationship. Not paying for the multiannual financial framework until 2020 and then every year during the transition – that's nonsense. The EU needs to get serious. [...] We will shut them out of the City of London.'

Some is more aggressive: 'The aim is to cut Barnier off from the twenty-seven, to get Barnier into a corner by himself.'

We shall see whether this note is true and whether we find these 'arguments' cropping up in the press or in British statements in the coming weeks.

Thursday, 31 August 2017: 'Your legal analysis is broadly without merit'

We are coming to the end of this third round. It is disappointing. The British position on the financial settlement even seems to be sliding backwards.

At the beginning of July, the British recognized international commitments that could run on after Brexit. Today they are sticking to a totally restrictive so-called legal analysis of these commitments. In their view, the last payment will be linked to the last commitment formally made in 2019. They deny any legal commitment for the multiannual period 2014–20. This includes the European Development Fund, which is intergovernmental and finances projects in Africa, the Pacific and the Caribbean.

The situation is deadlocked. But this extreme hard-line position places the British in a potentially weak position. It casts doubt upon the trustworthiness of the British signature in international agreements.

The British can sense our disappointment. One of their young civil servants yesterday was particularly flippant and arrogant, treating all the sound legal arguments of the Commission's and Council's legal services as null and void: 'Your legal analysis is broadly without merit.' Now we've heard it all! No doubt in order to give himself some leeway in future phases of negotiation, David Davis introduces a new concept, that of 'moral commitments'. I smile and ask him for a list of these moral commitments, but I am surely not going to agree to go down that road.

They need to move on and recognize that accounts must be settled. Otherwise, I do not and will not be able to see 'sufficient progress' to initiate the urgently needed discussion on the future relationship.

Saturday, 2 September 2017: No lessons to be learned

On the other side of the Alps, on the magical shores of Lake Como, I am thrilled to arrive back at the beautiful Villa d'Este hotel, occupied in its entirety by the annual Ambrosetti Forum. Many European, American, African and Asian leaders are invited to speak here every year. About three hundred Italian business leaders are regular attendees. A few journalists attend the debates, which are not public and are held under the Chatham House Rule.

Enrico Letta introduces a debate between Margrethe Vestager and Bruno Le Maire on growth and competitiveness. Although of different temperaments, the three have in common a remarkable knowledge of their subjects and a talent for presenting them with great elegance, fittingly for the setting of Villa d'Este.

I have been asked to explain the issues at stake in Brexit to attentive and worried Italian industrialists, in only thirty minutes.

In the middle of my short speech, I reiterate how this negotiation is pedagogical in nature, since it brings to light the benefits of the internal market, what it means to be in the Union, and what it means to be outside.

Referring to Geert Wilders, the leader of the Dutch sovereigntist party who was at the same table the day before, but also to the state of mind in my own country, I suggest that this way of explaining the matter may be useful for citizens.

The next day, I find this sentence distorted by certain British media, who accuse me of wanting to 'educate' the British and teach them a lesson. To avoid this controversy escalating, I decide to post a rather mild tweet to remind them of what I had actually said.

If further proof were needed of the UK's sensitivity on all issues related to Brexit, this incident provided it.

Thursday, 7 September 2017: A return to myth

This morning I read a long interview in *Les Échos* with Robin Niblett, director of Chatham House, the highly respected British international affairs think-tank. He knows his country well, and describes with great precision its historical and psychological mainsprings:

> With Brexit, we have reconnected with our old myth, that of a country whose government has never been defeated. The British are going through an incredible moment of excitement. And even if it comes at a price, they want to reconnect with that myth that they love and that makes them feel good.

As I read this interview, I think of what my Deputy Head of Cabinet said to me a long time ago when I was Commissioner for Regional Policy.

It was 25 July 2002, and I had gone to watch the opening ceremony of the Commonwealth Games in Manchester. The atmosphere was festive, comparable to the Olympic Games, with fifty-three countries and seventy-two nations in attendance. The Queen was there with her family, as was Prime Minister Tony Blair.

I found myself in the third row of the official gallery with my adviser Ronnie Hall, a Northern Irishman. As is always the case in such ceremonies, the athletes' delegations entered the stadium one by one, in an atmosphere at once solemn and joyous, each preceded by its flag. Several of these flags still featured the Union Jack. At the end of the long parade, Ronnie Hall tapped me on the shoulder and said mischievously: 'Now you understand better, Commissioner, why Europe seems too small to us.'

Sunday, 17 September 2017: Boris Johnson puts pen to paper

Boris Johnson is at it again. In a column published yesterday in the *Daily Telegraph*, which seems to have been written in some haste, Theresa May's Foreign Secretary seeks to place himself back at the centre of the negotiation game from which he has apparently been excluded.

It seems that the personal jostling within the Conservative Party is quite as complicated as it was last year among my own political family in France.

Above all, Boris Johnson once again brandishes, as he did before the Brexit vote, the figure of £350 million a week that could be spent on the NHS once it is no longer given to 'Brussels technocrats'.

In a rare communiqué, chair of the UK Statistics Authority Sir David Norgrove takes it upon himself to correct Johnson and to remind him that we must not confuse the UK's budgetary contribution to the EU with its net contribution. Once the UK leaves the EU, the UK national budget will have to take up the slack for regional or agricultural policies, for example, for which Europe will no longer pay.

Monday, 18 September 2017: English breakfast

The British Liberal Democrats are seeking to regain lost ground under their new leader, Vince Cable. At their conference this morning, the party's former chairman Tim Farron raised a laugh among his audience: 'Once upon a time, Michel Barnier would have croissants and coffee for breakfast, now he has David Davis, every flipping day.'

When the occasion arises, I'll let him know that I have always preferred English breakfasts to French croissants. And that, besides, I can chat with David Davis and have breakfast at the same time!

Tuesday, 19 September 2017: The British offensive

Olly Robbins, who has just left his post as Director of the Department for Exiting the European Union, remains full time with Theresa May and continues to lead the negotiations along with David Davis. He is currently spearheading a general offensive in all the EU capitals, ahead of Theresa May's speech in Florence.

This speech, which will be given not long before the Conservative Party conference in Manchester in early October, is extremely important for Theresa May. She is seeking to speed up the negotiations and is determined to meet the 'sufficient progress' deadline in October. For several days now, I have been repeating that this is less and less likely given the British position and their constant challenges over the financial question. Martin Selmayr, who has just received Olly Robbins, gives me a precise account of Theresa May's intentions. There are no real surprises: genuine progress on citizens' rights and, in particular – finally! – a step in our direction with recognition of the role of the EU Court of Justice, confirmation of the UK's positions on Ireland and, on the financial settlement, acknowledgement of the uncertainties created by Brexit for other European countries and a commitment to 'honour our promises'.

Above all, Theresa May wants to go as far as possible towards a political agreement on the parameters of the future relationship. Still the same strategy: by trying to link the negotiation on the future relationship to the financial negotiation, the objective is to buy pieces of the Single Market with debts from the past – and to warn that 'nothing is agreed until everything is agreed'.

Together with Jean-Claude Juncker's cabinet, my team and I decide to wait. On the day of the speech, I will simply say that we have received the British proposals but that we need precise and concrete documents in the next rounds. You don't negotiate on the basis of a speech.

Thursday, 21 September 2017: 'Where there's a will...'

Another consultation in a member state, and not just any member state. Here in the magical city of Rome, I meet one by one with the Minister for Economic Development Carlo Calenda, the trade unions, former President Giorgio Napolitano, members of parliament from both chambers, then with Prime Minister Paolo Gentiloni and, finally, with the President of Confindustria, the Italian business confederation.

The Prime Minister is a straightforward and direct man who has quickly earned the esteem and respect of his colleagues in the European Council. His style contrasts with the flamboyance of Matteo Renzi. He knows what he wants, and he confirms his confidence in me.

As for Giorgio Napolitano, we have been on first-name terms since he chaired the European Parliament's Committee on Constitutional Affairs from 1999 to 2004. This, he confides to me, is the only period in his past that he feels nostalgic about. This 92-year-old man admits to me that he is tired and growing weaker, but here in the apartment that the Senate has placed at his disposal, with a very large sunny terrace planted with trees, he seems to have lost none of his curiosity or intellectual vivacity. He hands me an article he has published today in a major newspaper, and asks me about the activities of Emmanuel Macron, who has been to see him. And he tells me: 'We must put an end to the hypocritical idea of a Europe of twenty-seven countries where everyone can do everything together.'

This day spent in Rome is not neutral since, somewhat by chance, it is the day before Theresa May makes her European speech in Florence. My team and I have therefore decided to set certain limits to the negotiations and to recall our principles, for future reference.

A genuine guarantee for citizens requires that they can assert their rights in direct reference to the Withdrawal Agreement, and that these rights are valid before a national court, which will be obliged to refer any questions of interpretation relating to European law to the Court of Justice of the European Union.

As for the potential transition period beginning on 30 March 2019, the day after the withdrawal, it must be short and well defined. This is what the European Council's guidelines indicate: during this transition, it states, we would expect 'existing Union regulatory, budgetary, super-visory, judiciary and enforcement instruments and structures to apply'.

And this transition period should be part of the Withdrawal Agreement under Article 50. Without this Withdrawal Agreement, there can be no transition. This is a point of law.

On the terms of the UK's withdrawal and on a possible transition period alike, I am convinced that rapid agreement is possible. And I call upon the United Kingdom to put proposals on the table next week that will make it possible to overcome the obstacles. As a final humorous touch, I quote Machiavelli in Italian: '*Dove c'è una grande volontà, non possono esserci grandi difficoltà.*'*

Friday, 22 September 2017: In Florence, Theresa May drives the point home

In the midst of numerous phone calls with sherpas across Europe, my team and I take a moment to watch Theresa May's speech. The setting for this intervention, which has long been kept secret, is rather unusual: since this morning, the British press has been telling us that the UK government will address the entire European continent from a place that is emblematic of European identity, which cannot be reduced to Brussels...

In the end, it turns out that the cloister of the Basilica of Santa Maria Novella has been chosen for the occasion, but that makes little difference to viewers; Theresa May stands in front of a white background showing a map of the world upon which are inscribed the words: '*Shared history, shared challenges, shared future.*' And this is the message the Prime Minister seeks to convey, using the formula she now uses in every speech she makes, namely that the UK may be leaving the EU, but it is not leaving Europe, with which it will continue to share its values and its future. From the outset, the emphasis is on the common challenges facing us and which we can only address together – which, incidentally, is in my view the most important justification for the unprecedented political project of the European Union...

On the eve of our fourth round of negotiations, however, it is Mrs May's remarks on the subject of withdrawal that are the most keenly anticipated. Having asked for and obtained the support of her principal

---

* 'Where there is great willingness, there can be no great difficulty.'

ministers Boris Johnson, David Davis and Philip Hammond, who are with her here, she makes numerous overtures in her speech towards reopening the discussion on citizens' rights. She signals her agreement as to the direct effect of European law, i.e. the possibility for citizens concerned to directly invoke the provisions of the Withdrawal Agreement before the British administrations and courts, and she lets it be known that the EU Court of Justice could also play a role.

On Ireland, the Prime Minister confirms the UK government's commitment to preserving the Good Friday (Belfast) Agreement and the Common Travel Area with Ireland without reinstating any infrastructure at the border, which is certainly a step in the right direction, although there is no mention of how we will put in place the controls necessary to protect the Single Market.

As for her remarks on the financial settlement, they are long overdue – and finally come only after Mrs May has reiterated her desire for a close security and defence partnership and a tailor-made economic partnership – halfway between a free trade agreement and the more beneficial aspects of the internal market, but without the constraints that go with it. Surely this is a deliberate attempt to tell us that everything goes together, and that the UK will only meet its financial obligations if it gets everything else it wants.

This doesn't surprise me, given my recent exchanges with David Davis. Mrs May does however make two game-changing remarks. Although there had been no discernible movement up until now, she declares that no member state should 'fear that they will need to pay more or receive less over the remainder of the current budget plan as a result of our decision to leave'. This is a step forward, covering the final two years of the multiannual framework of the EU budget, although there is still a long way to go. Second, she states, without further detail, that the UK 'will honour commitments we have made during the period of our membership'. This is a major shift in tone. We may be able to move forward.

She then calls for a transition period, which she calls the 'period of implementation'. I am not surprised by this request, since there is no way the British could be ready by March 2019 to take over administrative and technical responsibilities for all the organizations they have chosen to leave.

Monday, 25 September 2017: Round four

The first day of a new round of negotiations, the fourth.

At the end of the afternoon I meet David Davis, who confirms the advances set out in the Florence speech, and the request for a transition period. As if it were of some help to us, he finds it necessary to inform me twice over that he approves of Mrs May's speech. To which I reply that it never occurred to me to question this, since he is, after all, her minister…

Tuesday, 3 October 2017: A resolute Parliament

I attend the European Parliament in Strasbourg, as I do every month. And, as I have done before, after each round of negotiations, I have a private meeting with the Brexit Steering Group, whose task is to coordinate and prepare the European Parliament's deliberations and resolutions on Brexit.

The paradox here is that the meetings are held on the third floor – in the Margaret Thatcher room.

During the plenary debate, nearly sixty speakers take the floor. We come under fire from about fifteen British MEPs and sovereigntists from other countries. As if on cue, they all blame the Union for dragging things out with delaying tactics. Many speak of the UK as if they were still living in the nineteenth century, with a kind of nostalgia for what was once the British Empire.

By the end of the morning the debate has run over time and, as on every voting day, the Chamber fills up entirely within a few minutes. It is then that Antonio Tajani gives me the floor to respond. I set aside my notes and, spurred on by the attacks of the sovereigntists, rally all of my arguments in about nine minutes:

> [T]here are two words which I cannot accept because they are not at all part of my state of mind or attitude. They are: revenge and punishment. I have had the greatest admiration for the United Kingdom for a long time. […] I have the greatest admiration for your country and – honourable members from the United Kingdom – never, ever will you find the slightest bit of revenge or punishment in my attitude – never!

There is another word, Mr Farage, that I cannot accept and which you mentioned once again. And that is the word 'ransom'. There is no ransom. There is no exit bill. There is simply the fact that at the point in time that you leave, we are asking you to settle the accounts. No more, no less. To pay what you have committed to pay.

And I would add that this is an important point if – as you have wished – we are to begin a different, but solid and lasting relationship in trade, security, the fight against terrorism and defence. We need to have this trust between us if we are to create a lasting relationship in the future. And the key to this trust is that you accept to settle the accounts objectively.

There is something which you have said, ladies and gentlemen, which I do not understand: the idea that I, as a European negotiator, or the European Union as a whole, are delaying things, or are trying to keep the United Kingdom in the Union. Ladies and gentlemen, the referendum in the United Kingdom took place on 23 June 2016. We received Theresa May's letter notifying us of the UK's intention to leave on 29 March 2017. Because of the elections in the UK, we waited until the end of June 2017 to begin the negotiations. We are not using delaying tactics. You took your time, and we respected that, but frankly I cannot accept your criticism. We are ready to intensify the rhythm of the negotiations, as much as necessary.

In the wake of this somewhat improvised intervention, the European Parliament's second resolution on Brexit is adopted by an even larger majority than the first.

Wednesday, 4 October 2017: Agincourt

I am alerted to certain statements made by Jacob Rees-Mogg, a Conservative MP who has been mentioned in the British press as a potential rival to Mrs May, statements that were filmed by Sky TV. I listen to his rhetoric. Like many of those who spoke in Parliament yesterday, it is most decidedly the nostalgic view of the UK that dominates: 'We need to be reiterating the benefits of Brexit, because this is so important in the history of our country. This is Magna Carta […] it's the Bill of Rights […], it's Waterloo, it's Agincourt, it's Crécy. We win all of these things.'

All that's missing is Trafalgar!

As for Theresa May, her speech at the close of the Conservative Party conference was marked by several incidents: a coughing fit, a prankster brandishing a P45, the letters of the party slogan falling off the wall behind her…

I don't want to laugh at this, let alone mock her for it. She is a courageous and tenacious woman surrounded by a great many men who are more interested in their personal fortunes than in the future of their country.

Thursday, 5 October 2017: Stockholm

I arrive in this beautiful, romantic city, bathed in sunshine. *Vilken vacker dag!*

The day begins at the Parliament, where former Secretary of State Tobias Billström, whom I knew as president of the European People's Party (PPE), offers me a warm welcome. One by one, I meet the trade unions, the Minister for Trade and European Affairs Ann Linde, and then the Prime Minister, Stefan Löfven, a solid, calm, smooth-talking, efficient former steelworker. I get on well with his team and, in particular, his sherpa, the wise and capable Hans Dahlgren. Finally, I meet with the president of the Swedish employers' association.

Sweden is one of the four European countries that will be most affected by Brexit in economic and trade terms. All are keen to maintain a strong relationship with the UK. But what strikes me today, as it did three weeks ago with the French and German bosses in Évian, is that for them, the Single Market remains the most important advantage.

On the Prime Minister's table everyone has a piece of cake in front of them. We don't really have time to eat it. The photo of our meeting features in a number of tweets: 'They have the cake and don't eat it.'

Friday, 6 October 2017: Hard line from the ambassadors

From the outset, I decided to play things sincerely and transparently with the member states and their ambassadors in Brussels, whom we meet at least once a week for a Brexit working group. We tell them everything. This is how trust is built.

For weeks now, the British have engaged in a massive diplomatic and political campaign to convince EU leaders to open the second phase of negotiations without delay. Clearly, Theresa May needs to show that she is making progress, that the negotiations are moving forward, and that she has obtained trade talks without having made any concessions on the financial settlement. It even seems as if it is an 'existential question' for her. For weeks now, Sabine and Olly Robbins have been looking ahead to the next stage of the negotiations. It is clear that the British are desperate to obtain a firm commitment from us on a transition period during which the status quo of the internal market will be maintained. This morning Olly Robbins texted me at 7.23am: 'Dear Michel, good luck this morning. My hopes for our process rest on you! Kind regards.'

In my office at 8am, Sabine, Georg and I put the finishing touches to my speech to Coreper, the Permanent Representatives Committee, which brings together the EU ambassadors of the twenty-seven countries on whose behalf I am negotiating.

I do not intend to ask for more leeway from the member states today. I do not want to deviate from the mandate they have given me. And there is not enough progress on the package of the three major issues of the divorce, and especially on the financial settlement, which the British are trying to set apart. Recognition of a transition period would certainly be a considerable concession to make at this point.

Martin Selmayr, who has a good sense of the atmosphere among the member states, even from India, where he is currently with Jean-Claude Juncker, thought it necessary to warn me last night: 'There will probably be a change in London very soon, which will alter the organization of the negotiations on the British side, so we have to be prudent in the coming week. This is not the time to make concessions.'

So I just tell the ambassadors that we are stuck on the financial settlement and that, for the British, any further discussion inevitably implies linking it to the issue of a transition period. If they are going to pay, they need to be able to explain it to their electorate and they need to get the payments spread out over time.

The ambassadors remain wary. France and Germany ask that we maintain a strict line: no negotiations on the future relationship, or even on the transition, unless agreement is reached on the financial settlement. But I have at least opened up a path to avoid total blockage or breakdown of negotiations, and discussions will continue.

Thursday, 12 October 2017: Brussels – dinner with Theresa May

Theresa May makes the trip for a small working dinner with Jean-Claude Juncker. In the midst of a continuing political storm within her party and the government, the Prime Minister is desperate to shake up the negotiations, and to get the European Council to open the second phase this week.

I thank her for the Florence speech, which created a much-needed new dynamic in the negotiations. I tell her that we now need to work on a 'package' by the end of the year, which could go some way towards making the desired link with a potential transition period. But I also tell her that, in order to present such a package, I need to obtain firm agreement from her, if not on the figures, at least on the principal elements of the financial settlement: the UK contributions for 2019 and 2020, which she has already accepted, but also the outstanding balance at the end of the multi-annual period in 2020 and the outstanding liabilities, such as the loan guarantees in Ukraine or the pension system for EU officials. This is where we are furthest apart, I tell her.

She looks tired, as could be expected. She lets Olly Robbins and David Davis do a lot of talking, but insists: 'To sort out the financial issue, I need to get something in return.'

I choose to be very clear and frank during this dinner: 'This financial question is very difficult for you. We know that. We have to make it less dramatic in order to solve it as soon as possible. Half of the member states don't want to allow you a single euro more, the other half don't want to receive one euro less because of you.'

Jean-Claude Juncker has the good sense to add that a swift agreement on this issue will create a far better atmosphere for the British in the negotiations to follow on the future relationship.

All in all, this dinner, human and amicable, demonstrates goodwill on both sides, but no real movement.

Friday, 20 October 2017: European Council

The European Council is meeting, after four weeks during which the British have campaigned hard on the diplomatic front, trying to cut corners, open doors and bypass us, while simultaneously facing us across the table. In short, once again making the mistake of negotiating the wrong deal.

It has been a habit of the British, throughout the forty years that they have been members of the European Union, to use this method to fight, block and amend the proposals of the European Commission, which they consider to be the instrument of a federalism they detest. Since the beginning of the Brexit negotiations they have been doing it again, even though the Commission has no agenda apart from the interests of the twenty-seven and the integrity of the Union's legal regime.

Today, their aim was to obtain an early agreement on the transition period that Theresa May called for in her Florence speech, and also to infiltrate the work that the twenty-seven will be undertaking on the future relationship.

On both issues, they have been defeated. Instead of trying to lobby this or that member state to table amendments, creating confusion and counterattacks, it would have been more effective to have trusted me.

The conclusions of the European Council are adopted in three minutes without amendment. A fairly lengthy debate follows, during which twelve of the heads of state or government speak. They all support our work and reiterate their confidence in me.

Several prime ministers ask me about ways to break the deadlock and what they can do to help. In my response to all of their interventions, I confirm that I can work on the basis of these conclusions, and seek a way forward to present an extended package in December. This package would acknowledge the UK's agreement on the separation issues and in particular on the elements of the financial settlement, but would propose to spread the payments over a number of years following Brexit, including in this timetable a one- or two-year transition period.

This transitional period would be much more than a staggering of payments. It would be a year and a half or two years of maintaining the economic status quo and all the benefits of the internal market and European policies for a third country. And when you look at the economic flows between the UK and us, the UK has five times more interest in such a transitional period than we do.

Thursday, 9 November 2017: Rome

On the day that we resume negotiations with the British – our sixth round – I make a brief trip to Rome where I have been invited by the newspaper *Il Messaggero*. Antonio Tajani, always warm and friendly, is there too, and I meet the Italian Prime Minister Paolo Gentiloni, who is making headway not only in Italy but also within the European Council. Two Italians from opposite political camps and with different styles, both of whom defend the European project with great conviction against the populism that is on the rise here, as elsewhere: Tajani through his unlimited availability to interlocutors and his enthusiastic speeches, Gentiloni through his calm and compelling arguments.

For this trip I am joined by Georg and Matthieu, both 'Italians at heart': Georg via marriage to a charming and talented Italian woman from the European Commission; Matthieu via a cultural attachment – he spent his Erasmus placement in this beautiful city.

Together, we have decided that my speech should include a response to US Secretary of Commerce Wilbur Ross. Two days ago in London, he called on the British to diverge from Europe in order to better converge with others – with fewer environmental, health, food and no doubt also financial, fiscal and social regulations. He deliberately provoked us by giving the example of chickens that the Americans, who do not have the same chain of sanitary controls as we do in our farms, soak in a bath of chlorinated water before exporting them. We have never wanted these 'chlorinated chickens' on the European market, as they do not comply with our health regulations. Speaking in London, Ross warned that, in order to reach a trade agreement with the US, the UK will have to change those regulations.

In my speech, I ask: the United Kingdom may have chosen to leave the European Union, but will it also want to move away from the European model? That is another question entirely.

Behind the European regulatory framework proper, there are fundamental societal choices to which we all adhere: the social market economy, health protection, food safety, fair and effective financial regulation.

I am saying this in Rome, where the treaty upon which this model is based was signed: we will not accept this regulatory framework being called into question.

Monday, 13 November 2017: Warsaw

My tour of Europe continues, and Poland is obviously a key country, one whose politicians have been keenly courted by the British in recent weeks. It is they who have the greatest cause for concern about the situation of EU citizens in the UK, since there are almost 900,000 Poles living there. The paradox, and the injustice, is that their presence has been exploited by the partisans of Brexit to scaremonger, to induce a retreat into national self-interest, and ultimately to support the British position against free movement after the referendum.

I am reminded of the disgraceful episode of the 'Polish plumber', used shamelessly in 2005 in France to defeat the draft European Constitution. In the British case, what is all the more shocking is that many of these Poles were invited to come to the UK in order to keep the economy running. At the time of Poland's accession in 2004, the UK and Ireland were the only two EU countries that chose not to activate a clause available to them that would have suspended freedom of movement for seven years.

I see that British lobbying has had its effects, and that on certain issues related to citizens' rights, family reunification and the portability of social benefits, Poland is less intransigent than it was when negotiations began. Nevertheless, it remains on the side of European unity, and one by one Prime Minister Beata Szydło, Minister for European Affairs Konrad Szymański and, above all, the most adept and capable Deputy Prime Minister Mateusz Morawiecki confirm their confidence and support in me.

Friday, 24 November 2017: What remains to be done (in the first phase)

Thanks to the sequencing we put in place, the unity of the twenty-seven and the wonderful technical work of my team, which enabled us to constantly stay one step ahead in the negotiation, discussions are progressing.

On the financial settlement, we are almost there.

On citizens' rights, we still need some progress on the issue of family reunification, on the possibility of exporting family allowances and on the role of the European Court of Justice.

The Irish question is the stumbling block, because so much passion and emotion between the Irish and the British is bound up with it. My strategy has been to make sure that the British, who are leaving the Union, recognize their responsibility for the continuation of North–South cooperation in Ireland, set up under EU law, with EU funding, and supported by EU policies. Having recognized this responsibility, if they wish to preserve the Good Friday (Belfast) Agreement, then they will have to provide solutions. And these solutions, for each subject in question, will essentially consist in what I have called common regulatory areas covering the whole island of Ireland.

A few days ago at the Council of Foreign Ministers, I gave an example with which I became quite well acquainted as a former Minister of Agriculture, that of animal disease prevention. In 2009 I had to deal with the consequences of the bluetongue crisis and, in this emergency situation, we improvised coordination between European countries with extremely serious consequences at stake for livestock farms: we had to find a vaccine and vaccinate twenty-four million animals as fast as possible. And there are lessons to be learned here. In a territory as homogeneous as the island of Ireland, it is unimaginable that there should be two separate regulatory frameworks.

Monday, 27 November 2017: Tallinn

I am happy to be back in the capital of Estonia, which, since July, has held the presidency of the European Council with great authority. I am reminded of my very first visit here in 1995, ten years before Estonia joined the EU. As French Minister for European Affairs, at the time I made a point of going on a run very early in the morning with my security officer in the streets or parks of the capitals I was visiting, before the official start of meetings and appointments.

On that occasion, I was struck by the fact that there were ATMs everywhere in the streets of Tallinn, while there were none in the streets of Vilnius in Lithuania or Riga in Latvia. Estonia has always been ahead of the game in many respects, and this is especially true today in the digital economy. The administration works paperlessly, and the cabinet room is fully computerized.

First thing in the morning, I meet the President of the Republic for breakfast at her residence. Kersti Kaljulaid is a young woman who worked at the European Court of Auditors for a lengthy period. Her power is largely ceremonial and honorific, but she plays a role in foreign and defence policy.

During this breakfast, her adviser asks me a question which at the time seems a little incongruous: 'From a philosophical point of view, can we draw anything positive from Brexit?' Perhaps this daily diary will enable readers to find their own answer to this question!

Tuesday, 28 November 2017: Angela Merkel

On my return from Tallinn, I am looking forward to spending the next two days in the German capital and meeting there with my friend Peter Altmaier, a minister and trusted adviser to the Chancellor, who has taken on an interim role as Federal Finance Minister with great authority. I also spend some valuable time working with Sabine and the Chancellor's European adviser Uwe Corsepius, who is as precise, direct and competent as ever.

And despite her worries about the formation of the new government after the breakdown of negotiations with the liberals, Angela Merkel receives me for a good half-hour in her office before flying to Abidjan for the Europe–Africa summit.

We have known each other for a long time now. Since 1994, in fact, when she became Minister for the Environment of the Federal Republic of Germany, at the time I held the same position in France. Already during this period, I had ample opportunity to observe her tenacity, her straightforwardness, and her concern with seeing things in detail and taking the time to genuinely understand them.

We discuss the current state of the negotiations, the landing zones we are preparing on the financial settlement, on citizens' rights. She is worried, as I am myself, about the Ireland issue. She repeats to me what she said to Theresa May two days ago about the confidence she has in my work on the negotiations. 'It is up to you', she says, 'to tell us whether or not we are ready to move to the second phase.'

We then turn to what will come next. Like other German officials, she wants to be sure that the future political and economic status of the UK, which has decided to leave the EU, is clearly distinct. 'It can't be the same', she tells me, without raising her voice but making herself crystal clear. She says she is reassured by the preparations we are making with the member states for the next steps.

I talk with her about my speech the next day to the confederation of employers' associations, the BDA. 'We need to explain in simple, understandable language what it means to be a member of the Union and the Single Market, and what you stand to lose when you leave.'

The next day I will speak frankly to the BDA's business leaders: 'I don't know if British businesses have been told the whole truth about the practical consequences of Brexit. My responsibility before you, and everywhere else in Europe, is to tell the truth to European businesses.'

Any commercial relationship with a country outside the EU necessarily involves friction. With respect to VAT declarations, for instance. Or in relation to the import of live animals and animal products, which are subject to systematic controls at the EU border when they come from third countries.

In order to be prepared for these automatic consequences of Brexit, it is important that every company clearly analyses its exposure to the UK and is prepared to adapt, where necessary, its logistics circuits, supply chain and contractual clauses.

For example, many contracts give jurisdiction to the UK courts for the settlement of commercial disputes. Up until now, the judgments of these courts have been automatically recognized throughout the EU. Post-Brexit, there is no guarantee that this will still be the case.

Sunday, 3 December 2017: Finally, some progress...

This Sunday it's all hands on deck, and the corridors of the task force are bustling. We're almost there. The British have just confirmed their agreement on two points on citizens' rights that were still pending and which I and the European Parliament both wanted to see settled.

The first concerns the possibility for citizens covered by the Withdrawal Agreement to export family benefits and to bring their families – parents, grandparents, children and grandchildren – to their country of residence.

The British have also finally agreed to extend cover to the future children of a future couple: a Spanish citizen, living in the UK and benefiting from the rights recognized in the Withdrawal Agreement, is married to a Belgian. They have a child before Brexit. All three benefit from the protection of their rights. A divorce occurs after Brexit and this Spanish citizen remarries a French woman. A child is born to this new couple. This young child will be covered in the same way as their half-brother or half-sister. This is an important step forward for the citizens concerned.

Monday, 4 December 2017: The Irish trap

Finally, after a great deal of back and forth, advances and setbacks, we have managed to produce a Joint Report with the British on this first phase of the negotiations, which sets out the points upon which we believe agreement is possible. Theresa May is coming to Brussels today to approve the text.

I go up to Jean-Claude Juncker's office on the thirteenth floor shortly before lunch. Jean-Claude, as relaxed and friendly as ever, is smiling. As is Martin Selmayr, but in his case it's more like the excitement of a historic moment. To our minds, this lunch meeting must end with our reaching agreement with Theresa May on the content of our report.

We know that she would be taking a risk in accepting, on many issues, conditions that the British had stubbornly refused at the beginning of the negotiations – but our sequencing has had its intended effect.

At the beginning of lunch there is, in fact, an outstanding point of disagreement concerning the planned new British administrative body to monitor the protection of citizens' rights. European citizens in the UK must be able to appeal to this mediator just as British citizens within the Union can refer to the European Commission. Jean-Claude Juncker, at the instigation of Martin Selmayr, also wants this ombudsman to be able to refer cases to a court or tribunal in the UK.

This is a delicate point for the British because, from the beginning, we wanted to make the EU Court of Justice the ultimate arbiter of the consistent interpretation of rights on both sides of the Channel. We finally obtained agreement that the British courts would apply all the case law of the EU Court established up to the day of Brexit, that they will be invited to take into account the case law established post-Brexit and, moreover, that in new cases they can voluntarily request a preliminary ruling by the EU Court of Justice. The court's decision in such cases will of course be binding.

Under pressure from the most hard-line Brexiteers, who want the EU Court of Justice to play no role post-Brexit, Theresa May is seeking to set a time limit on this potential for preliminary rulings. Throughout the preparatory work for negotiations, France refused this limitation, and was supported by Germany in doing so. Since then, we have had extensive contact with the French on the matter, and yesterday I exchanged text messages with President Macron, who assured us that he would accept a compromise.

Jean-Claude Juncker suggests a period of fifteen years. Theresa May is starting from a very low base, proposing three years in exchange for a concession on the role of the ombudsman. This period is not acceptable either to us or to our legal services, because it would not allow us to 'wrap up' all potential cases of jurisprudence.

I speak immediately after Theresa May, telling her that, as a negotiator, I cannot accept such a duration because the European Parliament and several member states would find it unacceptable. Jean-Claude Juncker proposes nine or ten years and we leave it at that, without reaching any conclusion on these points.

Meanwhile, we sense feverish activity on the British side. A string of text messages is received by Olly Robbins, who, apparently irritated by them, reports tersely to Theresa May. By the third message we sense that something is going on. She looks dismayed and makes no attempt to hide her disappointment. 'I have a serious problem', she tells us, 'with my Northern Irish DUP allies, who do not approve of the report's text on Ireland.'

Every word in this part of the report had been carefully weighed up, and this morning we received the agreement of the British, passed on by Olly Robbins. Jean-Claude Juncker received confirmation of the agreement of the Irish Prime Minister, Taoiseach Leo Varadkar, at midday. So we thought the point was settled. Obviously, it is no longer settled on the British side, and this means Theresa May cannot approve the Joint Report – 'if you want there to be a British government to continue discussions with you', she adds.

So what's the problem? It is paragraph 48 of our Joint Report that is at issue. This paragraph commits the UK to continue to protect

North–South cooperation and to ensure the absence of any physical border. Any future arrangements must be consistent with these fundamental requirements. In order to achieve these objectives, Article 48 successively sets out three possible scenarios:

1. The future relationship between the EU and the UK could protect North–South cooperation and avoid a physical border. This is the UK's intention.
2. Should this not be possible, the UK will propose specific solutions to address the unique circumstances of the island of Ireland.
3. In the absence of any agreement on such solutions, the UK will maintain full alignment in Northern Ireland under the rules of the Single Market and the Customs Union which, now and in the future, are able to sustain North–South cooperation, the economy of the whole island and the protection of the Good Friday (Belfast) Agreement.

There are in fact nearly 142 points of cooperation between Northern Ireland and Ireland in all areas – trade in goods, agriculture, health, education, prevention of animal diseases – which are governed by European law and supported by EU policies and by the EU budget. The UK's withdrawal de facto calls into question or undermines most of these points of cooperation. It is therefore quite proper that the UK should shoulder its responsibilities and commit itself to proposing solutions. But it is this paragraph, which actually mentions the option of 'common regulatory areas' on the island of Ireland, that has provoked the ire of Arlene Foster and her colleagues in the DUP.

After a break, and many phone calls between London, Belfast and Brussels, Theresa May asks us to give her a little more time. It is agreed that we will suspend the discussion and that she will return on Wednesday or Thursday to try to conclude it.

In this phase, more than ever, 'the clock is ticking', as Donald Tusk will immediately confirm to Mrs May, who leaves to go and see him. The European Council takes place in ten days' time on 15 December, and if agreement is not confirmed on the whole of our Joint Report on Thursday, it will be too late to present it then.

My team is very disappointed, as I am myself, but there is nothing we can do except hope for an agreement between the British in London and the British in Belfast.

Tuesday, 5 December 2017: London in ferment

We are all a little stunned by the failure of yesterday's meeting and Theresa May's hasty return to London. We follow from afar the consultations she is holding so as to try and glue the pieces of her majority back together again.

But Arlene Foster is making her wait. Olly Robbins has promised us proposed amendments to the Ireland text by tomorrow. The Irish Taoiseach, like ourselves, has warned that not a single line of the famous Article 48 rejected by the DUP can be altered.

So it's a day of waiting, and preparing for Theresa May's return tomorrow. But we are also looking at the potential failure of this round of negotiations and the postponing of discussions on 'sufficient progress' to February or March, despite all the work that has been done. We thus have two possible scenarios, and two different texts for the press conference that I will have to hold whatever happens.

Wednesday, 6 December 2017: Olly Robbins in Brussels

Olly Robbins is back. He is definitely the key man on the British side. He takes a great many risks to salvage the situation. He sits in Sabine's office all day with coffee and cake.

Sabine and Robbins have developed a relationship of attentive trust. They have three things in common: remarkable intelligence, a talent for expressing their ideas, and a capacity for risk-taking. Undeniable qualities which sometimes serve to get them ahead of others and ahead of the political negotiation process. To her unparalleled negotiating skills, Sabine adds great elegance and an Art Deco look that makes her an easily recognizable character in these negotiations.

A day of non-stop redrafting. On the Ireland text, Paragraph 48 will indeed remain unchanged, but Mr Robbins proposes to add new paragraphs to ensure a 'belt-and-braces' approach. The risk we are taking, in full awareness, is that the final text on Ireland will be far less clear and operational, and that the only part of 'constructive ambiguity' that remains will be the ambiguity.

One of these additional paragraphs seems unacceptable to me, and I let Olly know it. Following in the spirit of David Davis's remarks yesterday in the House of Commons, this paragraph introduces the idea that regulatory alignment with EU rules being discussed in the context of Northern Ireland could affect the whole of the UK. This constitutes another attempt, by altering a single sentence, to keep what they want of the Single Market; more seriously, the British are now trying to use Ireland as a Trojan horse to do so. If this is how it's going to be, the discussions can stop right now.

On citizens' rights, Olly accepts the minimum eight-year period that we require during which a British judge can seek a preliminary ruling from the EU Court of Justice. Back in my office I tell Olly that I am happy for Theresa May to emphasize the voluntary nature of such rulings. It is indeed British judges who will interpret the law in the UK.

Thursday, 7 December 2017: An evening on the phone

Theresa May, through Olly Robbins, told us yesterday that she may return to Brussels to conclude work on the Joint Report today. The whole team is on deck. We know that negotiations are intense within the British cabinet on the Ireland issue and on Paragraph 48, which is causing such a stir among the DUP elected representatives in Belfast, but which the Irish government, with which we are in permanent contact, categorically refuses to modify.

The hours tick away. In the afternoon I retain the hope that Theresa May will join us for dinner, because tomorrow both Jean-Claude Juncker, for unavoidable personal reasons, and Donald Tusk, because he is leaving Brussels for Belgrade, will be unavailable after 9am.

Olly Robbins is in almost constant contact with Sabine by text message. His hopes that Theresa May will arrive this evening are finally dashed. We stay late into the evening finalizing the text of the Joint Report in liaison with the British.

Jean-Claude Juncker asks me to come and see him in his office. He too is in contact with both the British and the Irish, and finally it is agreed that the concluding meeting will take place tomorrow morning at 7am, which means that Theresa May will have to take a plane at 5am!

This is definitely a courageous woman who knows what she wants. She obviously needs an agreement on the Joint Report, which would unlock the second phase of negotiations. Her wager is that, by returning to London with this interim agreement on sufficient progress and agreement in principle from the European leaders to move on, in particular in regard to the transition period she is asking for, she will be able to make people overlook the concessions she has made to us, particularly on the budget. I believe her gamble may succeed. In this negotiation she has been forced to go for broke. She knows that, if she comes back to London without a deal, her government will not survive.

In the meantime, we ratify the compromises on the other outstanding issues apart from Ireland. British courts will be able to request preliminary rulings from the EU Court of Justice for eight years. This is neither the three years Theresa May suggested on Monday, nor the fifteen years we asked for. But according to two legal experts from the Commission and the Council, Luis Romero and Hubert Legal, eight years is an appropriate amount of time to build up case law where it does not yet exist.

Friday, 8 December 2017: Brussels at dawn

It is 6.30am and the task force is already in full swing. A number of journalists are already out on the Berlaymont esplanade at this unusual hour. I meet Jean-Claude Juncker in his office, together with Martin Selmayr. And, at the appointed hour, Theresa May arrives at the protocol entrance and we go back to Jean-Claude Juncker's office for breakfast. Agreement on the text of the Joint Report is confirmed, and the disputes that have plagued the whole week, on both the EU Court of Justice and on Ireland, are hereby concluded.

It is plain to see that Theresa May is expending all her energy in permanent negotiations with her own ministers and her parliamentary majority. She now wants to confirm with President Juncker, as she will do in a few moments with Donald Tusk, that the European Council will acknowledge that sufficient progress has been made. To this end, the President of the Commission has put in place emergency procedures and obtained authorization from the College of Commissioners for the Commission itself to propose that sufficient progress be recognized today.

The Prime Minister will then be able to return to London this morning having received that commitment publicly from the President of the Commission and the President of the European Council. We are well aware that she will present this in a way that makes things easier for her, placing the emphasis on the transition period that she is likely to be granted and the now more likely prospect that talks on trade can begin.

She thanks me and our teams for our commitment. I offer the same thanks to the British negotiators, placing the accent on the role played by Olly Robbins, who has been instrumental, rather than on David Davis, who is happy to simply follow on behind and play it safe.

Monday, 11 December 2017: Non-binding?

David Davis, who evidently never misses an opportunity, tells British television that this Joint Report is not 'binding' for the United Kingdom – as if the Prime Minister's word is provisional or contested. Reactions from the twenty-seven and from the European Parliament are not long in coming. And I will make it quite clear throughout the week that we will not accept any backtracking on the content of this Joint Report, and that every paragraph it contains, all ninety-six of them, will find its way into the legal text of the Withdrawal Agreement.

Tuesday, 12 December 2017: Meghan and Harry

Several British newspapers write today of Theresa May's 'betrayal' of pro-Brexit voters. Let's not forget that, during the referendum campaign, Boris Johnson claimed that leaving the European Union would free up £350 million a week for the NHS. And that, in reference to the 'bill' for Brexit, he also said that the Europeans could 'go whistle'.

Nevertheless, Mrs May, with great lucidity, has agreed to settle accounts and to honour the commitments made by her country. Thanks to the meticulous work of Stéphanie, Philippe Bertrand and Norbert Gacki on our team, but also Mark Bowman on the British side, we have managed to draw up a fair account of the commitments, without yet setting a figure. The British press nonetheless mentions a price to be paid of £50 billion, even higher than the £20 billion initially mentioned after the Florence speech.

The announcement of Prince Harry and Meghan Markle's engagement, however, swiftly relegates all talk of the 'Brexit bill' to the inside pages. As *Le Monde* writes, the engagement announcement acts as a 'powerful sedative against Brexit blues'. The wedding, scheduled to take place at Windsor Castle next May, is set to be 'a great opportunity for a display of national unity, even while the country remains split in two by the Brexit vote, its government prey to incessant chaos'.*

Friday, 15 December 2017: European Council and gastronomic competition

At the invitation of Donald Tusk, along with Jean-Claude Juncker I meet the twenty-seven heads of state or government at the European Council this morning.

Although we took an important step last Friday with the Joint Report, the situation remains delicate.

We have agreed with the UK on a jointly drafted, precise and detailed text that provides security in the areas where Brexit is creating anxiety: for citizens, for the island of Ireland and for stakeholders in projects financed by the EU budget. We must now avoid any backtracking. And we must look ahead to the future relationship, which will require clarity on the obligations the UK is prepared to accept.

For weeks now I have been asking my teams to produce a one-page summary of the possibilities and limits of the future relationship with the UK, taking into account its own red lines. Through sheer persistence, Georg has put his small team to work on the task, and they organize a competition. A number of representations are already in circulation among Brussels think-tanks, but we need to do better.

The aim is clear enough: to create a visually striking representation of the doors that the UK is closing on itself by insisting on its red lines. All entries are welcome!

In the end it is Uku Särekanno, a civil servant seconded by the Estonian presidency, who wins first prize. His slide shows that the UK, with its

* Philippe Bernard, *Le Monde*, 4 December 2017.

red lines, does not want to remain in the Single Market like Norway, or in a customs union like Turkey, or even in a deep and comprehensive free trade agreement like Ukraine. It finds itself at the bottom of the ladder, with a classic free trade agreement, of the type we have today with Canada or South Korea. Each step involves taking on rights and obligations. It is up to the United Kingdom to make its choice.

Future economic relationship
Consequences of the UK's red lines

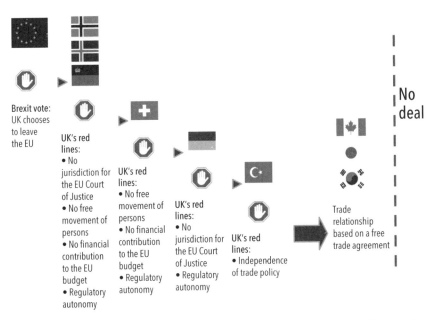

Speaking one by one, the heads of state or government welcome the Joint Report, but emphasize that there is still a long way to go to ensure the preservation of peace and stability on the island of Ireland, to clarify the rights and obligations of the United Kingdom during the transition period, and to negotiate a future relationship that will be distinct from member state status. Our little graphic is a big hit.

I leave the European Council glad of the atmosphere of trust. It is a good step forward for our whole team. I can imagine what the atmosphere would have been like without this agreement on the Joint Report. I am sure that a number of leaders, and especially journalists, would have laid the blame on us.

I go with Sabine and Stéphanie to Berlaymont, where the whole task force team is gathered for a Christmas meal. As always, Isabelle Misrachi has organized everything efficiently, and everyone has prepared a typical dish from their home country. Sixteen nationalities are represented within the task force, and the table is proof, if any were needed, of European gastronomic diversity.

It is our colleague Philippe Bertrand from Liège who, after having negotiated the financial settlement, now wins the prize for the best dish with his homemade foie gras…

2018

Monday, 8 January 2018: 'After Brexit, the EU will no longer exist'

The year 2018, and this first day back at work at the Commission begins with a very special conversation, as I receive Nigel Farage, the most visible and controversial figure in the Brexit campaign.

I have no problem in principle with this meeting. I have already met with many other Brexiteers over the past year, as well as members of the UK government itself.

Farage is as cordial and mild in private as he can be a violent demagogue in public.

The conversation lasts for thirty minutes. He is quite obviously not interested in me, but only in coming to see me so that he can show off about it later to the numerous journalists waiting for him in the pub opposite the Berlaymont.

I take nothing away from this conversation except confirmation that the members of UKIP, and he in particular, have behaved irresponsibly in relation to their own country's national interests. How else could you describe lobbying for such a serious decision without ever setting out and explaining the consequences of that choice to the public, and even campaigning on the basis of lies?

When he seeks to make sure that I have understood the reasons for the vote, I remind him that there are many reasons, in some cases contradictory ones, and that, in particular, false information has been propagated, such as the £350 million that he and his friends promised to get back from Brussels every week to reallocate to the health service. 'Yes, that was a mistake', he says. 'I told Boris not to do it.' How cynical can you get?

As was the case during the campaign, when he posed in front of a giant poster showing queues of migrants, Farage tries to accuse the European Union of an inability to control its borders, in doing so confusing external migration with free movement within the EU. I say to him that we will always be stronger in responding to crises of all kinds by being united, and that we have a moral duty of solidarity towards the refugees who seek our help.

His collaborator, Benjamin Wrench, who in a previous life worked with him in the financial industry, is determined to say that we want to protect European financial services, that we are protectionists. I insist: 'It's not about that. The only thing we want to protect, and which you should protect too, is the financial stability that we struggled so hard to regain after the 2008 crisis.'

Mr Farage is intrigued by the photograph his colleague has noticed of General de Gaulle greeting Adenauer on the steps of the Élysée Palace. I confirm to him that my commitment to Gaullism is indeed extremely longstanding.

'What would de Gaulle say', he asks me, 'about what goes on in Brussels?'

My answer is straightforward enough: 'It's hard to know what de Gaulle would say, but I'm convinced that in today's world, he would talk more about the independence of Europe than about national independence. As would Churchill or Adenauer.'

Before we leave, I have one last question: 'Since you wanted Brexit and have now got it, how do you see the future relationship between the UK and the EU after Brexit has happened?'

He answers without hesitation: 'Mr Barnier, after Brexit, the EU will no longer exist.' I knew that Nigel Farage and all his far-right friends wanted to destroy the Union from within. Today I received confirmation of this fact.

Wednesday, 10 January 2018: Gift basket

It seems that this is to be the week of Brexiteers marching into my office. Led by a former UKIP MEP, Steven Woolfe, who has always been straight with me, several former UK business leaders come to argue for the inclusion of financial services in the trade deal that is to be discussed. It seems to be their sole concern.

Around the table are Lord Digby Jones, Gordon Brown's former trade and investment minister and former Director-General of the CBI, John

Mills, boss of a large retail company and a longstanding Eurosceptic, and John Longworth, a financial consultant and chairman of a hard Brexit pressure group called Leave Means Leave. At the beginning of the meeting, they place on my desk a basket of goods that are supposed to prove the dynamism of the British economy and the quality of its products. In fact, most of these products are protected by EU designations of origin or geographical indications – cheddar, wine, tea, jam. Many are processed from European products.

I point this out to them with a smile, and also comment that the two books in the basket, Shakespeare's plays and an essay on Winston Churchill by Jeremy Havardi, concern a very Continental playwright and a very European British statesman...

The food basket aside, the rhetoric I hear from these Brexiteers is actually morally outrageous. In response to my stance to the general equivalence they want between the City's financial services and those of the EU – in principle hostile, although we are open to specific and conditional equivalences – Digby Jones dares to say to me: 'Mr Barnier, your position is contrary to the interests of the European economy. You are going to make life even more difficult for the worker in the Ruhr, the single woman in Madrid or the unemployed man in Athens.' Indeed!

Monday, 15 January 2018: Remainers

My door is always open to all British elected representatives and officials, and I invariably find these encounters interesting as they underline the intensity, the liveliness and also the great volatility of the British national debate.

Today I am joined by five British anti-Brexit parliamentarians, Conservatives Dominic Grieve and Anna Soubry, and Labour's Chris Leslie, Stephen Doughty and Chuka Umunna, with whom I had dinner two years ago at the Franco-British seminar on the outskirts of London.

Dominic Grieve, David Cameron's former Justice Minister and an enlightened Conservative, recently led a group of a dozen Conservative MPs who together forced a House of Commons vote obliging the Prime Minister to put the Withdrawal Bill – the law that will integrate the

Withdrawal Agreement into the British legal system – to a vote in the British Parliament when the time came. I heard him that day speaking on Europe 1, in impeccable French, explaining that this vote means that there is not really a majority in the British Parliament to approve withdrawal from the Single Market and the Customs Union, even if there is still a majority to confirm leaving the EU.

These Labour and Conservative MPs are courageous, all of them acting in opposition to their party leaders, and continuing to campaign hard to stop Brexit. Sabine, who welcomed them ahead of my arrival, emphasized that timing is crucial here: their belief is that there may well be a political crisis that will change the game, either next April or, more likely, in October, at the end of the Article 50 negotiations.

Thursday, 18 January 2018: Concerns in Luxembourg

For the past three days, amid the bustle of the European Parliament in Strasbourg, I have continued in my patient and tenacious work of making contact with MEPs. Every month, my team, in particular Georg and Nicolas Galudec, plan a continuous string of meetings with group and committee presidents, rapporteurs and coordinators. I am struck by everyone's attention to and interest in Brexit and the issues arising from it. With his spontaneous ability to forge connections, Nicolas is in his element dealing with the Parliament. He was already in my team as a trainee, and subsequently at the Directorate-General for the Internal Market. Today he plays a fundamental role, appreciated by all, in the ongoing dialogue with politicians from all sides of this great house, which is often complex but remains essential.

This morning I left Strasbourg very early by car to meet Xavier Bettel, the young, dynamic Prime Minister of the Grand Duchy of Luxembourg. He is waiting for me personally on the porch of his residence, and we spend a few moments together for a more political discussion in his office, where he surrounds himself with works of art and contemporary photographs. A hall full of colours.

A little later we get together with his team and Olivier Guersent and Ward Möhlmann. In a good Italian restaurant, the discussion continues, in the company of the principal leaders of the financial industry in Luxembourg.

Ward is an excellent Dutch lawyer whom I trust, and I have asked him to take a rigorous look at financial services and the separation of the City of London from the internal market.

In Luxembourg, however, the latest Commission initiatives aimed at coordinating and strengthening the coherence of financial market supervision, in particular through the reorganization of the three supervisory agencies, the ESMA for financial markets, the EBA for banks and the EIOPA for insurance, have not been well received.

Luxembourg alone accounts for almost 80 per cent of European transactions in a financial product that is recognized and highly valued worldwide: UCITS. Obviously, this concentration raises the question of just how rigorous or flexible supervision is in Luxembourg. There is real sensitivity on this subject, and even a slight sense of persecution.

With his usual aplomb, Olivier Guersent explains that this process of ensuring coherency has long been under way. The reform of the European supervisory agencies was announced as early as 2010–11 and the capital markets union obviously requires the strengthening of the Single Rulebook and regulatory consistency.* All of this started well before Brexit.

In fact, the fear expressed by Luxembourgers is that, when this increased regulation and strictness hits the Single Market, at the very moment when the UK escapes it by leaving the Union, investors will be tempted to leave Luxembourg.

On Brexit, my message is clear: if the British maintain their red lines and exclude themselves from the Single Market and the Customs Union, we will not be able to continue as if nothing had happened.

On this point I am backed up by what Emmanuel Macron is saying at the same time in London during an official visit to Theresa May:

> The choice is on the British side, not on my side. They can have no differentiated access to the financial services. If you want access to the Single Market, including the financial services, be my guest. But it means that you need to contribute to the budget and acknowledge European jurisdiction.
>
> There will be no hypocrisy in this respect, otherwise it would not work. It would destroy the Single Market and its coherence.

---

* The EU's single financial regulation is a body of common rules.

Monday, 29 January 2018: Transition under duress

Today constitutes a new milestone on the long road of this negotiation. I am meeting with the foreign ministers, or their secretaries of state, for a General Affairs Council. It's an opportunity to take stock of the negotiations and, on this specific occasion, to receive a mandate to open discussions with the British on the transition period that Theresa May has asked for.

The Council takes only two minutes to adopt its conclusions, but once again this speed belies all the work we have done in advance. It is almost a month since the Commission published a proposal for negotiating directives. There have been many exchanges on the subject, and three meetings of the twenty-seven ambassadors.

The line on this transition period is fixed. A number of governments have tightened the constraints on it. The transition will be short, twenty-one months, and logically it should end on 31 December 2020, at the same time as the 2014–20 EU budget programme.

After Brexit, scheduled for midnight on 29 March 2019, the UK will no longer be a member of the EU institutions. As a third country, it will no longer participate in decision-making, in particular within the Council.

However, during this twenty-one-month period, all the rights and obligations of membership will continue to apply to the UK, which will remain within the supervisory and enforcement framework of the Union and under the jurisdiction of the EU Court of Justice.

Since the UK will remain in the Single Market and the Customs Union during this transition, it will logically have to apply all EU rules.

This transition is the price to be paid to avoid a leap into the unknown on 30 March, to allow businesses a little more time to prepare, and above all to give the British government time to adapt, and even to create anew, services for customs, trade and product certification that it does not have at present, since it is Brussels and its 'bureaucracy' that does this work for all twenty-eight member states.

We all need this transition, and the British need it even more than we do. Nonetheless, I see a debate emerging in London about the harshness of our conditions. Conservative MP Jacob Rees-Mogg, being his usual self, accuses Theresa May of turning the UK into a 'vassal state'. David

Davis, in a speech last Friday, while accepting the EU's principal conditions, spoke of trying to 'build a dam'. He is going to ask us for a right of objection during this period for any legislation the UK may not like.

I head off this idea in advance in my press briefing this afternoon with the Bulgarian Deputy Prime Minister Ekaterina Zaharieva. There can be no divergence between us during this period if the UK is to participate in and benefit fully from the internal market.

Wednesday, 31 January 2018: Some rather belated studies…

Controversy is raging in London over a report of which I was unaware but whose contents do not surprise me. The Department for Exiting the European Union has commissioned a study on the economic consequences of Brexit. According to the leaked report, the impact in terms of growth would be –8 per cent of GDP in the event of a no-deal Brexit, –5 per cent with a simple free trade agreement, and –2 per cent if the UK were to remain in the Single Market without the Customs Union. The opposition is demanding that the study should be made public, but the government is not yet willing to release it.

Tonight I meet with Guy Verhofstadt, his loyal chief of staff Guillaume McLaughlin, and Georg for one of our regular dinners to prepare for the next round of negotiations. Guy always has good advice to offer and is an important force in public debate, where he can express himself far more freely than I can. These dinners, during which he shares his love of fine wines, are also an opportunity to take a break from our busy schedules and share a good many anecdotes and titbits of information about Brexit.

Friday, 2 February 2018: Global Britain?

Customs Union or no Customs Union? There are rumours in business circles of internal discussions in Theresa May's cabinet about a possible customs union agreement that could limit controls between the UK and the Single Market, preserve the bulk of trade and also facilitate the resolution of the Irish question.

Speaking from Shanghai, the British Trade Minister Liam Fox, whom I have never met, puts a stop to any such idea: 'It's very difficult to see how being in a customs union is compatible with having an independent trade policy. [...] We have to be outside that to take advantage of those growing markets. One of the reasons we are leaving the EU is to take control and that's not possible with a common external tariff.'

Quite! Here, once again we have the grand idea of a 'Global Britain' opening up to the great outdoors...

And again I wonder what has prevented the UK from being a 'Global Britain' up until now, if not its own lack of competitiveness. After all, Germany manages to be a 'Global Germany' while remaining solidly within the Union and within the Eurozone!

Monday, 5 February 2018: Back to Number 10

For once this winter, the weather in Brussels is fine as I take the Eurostar to London. This trip was the idea of the British, who probably want to show that negotiations are also taking place in London and not just in Brussels. I had no compunction about accepting. I just made sure that this week would also be the week of a new official round of negotiations in Brussels.

As a precaution, two police officers have been sent by the Commission's security service to accompany our small delegation, which includes Sabine, Stéphanie, Georg and Dan.

We finally arrive at the 'cul-de-sac' of Downing Street and have our first meeting at Number 8 with David Davis, who greets me.

As is always the case with him, the encounter is a cordial one. We rarely get into the substance of things. After a brief one-to-one discussion, we leave the building and walk to Number 10, where a forest of cameras and photographers awaits us.

A few moments later Theresa May joins us in a lounge for about twenty minutes. She seems tired, but still strong. The knocks she is taking from her own party, and often from within her own government, are many and harsh. She voices a rather hollow sentiment about the strong and friendly relationship between her country and an EU that must be built for the future. Surprisingly, though, she does not mention the current negotiations. These few moments that she devotes to me are a gesture that I appreciate because it shows personal attention, but they are no more than a diplomatic gesture, when we are at the heart of a fraught negotiation that is generating tension around her and between us. She might have taken this opportunity to pass on some kind of message to me...

The lunch that immediately follows brings together David Davis, Olly Robbins and Ambassador Tim Barrow, who is sometimes difficult for me to understand because of his accent, despite his having attended Oxford University. I have never really known what he actually thought about Brexit. Like his three predecessors in Brussels, Ivan Rogers, Jon Cunliffe and Kim Darroch, all of whom were experienced and capable diplomats, Tim Barrow is well versed in the arcana of Europe. Deep down, he must know that, by leaving the Union, his country loses leverage and a great deal of influence. But he is loyal, and quite close to Foreign Secretary Boris Johnson who, I am told, relies upon him. No doubt his sense of duty outweighs his personal convictions.

David Davis says nothing about the future relationship, even though the British debate, the media and the controversy within the cabinet have been focused all weekend on the possible demand for a customs union.

This morning, to put a stop to the controversy, Theresa May made it known that she did not want a customs union with the Europeans, or indeed any customs union at all. So we speak only about the transition period and, reading from a sheet of paper laid out in front of him, Mr Davis methodically spells out the points of disagreement with the conditions set by the twenty-seven.

There are seven such points:

1. The British want to see a commitment to act 'mutually in good faith' during the transition period, so as to protect against new developments in the agreement that may prove unfavourable to them. But the Treaty already provides for a duty of sincere cooperation.
2. Even though it will be a third country during the transition, the UK wants to be involved in decision-making process, and cites the example of Norway – but without declaring any intention of joining the European Economic Area, of which Norway is a member.
3. The UK wishes to differentiate between EU citizens who arrive in the UK before 29 March 2019 and those who arrive during the transition period.
4. On the duration of the transition, the British question whether the proposed twenty-one months will be sufficient. They would like two

years, which would raise the question of the price the UK would have to pay to participate in the internal market at the beginning of the new multiannual budget period that will start on 1 January 2021.

5. On trade, the UK wants to be able not only to negotiate, but also to conclude and sign trade agreements during the transition period.
6. On the replication of international agreements during the transition, the UK asks to be supported by the EU in its discussions with third countries.
7. Finally, in the domain of justice and home affairs, the UK is asking to be given the opportunity to join future EU initiatives (i.e. to maintain its opt-in right), even as it leaves the EU...

I answer point by point, all the while insisting on one requirement: if the Single Market and the four freedoms are to be extended, then it seems logical to us to also secure citizens' rights until the end of the transition period, on 31 December 2020.

David Davis tells me that citizens arriving in the UK after 29 March 2019 will know that they are coming to a third country; there will be no surprises. I simply say to him that this is an extremely sensitive point upon which the European Parliament will not budge.

Lunch draws to a close, and we prepare for a press briefing in front of a small pool of photographers. The British have demanded that we are seated, which is inconvenient for me and was probably intended to throw me off balance. Mr Davis has the linguistic advantage over me. I want to use notes and I can't put them down in front of me. But I decide that I won't be pushed around.

In his comments Mr Davis goes no further than a few generalities. But I didn't come here to exchange pleasantries. As for the future, I refuse to comment on the internal debates in the UK, but I remind those present of the fact that, outside the Single Market and without a customs union with the Europeans, there will be barriers to trade in goods and services. And we have prepared a succinct phrase to sum up the situation: 'The time has come to make a choice.'

We leave through a back door. However, I make sure to let David Davis know that a meeting has just been arranged with Jeremy Corbyn for this afternoon. We cross London to Canary Wharf and I visit Andrea Enria and Adam Farkas, the team that has been running the European

Banking Authority for the past five years, and who will be leaving London for Paris.

We review how financial actors and banks are preparing for Brexit and also for a no-deal scenario.

On our way out, on the Reuters building opposite among the scrolling dispatches that are doing the rounds of Europe, we see our little sentence from 10 Downing Street pop up. A good opportunity for a photo and a tweet!

And here again, I repeat quite frankly what I have said before several times over the past year, but which many traders still do not want to believe: 'When the UK leaves the Single Market, the financial passport is gone.'

The day in London ends with Jeremy Corbyn, whom I meet again for the third time. He is accompanied by Keir Starmer, Shadow Secretary of State for Brexit, and Emily Thornberry, Shadow Foreign Secretary. We have a rule of thumb between us: to talk to each other frankly and not to repeat anything outside. I can see that the Labour leader wants to avoid making certain choices and would rather leave all doors open.

Under the influence of Keir Starmer, who understands the issues very well, Labour was the first, last summer, to call for a four-year transition period. Among my British interlocutors, Starmer, always courteous and professional, is without doubt, along with Hilary Benn, chair of the House of Commons' Exiting the EU Committee, the one who impresses me the most for his ability to grasp in detail what is at stake in the Brexit negotiations. Listening to him I get the feeling that Keir Starmer will one day be UK Prime Minister.

Jeremy Corbyn, who has a short memory on this point, disputes having set that duration for the transition, but it doesn't matter. I don't think Labour will go back on Brexit itself – they are not in favour of a second referendum – but once in power, they may ask for a Norwegian-style status or at least to remain in a customs union – if it's not already too late.

On the way back to the continental mainland, the British steward comes to greet me and, quite touchingly, to thank me. 'I'm one of the 48 percent', he says.

Wednesday, 7 February 2018: In Frankfurt with Mario Draghi

This morning, on the cold and snowy platform of Strasbourg station I meet Valdis Dombrovskis, Vice-President of the Commission. We have chosen to go together to Frankfurt to meet the Executive Committee and the Governing Council of the European Central Bank (ECB).

Mario Draghi, President of the ECB, offers us a warm welcome. Around the lunch table are his vice-president, the Portuguese Vítor Constâncio, who will soon be leaving his post, the French Danièle Nouy, head of the supervisory authority for banks in the Eurozone, and the German Sabine Lautenschläger, head of the Resolution Authority. All of this brings back good memories of not so long ago in 2012, when I had to prepare the texts to create the banking union and these two authorities. Mario Draghi remembers this period too: 'Never before has the Commission proposed such a significant text in such a short time.' In that case, also, it was the urgency of a crisis.

I try to get two points across to this select committee: first, that there should be no official consultation between the European supervisor, i.e. the ECB, and the British supervisor, the Bank of England, until we have clear guidance on the future relationship from the European Council. This would be a bad signal for us to send on a subject that remains the main offensive interest of the British, namely financial services.

And then I also express my hope that the Central Bank, which is at the heart of the financing of the European economy, will be able to counter on objective grounds the claims made by British lobbyists that the financing of the European economy depends mainly on London. 'Indeed, it's a joke!' says Mario Draghi cuttingly. Mr Draghi is one of the most impressive figures on the European political scene. Thoughtful, independent-minded, incisive and always direct, he is not a politician in the classic sense, who has campaigned on doorsteps and won elections. He is from the banking world. But through his courageous and decisive action in 2012, he got the Eurozone out of the rut and earned himself a place among true European leaders – a breed which, alas, is all too rare.

Friday, 9 February 2018: An overheated press room

At the end of a rather chaotic week of negotiations with the British, I find myself back in the Berlaymont press room alone, since David Davis has chosen not to come this week.

I take my place at the lectern alongside the Commission's deputy spokesperson Alexander Winterstein as the opening ceremony of the XXIII Olympic Winter Games in Pyeongchang, South Korea, gets under way. And in a gesture towards the organizers and athletes, I wish them all well. Memories, memories!

Returning to Brexit, I take a firm line: 'If these differences persist, a transition is not a given.' Unsurprisingly, this simple sentence, which is simply the truth of the matter, immediately causes a downward movement in the price of sterling.

I also take care, once again, without getting worked up, to calmly respond to David Davis, who reproached me two days ago for my lack of courtesy.

Throughout this negotiation, you will not find in my attitude – on this subject, or any others – the least trace of discourtesy or willingness to punish. My mindset has been completely the opposite since the beginning of this negotiation and it will continue being so until the last day of the negotiation.

Wednesday, 14 February 2018: Boris Johnson's organic carrots

Key ministers from the UK government are out on the road. Like Theresa May who, at the weekend, will speak in Munich on security issues, they are carving up Europe between them to spread the word on their government's position. I hope that we will see it becoming clearer as a result, but I wouldn't bet on it!

At the Policy Exchange think-tank meeting today, Boris Johnson gives a speech that his team describe in advance as important. Listening to it, I garner no new information at all. It just provides further confirmation of a serious misunderstanding and cause for concern.

The major misunderstanding is one that was bound to appear among British citizens who voted for Brexit thinking they were voting against globalization, against a Europe that did not protect them enough, against a Europe that has deregulated and deindustrialized. The same reasons that so many French voters in Marseille and Picardy vote for Jean-Luc Mélenchon and Marine Le Pen. We must pay attention to this.

Boris Johnson's response is an 'internationalist Brexit': 'Global Britain', meaning more liberalism, openness and deregulation. At some point, this misunderstanding will come out, with serious political consequences.

In the same vein, Johnson argues for fewer rules, against the Brussels 'superstate': 'We can take back control of our agricultural policy, we can maybe do wonderful things with our own regulations to … promote organic carrots.'

European rules have the advantage of being fairly protective of organic produce and, above all, of being common to this large single market. Moving away from them means being less protective and closing off the European market for British organic carrots. This all brings to mind what the US Secretary of Commerce said a few weeks ago in London about chlorinated chicken…

Saturday, 17 February 2018: Security and defence in Munich

We arrived in Munich yesterday to attend the conference which every year in Bavaria brings together the world's leading foreign and security policymakers – a sort of Davos of the defence world. I take the opportunity to talk to German Defence Minister Ursula von der Leyen, Christine Lagarde and John Kerry, visibly distressed by current developments in transatlantic relations.

In order to avoid unnecessary controversy, I have decided not to attend today's speech by Theresa May on our future security partnership, preferring to listen from an adjoining room.

This is one of the areas of greatest convergence between us, and one that is particularly close to my heart. I am pleased to hear Theresa May reiterating the UK's unconditional commitment to the security of Europe.

In the face of the challenges of today's world, we must continue to stand together in the future and cooperate on sanctions, external operations and development aid.

On the other hand, when she talks about our future cooperation on the industrial development of defence capabilities, in particular through the newly created European Defence Fund, I find it difficult to imagine how the UK and its defence companies could continue to have access to it under the same conditions, especially in the case of the development of programmes as sensitive as Galileo, as she suggests.

The British are also manoeuvring to limit or curb the EU's ambitions for defence. They think it's a shrewd move to hide behind the United States, and so it was the US Secretary of State for Defense Jim Mattis, in a meeting of NATO ministers earlier this week, who warned Europeans that the defence of Europe was NATO's business alone.

Barely two years ago, Barack Obama said the exact opposite when he came to Europe. And not long before that, George W. Bush was the first to encourage Europeans to make a greater effort, by themselves and for themselves, in the field of defence.

The Norwegian NATO Secretary-General Jens Stoltenberg, whom I know well, echoes this speech and from the rostrum even enumerates the three risks that the EU's progress in the field of defence would represent for NATO – and indeed for British and American industry.

Jens Stoltenberg is a likeable and pragmatic man who has the unenviable task of dealing with the erratic and anti-European administration of Donald Trump. He is less prone to grandiloquence than his predecessor Anders Fogh Rasmussen, which has done the organization some good. But on the strategic challenges and the EU–NATO partnership, which must be developed, his vision is too short-termist and American. A little later, I bump into him in the corridor and take the liberty of telling him how disappointed and surprised I was. 'You spoke as we did twenty years ago.' For a moment he is taken aback and unsettled by my reaction.

French Prime Minister Édouard Philippe says it in his own way, too: 'European defence and NATO are complementary. Do I have to say this in Norwegian to make myself understood?'

I often prepare for these annual meetings on security and defence with MEP Arnaud Danjean. Beyond politics, Arnaud is a friend of mine. He is unanimously respected in the European Parliament because his judgement on major geopolitical issues is always informed and reliable.

Today I am also reassured to have at my side Guillaume de La Brosse, a lively and direct young Frenchman, very capable in security and defence matters. Equipped with experience both on the Council and in the European Defence Agency, he had already joined me in 2015 within the framework of the mission on this subject that Jean-Claude Juncker entrusted to me.

Wednesday, 21 February 2018: UK delegations

Following the House of Commons Select Committee and a delegation of mayors and Labour leaders from the major cities of the UK, this morning I receive a delegation from the House of Lords led by Lord Boswell, and made up mainly of Remainers.

One of the parliamentarians, Baroness Kennedy, asks me specifically about the degree of detail around the future relationship in the Political Declaration that will accompany the withdrawal treaty in October. 'When we vote', she tells me, 'we need to have the details of the future relationship.' Which is good news because, on the EU side, the member states and the European Parliament also want to know exactly where they are headed. I still remember Angela Merkel's warning in December: 'When I sign the Brexit treaty, I don't want there to be any last-minute surprises.'

Wednesday, 28 February 2018: Draft treaty

Today we take an important step by publishing a document that only the Commission's teams are authorized to produce: the complete draft of the Withdrawal Agreement, 168 articles and two protocols that translate all the negotiation points into legal terms. This is obviously a decisive leap forward. We now have a text, the result of many months of difficult and sometimes stormy negotiations.

As far as citizens' rights and the financial settlement are concerned, this legal translation reflects the agreement made back in December. On everything else, it is the positions of the European Union that we have integrated into this draft treaty. The thirteenth floor of Berlaymont, Martin Selmayr's floor, was generally reluctant to publish such a document so early. I therefore spoke directly to Jean-Claude Juncker. By publishing this text, I explained, we remain ahead of the game and will reap the advantages in our negotiations. 'If you think it's the right thing to do', he replied, 'I trust you.'

Friday 2 March 2018: Cherry-picking

After Lancaster House and Florence, and then Munich on security and defence, Theresa May continues to choreograph the negotiation in a very deliberate way. What she has to say today does not surprise us, but its tone is more constructive and it contains numerous new details.

In a speech given at Mansion House, the Prime Minister seeks to give assurances to the EU. She says that the UK will maintain high standards, for example by way of a potential alignment with EU competition and state aid rules, and will avoid any 'race to the bottom' in respect to workers' rights and environmental regulation. The Prime Minister also acknowledges that the UK will have less access to the Single Market and that UK courts will have to refer to the case law of the EU Court of Justice in some cases.

But apart from these few concessions, it is clear that Theresa May is seeking to piece together a specific proposal and to organize a generalized cherry-picking from the Single Market, for example by asking that we consider the UK's participation in certain EU agencies – in particular on chemicals and aviation security – and by arguing for a very broad agreement on services and on the recognition of professional qualifications.

Rather than reacting aggressively or negatively, we choose to push the Prime Minister to the brink and remind her of the tight corner she has backed herself into.

In a widely shared tweet, I welcome her speech for its clarity in confirming that the UK is leaving both the Single Market and the Customs Union. We shall now have to work on a free trade agreement. And it is in this direction that the European Council will have to set its course. In short, a free trade agreement and nothing else.

Saturday, 3 March 2018: With Danish fishermen

I have long felt at home in the Nordic countries. It is often cold, but the people are straightforward and solid, though often more expansive in the evening. So I felt pleased yesterday to be back in Copenhagen for my third meeting with the National Parliament here.

My friend Margrethe Vestager, the European Commissioner for Competition, welcomed me to her country with a tweet that read:

'@MichelBarnier welcome to Denmark – it is snowing and cold but warm at heart. Happy to have you as Brexit negotiator for all of us. Safe travel to Thyborøn.'

After meetings with, first, Foreign Minister Anders Samuelsen, and then Fisheries Minister Karen Ellemann, Liberal Prime Minister Lars Løkke Rasmussen welcomes me to his out-of-town residence with his team and in particular his sherpa Michael Starbæk Christensen, with whom I have a trusted relationship.

After our short meeting, the Prime Minister brings together Danish business and trade union leaders for a seminar on Brexit that we are running together. Of course, Denmark has a very close trading relationship with the UK and does a lot of business with the country, but they all confirm that it is the Single Market that is most important to them.

The Prime Minister thanks me for taking the time to visit the west coast in Thyborøn to meet the fishermen and elected representatives. The head of the Lego company, Niels Christiansen, gives me his business card, in the form of a Lego miniature. Very nice!

In the afternoon we take a long drive to the west coast, where the three mayors of the region and the Danish national and regional agriculture and fisheries officials are waiting for us. At dinner, I recognize an ambience that I enjoy greatly, and with which I was familiar as president of Savoie. In fact, I really need to get out of my office and meet people on the ground more.

This morning, up very early, the whole team is ready to be received at 8am in one of the two fish-processing factories on this coast that export their products to Norway and Scotland to feed farmed salmon. The centre of Thyborøn is an industrial fishery that uses British territorial waters for 40 per cent of its activity. When we look at the reciprocal use of waters, EU fishermen's use of UK territorial waters is five times higher than UK fishermen's use of EU territorial waters.

Accompanied by a number of journalists, we board one of the boats of this industrial fishery for a trip out to sea. Conversation with the fishermen is direct and easy-going. They are a family business, father and son. The captain, the owner of the boat, is with his business partner, who looks like he must be his brother. Their large boat was partly financed by

European funds; they take it out for eight to ten days at a time, bringing back hundreds of tonnes of fish. Five crew members are on board.

We end this visit with a lengthy meeting with all the local actors and the fishermen. Exceptionally, translation from Danish into English is provided. We take the time to listen to what they have to say. Bence Tóth, a Hungarian on my team who is responsible for the agricultural and fisheries sector, explains to them with precision and also with a dose of humour the legal framework in which we are going to approach these negotiations. Assistant to the Directorate-General of Maritime Affairs and Fisheries, Stijn Billiet, a young Belgian, has also accompanied me and answers all their questions skilfully.

Such attention seems quite proper to me, and reflects the signals I want to be giving out. I sum it up in sixty seconds in a tweet filmed on the deck of the ship, despite the bitter cold: Brexit is not just about London and Brussels. It is not just a high-level negotiation. Brexit affects the daily lives of many people, like the fishermen here in Thyborøn. I want to listen to and understand them in order to defend their interests and our values.

I have the feeling that everyone here is both surprised and touched by our attention and availability. We share a quick buffet and as we leave I receive a few boxes of mackerel stamped with the slogan '*Brexit – alle i samme båd*' – 'Brexit, all in the same boat!'

Monday, 5 March 2018: First Irish day

Before getting together with the leaders of the DUP, the Unionist party, I meet with the President of Sinn Féin Mary Lou McDonald and the party's leader in Northern Ireland Michelle O'Neill, as well as Martina Anderson, MEP, who, I am told, spent thirteen years in prison herself.

Sinn Féin, which campaigns passionately for reunification, welcomed our draft treaty and our proposal to include Northern Ireland in the European Customs Union so as to avoid a hard border, particularly for goods.

But Sinn Féin wants to go further and is calling for a 'special status' for Northern Ireland. I don't want to be led down that road, and we hardly discuss this prospect.

This does not prevent my interlocutors, who had taken care to write 'special status' in bold type on the documents laid out on the table, in full view of the photographers, from saying afterwards that this was one of the points in our discussions. When it comes to the Irish question, it's difficult to stick to the facts alone!

Olly Robbins suggests that we meet for a private dinner. We have already met once like this in December, the night before the Joint Report was concluded. But this invitation is of a different nature, coming as it does in the wake of Theresa May's latest speech, and just a few days before the European Council of 22 and 23 March.

The British are extremely anxious to get a result on the transition period at this European Council, just as in December Theresa May needed the agreement of the twenty-seven to open the second phase of negotiations. It's a kind of go-for-broke strategy. The political pressure she is under in her own cabinet and her majority force her to move forward in order to survive. But it is also the key to our reaching a deal.

Olly Robbins says that the cabinet will meet again next Tuesday and will have to agree to a proposal from Theresa May on transition that will be close to our requirements. He then takes an important step forward on the issue of citizens: as we and the European Parliament required, he now agrees to treat citizens who arrived in the UK before Brexit and those who will arrive after Brexit in the transition period until 31 December 2020 in the same way, and to grant them the same rights in perpetuity. In exchange, he wants the eight-year period during which UK courts can refer cases to the EU Court of Justice to begin on 30 March 2019.

On the duration of the transition, he does not press the point, but asks for a clause or a mutual agreement to extend it if necessary. I reply that such a 'one-shot' clause would have to be in the treaty itself, not in an annex, and would require the EU's agreement in order to be activated. And naturally, if the transition is extended, a new discussion will have to be opened on the budgetary contribution required from the United Kingdom as the price to pay for its participation in the Single Market for this additional period.

We also warn the British that many member states are reluctant to agree on transition unless parallel progress is made on all the other issues of separation. Stéphanie, as direct as ever, tells Mr Robbins that as a third state, the UK cannot be in the same or a better position than an EU member state – less now than ever before.

One day at a time. We will move forward on transition and separation, but the British must be prepared for strict guidelines from the European Council in response to Theresa May's speech on our future economic relationship.

At the very end of the meal, Mr Robbins, quite lucidly, tells us in a single sentence that obviously the United Kingdom would be better off choosing the option of a customs union with us. 'A Turkey-plus option', he says.

'Why "plus"?'

'Because, if you look at your staircase', he says, 'those at the bottom of the stairs, Canada, Korea and Japan, are all a long way away from Europe. We don't belong there, but higher up.'

I say: 'Of course, why not? But every option implies certain rules.'

A staircase is made to be walked down … or walked back up again!

Tuesday, 6 March 2018: With the 'iron ladies' of the DUP

As promised, I receive Arlene Foster, leader of the DUP, the Northern Ireland Unionist party which de facto holds sway over Theresa May's majority, as it brings her the ten votes vital to continue governing in Westminster. Mrs Foster is accompanied by the Dodds: Diane, an elegant and competent member of the European Parliament, very active in the Parliament's agriculture committee, and her husband Nigel, leader of the DUP in Westminster. Also with them is Sammy Wilson, a DUP MP known for his stormy temperament, and Timothy Johnston, Nigel Dodds's assistant, who seems to have his feet on the ground.

I let them know at the outset that we are implementing the decision they supported to leave the European Union, and that we wish to do so in a way that respects the constitutional order of the United Kingdom, including seeking practical solutions to avoid a hard border between the two Irelands, and to ensure respect for the integrity of the European internal market.

Strangely, it is not the DUP leader who speaks up, but Diane Dodds. It's not easy to know where the power lies in this party. The discussion is frank but on several occasions Sabine, who is at my side, and I have to bring them back down to facts and truths. The line they came to my office with is simply that of an appeal to motive. We are puppets of the Dublin government, which they hate, and we want to create a border between Northern Ireland and the rest of the UK so that there isn't one across the middle of the island.

I reply curtly that this is not our intention and that we have simply sought to operationalize one of the options in the December Joint Report because it is our responsibility, and this option directly concerns the tools and the rules of the Single Market and the Customs Union.

Clearly, the publication of the draft treaty last Wednesday came as a shock. According to Nigel Dodds, we may even have succeeded in uniting all the British people against us. I say to him that the more united the British are, the better, and that our concern is for the unity of the twenty-seven – and I do mean the twenty-seven!

After forty tense minutes, Nigel Dodds acknowledges that practical solutions for regulatory alignment have already been implemented between Northern Ireland and Ireland in the areas of agriculture, plant health and animal disease prevention. There are even controls at Northern Ireland ports and airports for products coming from Great Britain. I hammer the point home: these are the kinds of concrete and practical arrangements that we need for the areas of North–South cooperation described in the Good Friday (Belfast) Agreement (which the DUP refers to as the Belfast Agreement).

Deep down, they know it isn't possible to have no controls between the north and the south of the island while, at the same time, having no controls between the island of Ireland and the rest of the UK. As I tell them: 'It is the UK's decision to leave the Single Market that has created the problem. Help us to find concrete solutions to this problem.'

At the end of the conversation, Arlene Foster confirms that the formation of a new executive has been put on hold because Sinn Féin has been making new demands that she felt were 'unacceptable' to the people of Northern Ireland. I know, however, that agreement was reached between the two parties a fortnight ago, but that the DUP subsequently went back on its decision.

Monday, 12 March 2018: The outermost regions

A break in an otherwise full agenda. I receive the President of the Canary Islands region, Fernando Clavijo, who is also President of the Conference of the nine outermost regions of the EU. I have an emotional and personal attachment to these remote, isolated and, with the exception of French Guyana, island regions, born of my first meeting with the Sainte-Rose family in Martinique, whose eldest son, Christian, has become the respected head of the paediatric neurosurgery department at the Necker Hospital in Paris.

The Canary Islands produce a significant quantity of cucumbers, half of which are exported to the UK, with financial support from the EU, given the distance they have to travel. But while this aid provides economic support to the Canary Islands, within the Single Market it does not count as an export aid. Once the UK leaves the EU and the Single Market, it will become legally impossible to continue this support. In talking to Fernando Clavijo, I have a better understanding of the sometimes far-flung consequences of Brexit, and of all the issues for which we shall have to seek solutions.

Tuesday, 13 March 2018: Plenary session

Back to the hotbed of the European Parliament plenary for a debate on Brexit and a vote on a new Parliament resolution on the eve of the European Council. As usual, I stand next to Jean-Claude Juncker. Behind us, in the second row, are his inner circle, including his new Head of Cabinet Clara Martínez Alberola, and Martin Selmayr, whose hasty appointment as Secretary-General of the Commission was the subject of a long and arduous public debate in the same chamber yesterday.

President Juncker opens the debate. He is tired and his voice is weak and hesitant. As always, he is friendly towards me and publicly acknowledges the work of my team, which is first and foremost his own. In the concluding remarks to my own speech, I choose to cite Martin Selmayr for the work he is going to pursue, initiated by his predecessor Alexander Italianer, on contingency planning – the preparation for the scenario of an abrupt exit by the British, a no-deal Brexit.

He thanks me for this public testimonial. For myself, beyond the froth and the day-to-day difficulties of the work, from day one I have chosen to establish a direct and effective relationship with him. He has undeniable talents as a strategist and communicator, and he has a real vision for the future of Europe. It's just a pity that he has difficulty in accepting the limits of his role.

On the next bench, as always, Nigel Farage is there at the beginning and end of the debate. His mouth is on autopilot, with the same old stale arguments. Behind him, on the far right of the Chamber, another British MEP, an unconditional Brexit militant, rants and raves and, when the new US protectionist measures are discussed, exclaims: 'We vote Trump!'

After our meeting a few weeks ago, Farage told a journalist: 'I spoke with Michel Barnier this week. It's like telling a Christian that perhaps God doesn't exist.' But perhaps God does exist!

Thursday, 15 March 2018: Before the twenty-seven ambassadors

A long discussion with the EU ambassadors of the twenty-seven, in preparation for the European Council, the political context of which is somewhat comparable to that of December's. Pressure on the government from the British business community, disagreements within the cabinet in London and the rise of the Labour Party are forcing Theresa May to obtain a result so as not to find herself yet more embattled when she returns.

In December there was a commitment on the European side to open the second phase of the negotiations, particularly on trade. And this is how, at the last moment, we were able to conclude the Joint Report to secure the rights of citizens and settle the accounts.

Theresa May now wants to obtain an agreement in principle on the transition, so as to contain the anxiety, and even panic, of many British industrial sectors. In the UK, a great deal of investment has been suspended or even cancelled, and plans to relocate to the EU are becoming more definite.

My strategy is not to miss this 'window of opportunity'. I know that the British negotiators are now ready to move closer to our positions on the terms of the transition. By securing these advances, I tell the ambassadors, we can make major progress. We do not isolate the issue of transition from the other issues of separation. We maintain the momentum. We respect the spirit of the December Joint Report. We are not giving up anything on the substance. However, not everything will be settled, since there will remain points of real divergence on the governance of this agreement, on the role of the EU Court of Justice and, especially, on Ireland and Northern Ireland.

Each of the ambassadors thanks my team for their work. It is true that, since the publication of our draft treaty only a fortnight ago, we have been in almost permanent meetings with the member states. Over the entire course of a weekend, the task force answered and took into account almost 700 questions from the twenty-seven countries. It is this consolidated draft text that the ambassadors of the twenty-seven decide to approve today.

I begin by recalling our objective for the next few days: after the Coreper meeting, the Commission will officially send this draft treaty to the British, and our plan is to negotiate all weekend so as to 'colour' the document: in green, the parts of the text agreed between the negotiators; in yellow, everything that remains to be clarified or specified; in white, the points of disagreement.

In my speech to the ambassadors I also mention the 'guidelines' that the European leaders will have to approve, and which will constitute my mandate for the third parallel negotiation that will begin in April on the future relationship with the British. This is an opportunity for each ambassador to put forward their particular concerns. The French ambassador, Philippe Léglise-Costa, with the hard-headed intelligence for which he is often misunderstood, speaks at length. On several points, he goes back on the attack despite assurances given to us in Paris by Emmanuel Macron's adviser Clément Beaune. My team is taken aback by what appears to be a lack of trust on the part of the French. But for the other ambassadors, this exchange is probably just a reminder that their negotiator is negotiating on behalf of the twenty-seven and not his or her country in particular.

The Irish ambassador Declan Kelleher opens proceedings before the European Council, with the certainty that he will be heard by the British. The withdrawal treaty will have to include concrete and operational solutions to avoid a hard border on the island of Ireland. The British will have to understand this.

The fact remains that we must give a clear response to the British attempts at cherry-picking. A few days ago, Luxembourg's Prime Minister Xavier Bettel summed up the situation as follows: 'Before, they were in and they had many opt-outs; now they want to be out with many opt-ins.'

Monday, 19 March 2018 – David Davis is back

Beginning of a great day, as David Davis finally returns to Brussels. He has not been here since December, and in the meantime we have only met once, in London. Clearly, his method of negotiation for the British side is not the same as mine. And we now know that all the work of preparation, negotiation and arbitration is being done at the level of Olly Robbins, under the watchful eye of Prime Minister Theresa May herself. Mr Davis, whose agenda is more political and domestic, uses a technique that I have now understood. At any moment of negotiation and compromise, he deliberately steps back, and does not want to be bound by regular and multiple concessions. Instead, at every stage he accepts the package of compromises made by our teams and finds the words in which to dress them up, laud them or, in some cases, trivialize them.

I am neither surprised nor shocked by this method. From the beginning, it has not been marketing and froth that interests me, but substance. Step by step we are reaching agreement with the British on all issues. They often come around to our positions, which have been seriously prepared and are legally backed up. And that's what counts.

Since last Thursday, for three days and two nights the task force has been a hive of activity. All hands were on deck until 9.30pm yesterday, noting line by line, article by article the points of agreement, which we coloured green, the points to be clarified, in yellow, leaving the points of disagreement in white.

The whole grand tableau was projected onto the wall of our meeting room, so we could see the green making progress hour by hour. It was this that gave me the idea to illustrate our press conference today by projecting all 168 articles in three colours onto the big screen in the press room.

David Davis does not question any of the points of agreement. In our preparatory meeting he tries to trivialize the Gibraltar issue, but it is this draft treaty, 75 per cent of which is now green, that will allow me to justifiably claim, before some 250 journalists, that a decisive step has been taken in these negotiations.

At this stage, the key point for the British is that they have been able to colour all articles concerning the transition in green. In a few days' time, Mrs May will be able to return to London having obtained the agreement of the European Union for the transition period.

For my part, I will insist on this decisive step, which is only a step: 75 per cent is not 100 per cent. Obviously, all the points that have not yet been agreed are, and will remain, the most difficult. Even if it is now smaller, the risk of failure is still there, especially on the Irish question.

Wednesday, 21 March 2018: St Patrick's Day

I have a great fondness for Ireland and the Irish people. The French have always had a special affection for the country. For me, it brings back memories of the very last visit General de Gaulle made abroad after his resignation as President of the Republic.

Today is St Patrick's Day, the day when the Irish, wherever they may be, gather to celebrate and drink a Guinness or a Kilkenny.

After attending the reception of the two Irish ambassadors at the Palais des Beaux-Arts in Brussels, the 'Bozar', where I was very warmly welcomed, I take up the invitation of MEP Seán Kelly and his colleagues to the European Parliament.

The atmosphere is friendly, rather moving even. The Irish, who know that they can count on the solidarity of the other member states, are effusive in their thanks. There is clear concern that Brexit will derail the peace process and the Good Friday (Belfast) Agreement. It is well known that, on the other side, in Northern Ireland among the DUP Unionists, who never supported the Agreement, there is the thought, or the ulterior motive, of using Brexit as an opportunity to prevent the march towards reunification of the island.

I try to say a few words in Gaelic. It's no mean feat. '*Ní neart go cur le chéile*' – no strength without unity. And at the end of a very short speech: '*Go raibh maith agaibh*' – thank you for your attention. The gesture meets with great success.

Thursday, 22 March 2018: Mario Draghi

It's 7pm. I am alone in my office preparing for tomorrow's European Council. My mobile rings. It's Mario Draghi, urgently requesting a fifteen-minute meeting, 'anywhere in Brussels', he tells me. I ask him to be at his hotel on Place Jourdan at 8.30pm. He sounds worried. The subject is a communiqué that he has obviously promised to the Governor of the Bank of England, Mark Carney, announcing with great fanfare, tomorrow morning, at the very moment when the European Council opens, the setting up of a bilateral working group between the European Central Bank and the Bank of England. Indeed!

A few weeks ago, when he invited me to the ECB Governing Council in Frankfurt, we did indeed agree to set up a joint technical group with the British on the sole subject of a potential no-deal Brexit and its consequences. But now, under renewed pressure from the British, its remit, as if by magic, has suddenly extended to encompass all questions related to financial stability, and the group is to be announced at the same time as the European Council. The subterfuge is painfully obvious, the clear objective being to open up a parallel negotiating line to ours with respect to financial services issues.

I make it clear to Draghi, with whom I get on well, that such a manoeuvre is unacceptable, that there is no reason for such an announcement to be made at the same time as the European Council, and that the remit of this working group, in any case, must be limited.

He agrees, and we part with a commitment from me to send him a draft letter specifying the framework and mandate of the group very soon. The next morning, at the council of heads of state or government of the Eurozone, he goes back on the offensive with Jean-Claude Juncker, but as far as I am concerned, things are now set and there is no going back on them.

Friday, 23 March 2018: European Council

At around 9.30 this morning, I take up an invitation to join the table of the twenty-seven heads of state or government. I am able to report real progress, as the draft treaty delivered by my team just a fortnight ago has become the basis for discussions with the British. And over the past weekend we have managed to colour more than two-thirds of it green. We are now truly on the road to an orderly rather than a disorderly withdrawal.

But beyond these significant advances, I point out two serious points of divergence that should not be underestimated: the governance of the Withdrawal Agreement, since the Conservative Party's base will be opposed to any role for the EU Court of Justice, and the Irish question, to which we must give a legal and operational solution within the Withdrawal Agreement itself, even though Theresa May needs the DUP in order to preserve her majority.

And finally, I turn to the future relationship. In this new and undoubtedly more difficult stage of the negotiations, the key is still to maintain unity among the twenty-seven, even if there are different sensitivities and sometimes different interests at play. It was this unity, so unexpected for the British, that forced them to finally agree to pay their full share and to honour all of their commitments in the financial settlement. More recently, it was the unity of the twenty-seven that prompted Theresa May to enter into discussion on the basis of our Protocol on Ireland and Northern Ireland, even though she had said only three weeks earlier that no British Prime Minister could possibly accept it.

Along with this unity, I also remind those present once again that there is no agreement on anything until there is agreement on everything. This applies in particular to the transition period, which will not happen unless there is an agreement on withdrawal. And I then emphasize the major fundamental principles for this second phase of negotiations: the decision-making autonomy of the twenty-seven, the integrity of the internal market, the need for a 'level playing field' (a framework for fair and equitable competition), and the fact that the United Kingdom is becoming a third country. This applies to our future trade relationship, but also to our security and defence partnership.

At this point, I outline the idea that this partnership for the security of the continent could be put in place even before the end of the transition period. My intention today is simply to place this suggestion before the European Council in advance.

And finally, I allow myself a more political analysis of the state of play. Once we reach the Withdrawal Agreement in October, we will have a mutual interest in seeing it ratified. On the European side, ratification is the only guarantee that the British will pay what they owe and, above all, that the rights of citizens will be secured. On the British side, the transition period, which is vital both politically and economically, can only be locked in by this ratification.

But the two sides are diametrically opposed in terms of the political conditions for ratification. On our side, a few weeks before the European elections at the end of May 2019, we need clarity. We need to show businesses, administrations and citizens what will happen after the transition. We also need to clearly illustrate the difference between an EU member state and a third country. On the British side, though, what Theresa May needs is more ambiguity. She has no clear majority in favour of either version of our future relationship. We will therefore have to find the right balance between the precision we need and a certain flexibility so as not to close the door to future developments in the UK regarding its own red lines.

In the round-table discussion that then begins, Angela Merkel insists on unity: 'Our responsibility is the integrity and solidity of the Single Market. In October, we will have to be more precise and provide certainties.'

A little later, Emmanuel Macron and Dutch Prime Minister Mark Rutte, followed by some fifteen heads of government, take the floor in turn. Most of them reject any form of à la carte Single Market, express their solidarity with Taoiseach Leo Varadkar, and emphasize the work done by our task force.

Thursday, 5 April 2018: Helsinki

Back to Helsinki, where I start the day with a meeting with the Grand Committee of the National Parliament. All political parties are represented, including the True Finns, whose party line remains firmly anti-European.

Yesterday I again met the liberal Prime Minister of Finland Juha Sipilä. 'I like your style', he told me. Throughout the day yesterday I met the other coalition leaders, Finance Minister Petteri Orpo, who represents the National Coalition Party, and Minister for European Affairs Sampo Terho, one of those who split from the True Finns in 2017. Last night we had a good dinner with Finland's business leaders, whom I know to have been the focus of very special and pressing British attention for several months now. We speak frankly to each other and agree that the priority must remain the defence of the European internal market. Finland, in my eyes, has always been a very European country. I had a very close relationship with one of its former prime ministers, the wise Paavo Lipponen, and I once told him that his country could be seen as the 'seventh founding country' of the European Union.

Very early this morning, before flying back to Brussels, I meet Pekka Vauramo, the CEO of Finnair, which, like British Airways, is a member of the One World Alliance. We visit the airport's internal services and, of course, the control tower, which manages the landing and take-off of an average of 600 flights a day, around ten of them to or from London. In fact, Helsinki is a hub for many passengers from the region, as well as for British citizens travelling to Asia in particular.

By leaving the EU, the British and their companies are leaving not only the Single Market but also the single European airspace. We will therefore have to renegotiate a bilateral agreement with them so as to, at the very least, allow British aircraft to land in the EU and European aircraft to land in the UK.

The Finns obviously want to go further and open up this future relationship to the so-called fifth freedom of the air – which would allow BA planes to land in Helsinki, take on passengers or cargo and continue to take on more passengers in Paris or Rome before flying to Beijing.

I just ask my interlocutors not to expect me to set in stone now what will be the final outcome of the negotiations – but as a result of this visit I have a better understanding of their concerns.

Tuesday, 10 April 2018: Spitzenkandidat

Stefaan De Rynck, together with our press officer Dan, has gathered a new group of journalists for an on-the-record interview. Daniel Ferrie, a young, tall and enthusiastic Irishman known to everyone as Dan, has carved out a special place for himself in the team. Journalists unanimously like him, and rightly so, but he also knows how to hold fast to our communication strategy.

Around the table are European journalists from *Süddeutsche Zeitung*, *La Repubblica*, *Le Soir*, the Slovenian press agency STA, and *El Español*.

We have also brought in Laurent Marchand, a journalist in Paris for *Ouest-France*, the largest French daily newspaper.

Giving as much time as is needed, I answer all questions and explain where we are at in the negotiations and what is at stake over the next few weeks. In addition, today is very symbolic as it marks the twentieth anniversary of the Good Friday (Belfast) Agreement.

To journalists who allude to my possible candidacy as *Spitzenkandidat* of the EPP for the Commission presidency, I reply that I feel morally committed to seeing my mission through. A little later, I emphasize this point by answering another question: 'I am indeed thinking of several things at once: One, Brexit, two, Brexit, three, Brexit.'

Thursday, 12 April 2018: Prague

Back in the beautiful city of Prague for another visit. I found it remarkable to learn, years ago, that in 1914 this city was as rich as Paris... It has never lost its splendour and is gradually regaining its wealth. Investment has returned, as I see in the afternoon when I visit the Škoda factory, bringing with me our 'automotive' expert Fabrizio Sacchetti. An hour and a half from the capital, this ultra-modern plant built by the Volkswagen Group produces one car per minute on a continuous production line.

The new liberal Prime Minister Andrej Babiš speaks with me at length. A businessman who turned to politics relatively recently, he tells me in perfect French that he has invested in several hotels in the south of France.

I spend a good deal of time speaking with the European Global Navigation Satellite Systems Agency (GNSS) on a sensitive area of negotiation with the British, namely their participation in the Galileo project. Here again, the British are struggling to come to terms with the direct consequences of their decision to leave the European Union.

Tuesday, 24 April 2018: A new team in Berlin

A long day of meetings in Berlin.

Every time I visit the German capital, I regret not being able to speak to my interlocutors in their own language, despite my six years of German lessons.

But I keep in mind Valéry Giscard d'Estaing's plea to Helmut Kohl and the leaders of the EPP in justification of his not speaking German, when he called upon Konrad Adenauer to support his explanation: 'De Gaulle believed that he could speak German', Adenauer recounted. 'I didn't know him, and for our first meeting de Gaulle invited me to come and see him at Colombey-les-Deux-Églises. I was worried about this first encounter with him and what kind of welcome I would get. A car came to pick me up at the nearest military airport and soon we were approaching Colombey. At a certain point we saw a tall figure in a big coat accompanied by a soldier. The driver warned me that it was de Gaulle, coming to meet us on the road. And my first words of greeting to him were in German: "*Wie geht es Ihnen?*" Somewhat flustered, he replied: "*Zu Fuss!*"* After that, we decided to get an interpreter.'

At the start of the day, I meet with about thirty members of the Bundestag, where I have been invited by my friend Gunther Krichbaum, the French-speaking chairman of the European Affairs Committee. From there we go on to the Chancellery, where I meet Angela Merkel's European adviser Uwe Corsepius. The conversation is cordial, but I sense an irritation with the French positions, and a dialogue between France and Germany that is more complicated than might appear.

Having met the new strongman of the Chancellery, Helge Braun, and then the new Vice-Chancellor, Olaf Scholz, a member of the SPD, I meet the new Secretary-General, Annegret Kramp-Karrenbauer, at the CDU headquarters. She is a rather energetic, straightforward and direct woman. Angela Merkel chose her to take charge of the CDU at the time when this great new coalition was being formed. She has taken up her pilgrim's staff and is travelling around Germany, region by region.

We already know one another; our acquaintance goes back to a particular moment in Rome on Thursday, 7 February 2013. On that day, the German ambassador to the Vatican, together with his French colleague Bruno Joubert, organized a conference on the Élysée Treaty and Franco-German cooperation for teachers and students at the Jesuit College in Rome. The two ambassadors invited Annegret Kramp-Karrenbauer and me to be guests of the conference. Pope Benedict XVI,

---

* 'How are you?' (literally, 'How are you going?') – 'On foot!'

true to his German roots, had granted an audience in the morning to the young Minister-President of Saarland and, without being obliged to do so, she invited me to accompany her.

The audience of about twenty minutes took place in the Pope's library, and we were able to discuss the European issues of the moment and, on my part, the work we were doing to learn the lessons of the financial crisis. The Pope spoke alternately in French and German, with great intellectual vivacity, but I saw that physically he was totally exhausted, as if crushed by his role.

Returning to the Villa Bonaparte for the lunch organized by Bruno Joubert, I asked the two cardinals and diplomatic and ecclesiastical personalities gathered around the table: 'The Pope seemed extremely tired. Is it conceivable that a pope could resign?' I remember the unanimous denials of the ambassador and the bishops present in the face of this sacrilegious question. Three days later, on Monday morning, the Vatican announced the extraordinary resignation of Pope Benedict XVI.

Thursday, 26 April 2018: Sofia

After Hanover and Berlin, and before arriving in Dublin on Sunday, today I am in Sofia, having come here specifically to give a speech to all the major financial players and bankers in Europe, brought together by Eurofi. This association was chaired for a long time by Jacques de Larosière, whose advice I always have time for.

In the morning I meet the imposing Boïko Borissov in his office. The Bulgarian Prime Minister is a direct, straightforward man of impressive size. He has no truck with diplomatic precaution. For him, it is vital that Bulgaria belongs to Europe and, he hopes, one day soon, to the Eurozone. From the east he is under pressure from Russia, and to the south from Turkey, which is heavily financing the construction of new mosques.

The Prime Minister's main concern, beyond the situation in his own country, is the stability of the Western Balkan states and their integration into Europe. Taking advantage of the current Bulgarian presidency of the EU, he is organizing a summit of the twenty-eight heads of state and government of the EU countries in Sofia on 17 May to address these issues.

I remember my very first meeting with Mr Borissov in his office. One wall was lined with knives and another with icons. Smiling, he told me, 'over there is order, and over there is morality', before leading me onto the balcony to observe work on the Sofia metro below – a project which at the time had just begun, enabled by European subsidies.

In my current team, in honour of the rotating presidency, there is a young Bulgarian diplomat, Ivaylo 'Ivo' Iaydjiev, who speaks French perfectly. His judgement is acute and he has a good sense of humour. When organizing this trip, he suggested that we pay a visit, together with the mayor of Sofia, to the city's metro, the most tangible proof for Sofia's inhabitants of European solidarity. We meet at European Union Station, where dozens of journalists are waiting for us. The structural fund programmes that enabled this work are under threat of being cut by 14 per cent if we do not finalize an orderly withdrawal with the British.

A little later in the evening, I meet with representatives from the European financial sector. In financial services as elsewhere, Brexit creates a lose–lose situation, although the UK has more to lose than the EU. The argument that the EU absolutely needs the City does not correspond to reality, or to what we are being told by market participants and the European Central Bank. The EU is prepared to meet the costs of the fragmentation imposed by the UK's decision.

Until now, as a member state of the EU, the UK has benefited from the 'financial passport'. With this passport, a Japanese or Brazilian bank, once established in London, could offer its services throughout the Single Market.

Theresa May understands that this mechanism, which requires common rules, common supervision and a common Court of Justice, cannot apply to a country that has chosen to leave the EU. She has therefore given up any demand for retention of the financial passport.

At the same time, however, the British are asking for mutual recognition of our financial regulations via 'generalized equivalence', which would have a very similar effect to the financial passport. The suggestion is that financial institutions established in the UK would be able to offer their services throughout the EU on the basis of purely British rules, supervision and legal control, which is obviously not acceptable to us.

That being said, the EU is and will remain the most open market in the world: the EU treaty guarantees the free movement of capital, and our future free trade agreement with the UK should recognize the right of UK financial institutions to establish themselves in the EU. Finally, to facilitate trade in financial services, there is the possibility of recognizing 'equivalences' between EU and third country regulations. These equivalences, issued unilaterally by the European Commission one financial product at a time can be withdrawn at any time should the regulations of the third country in question no longer offer protections equivalent to those of European law.

Why should this system, which has proved to function with the United States, not work with the United Kingdom? And this system of equivalence will work all the better if the UK chooses not to diverge too much from the regulation and the supervision that we have built up together over the last forty-five years. Voluntary regulatory cooperation would help ensure this is the case.

Sunday, 29 April 2018: The General's Ireland

Another trip to Ireland, and an important step forward. In Dublin I meet Sabine and Nina Obermaier, the members of my team who with great tenacity have led the difficult discussions with the British on the Irish question, while maintaining a daily privileged link with the Irish government. Dan Ferrie, our dynamic and enthusiastic young Irish press officer, is also there. On an earlier visit I had briefly met his parents, Robbie and Emer, in front of the Dáil, the Irish Parliament.

I had hoped to arrive a day early with my wife Isabelle, to privately fulfil an old dream of mine to go to the south-west of the island, in the footsteps of Charles de Gaulle, who came here the day after his resignation on 28 April 1969. De Gaulle chose to stay in the small fishing port of Sneem, in the modest £500-a-week run-down Heron Cove Hotel, now a private home.* I have been told that in the main square of the village there is a memorial inscribed with the General's phrase: 'At this solemn moment of my long life, here I have found what I was looking for: to be facing myself.'

* Dominique de La Tour, 'L'Irlande du Général', *Les Échos*, 11 January 2013.

The images of General de Gaulle leaning on his cane, walking the windy Derrynane shore, of Yvonne and his aide-de-camp Admiral Flohic, are etched in the memory of all who admired the General. He had chosen Ireland, a country whose landscapes, culture and ruggedness corresponded well to his own sensibilities. And in fact he had ancestors among the McCartans, a South Belfast clan.

For all we young Gaullists, there was something moving in seeing this great old man, alone or almost so, withdrawing from France and from political life the day after the failure of the referendum. I will make the visit, but it will have to be another time.

This evening we travel instead to a comfortable hotel in Dundalk, and carefully prepare for tomorrow's speech and the sensitive steps to be taken during this visit.

Monday, 30 April 2018: A fragile peace on the island of Ireland

We gather with Taoiseach Leo Varadkar, and the Tánaiste (Deputy Prime Minister) Simon Coveney at the Dundalk Institute of Technology for an 'All-Island Civic Dialogue'. There are around 400 people present in the room, representatives of all political parties and communities in Ireland and Northern Ireland. It was the previous Taoiseach Enda Kenny who, in the wake of the Brexit vote, had the fine idea of creating a context for discussion and explanation of the consequences of the UK referendum. It is here in Ireland that these consequences will be potentially the most serious, as the UK's withdrawal from the European Union and the Single Market could theoretically lead to the re-establishing of a physical border in the middle of the island, bringing with it the risk of new tensions. In my speech I emphasize that, without a safety net, a 'backstop', which has been recognized as necessary by both parties, there will be no Withdrawal Agreement.

This is no EU strategy. The backstop is not about moving British red lines, it is a consequence of those red lines. Since we do not want a physical border on the island of Ireland, and since the UK has agreed to respect Ireland's position in the Single Market, goods entering Northern Ireland, which may subsequently end up in France, Belgium or Poland, must comply with the rules of the Single Market and the EU customs code.

After this, we go on to Northern Ireland, and therefore to the UK, as if we were just walking from one side of a room to the other, arriving in Newry where the first group of Northern Irish business leaders is waiting for me. I take the time to listen to each of them. They all speak briefly and precisely. It is clear to see how almost the entire economy is intertwined across a border that is currently invisible.

I begin to explain the only idea that is on the table, our proposal for a backstop. To avoid having to put customs controls in place between Northern Ireland and Ireland, we propose to bring Northern Ireland into the EU Customs Union on an exceptional basis. To avoid the need for regulatory controls in the middle of the island of Ireland, we propose a regulatory alignment of Northern Ireland with the rules of the Single Market, at least all the rules necessary to preserve cooperation and trade between the north and south of the island. But this also requires customs, regulatory and health and safety checks at Northern Ireland ports and airports for products entering the island from the rest of the UK.

We opt to take the approach of explaining this proposal, removing all the drama and stripping it of all the ideological and political dimensions in which the Northern Irish Unionists want to clothe it. This is not about challenging the British institutional order. It is about technical, practical, concrete controls, like those that already exist to ensure respect of veterinary and phytosanitary regulations. In Newry, I have the feeling that this pragmatic message is understood.

This evening, as I walk through Derry/Londonderry, I can't help but think of Bloody Sunday, and the tragic battles that took place on these streets. On 30 January 1972, on this very spot, fourteen people died.

Tuesday, 1 May 2018: A difficult job

This morning I get straight on with another round of meetings at the Guildhall in Derry/Londonderry, first with Mayor Maolíosa McHugh of Sinn Féin, then with MEP Martina Anderson, and finally with some thirty business and company representatives from across Northern Ireland.

In this reasonable and concrete dialogue, we have proof that our proposals for Northern Ireland are well understood and supported here. The tragedy is that the DUP, which represents just over 30 per cent of the electorate in Northern Ireland, is holding to ransom not just all the other players but the whole of British political life, just because its ten MPs provide Theresa May with the votes needed for her majority in the House of Commons.

Nothing constructive can be expected of this party, which fears movement towards reunification of the island.

Walking down the beautiful stairs of the Guildhall, I meet about fifty schoolchildren from four different schools in Derry/Londonderry, from both Catholic and Protestant families. In the simplest possible terms, I try to explain to them who I am and what I do. One of them asks me: 'Do you have a difficult job, Mister Barnier?' 'Yes, very difficult!' Difficult because there are so many questions, and I don't have all the answers.

Later, on the way back, I stop for sandwiches with a group of women who are part of the Northern Ireland Rural Women's Network in Dungannon. This small town is located next to the border, in the most rural and poorest part of Northern Ireland. Transport is scarce and the women, and some men too, all speak to me in very straightforward terms of what Europe is doing for education, social action, human rights and the environment. Two of them are on the verge of tears: 'You are our hope.' Action on all of these issues is indeed supported and made possible by European funds – not only the PEACE programme dedicated solely to Northern Ireland, but structural funds such as the European Social Fund, which Northern Ireland will be deprived of when the transition period ends. I promise to make the case in Brussels for preserving and even increasing the commitments of the PEACE programme in the next budget period.

Before boarding the plane back to Dublin, we read the editorial of the *Belfast Telegraph*, which, despite its Unionist credentials, welcomes our proposals and our approach, acknowledging that we have demonstrated 'a good understanding of the situation on both sides of the border' and that we are right to try and keep a cool head and make progress.

I am grateful to Nina and to the two Irish members of the team, Dan and Tadhg O'Briain, who ably covers energy issues, for helping to make this visit a success.

Perhaps, in the short time we have, we can convince the majority of Northern Ireland's economic and political leaders to support our backstop, even if it means making a few accommodations?

Monday, 14 May 2018: 'Little, not "very little"'

This morning I am pleased to join Federica Mogherini for a joint speech at the European Union Institute for Security Studies.

Our message is clear: in the fields of security and defence, solidarity between the EU and the UK is non-negotiable. There can be no 'trade-off' between security and trade.

The European Union will remain a global player after Brexit, and will continue to meet its responsibilities. But we have a mutual interest in joining forces to tackle common threats such as terrorism, and to shape the world order, for example by defending the deal with Iran.

Naturally, cooperation with the UK will not take place within the same framework as today. The UK will no longer participate in EU decision-making, it will no longer be able to help define and carry out EU actions, and UK entities will not have the same rights as EU entities. These are all purely mechanical consequences of Brexit.

However, the EU already cooperates flexibly with many partners. For example, twenty-five third countries have already participated in EU-led operations.

In the case of the UK, as set out in the European Council guidelines, potential future cooperation could extend to five different areas: close and regular consultations on foreign policy (e.g., information-sharing on sanctions); openness to UK contributions to our external actions; the possibility of the UK's participation in certain European Defence Agency research projects; and exchanges of information on cyber incidents and attacks. Finally, this future relationship should be underpinned by a security and information agreement between the EU and the UK, which would allow for the exchange and protection of classified information.

The level of ambition of this future security and defence partnership, which Guillaume de La Brosse is preparing with me, will depend upon the degree of commitment the UK is prepared to make. The EU will continue to deepen its defence and security policies, in particular through the initiatives taken by the Commission for the European Defence Fund, the European space programmes, and the centre of excellence in cybersecurity.

In the Q&A that follows, BBC journalist Adam Fleming is the first to ask me about the state of the negotiations. 'We are told that very little progress has been made in the latest rounds of negotiation. Is that your assessment?' I reply with a smile to 'the famous' Adam Fleming: 'I would say little, not very little.'

Thursday, 17 May 2018: Churchill meets Adenauer...

My assistant Barthélemy, always on the lookout for information and feedback on our work, brings me a book about Winston Churchill by a Dutch author, Felix Klos. The personal dedication inside reads as follows: 'I know that a group of Brexiteers have already given you a book about Churchill, but as was already the case with their tendentious claims during the referendum, their claiming of Churchill as a Brexiteer could not be further from the truth. In any case, his tireless work for Europe is a great inspiration. That is why I am sending you my book; as a Dutchman, as a European and one of the Maastricht generation, I want to thank you for all that you do for Europe and for representing Europeans in such a dignified and effective way.'

In the book I come across this phrase of Konrad Adenauer's addressed to Winston Churchill: 'Why is it that you, Sir Winston, became the champion for the European ideal? I believe this can be explained from two human qualities that also are the requisite qualities for states-manship: greatness of thought, depth of feeling.'

I have received so many letters – touching, ironic, confiding, critical – since I began in this mission. A small team within the task force, in particular Anouk Mertens de Wilmars, Giovanna Di Ruberti and Joel dos Santos Domingos, brings them to my attention and prepares answers for each one.

Throughout my public life, I have always demanded that the greatest respect should be paid to those citizens, often those of the most modest means, who take the time and trouble to write to me. The respect that is their due means that they should be answered. And that, as far as is possible, their ideas and criticisms should be taken into account.

Saturday, 19 May 2018: Royal wedding

Today is of course totally British, with the lavish wedding of Harry and Meghan.

An old friend of mine, Jean-Michel Naulot, a lifelong Gaullist, whose advice on financial regulation I have often listened to because he was a member of the board of the French Financial Markets Authority, sent me the following text message: 'What a magnificent people, these English! They always arrange everything so perfectly! Except perhaps for Brexit. But we must keep them by our side as a sure ally and continue to share the finer feelings with them.'

Tuesday, 22 May 2018: Poorer by £900

According to Bank of England Governor Mark Carney, speaking to a parliamentary committee, British households are already around £900 poorer than if the UK had not decided to leave the EU. And we are only just preparing for Brexit, the real effects of which will not be felt until the end of the transition period on 31 December 2020…

Saturday, 26 May 2018: Lisbon

A two-day visit to Lisbon ends under hazy sunshine. This morning I am at the International Federation of European Law for its annual congress. President of the Federation José Luís da Cruz Vilaça welcomes me, together with the President of the EU Court of Justice Koen Lenaerts and Advocate-General Melchior Wathelet, whom I have known for a long time.

I have decided to dot the i's once again for the British and, in a speech that is well received and applauded, I reiterate what we Europeans are about, and those things we will not accept being called into question just because the British are leaving.

There is no mistrust of the UK on our part. There is not – and there never will be – a spirit of revenge or punishment. But we must understand that, in the European Union, our strength lies in the trust that exists between member states.

This trust does not fall from the sky; it is based on a normative ecosystem, common rules, shared decisions, common supervision and implementation, and a common Court of Justice. Nowhere else in the world is there a common legal order for an entire continent like the one we have built together over the past sixty years. There is no reason, no justification, to accept a weakening of this community of law and this common destiny just because one of our member states has decided to leave it.

Coming around to the details, I remind listeners that an international agreement, however comprehensive, is of little value unless it is effectively implemented. The agreement with the British on a joint committee is an important and necessary first step, but it is not sufficient to ensure adequate governance of the Withdrawal Agreement. This governance must be built around three points that come as a set.

First, a jurisdictional system for settling disputes: unlike a classic international agreement, the Withdrawal Agreement will create rights that can be directly invoked by those individuals concerned, and it must be guaranteed that their disputes will be settled within a jurisdictional or arbitrative framework, and not by a simple political ruling.

Second, the role of the EU Court of Justice: logically, the bulk of the provisions in the Withdrawal Agreement comes from EU law. As far as these provisions are concerned, we cannot accept that a court other than the EU Court of Justice should pronounce on this law or impose its interpretation on EU institutions.

Finally, the role of the British courts, which we must respect. British judges will be responsible for applying the Withdrawal Agreement in the UK. For eight years they will be able to refer to the EU Court of Justice for a preliminary ruling. This mechanism allows us to ensure, in the long term, uniformity of interpretation of the Agreement on both sides of the Channel. I hope that the message is received loud and clear…

Monday, 4 June 2018: Budapest

Back on the banks of the Danube, in the beautiful Hungarian capital of Budapest, where I am accompanied by Sabine and Barthélemy, who has retained close links with the country since his Erasmus year.

In addition to the usual meetings with the national Parliament, then with trade union and professional leaders, I meet Prime Minister Viktor Orbán and his team in the huge Parliament building – a building inspired by Westminster. At the junction of several wings the crown of St Stephen is displayed, guarded by two soldiers on hourly rotation, its golden cross strangely askew. Hidden during the Second World War, the crown was recovered by the Americans and kept at Fort Knox, and was only returned to Hungary in 1978.

Viktor Orbán requests to meet me face to face in his large office where the walls are hung with maps of Bosnia-Herzegovina, Ukraine and the Balkans. We talk about the geopolitical situation in Europe, the changeover of power in Spain and, above all, the new populist government in Italy. Despite our differences, I have always enjoyed an honest relationship with Mr Orbán. We have always spoken frankly to one another. I listen to what he tells me and I tell him what I think. The EPP will never compromise on European integration and the rule of law, which are the values upon which it is founded.

Coming back to Brexit, he tells me: 'We let the British leave. We shouldn't have humiliated them by imposing Juncker on them in June 2014 when they didn't want him.' At the time, David Cameron did indeed express his opposition to the appointment of Jean-Claude Juncker, who he considered too federalist. But Angela Merkel, with the support of François Hollande, put the British in the minority in the European Council.

On the substantive issues of Brexit, we have no problem with Hungary. Its two main priorities were taken into account in the negotiations: the security of the rights of the 200,000 Hungarians living in the UK, and the funding linked to the Union's budget for the period 2014–20. To make sure things are clear, Mr Orbán has his spokesman say after our meeting that 'keeping the twenty-seven together is a priority' and that I have his support as negotiator.

Thursday, 7 June 2018: David Davis threatens to resign

This week of negotiations with the British has been a bumpy one. Once again, David Davis opted out. As for Olly Robbins, he only arrived in Brussels this evening for a working dinner, something we have become accustomed to. We meet at the Atelier, outside for once. It has been a trying week for him too, and he brings us up to date on the twists and turns that led to the publication, a few hours earlier, of a British White Paper on customs issues that brings back the idea of a temporary customs union between the EU and the UK.

David Davis, who is opposed to this arrangement, threatened to resign late this morning, and only backed down when he obtained the assurance that the proposed new arrangement would be temporary – which makes no sense at all.

Listening to Olly Robbins, I get a clear sense of both Theresa May's tenacity and the difficulties in which she finds herself. For her, this is not really a negotiation with the European Union but far more intense negotiation, on an almost hourly basis, with her own ministers and her own majority. And all the while, the clock is ticking.

Friday, 8 June 2018: Backstop means backstop!

Over the last few days we have made progress in agreeing on Euratom, goods placed on the market and customs issues related to separation. But we have agreed with the British that we would not give any detail on the points of progress, so that we can reap the benefits of these results a little later, before the European Council. At the end of this week's negotiations, I therefore mention to the press only the points that we still need to work on.

First, protection of EU citizens' personal data. We want long-term protection for data already exchanged under the same conditions that apply today under European law.

Second, protection of geographical indications, on which we still do not have a British position. This is an important issue for many producers and consumers both in the UK and in the other twenty-seven countries of the European Union.

There is still work to be done on infringement and administrative procedures concerning the UK that need to be in effect at the end of the transition period, for example on state aid. This is not a purely bureaucratic point; it is something that clearly involves the protection of the financial interests of the Union.

But apart from these three points, on which we still need to make a great deal of progress, there remain two major subjects of disagreement: the governance of the Withdrawal Agreement and, of course, the issues relating to Ireland and Northern Ireland.

The many journalists present today, however, are only interested in one thing: my reaction to the British document published yesterday concerning a temporary customs union. I risk disappointing them by not taking too strong a line on this, going no further than to pose a few questions. Is the British proposal a workable solution to avoid a physical border? Does it respect the integrity of the Single Market and the Customs Union? And, in particular, does the UK want to continue to benefit from our free trade agreements with countries outside the EU? Does this mean that we will have to re-open, renegotiate or even re-ratify our existing agreements? And finally, is the proposed solution a fool-proof backstop?

Apart from these questions, I issue a reminder as to why we need a permanent guarantee of this famous backstop unless and until the future relationship with the UK provides a better solution. *Backstop means backstop!*

Monday, 11 June 2018: Croissants for David Davis

At the end of last week, David Davis asked to see me urgently. In fact, I have not seen him since 19 March, and his visit, disconnected from the day-to-day negotiations we are conducting with Olly Robbins, is probably related more to tomorrow's House of Commons session. He needs to be able to tell the Commons that we have seen each other and that in some way he retains credibility as a negotiator. He has also been at the heart of the internal battle within Theresa May's cabinet, as evidenced by his threat to resign so as to obtain a guarantee that the customs union proposed by the Prime Minister will be explicitly temporary.

This morning, on my way to Exki to buy croissants for the British minister, I bump into the BBC's Adam Fleming, who is quick to relay the news. Flanked by Olly Robbins and Ambassador Tim Barrow, Mr Davis, who arrives punctually, asks to see me one-to-one. 'We need to see each other more regularly from now on', he tells me. 'The negotiations are entering a new, more political phase. We have to take things in hand at our level.' I confirm my availability. And I reflect to myself that it won't be too hard to see each other more often than we have done so far…

In the hour-long meeting that follows, referring to a document laid out in front of him, he continues with the same old rhetoric. 'We need a specific agreement. We will say what we are after in a 200-page White

Paper in July. Given our proximity in regulations, we want a comprehensive agreement, mutual recognition in a number of areas. If not, too bad.' Very calmly, in unison with Sabine and Stéphanie, I invite him to be more realistic about what will and will not be possible.

Once again, it seems to me that the tone of the discussion is rather out of touch.

For now, I say to him, but really to Olly Robbins, that we need further progress for the European Council in June. This European Council should be a kind of springboard. It must not be seen externally as backtracking. We are getting dangerously close to October and the risk of failure is still present.

Thursday, 14 June 2018: Isolating Ireland

Olly Robbins returns to Brussels with a mandate and British positions to be moved forward on several fronts: governance of the Withdrawal Agreement, data exchange and the protection of existing geographical indications. He hopes to settle all these points before the June European Council so that they can be 'green-lighted' in the draft treaty.

The British strategy is clear: isolate the Irish question so that, in October, at the concluding moment, it remains the only open question, in the hope that the twenty-seven will leave it for discussions on the future relationship. This is precisely what I do not want to happen. This question is so sensitive and serious for everyone involved that, come what may, it must be dealt with in the Withdrawal Agreement.

Monday, 18 June 2018: A beer on the Danube

It is 6am, and already I am at Brussels airport, ready to leave for two days of visits and work in Vienna.

On arrival, we have an hour to spare in this city in the architectural splendour of whose palaces and churches the heritage of the past is so visible. Together with Matthieu, I take the opportunity to prepare a tweet to mark the occasion of the anniversary of the Appeal of 18 June. Taking my lead from a text by the French Ministry of Culture looking back at the circumstances of the appeal, broadcast by the BBC with special permission from Winston Churchill, in my own message I voice a longstanding and firmly held conviction: 'Today, both de Gaulle and Churchill would be equally committed to the sovereignty and freedom of Europe.'

And then on to a string of meetings: the Minister of Foreign Affairs Karin Kneissl, a polyglot who knows the Middle East well and has even taught at the University of St Joseph in Beirut, where I still have close connections; President of the Republic Alexander Van der Bellen, a Green and a European, straightforward and sincere; and the former Socialist Chancellor, Christian Kern, with whom I have always had a good relationship.

Finally, in the early afternoon we meet the Minister for European Affairs Gernot Blümel, and are then joined by the Chancellor, Sebastian Kurz. As always, it is a friendly meeting. Even though Austria is not one of the countries most heavily impacted by these negotiations, the young Chancellor is following the situation with acute political awareness. The new Austrian presidency that is about to begin will play an important role in the second half of the year, when, one way or another, the Brexit agreement must be concluded.

My concern is to ensure that, during this sensitive period, the presidency remains vigilant so as to head off the parallel negotiations the British are trying to open up through every door and window in Europe.

As usual, I then go to the national Parliament where Austrian MPs have some good questions for me. They are well prepared and I sense no aggression, even from the three MPs from the extreme right-wing party FPÖ present at the table. After being received by Andreas Schieder, chairman of the Social Democratic SPÖ group, along with a delegation of MPs, I have the opportunity for an interesting dialogue with the President of the Parliament, Wolfgang Sobotka, a member of the Christian Democratic ÖVP party.

The last step in this long but by now customary itinerary is a meeting with socio-professional representatives and trade unions.

The sun is setting in Vienna, but the day is not over yet. After a beer and a salad on the banks of the Danube, I leave it to Matthieu and Magda Jagiełło, adviser on internal security to my team, to rework the speech I will give tomorrow to the European Union Agency for Fundamental Rights. I want to make it a precise declaration, laying out, in the area of internal security and citizens' rights, what is and is not possible for the British.

Tuesday, 19 June 2018: Brexit and homeland security

To the European Union Agency for Fundamental Rights. It's not always nice to be the bad guy, but my role here is to speak the truth about the mechanical and legal consequences of leaving the EU.

But first, I set out to recall what we, as twenty-eight, have already achieved together.

Together, on the basis of the European arrest warrant, we are able to extradite criminals or suspects – including our own nationals – from one member state to another.

Together, we created Europol to help national authorities. Europol collects information from all over the EU and helps to fight cross-border crime.

Together with our Schengen partners, including Norway and Switzerland, we have implemented the Schengen Information System. It was consulted more than five billion times last year to find out who was crossing Schengen borders. It has helped to stop criminals and terrorists. It has also helped not just to recover stolen cars, but also to find missing persons and children.

Together, via the framework of the 'European Investigation Order', we are able to collect factual data and exchange it quickly with one another in order to bring criminals to justice.

Together, we implement one another's court rulings in real time, for example by confiscating, or freezing, the assets of criminals.

To Europeans today, the availability of such means may seem quite natural. But is this really the case? Is there any other region in the world where sovereign states trust one another enough to establish such high-level cooperation on internal security? Is there any other region in which sovereign states have created a common space together without internal border controls? A region in which citizens can move freely and safely and can rely on common institutions to protect their fundamental rights? This degree of cooperation is both unique and unprecedented. It is made possible by the trust that member states have in one another.

Of course, we must continue to maintain strong cooperation with the British on all these issues, but their decision forces us to do so within another framework.

I spend some time on a controversial issue: extradition and the European Arrest Warrant. The European Arrest Warrant is linked to the free movement of persons. Its success depends upon mutual trust between states.

This trust rests upon several pillars: mutual respect for the fundamental rights set out in the Charter of Fundamental Rights; certainty that other member states will implement and apply the rules in the same way, under the authority of the EU Court of Justice; and the concept of European citizenship, which allows member states to suspend the constitutional prohibition on the extradition of their own nationals.

Today we know that the UK is not prepared to accept the free movement of people, the authority of the Court or the Charter of Fundamental Rights. The UK therefore cannot participate in the European Arrest Warrant programme.

But that does not mean that we cannot work together on extradition. We are ready to build on the existing Council of Europe Convention, signed by all member states. On this basis we might consider, for example, streamlining the procedure, facilitating the processes and introducing time limits. All of this is highly necessary.

This speech immediately provokes a great deal of comment and, of course, the incomprehension, whether feigned or sincere, of Brexiteers. The little 'blame game' with the EU continues. I even read a statement by DUP MP Nigel Dodds accusing me of promoting the spread of terrorism by refusing to cooperate with the British!

On my Twitter account I also find a message from a citizen who reacts as follows: 'How long will it take for the UK and in particular British MPs to start realizing that it is not Barnier or the EU that is erecting borders? It is the British government, with its red lines, closing the doors on itself.'

Saturday, 23 June 2018: With future customs officers at Schiphol

Last night I arrived at Amsterdam-Schiphol airport directly from Dublin. After a night in a grim hotel, at 7am I meet with the airport president Dick Benschop, whom I know, and the airport security services.

The Netherlands has clearly assessed the new control requirements that Brexit will call for. Like other major transit airports in Europe, they are seeking unilateral recognition on our part of the checks carried out in the UK for all passengers arriving in Amsterdam en route to another destination. This is the only way to avoid building expensive new infrastructure to handle controls on all of these passengers.

In addition to travellers, there are also goods, and a little later in the day I have the pleasure of greeting some thirty young Dutch people currently in training to become customs officers. Seven hundred and fifty new posts are being created in the Netherlands. I thank these young people for their commitment and tell them how important their mission is. 'You are the ones who will guarantee the integrity of the internal market and respect of the rules for all the products that enter the Union. We must protect consumers and businesses. That will be your job.'

Jos Hupperetz, a very friendly Dutchman who is the customs expert in our task force, and has accompanied me here, has created a new slide for our team which has been a great success. It lists all the controls that must be carried out on goods entering and leaving the Single Market. Some of these controls are financial, for example for VAT, or concern market supervision. Many others, involving safety and security, have to be carried out at the border – for example, on live animals, animal products, fresh fruit and vegetables, plants, or plastic cooking utensils from China and Hong Kong. The work of all these young trainees will be crucial.

Friday, 29 June 2018: European Council

Since yesterday the heads of state or government have been meeting again at the European Council for two days in a crisis atmosphere over the migration issue. Which is to say that Brexit is not the main priority of this summit.

The leaders left at 5am; I meet the twenty-seven at 11am. It is a pleasure to greet the new President of the Spanish government, Pedro Sánchez, and the new Italian Prime Minister, Giuseppe Conte, both looking smart and elegant.

Donald Tusk invites me to make my usual report. I begin by reminding him that we are four months away from the October European Council, at which we want to conclude the negotiation for an orderly exit from the UK in March 2019. As in any negotiation, these last few weeks are going to be the most difficult, and we have to take into account the British political context, which remains very unstable.

Not much progress has been made since the last European Council, although we have managed to 'green-light' nine new articles in the draft treaty, concerning goods placed on the market, ongoing customs procedures, VAT and excise issues, legal cooperation on civil and commercial matters, public procurement and Euratom.

None of these is negligible, but quite obviously Ireland remains the most difficult and explosive issue.

To avoid a hard border on the island of Ireland, EU leaders have agreed to an exceptional departure from their principles. In the absence of a customs union between the EU and the UK, which the latter has so far refused to consider, we have offered to integrate Northern Ireland alone into our customs territory. This is not enough to avoid controls on goods, though. That would require regulatory alignment in Northern Ireland with our rules and standards for goods and agricultural products, and the introduction of technical controls to monitor this alignment.

To explain the reasons for the controls that we will be obliged to put in place in Northern Ireland whatever else happens, I use the concrete example of American chlorinated chickens. We have never wanted them on the European market, but it is likely that the British will be obliged to accept them on their own market as part of any future trade agreement they want to sign with the US. We will then have to prevent such chickens not only from being produced in Northern Ireland, but also from arriving in Northern Ireland, as they would then immediately be on the European market. Hence the need for controls.

We know that, in order to avoid special treatment for Northern Ireland and to satisfy her Northern Irish DUP allies, Theresa May, who is meeting her ministers at Chequers on 6 July, will argue in a draft White Paper for a common UK-wide solution, and ask for access to the Single Market for goods only. This strategy would isolate the Irish issue in the negotiation, and ultimately instrumentalize it for the benefit of the whole of the UK. This, of course, would be the à la carte Single Market we do not want, and would amount to cherry-picking on a grand scale.

But above all, the British want to postpone any solution on Ireland until discussions on the future relationship begin. For us, the risk is clear:

the entire future negotiation could end up being a hostage to the Irish question.

After my presentation, several of the heads of government confirm their solidarity with Ireland and express concern about the prospect of a no-deal scenario.

This European Council has allowed me to confirm that the twenty-seven leaders and President Tusk have confidence in me, but I know that this trust must be continually 'cultivated'.

Thursday, 5 July 2018: Vilnius

Back in the capital of Lithuania, accompanied for this visit by Tristan and Thomas Lieflander, a young German lawyer from my team. What a difference compared to my first visit here in 1996, twenty years ago! The city has been rejuvenated, it is modern, the population is young. Here, as in all the capitals of the countries that joined us in 2004, but also in Romania, Bulgaria and Croatia, we see the concrete effects of European progress.

The President of the Republic, Dalia Grybauskaitė, is a strong and authoritative woman, who was formerly European Commissioner for the Budget between 2004 and 2009. I find her more cordial towards me than during our last meeting, and with more of a smile. She gives us her opinion: 'I know the British; it's all about communication. They will play the blame game.'

On substantive matters, the President and her ministers tell me that they are satisfied with the results achieved on citizens' rights and the financial settlement, two priorities for Lithuania. As for the future relationship, they emphasize the need for a close partnership with the UK on security and defence. And they reiterate their support for our negotiating team and for the unity of the twenty-seven.

On my way out of Lithuania, I choose to take a moment to look at the statue of the young Romain Gary. It's a statue of a child looking up to the sky, reminding us of the seven or eight years the future writer spent here with his mother, as described so well in *The Promise of Dawn*.

I have always loved Romain Gary – as a Gaullist and a Resistance fighter, and for the aura of mystery and of the epic that enshrouds him. My son Benjamin, now a publisher, and always passionate to find new horizons, has befriended his son, Alexandre Diego Gary. A nod toward this European literary heritage.

Also, I am always moved when I return to one of the three Baltic countries that until 1990 were Soviet provinces. I remember the incredible human chain that brought together millions of Balts between Tallinn, Riga and Vilnius to symbolize the popular movement for independence. I remember weeping when I saw on TV those simple wooden coffins on the airport tarmac, brought from Siberia. Parents, children, sisters of those deported by Stalin all desperately looking for the name of a relative on the coffins. And I also remember that these three countries first returned to the international stage under their own flags at the opening ceremony of the Albertville Olympic Games on 8 February 1992, eliciting an immense, spontaneous ovation from the whole stadium.

Friday, 6 July 2018: The battle of Chequers

The battle of Chequers is on. In fact, it's a battle on two fronts.

The first is the one Theresa May is waging against some of her ministers. Before the Chequers lock-in, she warned that if any minister wanted to resign, they would have to leave Chequers without their official car and take a taxi instead.

The second battle, of course, is the one on the horizon with the European Union. May's adviser Olly Robbins tells us that she wants her entire team to back a White Paper that marks a break with the clear-cut Brexit line. She is well aware of the dramatic consequences of her own announcements for the British economy. Leaving the Single Market and the Customs Union would come at a very heavy price for UK businesses.

Cornered by her hard-line Brexiteer ministers, she needs to square the circle. She is trying to preserve her red lines while asking Europe to change its own rules and accept an à la carte Single Market for goods and a customs system in which the UK would enjoy the benefits of the Customs Union while retaining freedom of commercial negotiation.

I am told at the end of the day that it was an arduous discussion. Some twenty ministers clearly supported the softer Brexit line proposed by Theresa May. Eight ministers opposed it. But finally, at the end of the day, all of them, out of solidarity, agreed on a three-page text prefiguring the White Paper.

I decide to react cautiously. In a single tweet, I say that the discussion in Chequers about the future is welcome, that I await the White Paper with interest, and that we will evaluate its proposals to see whether they are operable and realistic in light of the European Council's guidelines.

Saturday, 7 July 2018: David Davis calling

David Davis is trying to reach me. We speak at around 3pm. He thanks me for the openness shown in my tweet last night.

I tell him that I need to read the White Paper in detail. He confirms that it will be published next Thursday, makes it known that he would have liked certain points to have gone differently, and that he hopes to resume negotiations as soon as possible. In concluding, I tell him that I am available next week to meet him in Brussels.

Sunday, 8 July 2018: David Davis resigns

Stéphanie, Tristan Aureau, Stefaan De Rynck and I have just landed in New York for a week of meetings and conferences to try and make the 'European voice on Brexit' heard in a country where, for months, the only explanations of the situation have come from London.

Just as I am leaving for a friendly private lunch with François Delattre, the French ambassador to the United Nations who was my deputy chief of staff for a few months at the Quai d'Orsay, I hear news that David Davis has resigned.

It is midnight in London, 6pm here in New York. I am startled by this decision, of which there was no suggestion in my conversation with him yesterday. What happened? Why resign at midnight? The only explanation is that this decision is linked to the long letter written by several Conservative MPs against Theresa May's proposals, on the pretext that she is not respecting the commitments made to British citizens when they voted for Brexit. The letter accuses Theresa May of weakness in relation to the European Union for respecting EU rules. This marks a resurgence of the rejection of any idea that would turn the UK into a 'vassal state'.

By resigning, Mr Davis means to show that this is the side he is taking. I also imagine that, by announcing his resignation in the middle of the night, he wants to catch other ministers off-guard, particularly Boris Johnson, and thus become the leader of a potential manoeuvre against Theresa May. We shall see.

Monday, 9 July 2018: New York

In New York, where the weather is warm and sunny, I meet this morning with the twenty-seven European ambassadors to the United Nations, convened by João Vale de Almeida, the EU's ambassador. I had to fight to make sure that the British weren't invited to this meeting! Not all of our diplomats have yet understood that, after Brexit, in New York as elsewhere, it will no longer be 'business as usual'. My first words on this point are to tell the ambassadors: 'I know that you are not used to this format of twenty-seven. Unfortunately, it is a format that is set to become the norm.'

Meanwhile, in London, the battle of Chequers continues. Taken by surprise by David Davis's midnight resignation, Boris Johnson has also thrown in the towel. Other junior ministers follow. Throughout this year and a half of negotiations, not once have I met the British Foreign Secretary. Boris Johnson has treated this negotiation from a strictly domestic point of view and only according to the logic of the battle for Brexit which he himself led. I would have been happy to have got to know this baroque character better. In fact, we only spoke once when he was Mayor of London and we were seated in the same gallery for the opening ceremony of the 2012 Olympic Games. I wished him well and we talked about Europe, but we were a long way from the referendum and he was still European at the time – which is possible when you are British and conservative…

In truth, Boris Johnson has made so many blunders and let slip so many verbal 'witticisms' that his appointment as Foreign Secretary was regarded as incongruous in many capitals. And I can imagine that many British diplomats felt the same way. At this point I think that, deep down, Theresa May must be relieved to see him go.

And if further illustration of Boris Johnson's incongruity were needed, it is to be found in his clearly rushed letter of resignation, in which he describes his frustration when, as Mayor of London, he had been unable to protect cyclists from being run over by lorries because he had to wait for the EU to pass legislation to authorize a new model of lorry with a lower windscreen to improve driver visibility.

This is not a serious argument. There was nothing to prevent the Mayor of London from developing a network of cycle paths, enforcing better compliance to keep motor vehicles out of them, launching prevention campaigns aimed at lorry drivers, or even banning access to certain roads for lorries without certain equipment, such as electronic devices to warn of nearby pedestrians or cyclists…

Tuesday, 10 July 2018: France and Belgium

My team has scheduled two briefings in one day. It's too much. I have to make an introductory speech in English on both occasions, and for the first time in the United States I have agreed to a question-and-answer session in English with no safety net.

Before the Council on Foreign Relations and then at the European American Chamber of Commerce, my message is clear: despite Brexit, the EU will remain a large, coherent and regulated market, open for trade.

As if by some miracle, the agenda leaves a couple of hours free between 2pm and 4pm, the very time when the France–Belgium World Cup semi-final kicks off in Russia. A lucky break for our little delegation. Stefaan is wearing Belgium's colours, and we enjoy Samuel Umtiti's goal together, in a sporting spirit. Frankly, I'm happy that France won, but also disappointed for my 'second homeland' and its fine young team of Red Devils.

We take the train to Washington, where Olivier Guersent is waiting for us to take part in interviews in the federal capital, particularly on the theme of finance.

Wednesday, 11 July 2018: Donald Trump's ministers

During this long day in Washington, we meet, in turn, with Wilbur Ross, Secretary of Commerce, then Steven Mnuchin, Secretary of the Treasury, the new Chairman of the Federal Reserve Jerome Powell, and Robert Lighthizer, the US trade negotiator.

I have often visited the United States as a European Commissioner, but I have rarely been received by so many ministers and senior officials, which just goes to show the attention that is being paid here to European issues and to Brexit in particular.

I had been warned about the arrogance and brutality of Donald Trump's new ministers. In fact, on the contrary, I find them courteous and competent. However, it is clear that they are working with an unpredictable president.

Even if they do not really understand Europe, and sometimes harbour an animosity towards it inspired by their president, they all understand that the Union will not agree to unravel what it has built or to weaken what is its primary asset, the Single Market. All of them, more or less directly, let us know that they consider the UK to be acting against its own interests by leaving the Union. And, getting down to basics, they are easily able to tell the difference, as far as American interests are concerned, between a single market of 450 million consumers and a British market of 60 million.

Thursday, 12 July 2018: With Christine Lagarde in Washington

In Washington today I have the pleasure of meeting with Christine Lagarde, along with her team, to whom we explain the state of the negotiations. The IMF's analyses on the macroeconomic consequences of Brexit are always enlightening, and clearly show that we are in a lose–lose situation, that nobody stands to gain from this separation.

I am genuinely pleased have a chance to speak with 'the great Christine', as her staff affectionately call her. In June 2007, I succeeded her at the Ministry of Agriculture when she left for Bercy. Always ready with a smile, she has a very French elegance and a keen understanding of the world. 'The world is her oyster!' Some time later, we meet five congressmen on Capitol Hill who run the Friends of Ireland group. It is both fascinating and moving to see the attachment to the country on the part of so many American politicians who, like Kennedy, are descended from Irish emigrants. I reassure them of our determination to safeguard the Good Friday (Belfast) Agreement and to avoid a hard border.

Friday, 13 July 2018: Une grand dame

I always come back from the United States stimulated by the atmosphere of dynamism and the mobility of ideas. This morning I give my fourth speech to another think-tank, the Carnegie Endowment for International Peace. I call for institutions and the private sector in Europe to be encouraged to support – including fiscally – the development of such a network of think-tanks on economic issues and international relations. Public debate will have a part to play in building the Europe of tomorrow.

Madeleine Albright, who was Bill Clinton's Secretary of State from 1997 to 2001, personifies this passion for intellectual discussion. Now 80 years old, she is never jaded, always curious. She hands me a copy of her latest book, *Fascism: A Warning*, with a personal dedication: 'To Michel Barnier, who has probably the most difficult job in Europe today.' I have included Tristan in our lunch so that he has the opportunity to meet a *grande dame* of world diplomacy.

This lunch is in part devoted precisely to the rise of populist movements and the risk of a resurgence of fascism or authoritarianism. Born in Prague, in the former Czechoslovakia, Mrs Albright is well aware of the old demons that lie dormant in Europe. And I voice my conviction that, once we have dealt with the consequences of Brexit, we must learn from it and begin to respond to the popular sentiment, social anxiety and fear of a loss of cultural identity that populism exploits so effectively.

A conversation with Madeleine Albright is an important engagement for me whenever I visit Washington.

Sunday, 15 July 2018: White Paper

A somewhat trying day because of the time difference, but also an important one because of the World Cup final. I send a friendly text message to the Prime Minister of Croatia, Andrej Plenković: 'May the best team win! Our two teams have had a great run and have projected a great image of Croatia and France. Long live sport and long live Europe.' He replies at noon: 'Indeed, a great fixture and a huge success for both Croatia and France, but you are right, also for Europe whatever the outcome. So may the best team win!'

During our three stays in Belgium – a total of almost fifteen years – Isabelle and our children made many true Belgian friends. Before joining one of these friendly families to watch the match, I take the time to read the White Paper in detail.

What does it contain?

First, some concessions and a bit more realism: the UK recognizes that leaving the Single Market and the Customs Union would have negative consequences for trade flows. They accept that the core of our future economic relationship must be a free trade agreement, even if those words do not quite mean the same thing for the British as they do for us. They also accept that the final arbiter of the interpretation of EU law is the EU Court of Justice, and commit to ensuring that UK courts take account of the jurisprudence of that court. They send out strong signals on the level playing field, notably on state aid and mergers control. Finally, the British White Paper shows some real convergence on the scope of our future cooperation on external and internal security.

On economic matters, however, the two pillars upon which this White Paper relies raise many questions.

On customs, the UK is proposing a 'facilitated customs arrangement' in which they seek to secure all the benefits of a customs union without accepting the counterpart of a common trade policy. This contradicts the very principle at the heart of a customs union, namely a common external tariff. The British are thus seeking to retain an autonomous trade policy for goods. They want to be able to apply two tariffs to goods entering the UK – the autonomous UK tariff or the EU tariff – depending on whether their final destination is the British or the European market.

This proposal has already been presented once before by the British, last August. At the time, it was rejected by the member states and business sectors because it presented three risks, all of which would be borne exclusively by the Union.

A competitiveness risk: this system would give British companies a major competitive advantage over EU companies, since they would be able to incorporate imported inputs into their products at a lower rate. These products could then circulate freely throughout the internal market.

A fiscal and budgetary risk: lower British tariffs would be applied to materials from the UK incorporated into goods destined for the EU market. This would imply a loss of revenue for both the EU budget and the member states.

A supervisory risk: UK customs would then act as agents of the EU – an unprecedented situation – without being subject to the EU system of governance. In the case of VAT, this would go even further, as the UK has made it clear that it no longer wishes to abide by EU rules.

The result of all this would be a bureaucratic nightmare, all to the sole benefit of the UK. Further, this construction would have to rely on technologies that do not even exist today in order to trace the destination of goods circulating in the internal market, and it would generate extremely burdensome financial and administrative costs for all the European companies that would be forced to comply with it.

Alongside this customs arrangement, the British want a 'common rulebook' for goods, the aim of which would be to allow them to participate à la carte in the internal market, without the quid pro quo that member states have to comply with.

The British tell us that they would be prepared to align themselves with EU standards for goods. This goes without saying: any goods coming into the EU, wherever they come from, must conform to EU standards.

Furthermore, this alignment would be limited to border-controlled standards. This point is important because it leaves aside standards that are not controlled at the border. For example, on GMOs, the British are seeking mutual recognition between EU rules and future UK rules, which would give them more freedom than a member state.

In the sphere of services, the UK wishes to retain its potential ability to diverge from EU rules with a view to increasing its competitive advantage. Between 20 per cent and 40 per cent of the value of goods produced in the UK comes from services. If we were to allow UK-produced goods to flow unchecked through the internal market while allowing the UK to diverge on services, we would be granting UK businesses an immediate competitive advantage over our own businesses.

An extra word on the subject of financial services: the British say that they acknowledge that they will losing the 'passport', while seeking to recover it via a system of generalized equivalence that would in fact be co-managed by the EU and the UK. Behind this idea of generalized equivalence, we see the reappearance of the idea of mutual recognition, which is unacceptable, since it would be in direct opposition to our principle of autonomous decision-making.

Finally, if we add to the above proposals those concerning mobility – focused on short stays for certain categories of workers, students and tourists – we can clearly see what underlies the whole British approach: a generalized cherry-picking along with a refusal of the freedom of movement of persons.

Wednesday, 18 July 2018: Tony Blair

By chance, I have an appointment with Tony Blair today, and a little later with Nick Clegg, David Cameron's former Liberal Democrat Deputy Prime Minister, who is coming to meet Sabine. Two European Britons, sincere in their commitment and now marginalized within their own country.

Tony Blair has lost none of his charisma. He is precise in his questions. He remains convinced that the choice is between a no deal and keeping his country in the European Union. We last saw one another a year ago on the fringes of an EPP meeting in Ireland. At the time he thought that there should be a second referendum, but did not see how it could happen. Now, he tells me, the tide is turning, and a second consultation of the British people is no longer impossible. Any political declaration describing the future relationship would have to be very precise, though, and everyone would have to understand what the UK had to lose.

Thursday, 19 July 2018: Dominic Raab

The newly appointed UK Brexit Minister is in Brussels for the first time. I await him at the protocol entrance, as is customary. He's a forthright man, fairly young. He tells me straight away that he wants to put far more energy into the negotiations. Of course, I'm all for that.

In the one-to-one meeting in my office, from the start he tries to create a direct relationship. 'We need to do more politics, find political solutions for Brexit.'

There is something in his eyes that startles me, an almost messianic glow. He is undoubtedly driven by a duty to fulfil his mission and deliver

Brexit, but I am not sure how easy it will be to go into the details of the negotiations with him, and deal with the facts and hard realities.

Still, I understand that he wants to put his mark on the negotiations, to take over from Olly Robbins and to come to Brussels very regularly himself. And he will be most welcome!

Tuesday, 24 July 2018: Theresa May takes over

Theresa May has just announced that she is taking personal control of the UK negotiating team, having learned the lessons of the rivalries which, according to her, have weakened her exit strategy.

To tell the truth, from the beginning Mrs May's cabinet has controlled and managed the whole negotiation on the UK side. Since June 2017, my team and I have dealt only with Olly Robbins and the senior officials around him. The minister officially in charge of Brexit, David Davis, travelled to Brussels only once every three months. I myself met him twice in London. It's a shame, since I have a liking for him. In other circumstances, we could certainly have worked well together.

How are we to understand today's announcement, then? Perhaps the newly appointed Secretary of State, Dominic Raab, was being overly presumptuous or proactive when he told me at our first meeting, in front of Olly Robbins, that he would lead the negotiations himself and that he would come to Brussels every week if he had to. I sensed at that moment that Olly Robbins was not overly pleased with this 'new negotiating dynamic'. And so the Prime Minister, quite logically, has decided to set things back in order! We shall see – I will remain available to meet Dominic Raab whenever he wants, including in a one-to-one meeting. I even suspect that he might have his own ideas about Brexit…

Wednesday, 25 July 2018: Misunderstanding

This morning, five French, German and British economists whom we know well – Jean Pisani-Ferry, Norbert Röttgen, André Sapir, former Governor of the Bank of England Paul Tucker, and Guntram Wolff, director of the think-tank Bruegel – publish an article in *Le Figaro* and other European newspapers with the headline: 'Europe should avoid a no-deal Brexit.'

This text reads like it was written by a British author the day after the publication of the White Paper. In fact, it's a 'repeat', since the same five economists, on behalf of the Bruegel Institute, published a hasty report just a few weeks after the Brexit referendum. Already at that time they were pleading for a special agreement with the United Kingdom in which they could have their cake and eat it. This morning, with the same ardour, they defend the British White Paper, which calls for the division of the four freedoms and proposes a dysfunctional customs system that would work to the sole benefit of British interests.

I called Jean Pisani-Ferry yesterday to express my astonishment. Nothing doing. These five economists have an ultraliberal vision of the EU. This is the same André Sapir who, in the 2000s, produced a report at the request of the President of the European Commission, Romano Prodi, suggesting the dismantling of the European regional policy pursued by Jacques Delors, and the Common Agricultural Policy. And this morning he is arguing for the partial destruction of the Single Market for the benefit of the UK.

Pascal Lamy, interviewed this morning on France Inter, curtly rebukes the authors: 'The Europeans have always said from the beginning what was acceptable and what was not. What is not acceptable is to change the rules of the Union on the pretext that the United Kingdom is a special third country.' It is the UK that is leaving the EU, not the other way around.

I also hear the President of the European Space Agency, Johann-Dietrich Wörner, speak about Brexit on the occasion of the launch this afternoon of four new satellites, completing the Galileo constellation. The British are furious about one of the consequences of their decision to leave the EU – that they will no longer be able to participate in the technological development and control of the encrypted PRS signal, which provides the greatest accuracy for defence purposes. Wörner says simply: 'They are giving back the keys to the apartment but they want to carry on using the kitchen.'

Friday, 27 July 2018: Athens, scarred by fire

Back to Greece, where I arrived late last night, amid tragic circumstances for this great country.

For three days now, a fire has ravaged the area around Athens, and in particular the seaside town of Máti, claiming dozens of lives. The whole country is in mourning, and the first words I speak are to express my condolences and the solidarity felt throughout Europe with the Greek people. The European Commissioner Christos Stylianides visited the scene two days ago.

The distress of the Greek people can be read on the face of Aléxis Tsípras. And far more than Brexit, on which the Prime Minister supports our negotiating line, our conversation turns around the need to strengthen Europe's capacity for joint action in the face of such tragedies, whether man-made or natural, which are becoming ever more common.

Europeans must know that they can count on one another.

In 2006, I submitted a report to the President of the Commission proposing a European civil protection force. The idea is that Europeans should prepare, together and in advance, planned responses to future international crises in seven areas: earthquakes and tsunamis, forest fires, floods, industrial and nuclear accidents, terrorist attacks, maritime disasters and large-scale pandemics.

In the evening, before taking a few days of rest with my family on the magical island of Pátmos, my wife Isabelle and I are received for a friendly dinner by the leader of the New Democracy party, Kyriákos Mitsotákis, and his wife Mareva. It is a beautiful evening, also marked by a lunar eclipse.

I am struck by his determination, his willingness to make changes from the old order, and at the same time his confidence that he will be the next Prime Minister of his country.

Friday, 10 August 2018: Theresa May at Brégançon

Emmanuel Macron, who is beginning his short holiday in Brégançon, has invited Theresa May for dinner.

He took care to inform me of this via a call from his diplomatic adviser Philippe Étienne. He also warned the press and Theresa May that it was not a question of conducting negotiations behind my back. This was the message clearly conveyed by Clément Beaune, his European adviser, to a group of journalists.

No one is fooled by the manoeuvring of the British government, which, since the Chequers meeting, has been engaging in a cautious but large-scale diplomatic offensive...

The most caricatural figure in this exercise is the new Foreign Secretary Jeremy Hunt, who is making a tour of all the European capitals to blame the consequences of a possible no deal on the EU: 'Help us, otherwise Brexit will be a tragedy', he said in an interview in Paris on 31 July.

So, in order to 'help Theresa May', the Europeans are supposed to sacrifice the integrity of the Single Market, their principal asset in global competition? In order to prevent Brexit from becoming a 'tragedy', the Europeans are supposed to agree to take on a new customs system with a double charge at the external borders that the British themselves are unable to explain? In short, the Europeans are meant to pay for some of the economic consequences of a Brexit that they did not want and which they regret.

I've learned to keep my cool. What's the point in arguing with Jeremy Hunt? I didn't argue with Boris Johnson, when that would have been far easier and more fun!

This British offensive is being relayed by a number of academics, economists and think-tanks. The head of the British employers' association, Carolyn Fairbairn, is also sounding the alarm: 'The UK would not be the only one affected if the negotiations failed: 1.2 million jobs would be threatened in the EU...'

And in the midst of this offensive, the idea is still circulating that the 'Commission negotiator' must be forced to be more flexible, more pragmatic, more flexible, less dogmatic. The same Jeremy Hunt, whom I do not know and who has not asked to see me, said a few days ago: '[T]he European Commission [...] have this view that they just need to wait and Britain will blink. That is just a profound misunderstanding of us as a nation. [...] France and Germany have to send a strong signal to the Commission that we need to negotiate a pragmatic and sensible outcome that protects jobs on both sides of the Channel.'*

And so, from working dinners to bilateral visits, from interviews in the European press to telephone calls, the British are trying every way they can to break the unity of the twenty-seven and to present the

* Interview in the *Evening Standard*.

Chequers text as the 'pragmatic and reasonable' solution that it would be in the interests of the European Union to accept,

I know many EU leaders who want to be amicable and constructive with Theresa May. But quite frankly, I can't see why they would want to force their own businesses and administrations to bear the costs and consequences of London's proposed solutions to the overly hard Brexit that the Conservatives want.

Wednesday, 15 August 2018: The memoirs of Alain Prate

Our daughter Laetitia is an intrepid young woman. After training as a psychologist, she very soon became involved in international crisis management. Today, with great emotion, she announces to us her engagement to Augustin, a hugely likeable young engineer who, with a wink, offers me a book written by his grandfather, Alain Prate.

Reading the memoirs of this great public servant who, first in Paris and then in Brussels, played a part in each of the founding negotiations of the European Union, I am struck by the consistency of British positions over time. It's as if, from the 1950s to the present day, only the names and faces have changed, while the interests of the United Kingdom have remained the same, or nearly so.

The deep scepticism and even incredulity of British representatives towards the European Community in its infancy is well known; as early as 1954, it explains the UK's refusal to participate in the European Coal and Steel Community (ECSC). However, Prate very soon shows how a relative reluctance gave way to an interested curiosity about this Europe in the making, and more precisely to Britain's desire to be part of it while retaining its full freedom of action. Thus, in reference to the negotiations of the Treaty of Rome, he writes that, when British diplomacy 'realized that the discussions were progressing, the idea that a trading bloc was going to be formed on the Continent in which the United Kingdom would not participate began to seem intolerable. Not feeling able to participate in the system, but not wanting to be excluded, Britain came up with a project in line with its own interests, which was the creation of a free trade area, encompassing the Common Market, but without an external tariff or a common agricultural policy.' Even back then, Britain was demanding a 'made-to-measure' status.

Thursday, 16 August 2018: Jim Ratcliffe

Jim Ratcliffe is at the head of a £21 billion fortune. One of the richest men in the UK, like many advocates of deregulation, lower taxes and laissez-faire markets, he was also an active campaigner for Brexit.

The *Daily Telegraph* reports that he is now moving to Monaco…

Already, the ultraconservative MP Jacob Rees-Mogg, a leading figure among Brexiteers, has set up two investment funds in Ireland via his personal management company, Somerset Capital Management – in the Single Market.

And here lies the great misunderstanding – or the great hypocrisy – between Brexit campaigners, many of whom have links to financial services, and the majority of Brexit voters who took them at their word and voted for closed borders and limits on immigration.

The majority of Britons, by declaring themselves in favour of Brexit, were voting against globalization. But at the same time, Farage and Johnson, along with a number of financial and press bosses, on the same ballot paper, were opting for greater globalization…

Tuesday, 21 August 2018: Dominic Raab on the attack

After a short break at the beginning of August, which we all needed, our technical teams met again last week to begin clearing up the remaining issues and working on the future relationship. We are now carrying out a methodical comparison between the European proposal for a new partnership and the demands contained in the British White Paper.

Dominic Raab comes to see me again, eager to demonstrate his personal commitment. We review all the outstanding issues with his delegation. I remind him of the sensitivity of the issue of geographical indications, i.e. the protection of all the property rights granted throughout Europe for agricultural and agri-food products. There are more than 3,000 of them, ranging from Scotch whisky to Beaufort, feta and Gorgonzola cheeses.

Most importantly, we review the Irish question and the famous backstop that we need in order to conclude the agreement.

'The Irish issue needs to be addressed in a broader context. That is why we're asking for a comprehensive solution for the UK, with a special customs arrangement and the common rulebook for goods. If you don't agree to these arrangements, then it will be a no deal and it will be your responsibility to restore the borders', he says bluntly; 'not ours.'

My blood runs cold, and I see the astonishment in Sabine and Stéphanie's eyes. My response is swift: 'Theresa May never dared to make that threat; never, because she knows her responsibility and that of the UK. She acknowledged it: it is Brexit that is creating the problem in Ireland, nothing else. We are looking for solutions together. And Dominic, if this threat is your government's new line, then the negotiations can end right here. And I will be preparing in the next few days to inform the European Parliament and the member states. Which will mean the failure of the Brexit negotiation itself.'

A flutter runs through the British delegation. Dominic Raab realizes that he has gone too far. Olly Robbins is unhappy. Ambassador Tim Barrow is embarrassed. Dominic Raab is decidedly not a man of great subtlety. I proceed to hammer the point home. 'Theresa May has twice committed to the backstop, in December and then again in January. It may be a different backstop to ours. We can amend and improve our proposal. But there will be no agreement if there is no backstop in Ireland. I propose that our teams now work together seriously and precisely on the number, nature and location of each of the controls we need for goods, and also on who can implement them. We are prepared to allow the British authorities to carry out these checks, accompanied by EU officials. We need you to provide us with figures on the data and conditions of the controls you are already carrying out in Northern Ireland on trade from Britain.'

Sunday, 26 August 2018: The General and England

I am delighted to meet with Joëlle and Albert Gibello at their home on the heights of Albertville. Albert was my very first fellow traveller on my political journey in Savoie, from Jean-Moulin High School, where we led a small team of young Gaullists at the end of the 1960s, through to the Union des jeunes pour le progrès (UJP). He was later my assistant and then my deputy when I became an MP. Not to mention being, for two very active terms, mayor of the Olympic city of Albertville.

We listen together on the INA website to one of the famous press conferences of General de Gaulle, in whose cause we were both working at the time. It was 27 November 1967 and, responding to a question on the devaluation of the pound sterling and the prospect of England entering the Common Market, de Gaulle, who had obviously carefully prepared his answer, launched into a long argument, without referring to notes, on the differences that stood in the way of England's entry:

> It is a modification, a radical transformation of Great Britain that is necessary in order for her to be able to join the continental States. This is obvious from the political viewpoint. But today, to speak only of the economic domain, the report that was addressed on 29 September by the Commission in Brussels to the six governments shows with the greatest clarity that the present Common Market is incompatible with the economy, as it now stands, of Britain, whose chronic balance-of-payments deficit is proof of permanent disequilibrium, and which involves – as to production, to food supply sources, to credit practices, to working conditions – factors which that country could not change without modifying its own nature. [...]
>
> In these conditions, what could be the outcome of what is called Britain's entry into the Common Market? And if one wanted, despite everything, to impose it, it would obviously be the breaking up of a Community that has been built and that functions according to rules that do not tolerate such a monumental exception. [...] To have Britain enter and, consequently, to be committed now to negotiations to that end, that would be for the Six – everybody knows what this turns on – that would be for the Six to give their consent in advance to all the expedients, delays and façades that would be aimed at masking the destruction of an edifice that has been built at the cost of so much hardship and in the midst of so much hope.

In short, the General was opposed to the United Kingdom, too different from its Continental neighbours, entering the Common Market on its own terms. Sixty years later, the same United Kingdom is now seeking to leave the Single Market, but still on its own terms...

Friday, 31 August 2018: Misunderstandings

The summer is already long gone. It is ten days since we resumed negotiations with the British. Today, Dominic Raab calls loudly and clearly for six hours of talks – as if length were more important than substance!

A little later, before lunch, during a brief one-to-one that he has requested, he sets a trap for me by asking me to come to London. 'Why not!' I've already been to London for that famous dinner with Theresa May and another time for lunch with David Davis. 'But the negotiations are not taking place in London. We're not the ones leaving the UK', I say calmly.

Nonetheless, he will later report back to his team that I have agreed to a negotiation session in London...

Once again, at the end of our lunch, I clarify: 'There will be no formal negotiations outside Brussels.'

Monday, 3 September 2018: Thai shrimp and Chinese bikes...

A lengthy dialogue today, lasting almost two hours, with members of the House of Commons Select Committee on Brexit. The committee's chairman, Hilary Benn, is an enlightened Labourite, very clear-sighted on the consequences of Brexit. He asks good questions, in a very perceptive and British style, but always courteously. The group of British MPs is very diverse, and for the first time I have before me the famous Jacob Rees-Mogg, one of the most ideological and decidedly opportunistic Eurosceptic Conservative MPs, who cultivates a style that is more nineteenth-century than of the people.

In my introductory remarks I am careful to avoid our positioning in reaction to the White Paper being interpreted as a blanket rejection. In my interview yesterday with the *Frankfurter Allgemeine Zeitung*, I stated our strong opposition to any form of economic cherry-picking. British press reports, of course, have amplified this into a complete and utter rejection. This is inaccurate.

I reiterate to the MPs that our careful examination of the White Paper has enabled us to identify important areas of convergence: on internal and external security; on the UK's ongoing participation in a number of European cooperation programmes; and finally, in the area of our future economic relations, where the major area of convergence is that a free trade agreement is to be made between us.

I explain why, aside from this free trade agreement, it is the White Paper's proposals on customs and the common rulebook for goods only that are not acceptable as they stand.

But I make it clear that, with this serious reservation, we are ready to build an ambitious future relationship with the UK: 'If you put together all the areas in which we are ready to build cooperation between us, there is no doubt that we are envisioning an unprecedented partnership.'

Nevertheless, Jacob Rees-Mogg comes out of the meeting brazenly claiming that I agree with him in rejecting the Chequers plan. One observer even jokes on Twitter that Mr Rees-Mogg has become my spokesperson.

Hilary Benn, more intelligently, asks me about the option of a customs union between the UK and the EU. Is it still possible? My answer is immediate: 'Yes, of course, we have always said so.'

During the meeting, Sabine makes a strong impression when she explains to UK MPs why we need controls in Northern Ireland, on both sides, to protect our respective markets after Brexit: 'After Brexit, you will be signing trade agreements with other parts of the world. Let's say that, as part of one of those agreements, you import Thai shrimp into the UK that are produced with antibiotics that we don't accept on the European market. Who controls these shrimps so that they do not enter the single market via Northern Ireland, and where? The same question would arise for Chinese bicycles, on which the EU has imposed anti-dumping duties. For these bikes, which you might accept in the UK after Brexit, but which we don't want in our market, who will carry out the checks, and where?'

I can see in the eyes of the British MPs that the argument has hit home and that they realize they will have to accept these controls. I add that we are prepared to simplify, diversify and decentralize these controls, many of which can be carried out elsewhere and otherwise than at a particular physical point. I want us to make it quite clear that this in no way involves a border between Northern Ireland and Great Britain.

Thursday, 6 September 2018: Governance and Ireland

Dominic Raab returns to Brussels. Curiously enough, he wants to talk about the governance of the future relationship. I tell him that this discussion is premature because we don't yet know what the content of this future relationship will be. He is visibly disappointed.

On the other hand, I say to him, we must move forward on the governance of the Withdrawal Agreement. And here, this morning, the best thing we can do is to review the differences between us. In particular, we want British judges to be able to refer a question of interpretation of European law to the EU Court of Justice. This possibility has been agreed upon for questions relating to citizens' rights, for a period of eight years. We see no reason not to extend the provisions to all other matters arising from the separation. Especially since potential legal difficulties are likely to occur for a shorter period than problems concerning citizens' rights… Dominic Raab tells us that, on the contrary, the provisions on citizens' rights represent the limit of what is acceptable to the British government.

At the end of the meeting, I tell him that I am not happy with the British delegation's refusal to provide us with data on current controls on goods in Northern Ireland, including veterinary and phytosanitary controls. In order to establish precisely the controls we need for the backstop in Northern Ireland, we need to know the volume of trade between Northern Ireland and Great Britain and the nature of the products traded. Only then will we be able to detail all the controls needed: when, how, where and who? And to make it clear that these technical controls cannot objectively be presented as a border, contrary to the arguments of DUP Unionists and other British politicians.

Tuesday, 11 September 2018: A slice of potica

To Ljubljana this morning.

The new Slovenian Prime Minister, Marjan Šarec, is a former actor and comedian. He leads a relatively centre-left majority and has managed to sideline the winner of the elections, the EPP's Janez Janša. He takes office at the end of the week. I am also received by the outgoing Prime Minister Miro Cerar, who is to become Foreign Minister.

A little later, together with Nicolas and Georg, we are invited by the President of the Republic, Borut Pahor, to lunch on the shores of Lake Bled. Like many of the presidents of parliamentary regimes who, because of their duties at home, do not sit on the European Council, but with whom I have become acquainted – Marcelo Rebelo de Sousa in Portugal, Giorgio Napolitano in Italy, Frank-Walter Steinmeier in Germany, Prokópis Pavlópoulos in Greece and Sauli Niinistö in Finland – Borut Pahor has a real ability to take a distanced view of European issues. The discussion is frank and direct. At the end of the meal, he asks me a question: 'Where in Europe do you place Slovenia? In Western Europe, Central Europe, the Balkans?' The question speaks volumes about a Europe that was once dislocated, divided, and today is still searching for its identity.

I accompany this dynamic, sporty man to the Bled Strategic Forum, which Slovenia is trying to set up as a 'mini-Davos' for Southeast Europe. In answer to the German journalist Ali Aslan, who questions me during the plenary session, I say: 'If we are realistic, an agreement with the British is possible within six to eight weeks.'

This is my way of responding to the London government's new campaign, which the *Financial Times* ran on its front page this morning: 'EU to ask negotiator Michel Barnier to soften tone and find deal.' So as to save the trooper May by the time the Conservative Party conference comes around at the end of September...

This simple declaration immediately caused the pound to rise by one point! The financial markets in London are definitely in a feverish state.

More seriously, I remind those present that an agreement requires an operational solution to the Irish question, but also the settling of two or three other points that remain unresolved. In particular, the 3,000 geographical indications and registered designations of origin that must be protected in the long term after Brexit so as to prevent counterfeiting. Among them is the famous *potica*, a hazelnut cake, the best known of Slovenia's traditional specialities.

Wednesday, 12 September 2018: Three tweets

At the very moment that Jean-Claude Juncker is giving his last State of the Union speech to the European Parliament, I am in the Chamber on the benches of the Commission alongside Martin Selmayr.

The president is on his feet, willing but tired. Even so, speaking alternately in French, German and English, he gives a fine speech. His team has deliberately chosen to avoid the standard stocktaking... He devotes two pages to Brexit and quotes me amicably. I choose three sentences from his speech to make three tweets on three key aspects of the negotiations.

The first tweet, quite positive towards the United Kingdom, empha-sizes that, in President Juncker's words, 'after 29 March 2019, the United

Kingdom will never be an ordinary third country for us. The United Kingdom will always be a very close partner and neighbour in political, economic, and security terms.' Within twenty-four hours, this tweet is liked by 349 people and retweeted 219 times.

In the second tweet I repeat a sentence of President Juncker's confirming the solidarity of the Commission, the Parliament and the twenty-six other member states with Ireland. This tweet is liked by 2,234 people and retweeted 1,170 times.

Finally, in the third tweet I quote President Juncker saying that we respect the British decision to leave the Union, although we regret it. 'But', he adds, 'we also ask the British government to understand that someone who leaves the Union cannot be in the same privileged position as a member state.' This tweet is liked by 9,000 people and retweeted 4,000 times within twenty-four hours.

My followers may be characteristically more pro-European, but the reaction to that tweet shows me that debate in the UK is very heated and that there is something of a shift in public opinion.

Monday, 17 September 2018: Madrid

A short trip to Madrid and back. The new president of the Spanish government, Pedro Sánchez, has invited me to a working lunch at the Moncloa. He is friendly, straightforward and very direct. He receives me initially with his Foreign Minister, Josep Borrell. Two generations of Spanish socialists, one from Madrid, the other from Catalonia, but both with a strong commitment to Spain and to Europe.

He has placed his confidence in us, in particular to find an agreement on Gibraltar before 17 October. The Spanish line has not changed since the time of Mariano Rajoy. The Spanish are not so much concerned about the sovereignty of the Rock, although this is still a live issue, especially among the opposition, as about the settling of certain contentious issues: tobacco taxation to limit smuggling, environmental issues, and, above all, cross-border flows and the management of Gibraltar airport, which the Spanish would like to share with the British.

I understand and support Madrid's desire to use Brexit as an opportunity to reach settlements on the as-yet undecided points about Gibraltar, in particular in regard to sundry trafficking that has its source there and then finds its way into Spain and the rest of Europe. It's a good opportunity to bring some order and transparency to this tax haven. My task force is now working with the Spanish government to come up with a statement for the British that is legally unambiguous.

Thursday, 20 September 2018: A high-tension Salzburg

Salzburg looks a bit like a fortified camp. The opera arias will have to wait for another time! Hosting twenty-eight heads of state in a small city is no mean feat. But the Austrian government has done everything right and the organization is impeccable. Almost too much so! When I arrive, no doubt because I have to sit at the European Council table tomorrow, I am given a young liaison officer, an official car, two policemen, a motorcyclist and an escort car. Probably a bit over the top!

After two bilateral meetings with the Belgian Prime Minister Charles Michel, attentive and warm as ever, and then with the Cypriot President Níkos Anastasiádis, whose wisdom and confidence I appreciate, I meet back at the hotel with Sabine and Stéphanie to prepare my speech to the heads of state or government.

Stéphanie's computer is showing signs of strain as we begin to rewrite my speech to make it as effective and concrete as possible. The aim is to prove to European leaders that Theresa May's economic proposals run contrary to the interests of European business.

Around midday, confident in our work, we finish the preparation, thinking we have a good hour's margin before the start of lunch, when an urgent call warns us that everyone is waiting for me for the European Council and lunch, which has been brought forward by an hour. I panic a little because my text is not yet printed. On our insistence, the hotel concierge agrees as an emergency measure to print it out in the office, and I head over to the European Council building where the meeting is to begin immediately.

We sit at a huge oval table, myself to the left of Jean-Claude Juncker and to the right of the Polish Prime Minister Mateusz Morawiecki. In fact, throughout the morning, this has been Theresa May's seat for the European Council of the twenty-eight. She went out as I came in.

My presentation is to the point. On the Irish backstop, I explain how all the controls we need to protect the internal market, especially on goods coming from Britain to Northern Ireland, can be moderated, decentralized and simplified.

For customs and tax checks, for example, we can use the customs clearance form, which the producer fills in when the products leave for the UK. This declaration will have to be scanned on the containers or in the transit ports. It will then be used to calculate the taxes due.

In terms of regulatory controls, it is only sanitary and phytosanitary ones that, given the risks, will have to be applied upon entry into the island of Ireland, for live animals and products of animal origin. These checks are already carried out in Belfast and Larne, because the island of Ireland is a single epidemiological zone, but only on 10 per cent of trade. Without changing the nature of these controls, it will therefore be necessary to increase their volume to 100 per cent, thus avoiding any risk of importing animal diseases into the island.

Finally, on other products, we propose that regulatory checks are carried out in factories or workshops when products arrive in Northern Ireland.

All in all, it is clear that this is not a border but a set of technical controls, which can be made as unintrusive as possible.

I am well aware, however, that the UK will continue to refer to this proposal as a 'new Irish sea border' between Northern Ireland and the rest of the UK, and as an attack on the territorial integrity of the country. I know that this argument is not insignificant, and that it has struck a chord in many political circles, far beyond the DUP Unionists.

On the economic relationship, I aim to demonstrate to European leaders that the White Paper proposals are directly contrary to the interests of European business, and constitute blatant cherry-picking. The British are seeking to retain the benefits of the Customs Union while, at the same time, claiming the freedom to establish trade agreements with third countries.

For goods, they ask for freedom of movement, and in exchange propose a common rulebook by way of which the UK would align itself with most EU standards on goods – but would retain the freedom to diverge on all other regulations governing factors of production of these goods, such as the labour, energy and services that go into the manufacturing process.

I have chosen to illustrate this point with reference to the regulatory cost of chemicals. Thirty-one per cent of this cost is related to compliance with European product standards that UK exporters will in any case have to meet in order to enter the domestic market – for example, the REACH regulation for chemicals.

The remaining 69 per cent relates to the costs of compliance with other EU regulations, such as environmental rules. It is these rules that the UK would like to be able to diverge from.

For steel, the figures are even clearer, as only 1 per cent of the regulatory cost relates to compliance with product standards, while the other 99 per cent relates to compliance with rules that apply to the various production factors.

However, in some economic sectors where margins are low, minor differences in regulation could create significant competitive advantage for the UK if it remains in the Single Market for goods but diverges on everything else.

As is often the case, Angela Merkel is the first to speak. She thanks the Commission, emphasizes that any confusion has been averted, and that we must continue as we have begun. As is also often the case, in this forum she expresses what many heads of state and government think: 'This negotiation will largely determine the future of our relationship with the United Kingdom. Some of us are more lenient, others firmer. We need to be united, cordial and clear. On Ireland, I will follow what Leo says. As for the future of our relationship, there are points of agreement. We have some leverage, but the internal market cannot be touched. Theresa May will find it difficult to accept just a free trade agreement.'

A lengthy roundtable discussion allows everyone to make their views known. And in each case there is mention of the solidarity we owe to Cyprus and Spain, because of two specific situations: the British military bases in the middle of the island of Cyprus, and Gibraltar. The Irish dossier is also mentioned, of course. Ireland must not become a 'bargaining chip'.

I am struck by the justified confidence that all of them have in their colleague, the Irish Prime Minister Leo Varadkar: 'On Ireland, it is up to Leo to give the green light', many of them say.

Finally, we obtain the unanimous support of the European Council to try to speed up the negotiations in order to present, on 17 and 18 October, a draft treaty with agreement on all subjects, including Ireland,

and an outline of the Political Declaration with commentary. But it will take two to make this happen.

Upon leaving, in their respective press briefings Donald Tusk says unambiguously that the Chequers plan will not work, while Jean-Claude Juncker, less bluntly, leaves the door open for future negotiations.

The most hard-line is undoubtedly Emmanuel Macron, even though I have pointed out to him that the Chequers plan contains some useful and positive points. He publicly dismisses the British, sending them back to their red lines, in passing taking aim at the leaders of the Leave campaign in the United Kingdom: 'Those who told us that they could easily do without Europe, that everything would go well, that it's easy and would gain them a lot of money are liars. And what's more, they left the next day so they didn't have to deal with it.'

Friday, 21 September 2018: Dirty rats

Unsurprisingly, the British media and the tabloids are going wild, and they are all talking about some kind of humiliation for Theresa May. I can testify that neither was this the mood of yesterday's meeting nor is it the intention of EU leaders. But there is little that is rational or objective about the UK today. The *Sun* even caricatures Donald Tusk and Emmanuel Macron as gangsters, calling them 'DIRTY RATS'.

Theresa May is under yet more pressure and, in a very solemn improvised statement, she confirms her preference to exit with no deal rather than with a bad one. Strangely, she makes two unfair accusations: first, that we have failed to respect British positions, even though we have scrupulously respected the red lines set out by the government in London. And then the even more inaccurate argument that the EU never explained why it rejected the economic proposals of the Chequers plan.

In the midst of this, many journalists point out that in fact I have consistently, since July and the publication of the Chequers plan, explained why the customs arrangement and the common rulebook for goods stand in direct opposition to the integrity of the internal market and the indivisibility of the four freedoms.

There is now a kind of pointless and even somewhat desperate obstinacy in the British Prime Minister's adopting such an attitude on these points.

Saturday, 22 September 2018: A piece of cake?

I am still trying to understand why Theresa May reacted in such a tone yesterday, reproaching us for lacking respect for her government. Beyond Emmanuel Macron's rather blunt statements to the press, which were no doubt aimed at Boris Johnson and Nigel Farage, but which Theresa May could have taken personally, there was a slightly offbeat message posted on Instagram by Donald Tusk. Under a photo taken at the summit, where he is serving Theresa May a slice of cake, Tusk wrote: 'A piece of cake perhaps? Sorry, no cherries.'

All of this reinforces my resolve to avoid any form of aggression, emotion or passion, to shove my fists in my pocket after any provocation from the British, and to continue to stick to the facts, the figures and the legal bases if we want to succeed.

Wednesday, 26 September 2018: Port infrastructure

A meeting in my office with Jean-Marc Roué, President of the transport and shipping organization Armateurs de France. Obviously, French shipowners on the Atlantic coast and in the Channel have a direct interest in ensuring the fluidity of relations with the UK and Ireland.

To him also, I give the unvarnished truth. Barring the unlikely event of an agreement that would see the UK remain in the Single Market and in a customs union with us, any relationship with the British will involve new controls and friction. We will do all we can to simplify and moderate these controls, but they are mandatory if we want to protect the market.

The current emotion over these issues, in the northernmost Hauts-de-France region in particular, is also linked to a report published by the European Commission on maritime transport corridors and flows between Ireland, the United Kingdom and the Continent. Today, large-scale international shipping can only be accommodated in Rotterdam or Zeebrugge, because only these hubs have the necessary facilities. It is from there that the secondary transports, especially to Ireland, depart. In its report, the Commission simply takes stock of this situation, without ruling out future corridors between Ireland and the Continent, provided that the French ports are properly equipped.

Thursday, 27 September 2018: Jeremy Corbyn

Jeremy Corbyn makes another visit, accompanied by Keir Starmer. He is in Brussels the day after the Labour Party conference in Liverpool to attend a moving ceremony in memory of Jo Cox, a young Labour MP assassinated in cowardly fashion on 16 June 2016 while campaigning against Brexit. Jo Cox was a grassroots feminist MP who believed that Britons have far more in common than they have dividing them. She was also a committed European. She had lived in Brussels for some years and a small square in the centre of the European capital will now bear her name.

Jeremy Corbyn, who is participating in tributes to Cox, is a paradoxical character. He remains ideologically faithful to old, internationalist commitments. This is what led him to approve of Brexit, since he persuaded himself that Europe is only a vehicle for globalization, and a huge supermarket.

This view is not shared by his team, who are increasingly aware of the consequences of Brexit, particularly for workers' and consumers' rights. And the Labour Party is slowly but surely changing tack. In his speech yesterday, Jeremy Corbyn confirmed that Labour MPs would vote for a deal proposed by Mrs May if it included both a commitment to remain in a customs union with us and a level playing field for social rights.

He also wants to force an early election and, if he doesn't succeed, then Labour will campaign for a second referendum. From my first meeting with Jeremy Corbyn, I could see that he doesn't want to backtrack on Brexit and is trying to keep all doors open so as not to jeopardize his move into 10 Downing Street. Is this ambivalence, or a wait-and-see attitude on such a serious issue for his country? He is taking quite a gamble here.

Friday, 28 September 2018: Negotiation is the priority

For several weeks now I have been consulting and listening to all the EPP leaders, the presidents and prime ministers who are members, but also many MEPs and national party leaders.

Is my candidacy to become the EPP leader in the European elections at the Helsinki Congress on 8 November compatible with the Brexit negotiations?

I know that Manfred Weber and some German officials, as well as the British, are ready to score political points over this issue: the European negotiator cannot engage in personal politics, and if he were to do so, he would have to give up his mission as negotiator.

In fact, I don't need such pressure or threats to make a conscious judgement that my priority must remain the negotiations. It is a question of responsibility, a point of honour even. Over the past two years, I have created a strong and, in many cases, personal bond of trust with the heads of state or government, with President Tusk, with the members of the European Parliament and, above all, with Jean-Claude Juncker.

When I arrive at my office this morning, I decide to bring forward the announcement of my decision. Indeed, Jean-Claude Juncker has known about my choice since Wednesday, having been the first person I spoke to. It was probably he who told Martin Selmayr. Further more or less well-intentioned leaks are now likely.

I decide to take the lead in a letter to Joseph Daul, the EPP President. I tell my closest team, who advise me to make it public. I make sure to add by hand at the bottom of this letter that 'I will of course remain committed in the future and available to defend our values and renew the European project together'.

One hundred per cent focused on the negotiations as always, I note that, in London, Jacob Rees-Mogg is eating his hat. In an interview with the *Daily Telegraph*, he admits what everyone knows: 'The member states have not so far cracked under pressure from the efforts of our diplomatic service and have continued to support Michel Barnier.' No comment.

Wednesday, 3 October 2018: Dance moves in Birmingham

For almost a week now, everything has been somewhat suspended while the Conservative Party conference takes place in Birmingham. Apart from the Salzburg summit, which was certainly a disappointment for her, we have chosen to keep a low profile so as not to give any ammunition to those who want to bring Theresa May down.

Boris Johnson, as usual, was over the top, but refrained from attacking the Prime Minister head on. Jacob Rees-Mogg and David Davis were not on particularly fine form either. As for Jeremy Hunt, he certainly made an effort to stand out from the crowd! In a speech quite unworthy of a

UK Foreign Secretary, he compared the European Union to the USSR: 'What happened to the confidence and ideals of the European dream? The EU was set up to protect freedom. It was the Soviet Union that stopped people leaving. The lesson from history is clear: if you turn the EU club into a prison, the desire to get out won't diminish, it will grow – and we won't be the only prisoner that will want to escape.'

Even for the sake of stroking the egos of Conservative Party activists, comparing the European Union to the USSR like this is ridiculous and insulting. Donald Tusk and many others reacted strongly. The reaction I found most moving was that of Vytenis Andriukaitis, EU Commissioner for Health and Food Safety: 'Dear Jeremy Hunt, I was born in a Soviet gulag and was imprisoned by the KGB several times in my life. I would be happy to brief you on the main differences between the EU and the Soviet Union. And also about the reasons why we fled the USSR. Any time!'

Above all, Jeremy Hunt, who has spent a great deal of time over the past three months visiting the European Union, denigrating the European negotiating team and seeking to bypass it, has himself destroyed in two sentences what little credibility he had acquired throughout Europe.

Theresa May arrives at the podium with some dance moves, to the beat of *Dancing Queen* by ABBA. I like this kind of self-deprecating humour: a few weeks ago, in Kenya, she had been filmed dancing awkwardly with a local band. She was criticized and mocked. Hats off to the artist! I definitely have respect for this woman. She hangs in there, stands her ground, hunkers down and attacks when she has to. I don't know how long she can hold on, but you can be certain that, for us, this woman who doesn't like the Brexit she is obliged to implement, and who never wanted it, is infinitely preferable as Prime Minister to any of the Brexiteers.

Her speech today is conservative in terms of values and domestic policy, especially on immigration. It is, however, very liberal on the economic front. Mrs May does not mention the word Chequers, but continues to hold to the proposals of the White Paper. Her speech goes down quite well; she has gained a few weeks of political oxygen. I note, however, a sentence at the end that reveals the hard-line posture she is prepared to adopt: 'What we are proposing is very challenging for the

EU. But if we stick together and hold our nerve I know we can get a deal that delivers for Britain.' In short, if we want to get a good deal for the UK, we have to convince the Europeans to pay for some of the consequences of our decision themselves.

Her strategy is clear: she wants it to be us who budges. So it is up to us to keep our cool, remaining open to the future but vigilant on the foundations of the EU.

Thursday, 4 October 2018: Visit from the Taoiseach

Leo Varadkar, the Irish Taoiseach, is a courageous young man. He campaigned hard for his country to finally accept the law on abortion, and the 'yes' vote owes a great deal to him personally. We have established a relationship of trust and friendship with his team, especially his diplomatic sherpa John Callinan. As is also the case with the Tánaiste (Deputy Prime Minister) Simon Coveney, whom I see very regularly.

We take stock of the Irish question ahead of a crucial week of negotiations, and discuss all the details of the revamped and decentralized backstop that we have been working on. I make no bones about the fact that this negotiation will ultimately be very risky and difficult, and I also tell him that we must be prepared for the other option, which would be failure. I want us to be able to work quietly and confidently together on the measures to be taken, in the event of no deal, to protect the internal market in Ireland, and the country's consumers and businesses.

Of course, it is he who will set the tone on 17 October at the European Council by approving the final agreement, if there is one. In Salzburg, all his European Council colleagues made it clear that they would follow his recommendation.

After our meeting, he offers to greet the team members and, very casually, makes the round of all the offices, taking the time to thank each and every member of the task force.

Friday, 5 October 2018: Cyprus

Telephone meeting this afternoon with Níkos Khristodoulídis, the Foreign Minister of Cyprus. Our teams have worked well together to reach agreement with the British on the management framework for the relationship between Cyprus and the two British military bases on its territory.

The key issue is to protect the rights of the 11,000 Cypriot citizens who live in the villages around these bases, within British territory. We also need to ensure that people and goods leaving and entering the bases are controlled. The British have finally agreed to these controls being carried out by the Cypriot authorities, but I ask the Minister to confirm his government's acceptance of this text.

He is also satisfied with it, and promises me a definitive answer next Tuesday once he has discussed it with President Anastasiádis.

Tuesday, 9 October 2018: Northern Irish consultations

Together with Sabine and Nina Obermaier, I conclude a long series of consultations and dialogues on Ireland. After Taoiseach Leo Varadkar, we meet with the four leaders of the pro-European parties who are finally forming an alliance in Northern Ireland and who between them have a majority of the votes: leader of Sinn Féin in Northern Ireland Michelle O'Neill, leader of the Social Democratic and Labour Party Colum Eastwood, leader of the Green Party Steven Agnew, and Stephen Farry of the Alliance Party of Northern Ireland.

And yesterday in Brussels, my team worked for two hours with the economic and social representatives of Northern Ireland to explain what this famous backstop actually means.

Finally, today we blocked out two hours to receive DUP leader Arlene Foster and Diane Dodds, the party's MEP. They don't like one another much, and it shows. There is a kind of one-upmanship at work between them, with much use of slogans and ready-made phrases. But Arlene Foster is precise and pragmatic in her questions.

Listening to these two women, I find it hard to keep my composure, and wonder whether Theresa May will have the courage not to give in to their demands. We shall see whether the final Brexit deal, which they are not going to like, will prompt them to destroy her majority. They are opposed to everything, they don't want to hear any of the concrete proposals we make. But it is not a question of rebuilding a border, either on land or at sea. Over and over again I repeat the point: 'It is your vote for Brexit that has created the problem. We expect you to come up with ideas and proposals. You are not coming up with any. So when will you take responsibility for the consequences of your own actions?'

The interview ends rather abruptly. We don't have much more to say to one another, but I sense deep down that both of them are worried about losing public support in Northern Ireland. And their tweets after our interview are far more measured than what they said to me.

A little later, I meet a man whose sincerity I greatly appreciate, Jim Nicholson, MEP and Ulster Unionist Party (UUP) stalwart. We have established a good rapport in the European Parliament. He knows that I am looking for a solution for Northern Ireland. I think he will help us if we can present the backstop in the least intrusive way possible and perhaps place it in the perspective of the future relationship between the EU and the UK.

Thursday, 11 October 2018: A no-deal atmosphere

My wife Isabelle comes to have a quick lunch with me and I'm glad she has the chance to greet the team members during this intense and sensitive week.

There are British negotiators all over the place, meeting with our own representatives in a multitude of bilateral meetings to close the outstanding issues in the Withdrawal Agreement.

The Cypriot government has agreed to the Protocol on UK military bases in Cyprus. We have also worked hard with the Spanish on the Protocol on Gibraltar. There are now 'landing zones' in sight for the governance of the agreement and the famous issue of the protection of agricultural geographical indications. This essentially leaves the Irish question, which changes with each passing hour depending on the mood of the British and the multiple polemics and pressures coming from London.

British DUP MPs are issuing ultimatums to Mrs May, even to the point of threatening to vote against the budget if she tries to override their red lines on Northern Ireland, those famous red lines that DUP chairwoman Arlene Foster dared to call 'blood red'…

And therein lies the whole problem. Mrs May can probably take the risk of dispensing with the DUP in order to get Parliament to agree to the Brexit deal. But can she and will she risk doing without them if it means losing her majority?

In short, the mood in my team this morning is pessimistic. Even though we are close to a compromise with Olly Robbins on the backstop, I fear that the political situation in the UK makes it impossible.

In which case, a negative spiral would begin on Monday, and we will have to prepare for no deal.

Sunday, 14 October 2018: Dominic Raab blocks the process

This morning the corridors and the meeting room are still in disarray from last night's late meetings.

I can tell as soon as I arrive that things have not gone well.

In fact, Theresa May told us last night that she could not accept our latest proposals. There is too much turbulence and too many threats in her government team, and despite our efforts to simplify the Irish backstop, to dress it up and to put it in perspective, we did not succeed.

The causes of this failure lie in London, where Mrs May must now contend with two constraints.

First, the DUP, which rejects anything that might be read as establishing a difference between Northern Ireland and Great Britain, including therefore any idea of a backstop.

Second, the Brexiteers. Unlike the Unionists, they are not prepared to accept a customs union between the UK and the EU because the UK would then no longer have an autonomous trade policy, which would go against their vision of a 'Global Britain'. This group includes former members of the government (Boris Johnson, David Davis), but also current members (Andrea Leadsom, Esther McVey, Penny Mordaunt), as well as Dominic Raab. It was this latter group that, on Friday evening, threatened Theresa May with a mass resignation from the government.

As can be seen from this brief overview, Mrs May now has no majority to move forward.

While at the end of last week it seemed that she was ready to drop the DUP, we worked with the British negotiators on a solution to deal with the other constraint. This solution consisted of what could be described as a 'two-stage backstop' with, on the one hand, an alignment of Northern Ireland with the rules of the European Union and, on the other, a customs union for the whole of the United Kingdom, with specific customs arrangements for Northern Ireland as a last resort.

As we have always said, such a customs union cannot be built on the basis of a Withdrawal Agreement for legal reasons, since Article 50 cannot be the basis for our future relationship. But also for economic reasons, insofar as it would entail anticipating what would lie at the very core of our future economic partnership without settling the absolutely essential questions associated with it, in terms of the level playing field, governance and related subjects such as fisheries.

That is why, together with the British negotiators, we made every effort to ensure that taking the path of a customs union in a future agreement was a credible approach. But this would require Theresa May to choose the Unionists, who are not opposed to a customs union, over the Brexiteers, who offer no solution.

Monday, 15 October 2018: Derry Girls Against Borders

Dan Ferrie and Nina Obermaier have organized a short meeting on the esplanade of the European Commission with four young women who had come especially from Northern Ireland, the 'Derry Girls Against Borders'. They got lost on the way and arrived out of breath but happy to hand over a petition against the return of a border between the two countries. I tell them that we are still negotiating to avoid a hard border, but that we have to find a way to apply controls somewhere, for products coming into the Single Market.

Every day I see evidence that Brexit is a step backwards, and it is in Ireland that this step backwards is the most serious and is felt the most strongly.

Wednesday, 17 October 2018: An exercise in futility

Another European Council meeting, which we hoped would prove decisive, but which will not be since no real progress has been possible on the Irish question.

Martin Selmayr is nervous. 'The leaders are very tense', he tells me, true to his habit of putting pressure on his interlocutors. But I am sure that the European leaders have confidence in me, and I tell him that many governments are now worried about the Commission's lack of readiness in preparing for a deal or a no deal. It is a subject for which he is responsible, but which the Commission is managing without sufficient consultation with the member states.

Theresa May is announced at 4.30pm in Jean-Claude Juncker's office. I take part in the meeting, which is quite cordial. President Juncker hopes that 'what happened in Salzburg won't happen again this time'. We can of course be formal and respectful, and we are, but the substance of our disagreement remains the same.

Mrs May emphasizes the progress made on several points of the negotiation: governance, geographical indications, military bases in Cyprus, and even Gibraltar. On Ireland, her words are still ambiguous. The conversation is one that takes stock of things already known and simply seeks to demonstrate a positive state of mind.

The European Council hears her later in the evening, with courtesy as always, but there is a kind of weariness among many heads of government. Mario Monti had the right expression a few years ago when he spoke of the 'fatigue' of the internal market...

I am invited to dinner, without her, and I feel a sense of trust and even friendship in my contact with the heads of state or government. We have worked hard on my speech, as we did in Salzburg, so as to be as concrete and effective as possible.

It is now clear, I say to the heads of state and government, that the Irish question is the central issue in this negotiation. And this issue goes far beyond Ireland. The solution proposed by the British for the absence of a border in Ireland is 'frictionless trade' for the whole of the United Kingdom. This solution, as proposed in the Chequers plan, amounts to half of a customs union – together with an autonomous British trade policy – and a quarter of the internal market, for goods only – without the freedom of movement of people and with the potential to diverge on services, with all the risks of unfair competition this implies for our companies. Without being dogmatic, we must remember that there is no such thing as 'frictionless trade' with nations outside the EU: two distinct regulatory and customs territories necessarily require controls between them.

Given these conditions, what have we done to find a solution? We have worked in two directions.

First, we have worked hard to minimize, moderate and decentralize controls so that they do not constitute a border between Northern Ireland and the rest of the UK.

Second, we have sought to address British concerns, by stating in the Withdrawal Agreement that the future relationship would allow as many elements of the backstop as possible to be replaced, including through a customs union.

Obviously, the establishment of such a customs union must respect our principles and requirements. Since a customs union involves a free trade area, without tariffs or quotas, and with a common external tariff, we need to address the key issues of state aid, social, fiscal and environmental issues, governance, and related issues such as fisheries.

Angela Merkel sums up everyone's feelings: 'We will only meet again when we are ready.' And indeed this is what Donald Tusk will say quite clearly to the press about this dinner. The German Chancellor approaches me after dinner and gives me a useful piece of advice: 'When I come across a problem that I don't know how to solve, I always act like a scientist: I take three steps back to place myself in a wider context and find a solution.'

I am not surprised by this advice. That's the impression she has always given me. Extremely methodical and thorough, she looks at things in detail and leaves nothing to chance, never losing sight of the big picture.

I reply: 'This is precisely what we are trying to do with the British, by placing this famous backstop within the broader perspective of the future relationship and the option of a customs union with the British.'

Monday, 22 October 2018: Parallel negotiations?

This morning I take time out for a lengthy meeting with the leaders of the European Research Group (ERG). This group of hard-line Brexiteers is pushing for a hard Brexit and a permanent exit from the Single Market and the Customs Union.

Their delegation is led by Iain Duncan Smith, former minister and former leader of the Conservative Party, and Owen Paterson, former Secretary of State for Northern Ireland, as well as Lord David Trimble, former First Minister of Northern Ireland, who, together with John Hume, was awarded the Nobel Peace Prize for their role in the negotiations leading to the Good Friday (Belfast) Agreement.

It's an interesting meeting. At length, and with the help of several experts, they argue for a fully technological solution to implementing border controls in Northern Ireland. Like all Brexiteers and DUP politicians, they are opposed to any division of the British customs territory and therefore to the backstop. I tell them that we will never be able to control the health of cows entering our internal market with drones!

These characters have their convictions, though. They are all opposed to Theresa May's White Paper, but are also aware of the British responsibility in Northern Ireland.

The same day, I have a telephone conversation with Martin Selmayr to discuss the substance of the negotiations and also questions of method. I know that he sees Olly Robbins directly and speaks to him, despite the formal request made by Jean-Claude Juncker in my presence in his office. Such discussions in themselves do not shock me, except when it is a question of his expressing directly to the British ideas that are his alone and that we have not discussed together. Since the beginning, the British have been playing both sides against each other and trying to open up a second line of negotiation with Martin Selmayr. And I can see that he is finding it hard to resist…

With his usual aplomb, he tells me that he doesn't have time to deal with Brexit, that he has many other things to do, in particular saving the draft trade agreement with the United States that Jean-Claude Juncker recently outlined in Washington, and that he isn't talking to the British.

No one is being fooled here. I tell him that his opinion and advice are important to me so long as they feed into a common and unique line for the Commission. We leave it at that.

Monday, 5 November 2018: A major conference in Brussels

I have been invited tonight to speak at the Grandes Conférences Catholiques in Brussels. This is a great opportunity not only to talk about Brexit but also to place this negotiation into the broader perspective of the political divide between citizens and Europe, and the question of how to rebuild trust.

In Brussels, at the Bozar, I find Herman Van Rompuy, former Prime Minister of Belgium and former President of the European Council, as humble and mischievous as ever, who introduces me in a friendly and benevolent manner. The room is full, with 2,400 people in attendance, and Matthieu, Georg and I have chosen to write a structured, well-argued, programmatic, fairly lengthy speech. Perhaps rather a little too lengthy! So, at the end, I simplify and summarize the last proposals I wanted to make on the four major areas of European renewal: an EU Green Deal, a digital economy for all, controlled borders and a global ambition.

At the very beginning of this lecture, I read one of many letters I have received since the UK referendum. It is from Bernard, a 69-year-old British lorry driver who has driven all over Europe since 1973, and who would like to continue living his life as a European citizen. 'That was the vision of my forefathers and of my own generation', he writes. A few days later, a suspicious British journalist tries to check whether the letter was real.

I also take this opportunity to mention three enduring landmarks that lie at the heart of our European commitment.

Peace, first of all. For a long time, the European project was justified by a promise: to put an end to wars between our nations. For seventy years this promise has been kept between the countries of our Union. But peace is more recent in some parts of Europe, such as Northern Ireland, where it is just twenty years old, or some of the countries that joined the Union in 2004, 2007 and 2013. And peace is not a given. In many of our countries, nationalism is set to overtake the promise of Europe. This, I believe, would be a historical misjudgement and a great error.

The second major European landmark concerns respect for our identities. We are proud of our histories, our national identities, our languages and our cultures, and quite rightly so. But alongside our national identities, we must also be proud of our European identity. This identity has been forged over the centuries through trade, religion, artists and philosophy. And yet that has not prevented it from being torn apart by racism, war and dictatorships. In 1950, for the first time, we decided to affirm this identity together, through a contract between our nations and peoples, a mutual commitment, the European contract. This contract is a source of rights and obligations for all of us. 'Brussels', the target of so much idle talk, is each and every one of us! And this contract should not be called into question every time a government changes hands. This contract was not concluded between political parties, but between countries. In 1958, General de Gaulle implemented and defended the Treaty of Rome signed a year earlier, before he was elected, even though he had opposed it.

Finally, the third landmark is the need to be united. If Donald Trump receives Jean-Claude Juncker in Washington to talk about trade, or if the Chinese respect the EU, it is first of all because we speak with a single voice, because we have a single policy when it comes to trade or competition rules, and a Single Market on the scale of an entire continent.

At a time when the movement that was thought to be inevitable towards achieving liberal democracy – respect for human rights, for the rights of man and woman, for freedom of expression, independence of the judiciary and freedom of the press – is being called into question in too many places around the world, we have every reason to defend the European flag, and the values that it represents.

All in all, despite the length of this speech, its conclusion is warmly welcomed and applauded. For me, speaking to citizens and audiences seriously and comprehensively, as I wanted to do this evening, is a way of paying them the respect they are due. And I feel that this substantive speech will be useful in one way or another in the debates that lie ahead and for the action of the European institutions in the coming years. I also believe that I am the first person, today, to import the idea of the Green New Deal, promoted in the United States by Alexandria Ocasio-Cortez, into the great European debate.

Tuesday, 6 November 2018: Bratislava

Another field trip to Bratislava enables me to meet the new socialist Prime Minister Peter Pellegrini. The Slovak capital is sunny and upon arrival we take a short break at the foot of the fortress overlooking the city.

The Head of the European Commission Representation in Slovakia, Ladislav Miko, and his deputy, Jana Cappello, accompany me. They have done a very good job in preparing for this visit, as have all the teams in our representations throughout Europe, on whom we call every week for information and to organize my visits.

I meet the Prime Minister in his residence. I recognize the long room where he receives me well. I have a clear memory of my very first visit to Slovakia in 1996 as French Minister for European Affairs. My German colleague and friend Werner Hoyer decided to make a symbolic joint visit to one of the European capitals. We chose Slovakia, almost ten years before the country joined the EU! The Prime Minister, Vladimír Mečiar, was a man from another era, that of authoritarianism, and he really did not understand the idea that two ministers, German and French, were coming to see him together, with the same language. He was definitely not prepared for his country's accession to the European Union.

The atmosphere today is much warmer. The Minister of Foreign Affairs, Miroslav Lajčák, stands alongside his Prime Minister. Miroslav Lajčák is a serious and capable man. There is even talk of him running for the presidency of the Republic, but he tells me that he wants to stay in international affairs. In 2007, when he was the High International Representative in Bosnia, I received him for a dinner at the Ministry of Agriculture on the advice of my friend Arnaud Danjean, who knew him well.

Leaving Bratislava, we head for Vienna airport on a very modern motorway. Just thirty years ago, the Iron Curtain passed right down the middle of this road…

Friday, 9 November 2018: All hands on deck to fine-tune the backstop

David Davis is back on air.

He tells BBC Radio 4's morning show that Brexit is just like buying a house, and that '[i]f you buy a house, you don't just take the first price offered'. In the process, he calls for the government to put pressure on the EU to improve the terms of our offer.

The British have clearly not understood that this is no normal negotiation, and that it is not a question of bargaining.

We do not have to 'sell' anything from the Single Market, nor do the British have to 'buy' their departure from the European Union. This is, let me repeat, an exit process that we must organize as best we can.

As for Dominic Raab, he appeared in front of an audience of worried business leaders this morning, no doubt with the aim of reassuring them. I'm not sure he succeeded, saying: 'I hadn't quite understood the full extent of this, but if you look at the UK and look at how we trade in goods, we are particularly reliant on the Dover–Calais crossing.'

I don't even want to crack a smile at this, but there is most definitely something wrong with the British system. It is now almost two and a half years since a majority of British people voted for Brexit under the leadership of politicians like Dominic Raab, and every passing day shows that they have not realized the consequences or what is truly at stake here.

In Brussels, meanwhile, the task force is in full swing. The small legal team, Eugenia Dumitriu-Segnana, Thomas Liefländer and Liana Bratusca, and the trade and customs experts, Antonio Fernández-Martos, Jos Hupperetz and Nicolas von Lingen, are hard at work. They are doing an incredible job of adapting to the permanent shifting of the negotiations. And today they are working to integrate into the Withdrawal Agreement and into an annex to the Irish Protocol the content of a customs union and the whole arsenal of guarantees that usually accompanies it.

Under normal circumstances, such a construction would take months or even years of negotiation. But we are under time pressure, 'the clock is ticking'. The British are pushing for a deal in the next few days. Theresa May needs it. She emphasized this again yesterday morning on the phone to Donald Tusk, and I know she is giving the same message to every prime minister she sees or calls. Donald Tusk replied that it would be 'Michel Barnier's responsibility to say when an agreement is ready'. Even if they always try to bypass us or influence us, the British, in this final stretch, have understood that it is here, with us, on the fifth floor of the Berlaymont, that it will happen.

So the idea we are working on is a customs union that, if a solution to the Northern Irish problem is not found by then, would be put in place for the whole of the UK after the transition period.

Frankly, this morning we are on a knife edge and anything is possible. I still think it's insane that a great country like the United Kingdom is conducting such a negotiation and taking such a decision, so gravely serious for its future, without having any clear vision of it or a majority to support it either in the government or in Parliament.

Sunday, 11 November 2018: Ypres

My wife Isabelle and I choose to go to Ypres tonight, where almost 500,000 Belgian, British, Commonwealth, African and, of course, French and German soldiers lost their lives during the Great War.

Since 1928, the Last Post ceremony has taken place every day at 8pm in this city in West Flanders, which was utterly destroyed by bombing and has been completely rebuilt. For this hundredth anniversary of the armistice, King Philippe and Queen Mathilde are here, as is Prime Minister Charles Michel. We stand alongside them to lay a wreath in memory of the soldiers.

There are many English people there and several of them greet me in the bar where we share a drink after the ceremony.

Earlier in the afternoon, we took the time to make a moving visit to the museum, which does such a good job of recounting the tragedy of Ypres and its Salient, the front line that was the scene of ceaseless confrontations throughout the war, forcing the inhabitants to evacuate the town as early as 1915, leaving behind them a field of ruins.

Tuesday, 13 November 2018: Eve of battle

We're almost there! At least I hope so.

The last few days and nights have been intense. On Friday evening, up until 11pm, the task force was preparing itself. I remain admiring and proud of the professionalism and adaptability of my entire team. That evening, Sabine and Stéphanie took up point by point the areas of negotiation on the withdrawal treaty that were still open. Tasks were distributed. Everyone was given a to-do list.

All day Saturday and again on Sunday morning, each point was validated and set out in our final negotiation line. And above all, all the Directorates-General were mobilized alongside us to provide the necessary expertise, such as the legal department headed by Luis Romero. Teams from the Commission's Directorates-General for Competition, Trade, Transport, Employment, Fisheries and Taxation were also present.

Everything was ready for the return of Olly Robbins at 2pm on Sunday, accompanied as always by the most distinguished of British officials, including Kay Withers and Sarah Healey. All are from the Treasury or the Foreign Office. One can only regret the absence of experts from sectors such as fisheries or agriculture, which weakens the British position and its responsiveness.

The discussion continued on Sunday until 3am and then all day yesterday. We sense that Olly Robbins's mandate here is to bring negotiations to a successful conclusion. I am not surprised. My analysis has long been that, with each passing day, the danger for Mrs May grows greater. The risk she takes is that, if she waits too long, the Remainers, who are getting better organized in their demand for a second vote, and the Brexiteers, who want a clear end to the UK's relationship with the EU, will coalesce. Her only chance of survival is simply to be the Prime Minister who 'makes Brexit happen', thus taking the wind out of the sails of the most hard-line Brexiteers who want her out.

So this is how, at the end of the day yesterday, Sabine and Olly managed to arrive at an equilibrium on the Draft Withdrawal Agreement. And Olly was able to take the text back to London, where a cabinet meeting is taking place this morning. Theresa May, as I understand later, has decided to give herself a little more time. She has just called her ministers one by one to familiarize them with the draft agreement in advance of a historic cabinet meeting tomorrow afternoon at 2pm.

The choreography that I have agreed to is for the Brexit Minister, Dominic Raab, to leave London immediately after the cabinet has given the go-ahead and to come back to Brussels, where we will hold simultaneous press conferences early tomorrow evening. If all goes well, the Draft Withdrawal Agreement and the annotated structure of the Political Declaration will be published in London and Brussels.

Throughout these last few days, among ourselves and with the British, there has been a sense of urgency that has pushed everyone to give their best. Isabelle Misrachi was very efficient in organizing the reception of the British, the meeting rooms, the drinks and buffets needed throughout these days and nights to ensure that everyone could cope. When Olly Robbins returned to London, the long wait began for the white smoke to come out of 10 Downing Street tomorrow.

Wednesday, 14 November 2018: Deal!

As a decisive cabinet meeting begins in London, Sabine crosses the rue de la Loi to Coreper to brief the ambassadors on the final outcome of the negotiations and the content of the Draft Withdrawal Agreement. Many governments are nervous that UK ministers will now be able to read the text, but not EU ministers. I understand their sensitivity, and the desire to remain in the loop, but frankly the ministers who want to know more, like the ambassadors, are fully aware of the agreement's essential content already. Above all, I cannot risk leaking the document before it has been approved by the British cabinet. I know that the discussion at Downing Street will be very tough, and our policy is to make things no more difficult than they need to be for Theresa May.

However, at around 8.30pm, I ask Clara Martínez Alberola, Jean-Claude Juncker's Head of Cabinet, if I can show him the draft treaty first, alone. It is an impressive text in terms of its volume: 185 articles, three protocols, and a dozen annexes, adding up to a total of 585 pages.

It is during this brief meeting in President Juncker's office that I learn that the cabinet in London has approved the draft. I rush back downstairs to tell the team. The atmosphere on the fifth floor is one of joy, relief and pride in the work we have done. Upon learning of the agreement via a message from Olly Robbins, Sabine sheds a few tears, and not just tears of exhaustion. Stéphanie can't hide her excitement.

But once these understandable feelings have been expressed, we get back to work. Along with Matthieu, Stefaan and Dan, I reread my text for the press conference initially planned to be delivered alongside Dominic Raab. The last Eurostar has left. Will he take a special flight? Very quickly we learn that he will not be coming. The decision is taken to give a parallel but consistent joint briefing with the British. I wait for Theresa May to make her statement before joining the press room, along with the whole team, at 9pm.

We choose sobriety and pedagogy. There is no room for complacency. We know that the situation in London is extremely fragile. When Adam Fleming of the BBC asks me 'So, champagne?', I answer: 'Certainly not, we're going to drink water and continue with our work.'

Thursday, 15 November 2018: Flash visit to Strasbourg

The day begins early. Donald Tusk receives me at 7.45am. As I did last night with Jean-Claude Juncker, I present him with the draft treaty. I have worked in confidence with Donald Tusk since the beginning. He understood very quickly that I would not play the usual game of competition and rivalry between the institutions, that I would work with him to make sure we could succeed together.

Obviously, this morning he is happy with the hard-won agreement reached yesterday with the British government. He suggests a brief statement to the press to present the document and to announce that he can now convene the European Council on 25 November, since yesterday I made the long-awaited announcement: 'I consider that we have now made decisive progress in the negotiations.'

Just after the European Council meeting, Martin Selmayr tries to contact me to let me know 'as a friend' that the President of the Commission is furious about having seen me on television with Donald Tusk. The same old method of adding fuel to the fire, piling on the pressure by destabilizing his interlocutors. I know him well enough by now not to be thrown by it. In this case, I took care to see Jean-Claude Juncker first. I had a photo taken together with him yesterday, as I did this morning with Donald Tusk, but his communications team did not follow up. Later in the day, I check in with President Juncker about his real feelings on the matter; in fact, he was not bothered about it.

On this very special day, it is essential to me that the three institutions, which have worked so well together, are informed immediately. The European Parliament is in plenary session. In these exceptional circumstances, President Juncker authorizes me to take a special flight to Strasbourg this morning. Nicolas, Georg and I are used to travelling by train with a change in Paris, but this unaccustomed mode of transport allows us to arrive promptly for the conference of group and committee chairmen with President Antonio Tajani and Guy Verhofstadt. All of them praise the work that has been done, expressing confidence in an ongoing dialogue with Parliament.

Wednesday, 21 November 2018: Theresa May

This morning, I am delighted to accept Jean-Claude Juncker's invitation to present to the College of Commissioners the complete draft agreement on an orderly withdrawal and the draft Political Declaration on the future relationship. The last outstanding points are to be settled this evening at 5.30pm between Jean-Claude Juncker and Theresa May, who is coming to Brussels especially for the purpose.

I emphasize the very sensitive political context in which we find ourselves. Theresa May is under strong pressure, from her own party above all, to reopen negotiations on the text of the Withdrawal Agreement. We have to be very careful and maintain a 'collective spirit of responsibility'. This morning, as I speak, the only reservation is in relation to the Spanish government – and we are in intensive discussions with Madrid and the government of Pedro Sánchez to find a solution in the next few days.

There is also a question that has been left open in the Withdrawal Agreement: the deadline up until which the transition period can be extended. On Monday, I suggested to the General Affairs Council that this extension could last until the end of 2022 at the latest, i.e., two more years.

I mention to the Commissioners the points that have been the most difficult: first, trade in goods, which will no longer be frictionless.

Second, the 'level playing field'. The inclusion of a common customs territory between the UK and the EU in the Protocol on Ireland and Northern Ireland has enabled us to obtain guarantees that are unprecedented in this type of partnership.

On fisheries, where they know they are in a strong position, the British want annual negotiations on access to their waters. We have maintained our demand that access for European fishermen to British waters be negotiated at the same time as access for British fisheries products to the European market. I am aware that this negotiation will be very difficult.

An appropriate solution has been found to protect the three thousand geographical indications. Scotch whisky and Savoyard Beaufort alike will be safeguarded until equivalent protection is provided as a part of our future relationship.

On the movement of persons, British ambitions for the future relationship are very slight. They want to keep this as leverage, to treat

European citizens like all other third country nationals and to let into the UK only those people who interest them: students, researchers, bankers or tourists. We must prepare ourselves for an uphill battle here too; our line will be to refuse any discrimination, and to demand reciprocity between our citizens and British citizens who want to come to Europe.

Later in the day, Theresa May arrives in Brussels.

Although tired, she knows her subject and her text. She insists on changing one word, so as to express the 'determination' of both parties to find a solution in Northern Ireland that makes the backstop unnecessary. As expected, she fights to reintroduce the 'frictionless' relationship in trade, without using the word, subtly referring instead to the need to avoid controls. On this point, I intervene to say that stating this would simply not be true. You can't lie to people. There will always be controls unless the UK remains in the Single Market and in the Customs Union. We alter the sentence a little, but she understands that we will not give in.

In fact, it seems the Prime Minister arrived this evening with the idea of continuing to negotiate, to show that she is extracting new concessions from the Europeans. And yet she understands that no one on the European side wants to reopen negotiations on the text of the treaty and that the Political Declaration must be completed tonight or tomorrow. Several heads of state, including Angela Merkel and Emmanuel Macron, have indicated that they will not come to Brussels on Sunday if there is an expectation of reopening negotiations.

Afterwards, Theresa May measures her words carefully. She repeats over and over again in an interview with the BBC that very good progress has been made tonight, and that negotiators will again be working through the night:

> We have made further progress and, as a result, we have given sufficient direction to our negotiators. I hope for them to be able to resolve the remaining issues and that work will start immediately. I now plan to return for further meetings, including with President Juncker, on Saturday to discuss how we can bring to a conclusion this process and bring it to a conclusion in the interests of all our people.

Sunday, 25 November 2018: European Council

A serious and significant day, and the weather in Brussels is appropriately dour this morning. A thick fog envelops the buildings in the European quarter, and it is raining. Sabine, Stéphanie and I had planned to arrive together for the usual statement to journalists at the entrance to the building. Both of them are at my side as I say a few words in front of a forest of microphones:

> All along this extraordinary, very difficult complex negotiation, we have worked to reach a deal. That has meant organizing in an orderly fashion the withdrawal chosen by the UK.
>
> We have negotiated with the UK, never against the UK. Now it is time for everybody to take responsibility, everybody.
>
> This deal is a necessary step to build trust between the UK and the EU. We need to build the next phase of this unprecedented and ambitious partnership. We will remain allies, partners and friends.

I then proceed to the European Council room on the seventh floor. The council will meet in two sessions. First a meeting of the twenty-seven, then at 11am a second session with Theresa May. The dice of the negotiation have been rolled, the chips are down. The atmosphere is solemn. Everyone has the feeling that we are living through a historic moment, the moment of a break-up desired by a member state and a divorce that we have tried to deal with as well as possible. The leaders express great warmth towards me and thank my team, in person and in their speeches.

Emmanuel Macron recommends that we continue to use this method, which has been successful and has preserved unity. Angela Merkel, very relaxed, even speaks of a 'masterpiece of diplomacy'.

I am pleased to welcome Pedro Sánchez, given the dispute that has been going on for some days over the issue of Gibraltar. Last Thursday, the 'drama' centred on Article 184 of the draft treaty, which was introduced at the request of the British, and which is the only article that establishes a link between the separation and the future relationship. In this article, we commit ourselves and the British to making 'our best endeavours' to build that future relationship.

In disagreement with the legal services of the Council and the Commission, the Spanish consider that this article prejudices the territorial remit of the future relationship, which would necessarily extend to Gibraltar. They see this article as a British manoeuvre, a trap into which we have fallen through a lack of vigilance.

After several phone calls between Pedro Sánchez, Jean-Claude Juncker, Donald Tusk and Theresa May, we agreed to simultaneously publish a statement confirming that this article does not prejudice any territorial issue. The British, with their backs to the wall, faced with the risk of a Spanish veto, agreed yesterday to brief on the same interpretation on their side.

Meanwhile, the Spanish Prime Minister obtained another declaration from the twenty-seven guaranteeing that the negotiation with Gibraltar would be different, and that Spain would have approval on any agreement covering Gibraltar to be signed by the EU and the United Kingdom.

The Spanish have not forgotten or forgiven their humiliation in 1986, when they joined the EU and London demanded the consolidation of British sovereignty over and the granting of special status to Gibraltar. They simply want to reciprocate as the British leave, and understandably so.

The roundtable is interrupted at 11am at the request of Donald Tusk to allow Theresa May to take part in a meeting with her counterparts of at least the same duration as that of the twenty-seven among themselves. At the beginning of this second meeting, Jean-Claude Juncker says a few sentences he has prepared for the occasion. No doubt inspired by Martin Selmayr, he believes it is appropriate to recall that the result obtained was achieved by 'the whole Commission and not by the negotiator in his personal name'.

This phrase raises a smile for many heads of state or government. No one is fooled. It is just another bit of pettiness, and I take note of it.

President Juncker quickly realizes that his comment was unfair and takes the trouble to get up, go around the table and tell Donald Tusk, as an aside, that he wants me to take part in the final press conference with them, something that was not at all planned.

In my own short speech, after thanking all those who deserve recognition, I seek above all to impress upon those present that this draft treaty is only a stage in the process. The 'meaningful vote' on 11 December will be the moment of truth for Theresa May.

> I should like to warn you of the difficulty of the next stage, based on the experience of the last two years. The negotiation of our future relationship will be extraordinarily difficult, because of the complexity and the number of issues to be dealt with, the short time we will have – twenty-one months, perhaps a little more – and the uncertainties on the British side about the fundamental choices it will involve.

Finally, Theresa May, in this rather solemn atmosphere, thanks the two negotiating teams. 'It is important that the Europeans have been united', she says, after she and her ministers had done everything to divide us. 'This is the best deal possible, there will be no going back on this negotiation. We will never', she adds, 'be a third country like any other' – no doubt with the hope of extracting, in the coming months, further concessions from the Europeans, and perhaps returning to her ambition to cherry-pick.

Tuesday, 27 November 2018: The fifth baby of the task force

A new jibe from Donald Trump this morning. In response to a reporter's question, he says: 'Right now as the deal stands, they may not be able to trade with the US, and I don't think they want that at all.' To which he adds: 'That would be a very big negative for the deal', before expressing his hope that British Prime Minister Theresa May '[will] be able to do something about it'.

It is quite clear that the only thing that gets the American president motivated is the making of deals. His criticism of the agreement we have just concluded is based purely on the fact that, during the two years of the transition, and perhaps longer if we have to implement the backstop for Northern Ireland, the Americans will not be able to conclude a free trade agreement with the UK.

I have long believed that it is in the best interests of the UK, its businesses and its consumers, to be wary in any bilateral negotiations with the Americans. Trump will not give away anything, either on cars or on chlorinated chickens.

1. The first lie of the Brexit campaign: in May 2016, Boris Johnson alleges that the £350 million per week relinquished by Brussels would be used to fund the NHS instead. © Darren Staples/Reuters

2. A hateful conflation from Nigel Farage in June 2016, which intentionally misattributes the cause of the flow of Middle Eastern refugees to freedom of movement within the EU. © Daniel Leal-Olivas/ Stringer/Getty Images

3. Thyborøn, Denmark, 21 April 2017, a trip out to sea in minus 22 degrees Celsius, to listen to fishermen who work in British waters. © Henning Bagger/Denmark OUT/AFP/Getty Images

4. 12 May 2017, on the yellow line that divides Northern Ireland and the Republic of Ireland, or the 'invisible border' between the EU and the UK. © Michel Barnier

5. With Brian Burgess, an Irish farmer, and his 'European cows', several metres from the Northern Irish border. © Michel Barnier

6. Patrick Blower, *Telegraph*, 19 June 2017. © Garland/Telegraph Media Group Limited 2021

7. My two deputies, Sabine Weyand and Stéphanie Riso, and I received David Davis, Tim Barrow and Olly Robbins on 17 July 2017 – they had left their papers behind! © Thierry Charlier/Reuters

8. At Berlaymont, seat of the European Commission, a convivial moment on my birthday with my whole team, 9 January 2018. © Michel Barnier

9. In May 2018, at the Derry/Londonderry Guildhall. A spontaneous discussion with Northern Irish school pupils. © Michel Barnier

10. For four years we visited a new capital city each week in order to meet their nation's government, the national parliament, trade unions or businesses. Here we are in Lisbon with the Prime Minister Antonio Costa, 26 May 2018. © Michel Barnier

11. A frank and direct discussion with the Hungarian Prime Minister Viktor Orbán in his office in Parliament in Budapest, 4 June 2018. When it comes to Brexit, he always supported the EU. © Government of Hungary. Photographer: Balázs Szecsődi.

TAKING BACK CONTROL

12. Ingram Pinn, *Financial Times*, 27 July 2018. © Financial Times

13. Christian Adams, *Evening Standard*, 4 March 2019. © Christian Adams/Evening Standard

14. Jean-Claude Juncker and I meet Theresa May in Strasbourg. Demanding negotiations don't preclude courteous manners! © Alex Kraus/Bloomberg/Getty Images

15. Meeting of the Brexit Steering Group at the European Parliament, chaired by the Belgian Prime Minister Guy Verhofstadt. European unity is founded on transparency and trust. © EU/Étienne Ansotte, 2019

16. Teatime! The role of Leo Varadkar, the Irish Taoiseach, was decisive throughout the negotiations. Photo taken 8 April 2019 in Dublin. © Charles McQuillan/Stringer/Getty Images

17. No-one, not even Nigel Farage, ever convinced me of the added value of Brexit. Here we are in Strasbourg at the European Parliament, where we had many tussles during the plenary session. © EU/Étienne Ansotte, 2019

18. Andy Davey, *Evening Standard*, 16 September 2019. © Andy Davey/Evening Standard

19. 17 October 2019, in the early hours. After three years of effort, we had reached an agreement with Boris Johnson and his negotiator Stephen Barclay on the UK's exit from the EU. © EU/Jacqueline Jacquemart, 2019

20. During this long journey, I felt the need to return to Savoie, my 'homeland' and the place where my roots lie. © Michel Barnier

21. 28 January 2020, with my two new deputies: Clara Martínez Alberola and Paulina Dejmek Hack. The task force takes up the reins of negotiation over our future relationship anew. © Michel Barnier

22. At the Élysée with Emmanuel Macron on 31 January 2020, the day of the UK's exit from the EU. © Ludovic Marin/AFP/Getty Images

23. Patrick Blower, *Telegraph*, 3 March 2020. © Garland/Telegraph Media Group Limited 2021

24. In Brussels on 29 June 2020. One of the official negotiation sessions between the British and the Europeans. © John Thys/AP/SIPA/Getty Images

25. Peter Brookes, *The Times*, 18 September 2020. © The Times/News Licensing

26. In Berlin on 12 October 2020, with Chancellor Angela Merkel. We were both environment ministers for our respective countries in 1994. In her words: 'Europe's future is more important than Brexit.' © Bundesregierung/Steffen Kugler

27. In London, 27 October 2020. En route between our hotel and the conference centre where the negotiations were taking place; remaining anonymous was not easy. © Michel Barnier

28. In the basement of the conference centre in London, in the room we were assigned by the British. Our teams worked here, night and day, for weeks. © Michel Barnier

29. 10 December 2020, fifteen days away from a deal which at that point still seemed unlikely. PM Boris Johnson and David Frost were in Brussels for a business dinner with the President of the European Commission, Ursula von der Leyen. © EU/Etienne Ansotte, 2020

30. In the late hours of 23 December 2020, my adviser Matthieu Hébert and I prepare the speech for my last press conference. © Michel Barnier

31. Elena Mongiorgi, *Lacrima Europa*, January 2020. © Elena Mongiorgi

Strangely, Brexiteers in London remain silent in the face of Trump's outburst, even though they had protested violently against Barack Obama's intervention in the referendum campaign.

A friendly meal for the whole team in the negotiation room. The members of the task force are both very tired and very happy. Six members of staff have already left the team for other departments, and I take the opportunity to thank them along with the others. 'You have been formidable in your competence, dedication and motivation. I feel very proud to lead such an exceptional team. Sabine, Stéphanie and each and every one of you are a credit to the European civil service. Nevertheless, we are not at the end of the road. Take some rest in the next few days. We don't know what will happen in the week of 10 December' – except, that is, for the birth of Thomas Liefländer's baby, the fifth new-born of the task force since its inception.

Monday, 10 December 2018: London vote postponed

Two ministers confirmed this morning that the meaningful vote on the Withdrawal Agreement will take place tomorrow evening.

But at 4pm, in the middle of Prime Minister's Questions in the House of Commons, Theresa May announces her decision to postpone the vote to a later date, stating that, while she believes there is broad support for many of the key aspects of the deal, she is aware of widespread and serious concerns about the backstop. She therefore believes that, if put to the vote tomorrow, the text would be rejected by a significant margin.

In her speech, however, she defends and explains the deal she has obtained, in particular reviewing the reasons why the backstop is needed and the four guarantees obtained so as to avoid the United Kingdom being permanently trapped by it:

> The customs element of the backstop is now UK-wide. It no longer splits our country into two customs territories. This also means that the backstop is now an uncomfortable arrangement for the EU, so they won't want it to come into use, or persist for long if it does.
>
> Both sides are now legally committed to using their best endeavours to

have our new relationship in place before the end of the implementation period, ensuring the backstop is never used.

If our new relationship isn't ready, we can now choose to extend the implementation period, further reducing the likelihood of the backstop coming into use.

These factual arguments are not enough to prevent outcry from the opposition and from some of the Prime Minister's own party, who accuse her of treason and cowardice. Brexit is looking more and more like a tragicomedy in which it is impossible to know whether the ending will be truly tragic, or somewhat happier.

Wednesday, 12 December 2018: Motion against Theresa May

A new episode unfolds in London: the forty-eight letters needed to trigger a vote of no confidence have been tabled, and this evening Theresa May will have to face this new internal front within her own party. This woman is really up against it, but I think she'll win. It's madness to see the extent to which the future of this great country, and our relationship with it, has for three years now been dependent upon the bickering, backstabbing, serial betrayals and thwarted ambitions of a handful of Conservative Party MPs.

Boris Johnson, who since yesterday has been sporting a new haircut, will, along with David Cameron and a few others, carry a real burden of responsibility in their country's history.

Thursday, 13 December 2018: European Council

Another European Council day taken up largely by Brexit, despite all my best efforts!

In the afternoon I arrive at the European Council to hear Theresa May speaking. The Prime Minister is tired.

If I had held the vote in the House of Commons last Tuesday, the text would have been rejected. Nothing insoluble, though. The whole debate is crystallizing around the backstop. A certain number of MPs do not want a deal. Others want a second referendum. I am not asking for new commitments.

The backstop remains. But we must be able to say that it will never be used, or only for a short period of time.

Donald Tusk offers EU leaders the opportunity to question Mrs May, so long as they don't go into internal discussions on the EU's positions. The questions are numerous: 'Are any Labour members prepared to support you?' 'What are your concrete plans?' 'What do you need beyond what is already written in Article 19 of the Treaty? The Treaty cannot be picked apart.'

In her response, Theresa May insists: 'I need my party. We need to find a way out, or an end date for the backstop. We need to be able to show more than goodwill, and more than our "best endeavours", to find an alternative to the backstop. We have to show absolute determination for a fixed date, 2021.' And she adds: 'There is a great deal of mistrust in the UK towards the European Union. We need to reassure people by setting a date. If this fails, then Parliament will take over. There is no majority for another scenario.'

Several heads of government run with this: 'We can find a later date, but we can't stop the backstop. The border in Ireland is our border too', says one of them.

One final time, Theresa May reminds us that she is committed to the Good Friday (Belfast) Agreement. 'The firmer the terms of the statement I am asking you for, the more confidence it will inspire. It's a question of perceptions. We need to show that there is no conspiracy against the UK, that we will not be trapped in a customs union against our will.'

Evidently, she fails to convince her audience. Most European leaders feel as I do: the UK has decided to leave the European Union, the Single Market and the Customs Union. No one properly considered the consequences of the decision. And today, Europeans cannot and will not pay the price and suffer the consequences of decisions they did not take, even if many feel a close affinity to the UK and sympathy for its Prime Minister.

A little later, during dinner, Jean-Claude Juncker and Donald Tusk ask me for my view of the situation. I reaffirm that, faced with the British request for additional assurances for the month of January, we must be extremely clear on the substance: the backstop cannot be time limited.

If it were to be, and if we went on to fail to reach a future agreement to ensure that there is no border on the island of Ireland before the final date, an arbitration panel, as provided for in the Withdrawal Agreement, could find that the Union was acting in bad faith and allow the UK to unilaterally suspend all or part of the Ireland/Northern Ireland Protocol.

In that situation, the EU would have to make a choice between two equally unacceptable options: agreeing to a future relationship that would guarantee frictionless trade, in which case the British would have finally succeeded in holding the whole negotiation on the future relationship to ransom by instrumentalizing the Irish question. Or setting up a physical border on the island of Ireland, with all the obvious consequences, particularly in terms of civil peace between the different communities.

The only way to avoid this twofold risk is to stick to the content of the Withdrawal Agreement and the Political Declaration. We could, however, make more explicit all the elements contained in these texts – and there are many – that demonstrate our determination to find this alternative solution so that the backstop never need be used.

The heads of state or government who speak support this line. Some of them insist on the need to support Ireland, stating that they will not accept any change to the backstop unless Leo Varadkar has agreed to it.

Friday, 14 December 2018: Oriana

A special day, and one of great personal and familial emotion, as Isabelle and I become grandparents for the first time. At 5pm, little Oriana was born, the new daughter of our youngest son Benjamin and his partner Flora.

2019

Monday, 7 January 2019: New year, new vote?

Following a few days of well-deserved rest, the whole team is back on the fifth floor.

The Brexit process is somewhat suspended until the vote on the draft treaty in the House of Commons on 15 January. And on the British side political debate has resumed with a vengeance, chaotic and sometimes even hysterical. We need to remain calm for the sake of both sides; the best thing we can do is to be constructive.

Discussions have taken place in recent days between Olly Robbins and the two Secretaries-General of the Council and of the Commission, Jeppe Tranholm-Mikkelsen and Martin Selmayr, on the idea of providing these clarifications via an exchange of letters.

President Tusk, who is very cautious, cannot and does not want to go beyond the conclusions of the European Council. Martin Selmayr wants to go further, however, and is pushing Jean-Claude Juncker to provide more clarification. The result: rather than a letter co-signed by the two presidents, each will give their own response, within the framework of their respective competences, to the letter that the British are preparing.

Olly Robbins prudently consulted the Europeans on a first draft version of this letter and quickly came to understand that, as far as we are concerned, negotiations on the Withdrawal Agreement are over. Both Presidents are, however, able to provide clarification and information to reassure British MPs, for example, that negotiations on the future relationship can start very soon after the treaty is signed, without having to wait the actual exit from the European Union. The Commission can guarantee that it will ready itself with this objective in mind.

Jean-Claude Juncker is willing to confirm in his letter that both parties will make their best efforts either to reach a specific agreement for Ireland or to establish a new relationship between the Union and the United Kingdom that guarantees the absence of a border in Ireland.

I know that in their private discussions Olly Robbins and Martin Selmayr have agreed that these efforts should bear fruit before 2021, as the British would like. A new date, in my view, would change the nature of the agreement. The duration and use of the backstop can only be conditional on the concluding and signing of a final agreement to settle the issue.

Tuesday, 8 January 2019: Martin Selmayr

I meet with Martin Selmayr again, and we wish one another a Happy New Year... He is friendly and tries to be attentive. We talk about the exchange of letters between the British and the EU and I reiterate to him my clear reservations about setting a date that would force us to settle the Irish border issue at a particular point in the process.

He argues that he is a lawyer, and that we can find a way of phrasing it that would not be binding on us. I repeat my concern that, on the basis of this letter, and after a negative vote in the House of Commons, Mrs May will come back to obtain a legal guarantee by leaning on a few member states: 'If we take that risk, we are gambling with the interests of the European Union and the Single Market.'

Wednesday, 9 January 2019: British beef in Japan

On the sidelines of Japanese Prime Minister Shinzo Abe's official visit to the UK, International Trade Secretary Liam Fox takes to Twitter to welcome the fact that 'British farmers & food producers will be able to export beef & lamb to Japan for the 1st time in over 20yrs, opening access to one of the world's fastest growing markets.'

Under the hashtag #FreeTradeUK, he adds: 'Another example of the DIT's banging the drum for top-quality British produce.'

The one thing he forgets to mention is that this is an agreement negotiated by the European Commission and concluded by the European Union! Not by the UK on its own...

Every day that passes brings further proof that the British people are not being told the truth, and that ministers themselves are lying by omission when it suits their purposes, just days before a historic vote on Brexit in the House of Commons.

Thursday, 10 January 2019: Theresa May calling

At 7.15pm, Theresa May telephones me. An unusual call, since, although we see one another regularly when she comes to Brussels, she tends to keep her direct calls for presidents of the EU institutions or heads of state or government.

Is this a courtesy call at the start of the new year? Is it to head off any negative reaction on my part to the content of the assurances she needs before the vote on Tuesday? Is it a call to close a chapter in our relationship, at an important moment when she is not sure how much longer she will be in office?

In fact, she thanks me for my cooperation and the spirit in which we have conducted the negotiations. I ask her how she expects the vote on Tuesday to go. 'It's a very sensitive and difficult time, but I'm determined.'

'On our side', I tell her, 'the negotiations are over, but we want to be constructive. Olly knows exactly what clarifications are possible on our side, but my question to you, Theresa, is: At what time will these clarifications be useful for you? *We only have one shot.*'

His response is clear: 'I need these clarifications before the vote, Sunday or Monday.'

I take the opportunity to mention the backstop: 'Nobody on the European side wants the backstop to come into force, but whatever the solution, there will have to be an agreement between the UK and the EU. A unilateral exit from the backstop offers no solution.'

On this point, she simply repeats that the backstop is the most difficult issue and that she needs a 'guarantee' that it will not be used.

Finally, since if all goes well we will have to start negotiating the future relationship very quickly, I confirm to her that, in his letter, Jean-Claude Juncker will specify that the Commission is ready and will get organized to start negotiating as soon as the agreement is signed. I add that the President has asked me to do the preparation for the Commission in view of these future discussions.

We leave it at that, and I wish her well for the next few days.

Tuesday, 15 January 2019: A meaningful vote at last?

Tonight I find myself sitting in my small office in the Winston Churchill Building of the European Parliament in Strasbourg, listening to the debates in the House of Commons and awaiting the vote. I am always fascinated by the way these debates are conducted, by the authority and firmness shown by the Speaker John Bercow and by the fact that, unlike in other parliaments, British MPs are not allowed to applaud, and therefore express themselves in a different way, with a hubbub that forces the Speaker to intervene frequently.

Nicolas Galudec has ordered takeaway, which I share with Georg and my press officer Dan in front of the computer screen as we watch the vote live on ITV.

The first amendment put to the vote would give the UK Parliament unilateral power to end the Irish backstop. It is clearly at odds with the draft treaty and, fortunately, is defeated by 600 votes to 24.

Then voting on our draft agreement begins. The question is not whether Theresa May will win or lose this vote. It is lost: the question is, by what margin? And finally, the verdict comes in. It is far harsher than the Prime Minister feared, with 432 MPs rejecting 'our' proposal, and only 202 in favour.

This confirms the analyses of Georg, Nicolas and Dan. There are indeed two negative majorities in the House of Commons: one massive majority against the deal and another against a no deal. Stuck between the two, Theresa May has never really managed to open a dialogue with her opponents, and today's vote, on the basis of conflicting or contradictory reasons, brings together the 'antis' from all sides.

Of course, there are those who reject the backstop, including the DUP and certain Brexiteers who have criticized Theresa May for seeking a deal that keeps the UK too close to the European Union. Then there are the Remainers, who don't want a deal because they don't want Brexit. And in the middle of all this, there is a Labour Party which, for the moment, is playing only one card, which is to destabilize Theresa May at any cost and trigger another election.

I immediately join members of the Brexit Steering Group convened by Guy Verhofstadt. To get to them I have to run the gauntlet of a group of journalists, to whom I simply say: 'Now it's up to the British government to tell us the next steps. On the European side, we will remain calm, united and determined to find a deal.'

Wednesday, 16 January 2019: Three possible outcomes

There are three possible outcomes following yesterday's vote: deal, no deal or, as some would still like to believe is possible, no Brexit.

If no action is taken, the default outcome will be a no-deal Brexit on 29 March 2019, ten weeks from now…

For one of the other two scenarios to apply, an extension of the negotiation period under Article 50 of the Treaty on European Union seems almost inevitable. In order to allow the twenty-seven, who will have to decide unanimously, to take an informed decision on such an extension, they must receive clarification from the British on two issues.

First question: what would the purpose of an extension be? What would the extra time be used for?

As lack of clarity on the future relationship seemed to be a more significant factor than the backstop in the vote against the agreement, an extension may first of all serve to renegotiate the Political Declaration on the future relationship. This would require clear UK positions and a review of the UK's red lines so as to allow for a more ambitious future relationship, for example through UK participation in a customs union.

An extension could also be justified by a new general election or by the holding of a second referendum (but that would require the British to agree on the question to be asked).

Second question: what would be the ideal duration in order to make sure there is a clear outcome from this process, while preserving the integrity and proper functioning of the EU institutions?

Naturally, the answer depends upon the purpose of the extension requested. Whatever the case, though, if the UK is still an EU member state on 23 May, it will have to hold European elections. Which would only further add to the absurdity of the situation.

Thursday, 17 January 2019: Henry the Navigator

Henry the Navigator, Duke of Viseu, was born in Porto on 4 March 1394 and died in Sagres on 13 November 1460. A scholar of mathematics and cosmography, he was responsible for financing the great Portuguese voyages of discovery in his capacity as Grand Master of the Order of Christ.

It is with a badge of this order that the President of the Republic of Portugal, Marcelo Rebelo de Sousa, honours me today, in a very formal ceremony at his beautiful residence in Belém. The Portuguese President is a warm, perceptive man with a keen political instinct, who is doing a good job of managing his cohabitation with the popular socialist Prime Minister António Costa, former mayor of Lisbon. I am obviously very touched by this honour, which in reality rewards and encourages the work of a whole team.

The President then asks me to attend a meeting of the Portuguese Council of State, which includes former presidents and prime ministers, including General António Ramalho Eanes, who in 1976 became the first President of the Republic after the Carnation Revolution of 25 April 1974.

It is a long meeting, with everyone speaking in detail from prepared notes. All of Portugal's great political bodies are present, and I can feel the tug of war between the preservation of the necessary unity among Europeans on one hand and, on the other, the fear of weakening the Anglo-Portuguese alliance, which goes back to the Treaty of Windsor in 1386, making it the oldest alliance of nations still in force today.

At the beginning of my speech, thinking of the great Portuguese explorers of the fifteenth and sixteenth centuries, Magellan, Vasco da Gama, Pedro Álvares Cabral and Bartolomeu Dias, I quote a beautiful sentence of General de Gaulle's: 'We are a people on the march, we have been forced to do so, the century has forced us to do so, but we are on the march towards an unknown sea, towards an unknown destiny, and for this march the people must be together.'*

Wednesday, 23 January 2019: Preparing for no deal

I use the occasion of a speech to the European Economic and Social Committee, chaired by Luca Jahier, to remind everyone of the need to prepare for a no-deal scenario, which still cannot be ruled out.

---

* Speech to RPF leaders, 11 February 1950.

On 19 December last, the Commission presented fourteen measures that the Union will be able to activate unilaterally in domains where no deal would be a source of major dysfunction for the citizens and businesses of the twenty-seven.

For example, in order to avoid major problems in the airline sector, the Commission proposes to allow for the provision of certain air services between the UK and the EU for one year, subject to reciprocity.

On customs, the Commission proposes adding the UK to the list of countries to which EU countries can export dual-use (both civilian and military) goods.

On financial services, the Commission proposes conditional equivalence for twelve months to ensure that there will be no immediate disruption to central clearing of derivatives.

What all these measures have in common is that they would be temporary, limited in scope and unilaterally adopted by the EU. Their purpose is to protect European interests, not to enable the negotiation of mini-deals with the UK.

Thursday, 24 January 2019: Angela Merkel

Lightning visit to Berlin with Sabine. As usual, Angela Merkel receives us exactly on time, accompanied by her faithful adviser Uwe Corsepius. She seems more serene, more relaxed, despite being tired from her trip to Davos earlier today. The Chancellor is precise and direct on the essential questions. She takes her time and, in the end, the meeting, scheduled to last forty-five minutes, lasts more than an hour. Like all European leaders, she is suffering from a kind of Brexit fatigue: 'Now, they have to leave.' But like me, she still hopes for an orderly exit.

On Ireland, her position is clear: we cannot reopen negotiations on the Withdrawal Agreement, nor can the backstop be touched. If, at the very last moment, the Withdrawal Agreement has to be accompanied by a roadmap on the exit mechanism for the backstop, as we are considering, she is open to this.

Mrs Merkel seems reassured that we are looking for a way to facilitate an agreement with the British. On the potential extension of negotiations, her opinion is that it should be limited to a few weeks, until 30 June or even July.

What this would mean is that any extension could be decided upon by the twenty-seven only with the assurance and guarantee that Brexit will take place by 30 June. Such assurance and guarantee can only be supplied by a House of Commons vote in favour of the treaty. Which just brings us back to the first corner of the squaring of this circle.

Clearly, Angela Merkel, like other leaders, is anxious to avoid the blame game that the British want to start playing.

Friday, 25 January 2019: Royal wisdom

Since the beginning of the negotiations, Queen Elizabeth II, properly observing her duty of reserve, has been careful not to voice any opinion on Brexit.

But her statements yesterday to a women's group near her Sandringham estate sounded like a call for calm:

As we look for new answers in the modern age, I for one prefer the tried and tested recipes, like speaking well of each other and respecting different points of view; coming together to seek out the common ground; and never losing sight of the bigger picture. [...] To me, these approaches are timeless, and I commend them to everyone.

Wednesday, 30 January 2019: Back to square one?

Yesterday, for the first time Mrs May openly argued for the Withdrawal Agreement to be revisited. She declared herself in favour of significant and legally binding changes concerning the backstop, by way of 'alternative arrangements' that she did not detail at any point.

She made this declaration while announcing the UK government's explicit support for the amendment tabled by Sir Graham Brady and Dr Andrew Murrison, which itself refers to these 'alternative arrangements' without any further elaboration.

This position marks an important shift on the part of the British government, since it amounts to a direct calling into question of the outcome of two years of negotiations, without any detailed indications as to what they want instead. This is not acceptable.

As for the two other options circulating in London – a time-limited backstop and the possibility of a unilateral withdrawal by the United Kingdom – they have been explicitly excluded by the European Council, as they stand in direct contradiction to the very idea of a backstop!

Wednesday, 6 February 2019: 'A place in hell'

'I've been wondering what that special place in hell looks like, for those who promoted Brexit, without even a sketch of a plan about how to carry it out safely.'

In his press briefing to welcome Leo Varadkar, Donald Tusk surprises everyone with his frankness. We can be sure that his statement will have been used, exploited and distorted by this evening. Perhaps it will even be perceived as an attempt to humiliate the British.

Over in the Commission, some are amused by this clumsy move by the President of the European Council. But with his trademark spontaneity, in these words Donald Tusk is just telling the truth. In my own words, I would say that we are dealing with far too many British political leaders who do not want to face the consequences of their vote for Brexit. And frankly, there is growing fatigue. We must now put an end to this soap opera.

Later, Leo Varadkar comes to the Berlaymont for a discussion with Jean-Claude Juncker. I tell him of the sensitivity of the member states on the issue of the internal market, which is directly linked to the issue of the border in Ireland. We must be clear among ourselves. Controls to protect the internal market must be implemented somewhere, whether around the island or within it – or on the mainland, with the risk of excluding Ireland from the Single Market, which we do not want.

The joint declaration reaffirms solidarity with Ireland and the impossibility of reopening negotiations on the backstop. It also emphasizes our intention to step up preparations for the no-deal scenario.

The Commission's Deputy Secretary-General, Céline Gauer, has conscientiously visited each of the capitals in order to better coordinate preparations by member states, in close collaboration with Stefan Fuehring, who is responsible for this subject within my team. The day before yesterday she was in Dublin, where representatives of the Irish government told her that, in the event of no deal, their objective would remain the same: to preserve the peace process and to anchor Ireland firmly within the internal market alone, which for them implies the rejection of any new control infrastructure in ports and airports.

In the event of no deal, what these senior Irish officials envision is a return to the original concept of the backstop: controls between Great Britain and Northern Ireland, and the inclusion of Northern Ireland in the Customs Union and the Single Market. This solution, they believe, would ultimately be accepted by London because it would be in Northern Ireland's best interests.

While this solution is being put in place, they envision stronger controls based on the existing controls, and a call for flexibility on the part of other member states and the Commission. In no scenario do they want to begin preparations to put a physical border back in place.

Thursday, 7 February 2019: Theresa May returns

Theresa May arrives at 11am sharp. For some days now, I have been hearing that she does not know where to turn or which direction to go in. On all sides, doors are being shut on her and the walls are closing in. And yet she seems unsinkable.

I tell her that we are ready to look for alternative arrangements to the backstop during the transition period, but point out that it is not possible to set a time limit for the backstop or to provide a unilateral exit clause.

As Jean-Claude Juncker insists, 'the problem seems to be the customs union for the whole of the UK, which is something you wanted. I am prepared to propose to the twenty-seven to go back to the backstop only for Northern Ireland if that helps you. But if we are to consider a new round of discussions between us, it must be limited to the Political Declaration alone.'

The conversation is cordial but quite frank and hard-line. At one point it becomes focused upon the word 'confidence', used by Olly Robbins. 'We cannot', Mr Robbins says, 'get into a situation where the EU is aggressively using the backstop to keep our country permanently in a customs union that it doesn't want. A commitment to do our best is not enough. The EU might change its mind. What would happen if Salvini became Italian Prime Minister?' Theresa May adds: 'Why not set a final date for the backstop? I need a legally binding commitment.'

In turn, I also focus on this 'confidence': 'Conversely, we may also fear that one day the UK will aggressively use an end date for the backstop to put us in a situation where, with our backs to the wall, we would be forced to accept your Chequers plan and your cherry-picking. We will not take any risks with the integrity of the internal market.'

To my question about a possible extension of the negotiation period, Theresa May replies that she does not intend to ask for such an extension. 'That could open up other issues. We must focus on one thing at a time.'

A rather disappointing meeting, ultimately. Disappointing for them because we will not budge, and disappointing for us because we are faced with a country that is clearly refusing to accept the objective consequences of its decision to leave the Union. On Monday, as Theresa May has requested, I will meet with the new Secretary of State for Brexit Steve Barclay, and we will work with the experts whom she appoints.

Monday, 11 February 2019: Enter Steve Barclay

With Sabine and Stéphanie, to the beautiful residence of the Permanent Representative of the UK to the EU Tim Barrow, on the edge of the Royal Park in Brussels, to meet the third British minister to be placed in charge of Brexit since negotiations began. Steve Barclay is a former military officer who subsequently worked in the private sector for the Axa group. He is a straightforward and warm man, one of Theresa May's loyal soldiers. Unlike his predecessors, David Davis and Dominic Raab, he harbours no ambitions to replace the Prime Minister, and it shows. He strikes me as being less of a politician.

As a sign of welcome to the negotiations, Barthélemy, who with his great sense of culture and diplomacy took care of the gifts offered to previous British negotiators, found a beautiful book in English on Leonardo da Vinci, on the occasion of the 500th anniversary of his death at Amboise. But before dinner, the British tell us that there will be no exchange of gifts. Too bad, I'll keep the book for another British minister...

During our one-to-one conversation and then later over dinner, it becomes clear that nothing has really changed. Mr Barclay explains to me at length the constraints of parliamentary debate in the House of Commons. We are quite aware of them. I tell him that we will not reopen negotiations on the Withdrawal Agreement and that we will not do anything to undermine the backstop that we have agreed with his government. I am given to understand that the position of the Attorney General, Geoffrey Cox, is decisive in this debate. It is he who will set the tone.

Theresa May's calculation is risky. She needs to bring over to her side between 115 and 120 of the 432 MPs who rejected the deal. She wants to convince the ten DUP MPs, who are not the easiest to win over. But their party is losing ground in Ireland and they have no interest in seeing negotiations fail. About fifty Tories could follow on behind the DUP, although the most hard-line Brexiteers, those in the European Research Group, will remain opposed to the agreement.

On the other side of the house, Theresa May is looking to win the vote of about fifty Labour MPs, those whose constituencies voted for Brexit. She is prepared to give guarantees on workers' rights in the future relationship and, in addition, has promised grants and investment in each of the constituencies concerned. This is a tactic, not a strategy. I really don't understand how a decision as serious, as historic, as Brexit can be implemented without a minimum of national dialogue and consensus.

The Tory Prime Minister and the leader of the Labour opposition are pretending to talk, but unfortunately are unwilling to do what is necessary to achieve a comprehensive cross-party agreement. Theresa May will probably make tactical use of the threat of a long drawn-out negotiation. This is the way to give cold sweats to the most hard-line Brexiteers, who may fear that such an extension would give further time to the supporters of a second referendum and fuel their arguments. And then the line would be: 'Either vote for my deal, or run the risk of a no-deal Brexit.'

We agree to meet again next week. I tell Barclay that there is growing Brexit fatigue on the European side. Governments are now preparing for a no deal, and some think that this would be preferable to a long period of uncertainty and instability. A kind of fatalism or realism is at large. I recommend that he does not underestimate this state of mind.

Tuesday, 12 February 2019: Walls have ears

Several newspapers report on a discussion between Olly Robbins and two others in a Brussels hotel bar last night. Which goes to show the importance of never talking too loudly in a restaurant or on a train… Nothing particularly surprising is said, though, as the conversation simply finds Olly Robbins confirming that Theresa May's tactic is to achieve a deal by the skin of her teeth, having edged as close to the precipice as she can afford to.

Thursday, 21 February 2019: Concessions at last?

Steve Barclay is back, along with Attorney General Geoffrey Cox and a far more constructive attitude than last time. In the meantime, we have managed to identify three areas to work on: guarantees on the temporary nature of the backstop, work on alternative arrangements, and potential changes to the Political Declaration.

Geoffrey Cox's concern is clear: he wants to find a solution that will allow him to play down to MPs in the House of Commons any risk of establishing a single customs territory that might turn out to be permanent.

Saturday, 2 March 2019: Nick Timothy

In an interview with Channel 4, Nick Timothy, Theresa May's former Joint Chief of Staff, denies that he secretly drew up the UK's red lines with the Prime Minister, but nevertheless confirms his wholehearted support of them:

> The red lines, as described, are that Britain should leave the Single Market and the Customs Union. My counter-question to that is: what is the European Union? The European Union was created by the Treaty of Rome which set up a customs union; through a series of processes, subsequently it created a single market. It also created a single currency, which we didn't join. It has laws and institutions that uphold the Customs Union, Single Market and Single Currency. So, as the country voted to leave the European Union, if we're not leaving the Customs Union or the Single Market, what is it we're leaving?

This is to forget that a country can be outside the Union but still participate in the Single Market, like Norway, or can be outside the EU but in a customs union with us, like Turkey. It is also to forget that the benefits of the Union, for farmers, for regions, for food security, are not limited to the Single Market and the Customs Union, as essential as those two are...

Wednesday, 6 March 2019: A royal visit for the task force

For the first time, we receive a royal delegation. King Carl XVI Gustaf and Queen Silvia of Sweden are visiting the European institutions. They have met the presidents of the Commission, the Council and the European Parliament, including Swedish Commissioner Cecilia Malmström. And their programme includes a lengthy stop at the task force HQ.

We welcome them over coffee and pastries. To ease the somewhat solemn atmosphere, I comment on the photo on my wall of Albertville schoolchildren bursting with joy and waving the Savoie flag on the day Juan Antonio Samaranch, President of the IOC, announced that we had been chosen to host the XVI Olympic Winter Games. That was on 17 October 1986 in Lausanne, and one of our main competitors was Sweden, with a bid for Falun.

Knowing that the King and Queen themselves have a personal history with the Olympics, I recall this friendly sporting rivalry between Falun and Albertville, and the King tells me that Sweden has not given up on its Olympic ambitions.

The Queen goes on to ask a number of questions about the UK, and both take time to personally greet each member of the team, who are dressed to the nines for the occasion.

Friday, 8 March 2019: Theresa May appeals to the people

We are a week away from the second House of Commons vote on the Draft Withdrawal Agreement. In a speech this afternoon from a warehouse in the port town of Grimsby, where the population voted 7–3 to leave, Mrs May seeks to throw her final arguments into the balance, hoping to tip the scales in her favour.

Her strategy is now clear: to dramatize the situation at any cost. She does this by putting forward a clear alternative: either you support the deal and we get out, or you reject it and there will be chaos. Above all, she adds, 'Brexit does not belong to MPs in Parliament but the whole country.'

It seems to me that, by expressing things like this – and especially by choosing to address British citizens directly rather than parliamentarians – she is embarking upon a perilous path, namely bypassing the House of Commons, something which, in the world's oldest parliamentary democracy, is a cavalier move to say the least.

On substantive matters, she is more combative than ever and reiterates each of her red lines. The only new point compared to her previous interventions is that she now rejects any possibility of extending the negotiation period, except for an exclusively technical extension to allow for the adoption of the legislation necessary for the implementation of the Withdrawal Agreement.

Putting parliamentarians on the spot by calling on public opinion is a bold move. I am not sure this will help reduce the antagonisms that have paralysed the House of Commons for more than four months now.

On our side, we are always ready to do what we can to help Theresa May, not least by reassuring British MPs who fear that the EU is not negotiating the future relationship or subsequent agreements on Ireland and Northern Ireland in good faith.

And so we find ourselves in the strange position of having to help the British government convince British MPs that what the UK has asked for, a single customs territory, is not some trap that we have designed… In order to achieve this, we are able to give the British three additional assurances.

First, we recall that, under the terms of the Withdrawal Agreement, an arbitration panel may give the UK the right to suspend its backstop obligations proportionately, as a last resort, if the EU fails to meet its obligation to make 'best efforts' and act in good faith to negotiate alternative solutions.

Second, we are prepared to give legal force to all the commitments made by Presidents Tusk and Juncker in their January letter, through a joint interpretive declaration that will facilitate the task of the panel of arbitrators in its monitoring of compliance with the obligations of best efforts and good faith.

Finally, the EU commits to giving the UK the option to exit the single customs territory unilaterally, while respecting the other elements of the backstop. The UK, then, will not be forced to remain in a customs union against its will.

A few hours later, the British reject this third point, which would mark a return to a single customs territory between the EU and Northern Ireland alone, which the DUP does not want. This leaves the first two points, which represent solid guarantees.

Monday, 11 March 2019: An evening in Strasbourg

This negotiation certainly calls for flexibility and adaptation. The British are incapable of planning things in advance. London is frantic in its attempts to achieve a positive second meaningful vote tomorrow.

Theresa May has made it known that she wants to renegotiate with us so as to formalize the guarantees discussed in recent days on the provisional nature of the backstop. In particular, she hopes to convince Attorney General Geoffrey Cox to issue a favourable legal opinion on the Withdrawal Agreement.

To lend strength and credibility to this latest negotiation, she is ready to come to meet Jean-Claude Juncker. Except that it is a week of plenary session in the European Parliament, in which the President of the Commission is participating. Theresa May therefore informs us early this afternoon that she intends to meet us this evening in Strasbourg, leaving me just enough time to drive there from Brussels.

In the end, the Prime Minister arrives quite late, and together with Jean-Claude Juncker we finalize an 'instrument relating to the Withdrawal Agreement' and a joint declaration that complements the Political Declaration, texts for which the President has made sure to obtain the support of Taoiseach Leo Varadkar.

In his letter to accompany these documents when they are sent to Donald Tusk, President Juncker writes that he hopes that this last effort will allow the withdrawal process to be concluded before the date chosen by the United Kingdom, and that negotiations on the future relationship can begin as soon as possible thereafter.

The President also recalls that if the UK is still a member of the Union at the time of the European elections on 23–26 May, it will have to organize these elections in accordance with the rights and obligations of any member state.

Tuesday, 12 March 2019: Meaningful vote #2

Bombshell! In an opinion published late this morning, Attorney General Geoffrey Cox acknowledged that the provisions of the treaty agreed in Strasbourg are legally binding, and reduce the risk that the United Kingdom could be trapped in the backstop through the fault of the European Union.

He also believes that it is highly unlikely, should the parties demonstrate a genuine desire to reach agreement, that they would fail to reach a subsequent agreement to replace the backstop within the appointed timeframe.

However, above and beyond this political judgement, he considers that the legal risk remains unchanged, since, without any breach by either party, but simply because of irreparable differences, the UK could find itself without the legal means to withdraw unilaterally from the backstop.

Despite calls from Theresa May, who meanwhile has lost her voice, the consequence of this opinion, particularly eagerly awaited by the Brexiteers of the European Research Group led by Jacob Rees-Mogg, is clear: the House of Commons is on its way towards a new rejection of the Withdrawal Agreement, as indeed is confirmed this evening by a clear majority of 391 votes to 242.

Wednesday, 13 March 2019: No to no deal

A second day of voting in the UK. After yesterday's rejection of the deal, MPs are to vote upon whether or not a no deal is acceptable.

The government motion, planned to be a free vote, proposes to reject a no deal on 29 March but to keep it on the table for a later date.

There is a new twist as Labour MP Yvette Cooper proposes amending the motion to exclude a no deal in all circumstances. This amendment is passed by four votes. In a panic, the government then decides to scrap the free vote and tells Conservative MPs to vote against its own motion with this new amendment – which a large majority of Tories refuse to do, preferring to abstain.

The result: Mrs May's government is once again outvoted on a motion it itself had proposed, as a no deal in all circumstances is ruled out by a majority of 321 to 278 MPs.

However, voting against a no deal is not enough to exclude the no deal that will automatically result under Article 50 in the event that the Withdrawal Agreement is not voted on before 29 March, in the absence of any extension of the negotiation period. As the Dutch Prime Minister Mark Rutte sums up the situation: voting against no deal is a bit like the *Titanic* voting for the iceberg to move…

Thursday, 14 March 2019: A positive vote!

Third major vote of the week in the House of Commons. The question today is whether to ask the EU for an extension of the Article 50 period.

And once again both Conservatives and Labour are divided.

But perhaps the most inscrutable position is that of Steve Barclay, who, having urged MPs to vote in favour of the extension, chooses to vote against it himself, along with seven other ministers… This does not prevent the motion in favour of the extension from passing by 413 votes to 202.

Monday, 18 March 2019: Revenge for Crécy!

David Davis is back in the news: after having voted against the Withdrawal Agreement on 15 January, then in favour of it on 12 March, this morning he declares in the British press that he may vote against it again in the event of a third meaningful vote…

Meanwhile, on the Russian channel Rossiya 1, presenter Dmitri Kisselev reveals that I am using Brexit to 'avenge the French for the defeat by the English at the battle of Crécy in 1346'. Now we really have heard it all!

Tuesday, 19 March 2019: J-10?

This morning, the press are reporting that the Permanent Representative of the UK to the EU, Tim Barrow, wrote a few days ago to the Romanian Presidency of the Council of the European Union to express the UK's intention to accept recent changes to the rules governing Eurojust, the EU agency that coordinates judicial cooperation between EU countries.* The UK apparently also wants to strengthen Eurodac, the EU database that records the fingerprints of migrants arriving at the EU's external borders.

In other words, the United Kingdom, which wanted to be outside the Union's justice, security and freedom policies, but to have the right to participate in certain projects on a case-by-case basis, wishes to make full use of this opt-in right, two weeks before its planned exit from the Union... It doesn't take a great leap of imagination to see this as a last-gasp attempt to gain access to European Union data...

Wednesday, 20 March 2019: What extension?

Olly Robbins, with whom I spoke this morning, shares my preference for a short extension until 11 April, even if it means taking a weightier decision on that day, either to confirm the exit without an agreement or to opt for a longer extension.

'But there is no real support for this option', he tells me. 'The cabinet meeting was very difficult yesterday and we are preparing a short letter asking for a short extension.' I detect a sense of resignation on Robbins's part. And his position in London has become weaker. It is even rumoured that Theresa May is planning to sacrifice him in order to secure the support of the hard-line Brexiteers.

One thing is certain: we cannot risk finding ourselves, at the end of an extension, in the same or an even worse situation than the one we are in today.

To avoid this, it will be important for the European Council to make clear that no negotiations on the future relationship can take place during an extension. Otherwise, the UK could seek to use the financial settlement and the Irish border as leverage to make the future relationship subject to its conditions. This is not a purely theoretical risk: we know that some ministers have already discussed this strategy with third countries.

On the other hand, during an extension, the UK would remain a full

* *Politico Playbook*, 19 March 2019.

member state with all the attendant rights and obligations. This means that it would participate in the Union's decision-making process as the budget for the next seven years is negotiated. The UK would also take part in trade negotiations conducted by the Union while at the same time preparing for its future as a third country. Moreover, we are well aware that the British are not informing us, as they should, of the negotiations they have opened or even already concluded with Chile, Switzerland, the Faroe Islands, South Africa, Israel and Canada.

What all of this shows is that no deal is not the only scenario that has a cost. Prolonging uncertainty by granting an extension of negotiations also brings with it a non-negligible political and economic cost. This is why I am not in favour of a lengthy extension.

The dangerously paradoxical situation in which we find ourselves is that, in a heated and polarized House of Commons, and even within the Cabinet, British Remainers are calling for a long extension to prevent Brexit, while at the same time the most hard-line Brexiteers are calling for a no deal to ensure that Brexit happens. As a result, on both sides there is less support than ever for the actual deal itself.

At 7pm we cross the street once more to meet our 'cousins' from the European Council, so as to prepare our response to Theresa May's request for a short extension of the negotiations until the end of June.

The European elections that will take place between 23 and 26 May are a key element in this discussion. Our legal services have made it clear that should the United Kingdom remain a full member of the Union at the time, it will have to hold these elections. Failure to do so would pose a major risk of legal uncertainty for the new European Parliament, whose decisions could be challenged in the EU Court of Justice, particularly by European citizens living in the UK who would have been deprived of their right to vote.

And here we come up against another problem, which is the deadline, 11 April, after which the UK can no longer materially and legally hold European elections upon its territory, according to its own internal procedures.

For this reason, I mention the possibility of a 'ratchet' mechanism. The extension requested by the UK should automatically end on 23 May if the UK has not taken a decision by 11 April to hold European elections. If it wishes to extend further, then it will automatically have to hold European elections.

I sense that Jeppe Tranholm-Mikkelsen is interested in this idea of a two-stage response to the British. Indeed, later in the evening he will adopt it and I will express my support for it. Next to me in the meeting, Martin Selmayr does not look very happy.

In an aside, Jeppe Tranholm-Mikkelsen lets me know that he has another meeting planned that evening with Mr Selmayr, and that they will also have a discussion with Olly Robbins. This comes as no surprise. It is now a habit of Mr Selmayr's to try and organize secondary meetings like this. What worries me most is the line he will take, if I am to believe his own draft conclusions, which he has sent to the General Secretariat of the Council – a seven-point text that is a plea for a long extension, with European elections held in the UK.

In a text message at the end of the evening, I remind him that in the afternoon I had taken the line agreed with Jean-Claude Juncker in his office, warning governments against the economic and political costs of a long extension without any guarantee of a resolution. In any case, the most likely common position of all member states will be to opt for a short extension. I ask him to keep me apprised of his dialogue with Mr Robbins that evening.

At 2.38am, he replies: 'The situation has changed, we will have to be very careful, but there are only two possibilities: either no deal or a long extension. The proposal for a short extension until 11 April was rejected by Tusk this evening.'

Once again, I feel that he is wrong to privilege tactics over strategy.

Thursday, 21 March 2019: A thousand days' work

Before the heads of state or government of the twenty-seven, Theresa May gets back down to work with impressive tenacity, explaining why she needs an extension and what she intends to do with it. A dozen heads of state or government then question her about the chances of finally getting a positive vote: 'We've now been working on this for a thousand days, since the referendum.'

Another participant dares ask: 'Is it possible to reverse Brexit?' while a third insists: 'We have arrived at this impasse because of your red lines

– they have to move.' A fourth wonders: 'Is your country ready to face all the consequences of a no deal?'

Theresa May laboriously repeats the same answers over and over again, adding that it is possible that Parliament might consider alternative solutions: 'MPs are free to propose changes during the ratification process. We have to give them time.'

She even mentions that there are other new elements that she wants to present to Parliament. I know that this means a unilateral statement on the interpretation of the backstop in Ireland in order to try to win the votes of the ten DUP MPs. One can sense that the EU leaders, while always courteous, do not believe that a yes vote is a realistic scenario.

One particular Prime Minister, who always speaks spontaneously, tells Mrs May that Europeans are tired of all this procrastination and that he often hears people saying, 'Let them go, since they want to leave!'

Another takes up the baton: 'We're not going to change a comma in the draft treaty in the next eight days. Does the British Parliament know that in the event of a no deal, Leo [Varadkar] will be obliged to install controls between Ireland and Northern Ireland? Shouldn't the House of Commons be informed and asked the question?' On the defensive once more, Mrs May replies that for a certain period after a no deal, 'in Ireland, on our side, we won't be doing checks'.

After ninety minutes of such exchanges, Theresa May shakes my hand and leaves the chamber.

A sense of resignation is spreading amongst the twenty-seven. But we must continue to be amicable, we must not give in to the blame game, and we must take matters into our own hands. The British cannot be allowed to impose their own timetable right at the very end of negotiations.

Donald Tusk proceeds to circulate the draft conclusions. Paragraph 3 of these conclusions states that the European Council agrees to accept, before 29 March, eight days from now, an extension to 22 May, provided that the Withdrawal Agreement is approved by the House of Commons before then. The conclusions add that, as the UK does not intend to hold European elections on its territory, no extension beyond that date will be possible. The European Council also reiterates that there will be no reopening of negotiations on the Withdrawal Agreement agreed in November 2018 between the United Kingdom and the European Union.

So begins a very lengthy discussion. Some insist on the need for clarity on 11 April, given the procedures for organizing the European elections in their own countries. Emmanuel Macron, to the surprise of many, expresses his hostility to a long extension and proposes 7 May as the cut-off date, without conditions. Why 7 May? Because it is the day before the extraordinary summit in Sibiu, Romania, where Europeans are scheduled to meet to discuss the future of Europe. 'Then it will be time to make a decision', he says. Deep down, I also feel that a UK withdrawal on 7 May would not provide the most auspicious circumstances for the 9 May discussion among the twenty-seven.

President Juncker has chosen to let me take the lead when Donald Tusk asks the Commission to speak. On the extension period, I argue in favour of conditionality: 'Theresa May herself needs it in order to put pressure on her Parliament.'

I conclude with an enumeration of the three scenarios we will be presented with if this third meaningful vote is lost: either the revocation of Article 50, or, by some miracle, a new process of dialogue between the majority and the opposition via transparent agreements, or else a disorderly exit from the EU. This last scenario is something we did not and do not want, but we are prepared for it.

The heads of state or government then resume their discussions, which go around in circles until, at 9pm, Donald Tusk proposes to adjourn the session and work on a draft of new conclusions before dinner.

Factions are forming. There is visible tension at the end of the table around Donald Tusk. The general feeling is that we should not take any chances with the European elections, but should nonetheless leave some doors open.

Jeppe Tranholm-Mikkelsen paces back and forth behind a group of advisers huddled around a computer on the other side of the door. And then, as is often the case in European meetings, after a somewhat tragic moment of tension and deadlock, a new text is proposed. The European Council agrees to an extension until 22 May on condition that the Withdrawal Agreement is approved next week by the House of Commons. Should the Withdrawal Agreement not be approved, the European Council stipulates an extension until 12 April, and will expect the UK to indicate, before that date, which way it will go.

I go back to the idea of the 'ratchet'. The draft is carefully worded. It satisfies the British on the short extension they are asking for. It is limited to the day before the elections if there is a positive vote in the Commons. If not, the extension will end on 12 April, which means that on that date the UK will have to commit to an exit without an agreement, or else ask for another extension and commit to holding European elections. In either case, the EU regains the upper hand.

Gathering around Donald Tusk, all the European leaders sign their agreement to the text. A little later, my place setting is added around the table for the dinner, which was supposed to be devoted to relations with China but will instead be entirely dedicated to Brexit. The atmosphere is far more serene now. The twenty-seven have preserved their unity by agreeing to the new conclusions. Dinner conversation revolves around the risks and consequences of a no deal.

One Prime Minister questions the future policy of cooperation with the UK on defence. Two others are concerned about preparations for a no deal in Ireland. Everyone understands that the risks and consequences of a no deal must be emphasized over the next few days.

Friday, 29 March 2019: In Natolin, Poland

It has now been two years since Tim Barrow, in his three-piece suit as always, came to deliver to Donald Tusk the letter notifying him of the UK's intention to leave the European Union.

Now, on 29 March 2019, long announced as the date of Brexit, I am in Poland for further discussions in Warsaw with Prime Minister Mateusz Morawiecki, with whom we have a direct and trusting relationship, Minister of European Affairs Konrad Szymański, a delegation of national parliamentarians, and representatives of business and civil society.

After these meetings, we head to the College of Europe campus in Natolin, in the people carrier of the Commission's representation in Poland. Matthieu points out that the car in front of us in the fast lane is a Jaguar with a small British flag on the bonnet – apparently, my speech is of interest not only to students! I'll be sure to mention the British ambassador to Poland, Jonathan Knott. And also to emphasize the debt I owe to the College of Europe, where Sabine Weyand and several members of my team studied, in Bruges and in Natolin.

At the end of the day, while awaiting our plane at Warsaw airport, we watch the third vote in the House of Commons on the Withdrawal Agreement. The government loses again! This time by 344 votes to 246.

Tuesday, 2 April 2019: Another extension request

After seven hours of meetings with her ministers, Theresa May speaks briefly. She begins by saying that, in the long term, the UK could make a success of a no deal. However, she believes that leaving the EU without a deal is not the best solution, and acknowledges that a further extension of Article 50, 'as short as possible', will be necessary.

The new deadline will aim to ensure that the UK leaves the EU 'in a timely and orderly way'. To this end, Mrs May is proposing to the leader of the opposition, Jeremy Corbyn, that they sit down and seek to agree a plan for the UK's withdrawal. If early agreement on a common approach proves impossible, discussions with the opposition could open up a number of options for the future relationship, which the House of Commons would have to approve, and the government would have to commit to respecting the House's decision.

The UK government's objective remains to get the Withdrawal Agreement Bill passed before 22 May, so as to avoid the UK being required to hold European elections.

Listening to the Prime Minister, as courageous as ever in the face of adversity, I can't help thinking that, on this issue of 'national interest', a genuine dialogue between the government and the opposition is long overdue.

Friday, 5 April 2019: European elections?

In a letter to President Tusk this morning, Theresa May formally requests a second short extension until 30 June. She pledges to hold European elections in the UK if the Withdrawal Agreement is not ratified by 22 May.

The European Council, which meets next Wednesday, will have three choices: to refuse this new extension and force a no-deal Brexit at midnight on 12 April; to accept this extension until 30 June; or to propose a longer one, as suggested by Donald Tusk.

Any new extension has to serve a purpose. It must maximize the chances of a deal, which means keeping up the time pressure. It must also minimize the impact on the EU by ensuring that Brexit does not monopolize the heads of state or government at every summit, impede the smooth running of our institutions or prevent the Union from acting. In my view, the heads of state or government will have to make a decision on the basis of the plan to be presented by Theresa May next week. If we are convinced that there is a chance for this plan to succeed, then we should give her the short extension she is asking for. If, on the other hand, we are not convinced by the proposed plan, we should indeed offer them a longer extension to allow a solution to emerge.

Wednesday, 10 April 2019: Halloween Brexit

Today, speaking before the heads of state or government of the twenty-seven, Theresa May seems more confident than on previous occasions:

> The UK Parliament wants to avoid a no deal but has not achieved a majority for any of the options so far. A delay is the best solution, but patience is wearing thin. That is why I have opened a dialogue with Jeremy Corbyn. We need to give this dialogue a chance. It is not about the Withdrawal Agreement, but about the future relationship: the customs issue, regulatory alignment, UK participation in EU agencies, alignment of workers' rights with EU rights. I hope to conclude this by 22 May. But if we can't meet that deadline, then we are prepared to hold European elections. If there is a longer extension, it must be possible to end it as soon as an agreement is reached. We will remain a loyal and constructive partner. During any extension, we are bound by the obligation of sincere cooperation.

One by one, a dozen heads of government question Theresa May on the possibility of keeping to her timetable and reaching an agreement with Labour: 'Does a further extension help you in your process? And will the discussion with Labour include the idea of a customs union?'

Theresa May responds without ever saying the words 'customs union' herself, simply repeating variations on the same answer and talking about lowering barriers to trade, simplifying checks and controls, and cooperation. She reiterates her preference for a short extension, until 30 June.

Mrs May then leaves the chamber but remains in the building, and discussion quickly resumes. One Prime Minister opens the debate rather bluntly: 'I've had enough of all these meetings on Brexit. Of course we want to avoid a no deal, but it's still on the table. We shouldn't imagine that a long extension is going to lead to the revocation of Article 50: that would be undemocratic. It will certainly be very strange to see the UK holding European elections.'

A majority of the heads of state and government are in favour of a long and flexible extension, as proposed by Donald Tusk. Their message is clear: this is a historic moment for Europe, eighty years after the Second World War. We need to reassess our relationship with the UK. This is a moment of truth. What is another twelve months when we are at such a crossroads? If we don't give them more time, it is the British who will impose their timetable on us.

Others, however, propose to give Theresa May what she is asking for, without going any further: 'It's been thirty-four months since the UK voted and now, with a long extension, we're going to ask them to hold European elections. There is popular contempt. We have done a great deal of negotiating. Theresa May is asking us for a delay. She needs pressure, she told us, so let's give it to her! If we give her a different deadline to the one she has asked for, they'll say we are afraid of a no deal. I don't want to give out that signal. I regret that this message about a longer delay has been sent without consultation. I'm sure that if we decide to put on this pressure, they'll come to an agreement soon enough.'

The discussion continues for some time. Donald Tusk stands by his conviction: 'Our previous decision to extend for a short period of time brought us here. If a short extension is decided upon again, we will come back in June to decide on yet another extension.'

Before dinner, the President of the European Council decides to suspend the session. Around the table, discussion is lively within the groups that have formed. Finally, a compromise emerges on an intermediate date between 30 June 2019 and 31 March 2020: 31 October 2019.

This is a logical date as it marks the end of the Juncker Commission. However, it is also the date for the holding of European elections in the UK and the return to Strasbourg of the seventy-four British MEPs, who will take part in deciding appointments for all posts in the European Parliament and the appointment of the President of the Commission.

During dinner, Theresa May agrees to this deadline, slightly longer than she had requested. In the end, for better or worse, the European Council ends in unanimity.

Basically, the choice tonight was between putting two kinds of pressure on the British: the pressure of a short deadline and the perceived risk of a no-deal exit, or the pressure of a longer extension and, for Tory Brexiteers, the risk of facing European elections at home. My team and I considered that the pressure of a short extension would be the greater one.

Friday, 19 April 2019: Brexit break?

I am happy to be back in our house in the middle of the woods of Sologne. At the top of the barn I have set up a small office the window of which opens onto the beautiful lawn and the pond. The whole family is here, including the latest addition, Oriana, now four months old. It's spring and there are as many birds in the trees during the daytime as there are frogs croaking at night.

I work on what used to be my desk when I was a Member of Parliament. A solid pine table, simple and heavy, behind which I listened to and advised so many citizens in Savoie.

On the wall I have hung an assortment of photos in a deliberately disorderly arrangement, especially faces that mark the stages of my political life and its key moments. My first lunch at the Élysée Palace, invited by Georges Pompidou in 1971: I was twenty years old! The audience with John Paul II at the Vatican, where I went with Jean-Claude Killy to talk about the Olympics. The audience with Benedict XVI just before his resignation, with Annegret Kramp-Karrenbauer, then Minister-President of Saarland. On these walls there are also photos of Jacques Chaban-Delmas, Resistance fighter, a Gaullist and a European. And of Jacques Chirac, Alain Juppé, Jean-Pierre Raffarin and Nicolas Sarkozy, all of whose trust and confidence I enjoyed at one time or another. And of course, the tutelary figure of General de Gaulle, to whom I owe my first involvements in politics and my greatest pride. At the top is the front page of the newspaper *Libération* from 13 June 2005, with the beautiful smiles of Florence Aubenas and Hussein Hanoun, finally freed from captivity in Iraq after so much patient effort and active solidarity – with their personal dedications.

But enough nostalgia! Nostalgia is never a good counsellor in politics, although there is nothing wrong with memories, remembrance and recognition. And these photos serve as so many markers of a certain idea of what politics should be.

This morning, my first day of relaxation was disturbed by some sad news. In Northern Ireland, a young woman, a committed journalist, was shot dead last night, the victim of clashes between Republican militants and the police. Her name is Lyra McKee. In an unusual joint statement, all parties in Northern Ireland condemned the murder.

The 'Brexit Break' decreed in Brussels at the beginning of the Easter holidays will not be so serene in reality…

Sunday, 21 April 2019: Churchill's political diary

In my library, I pull out the diary written by Winston Churchill throughout the years 1936–1939.

In the aftermath of the Munich Agreement, he wrote: 'It is not unlikely that we are moving towards a General Election in the coming year.' He continues:

> If there is an election in the near future it will be a very strange and unhappy one. It's not so much a question of who wins or loses but what would happen to the country. I have never seen it divided as it is to-day. The division does not follow exactly regular party lines, but cuts very deep and will sever many ties and friendships.

The situation in 1938 was serious in quite a different way, and therefore by no means comparable, and yet those lines could have been written yesterday…

Thursday, 9 May 2019: 'This precious stone set in the silver sea…'

At one of the few Brussels dinners that Isabelle and I attend together, I meet Bernard Snoy et d'Oppuers, a passionate campaigner for European integration who has been an official at both the World Bank and the European Bank for Reconstruction and Development.

Whether to encourage or forewarn me, he recommends that I read *This Blessed Plot: Britain and Europe from Churchill to Blair* by Hugo Young, a journalist and keen observer of British political life. It just so happens that a British journalist in Brussels sent me the same book some time ago.

In this book, published in 1998, the author argues that, since 1945, 'Britain has struggled to reconcile the past she could not forget with the future she could not avoid'. He is speaking of the mythology of what Shakespeare described as

This royal throne of kings, this sceptred isle,
This earth of majesty, this seat of Mars,
This other Eden, demi-paradise,
This fortress built by Nature for herself
Against infection and the hand of war,
This happy breed of men, this little world,
This precious stone set in the silver sea,
Which serves it in the office of a wall
Or as a moat defensive to a house,
Against the envy of less happier lands,
This blessed plot, this earth, this realm, this England.*

So deep-seated is this mythology for many Britons, that it leads Young to question whether the UK could ever have truly accepted that its modern destiny was to be a European country.

For the makers of the original 'Europe' [...] their creation was a triumph. Out of defeat they produced a new kind of victory. For Britain, by contrast, the entry into Europe was a defeat: a fate she had resisted, a necessity reluctantly accepted, the last resort of a once great power, never for one moment a climactic or triumphant engagement with the construction of Europe.

Yet this did not stop Churchill from being one of the pioneers of Europe, from the time of his Zurich speech on 19 September 1946: 'If

---

* William Shakespeare, *Richard II*, Act II, Scene 1.

Europe were once united in the sharing of its common inheritance there would be no limit to the happiness, prosperity and glory which its 300 million or 400 million people would enjoy.'

Sunday, 12 May 2019: Documentaries

Media interest in the Brexit story continues unabated. Along with the European Parliament, we have facilitated the work of a number of film crews. The director Alain de Halleux followed my team for two years, for Arte and RTBF.

Our first encounter was frank and direct. He made no bones of the fact that I was not his 'cup of tea' and that he would have voted Leave in the Brexit referendum. And yet over the months, a certain complicity developed between us, and his long, carefully constructed and very instructive report is proof of it.

Ultimately, what we see in his film *Brexit: The Clock is Ticking* is the patience and tenacity of the whole task force. And above all, how throughout these two years, we have 'cultivated' the unity and cohesion of the twenty-seven member states and the European Parliament. On a more basic level, I am simply pleased that it is there as a living trace of the commitment of our entire team, of its professionalism and of the 'collective morale' that drives it.

I cannot say the same about the documentary by Lode Desmet, to whom Guy Verhofstadt, for two years, opened the doors of his office, his residence and, above all, those of the Brexit Steering Group he chaired in the European Parliament. It is not about the negotiations themselves but about the debates and the parliamentary teams. As the film goes on, there is far too much mockery of the British. Theresa May's chief of staff is even recorded without his knowledge at one point, which is not right.

At another point we hear Olly Robbins, in a relaxed moment, joking about applying for Belgian nationality. It seems that many British people do not share his sense of humour. Following the BBC's broadcast of the film, Olly received threats and insults, which is obviously unacceptable. I expressed my solidarity with him in a text message: 'Dear Olly, I hear that the BBC's programme on the European Parliament and Brexit has had a very negative impact on you personally. I am sorry to hear this. The film is an unfortunate distortion of the reality of these negotiations, which have always been characterized by respect and professionalism between us. I hope the dust settles quickly.'

Monday, 13 May 2019: Berlin

Together with Sabine, Georg and Christian Krappitz, a European civil servant of German nationality who is the member of our team responsible for keeping in touch with the national parliaments, I am pleased to return to Berlin for a series of meetings with the government, industry, the Bundestag, several think-tanks and, finally, the press.

I know how important the trade organizations are in Germany: the Federation of German Industry, the BDI, chaired by Dieter Kempf, and the Confederation of Employers' Associations, the BDA, chaired by Steffen Kampeter, as well as the chambers of commerce and industry.

Our meeting with them is most cordial and constructive. The participants seem ready to take the risk of a no deal if it means defending the Single Market, which they consider to be the priority. I ask them to continue to prepare for this and to use the time remaining between now and 31 October effectively. It seems to me that they are well aware, probably more so than some politicians, of the cost of prolonging the negotiations with the British. 'This extension spells instability, and that's something we can do without.'

A little later I meet Mathias Döpfner, the charismatic boss of the Axel Springer Group, owner of *Bild*, *Die Welt*, and a number of newspapers in several other countries, including Poland. His office, which is completely transparent, is located on the very street that, until 1989, marked the boundary between East and West Berlin. I am told that Axel Springer chose to build his company's historic building on this spot facing the GDR as a symbol of the freedom that was close by.

Thursday, 16 May 2019: Theresa May throws in the towel

Theresa May has announced that she will step down from government in June, after holding her fourth crucial vote on the draft treaty in the week of 3–8 June. This time it will be far more than a meaningful vote – it will be a vote on the legislative ratification of the draft treaty, and therefore a real 'double or quits' situation.

For several days rumours of her resignation had been growing in London. Her cabinet was in a feverish state and her last remaining supporters were drifting away. Her belated efforts to forge some sort of alliance with Labour on the Withdrawal Agreement were all in vain. And as if that were not enough, Conservative Party officials had called for an extraordinary general meeting on 15 June where they intended to raise concerns about the Prime Minister's leadership.

Olly Robbins returned to Brussels yesterday to report on the ongoing negotiations with Labour. He seems to be more optimistic than media reports would suggest is justified. According to him there is a 40–50 per cent chance of achieving a cross-party agreement.

Nevertheless, chances of such a positive majority are low. In any case, we will soon have a new Prime Minister. It will be either Boris Johnson, or Dominic Raab, or another Tory Brexiteer. And if the treaty has not been ratified, this new Prime Minister will of course immediately start trying to blackmail the European Union. They will confirm that the UK will leave the EU on 31 October and will seek to reopen negotiations with the aim of removing the backstop, if nothing else, from the treaty.

Monday, 20 May 2019: Turkish provocations in Cyprus

Even during this period of suspended negotiations I continue my visits to each of the member states: this morning, to Nicosia for a meeting at the Chamber of Deputies and then a meeting with Níkos Anastasiádis, the President of the Republic of Cyprus.

I receive a genial welcome, and both the President and his Minister of Foreign Affairs, Níkos Khristodoulídis, reiterate their confidence in me. The atmosphere here is electric because of Turkey's provocative announcement that it wants to begin underwater oil explorations in the Exclusive Economic Zone of Cyprus, as the Minister of Foreign Affairs and his team explain to me with the aid of maps.

In addition to these provocations, since yesterday there have been large-scale military manoeuvres. Immediately, President Donald Tusk, followed by Federica Mogherini, reaffirmed the EU's solidarity with each of its states.

This concern obviously outweighs the issue of Brexit. We are in Cyprus, 170 kilometres from Lebanon and 105 kilometres from Syria.

Nearly a thousand refugees per month enter Cyprus illegally by boat and live there in precarious conditions.

Friday, 24 May 2019: Theresa May's regrets

At 11am, Theresa May takes her place at the lectern outside 10 Downing Street. Her tone is serious and resolute.

> I have done everything I can to convince MPs to back [the] deal. Sadly, I have not been able to do so. I tried three times. I believe it was right to persevere, even when the odds against success seemed high. But it is now clear to me that it is in the best interests of the country for a new prime minister to lead that effort.

She expresses her 'deep regret' that she has 'not been able to deliver Brexit', and announces that she will resign as leader of the Conservative Party on 7 June, so that a successor can be selected.

As Mrs May expresses her gratitude for the chance to 'serve the country I love', she cannot suppress a sob. And frankly, who can blame her, except the writers of a few unworthy tabloid headlines?

For my part, as I have written several times in this Diary, I admire the courage of this woman of politics who did not vote to leave the European Union. She nonetheless made it her mission to implement Brexit, in order to respect that democratic decision, despite the many obstacles placed in her path, not least by Brexiteers who have done their best to shirk their responsibilities for the last three years.

Sunday, 26 May 2019: European elections

Late last night the results of the European elections in the UK, where there are no exit polls, began to come in. The result is clear-cut for the two major governing parties, with 14.1 per cent for Labour and 8.7 per cent for the Tories. The two big winners were Nigel Farage's new Brexit Party, which, with 37.7 per cent of the vote, could become the largest national party in the European Parliament in terms of the number of MEPs, and the Liberal Democrats, who came second with 18.6 per cent of the vote. Clearly, the divide between Brexiteers and Remainers is still very much in force, to the point of eclipsing the traditional divide between the Tories and Labour.

For the next Conservative Prime Minister, whoever that may be, this should serve as a clear incentive to avoid the marginalization of their party by settling the Brexit issue as soon as possible. This latest turn of events may end up increasing the possibility of a no deal.

On the other end of the political spectrum, those who want to hold a second referendum with the hope of remaining in the EU, led by the Liberal Democrats, will no doubt be heartened by the results.

Between the partisans of no deal and the promoters of a new referendum, what room is left for supporters of compromise, i.e. of the agreement that we patiently negotiated with Theresa May's government? Everything will depend upon Labour's attitude and, above all, on the position taken by whoever succeeds Mrs May in a few weeks' time.

In the Conservative Party the game is already afoot, and the contenders are numerous, almost too many to keep track of. Boris Johnson remains the front runner, but candidates also include the former Brexit negotiator Dominic Raab, the environment secretary Michael Gove, and the leader of the House of Commons Andrea Leadsom. As well as Jeremy Hunt, the rather odd foreign secretary.

Meanwhile, the seventy-three British MEPs elected today will join the European Parliament. What a paradox! Seventeen of them will join the ranks of the liberal Renew Europe group, while Farage and his friends will join the Eurosceptic group. And all of these MEPs, elected from a country that is preparing to leave the Union, will participate in the appointment of the President of the Commission and the College of Commissioners in a few weeks' time. That is the Treaty, and that is the law!

Wednesday, 5 June 2019: Donald Trump in London

Donald Trump is back in London, this time for a state visit.

Yesterday, as in 2018, standing alongside Theresa May, he assured journalists that the United States is ready to negotiate a 'huge' free trade agreement with the United Kingdom. And soon afterwards he indicated that this agreement could include the NHS – before backing down a little later in the face of the emotional responses this provoked. The

British public health service is certainly a major purchaser of medicines and manages a great many hospitals, but it is above all an institution which, for many Britons, is emblematic of their country, as we saw during the 2016 referendum campaign. Yesterday, Andrew Adonis summed up the connection in a tweet: 'The NHS is the alpha & the omega of Brexit. It was there at the birth on a bus & it is now organizing the funeral.'

Today, Air Force One lands at Shannon Airport in Ireland. And as soon as he gets off the plane, in the airport lounge where he meets Leo Varadkar, Donald Trump declares that Brexit could be 'very, very good for Ireland – I think that will all work out, it will all work out very well and also for you, with your wall, your border', before launching into a parallel between the Irish border and the one between the United States and Mexico.

Leo Varadkar helpfully – and tactfully – reminds him that Ireland wants to avoid any wall or border with Northern Ireland after Brexit.

Friday, 7 June 2019: Russian border

Ivaylo Iaydjiev, Jos Hupperetz and I arrived in Helsinki yesterday for a visit to Finland. The heat is stifling, and yesterday evening, as soon as we arrived, the new Prime Minister Antti Rinne received us for a working dinner. He only officially takes office today.

Before dinner, the Border Guard Service provided us with a helicopter to fly to Vaalimaa on the Russian border. We wanted to see at first hand how, by making maximum use of new technologies, an EU country can ensure efficient and smooth border control with a large third country like Russia.

The land border between Finland and Russia is 1,340 kilometres long. It is not so much the Irish question that I have in mind as I make this visit, since there is heavy infrastructure at the border crossings here, but the fact that, whether Brexit ends up being hard or soft, it will in any case be necessary to put in place new controls for people and goods in each of the countries of the Union, as the UK becomes a third country. And I am interested in the Finnish experience of implementing technologically sophisticated controls integrated across different services.

Monday, 17 June 2019: Finalists in the campaign

Of the six candidates still in the running for Conservative Party leader, Rory Stewart is the only one not calling for a renegotiation of the Withdrawal Agreement. The others all want changes to the backstop.

What differentiates them is their methods. While Dominic Raab and Boris Johnson believe that the best strategy is to take seriously the likelihood of a no deal (something that Dominic Raab is in fact quite happy to envision…), Michael Gove wants to argue for a further extension to find a new deal, and Jeremy Hunt insists on the need to overhaul the negotiating team by including representatives of the European Research Group and the DUP, as well as Scottish and Welsh politicians. As for Sajid Javid, he proposes to cover all the costs that would be incurred by setting up alternative border arrangements in Ireland.

Wednesday, 26 June 2019: Sabine Weyand in the spotlight

Politico has a front page story on Sabine Weyand, my deputy from the very beginning of the process, who has just been appointed Director-General for Trade at the European Commission.

It is a source of great pride for all of us to read the glowing portraits of Sabine published on the occasion of this well-deserved promotion. In this one, she is described as 'the exemplar of a new breed of Brussels Eurocrat – faceless no more and empowered by social media to push their messages and agendas out from behind closed doors into the public discussion.' *Politico* goes on to describe her ability to take the wind out of the sails of her opponents.

We will miss her technical mastery, her political instinct and her humour, even if, fortunately, she will not be going far: just across the street, in fact…

Monday, 8 July 2019: Labour wants a second referendum

A minor earthquake within the Labour ranks.

Yesterday, the leaders of the trade unions, which have an intrinsic link to the Labour Party, argued in favour of a second referendum should the new Conservative government propose to Parliament a deal or a specific date for an exit without a deal. Labour would then campaign to remain in the EU.

That said, the trade unions are careful to point out that Labour does not want to remain in the EU at any cost. Indeed, should Labour win an election before Brexit and take over from the Conservatives, it would reserve the right to campaign to leave the EU on the basis of a deal it had itself struck with the EU. One thing is clear: Labour now favours a referendum on the deal – or no deal – that will be presented to Parliament.

Parliament would still need to have its say, though! And yet even this does not seem to be a given, if we are to believe the remarks of Boris Johnson, who says he does not rule out suspending the parliamentary session if MPs try to block a no deal on 31 October.

Thursday, 11 July 2019: James Dyson votes for Singapore

At the beginning of the year, James Dyson, British captain of industry and fervent Brexiteer, announced to general surprise that he had decided to transfer his company's headquarters to Singapore. I read in *Le Figaro* this morning that he himself has also decided to move to the city-state, where he has just bought a gigantic apartment. According to the newspaper, Singapore is also where Dyson is considering producing his planned electric cars, much to the chagrin of the north of England, which had hoped the company would place its factory there.

A string of decisions that are not going down well in the UK, to which Mr Dyson promised a bright future once it was released from the 'restrictions of the European Union'…

Friday, 12 July 2019: The Queen to the rescue of Parliament?

John Major has just threatened to take Boris Johnson to court if he follows through on his threat to suspend Parliament so as to force a no deal. Already all eyes are on the Queen. What would she do in such a scenario? Would she risk refusing to suspend Parliament, since she is supposed to set the agenda at the suggestion of the Prime Minister? Or would she have to stick to her role as a sovereign distanced from politics?

The new political year in the UK is shaping up to be a very eventful one.

Monday, 15 July 2019: A letter to Theresa May

In a few days, Theresa May will leave 10 Downing Street.

This is the moment for me to write to her to thank her personally, but also on behalf of my whole team, for the good cooperation we have enjoyed over the last two years.

I also thank her team, in particular Olly Robbins and Kay Withers, who in our discussions have always shown themselves to be highly capable and committed, and have loyally defended the UK government's positions throughout these negotiations.

I recall how together we constructed the Withdrawal Agreement, which I believe is the best possible agreement for citizens, businesses and governments, as well as for protecting the achievements of the Good Friday (Belfast) Agreement.

I also express my regret that political circumstances prevented the Withdrawal Agreement from being ratified during Mrs May's term of office as Prime Minister, and add that, on a personal level, I have admired her courage and determination throughout the parliamentary process in the House of Commons. Finally, I wish her all the best in her future endeavours.

Her office contacts me a few days later to let me know that Theresa May was touched by the message.

Tuesday, 16 July 2019: Ursula von der Leyen elected

An important speech in Strasbourg for Ursula von der Leyen, who has been nominated by the European Council for the post of President of the European Commission.

She is an experienced and determined woman. We have known each other for several years, in particular from the time I became special adviser to Jean-Claude Juncker on defence.

I have no doubt that today she will succeed in convincing the demanding audience of the European Parliament in plenary session, even though every vote will count!

Her opening statement is precise and enthusiastic, and draws on her personal experience. On Brexit, she speaks of how, since the 2016 referendum, the EU has worked hard with the UK government to ensure an orderly withdrawal: 'The Withdrawal Agreement concluded with the government of the United Kingdom provides certainty where Brexit created uncertainty: in preserving the rights of citizens and in preserving peace and stability on the island of Ireland. These two priorities are mine, too.'

'However', she adds, 'I stand ready for a further extension of the withdrawal date, should more time be required for a good reason', concluding that, '[i]n any case, the United Kingdom will remain our ally, our partner and our friend.'

Wednesday, 17 July 2019: Final speech

Theresa May makes her last major speech as Prime Minister at Chatham House today.

After reviewing the positive developments that have taken place in the world during her fifty years in politics, Mrs May declares that she is 'worried about the state of politics.' '[G]etting things done rather than simply getting them said requires some qualities that have become unfashionable of late', she says, such as 'a willingness to compromise', which 'does not mean compromising your values'.

The Prime Minister goes on to recall how the creation of the NHS was the result of a compromise between British political parties, that the UN Charter was also the result of a compromise between the nations of the day, and that it is also only through compromise that the Brexit impasse can be resolved:

> [M]ost people across our country had a preference for [leaving the EU] with a deal. And I believe the strength of the deal I negotiated was that it delivered on the vote of the referendum to leave the European Union, while also responding to the concerns of those who had voted to remain.

It's a courageous, well-written and necessary speech, which takes a step back, but does not necessarily encourage optimism, either about political life in general or about the Brexit negotiations in particular.

Thursday, 18 July 2019: Riga

Another Baltic day!

In Riga this morning, I am pleased to meet with Prime Minister Krišjānis Kariņš and his Deputy Prime Minister and Defence Minister Artis Pabriks. Both have been active Members of the European Parliament. They symbolize the new generation of politicians who are now taking charge, especially in the Baltic States. Further meetings are planned with parliamentarians and representatives of trade unions, the chamber of commerce and representatives of civil society.

During this period of uncertainty, I want to reiterate that the EU's priorities remain the same: to ensure an orderly withdrawal on the part of the UK, to safeguard the rights of citizens, including the tens of thousands of Latvians living in the UK, and to preserve both peace and stability in Ireland and the integrity of the Single Market.

Friday, 19 July 2019: Smoke and mirrors

On Wednesday evening, in the middle of a campaign meeting, Boris Johnson crouched down behind his lectern and stood up brandishing … a kipper.

According to the UK's potential future Prime Minister, an Isle of Man-based kipper smoker is 'utterly furious' about new EU regulations which, after years of simply sending his products through the post, would force him to accompany them with an expensive and environmentally damaging plastic ice pillow.

The problem with this story is that the regulation cited by Mr Johnson is in fact a British one, in force on the Isle of Man, which is a dependency of the British Crown… The EU's regulations, which aim to effectively protect consumers, are not the same and were in no way involved in the case in question.

'Yet another smoke!', as European Commissioner for Health and Food Safety Vytenis Andriukaitis puts it.

Tuesday, 23 July 2019: Transfer of power

Unsurprisingly, 'BoJo' has triumphed in his duel with Jeremy Hunt, receiving 66.1 per cent of the vote in the second round of the Conservative Party leadership election.

The announcement is made in front of the party's top brass at the Queen Elizabeth II Centre in London. Both candidates try to put a brave face on it. The future Prime Minister utters a few rather standard sentences in a tone that is still that of the hustings.

Nevertheless, behind the slogans I detect a strategy that comes as no surprise: 'Deliver Brexit; unite the country; defeat Jeremy Corbyn.' This is clearly the route he has chosen and that should allow him to reach an agreement with us for an effective and orderly exit on 31 October. After this, having deprived the Brexit Party of any raison d'être, it would then be in his interest to call the expected early general election and win it.

Even if he often leaves himself open to ridicule with his attitude and his jibes, I am well aware that Boris Johnson is not to be underestimated. He will be more pragmatic and more effective than some people think. I am sure he needs a deal with us to survive. And all posturing and lobbying aside, it is in his logical interest to put Brexit behind him, get a 'repackaged' deal passed and, immediately after Brexit itself, go to the country in a general election which he would then be in a position to win.

On the contrary, a no-deal exit would occasion strong opposition in the House of Commons, and would probably lead to a break with a number of his Tory colleagues, thus creating the risk of a political crisis.

On the eve of the handover, at what must be a difficult moment for her, Theresa May has taken the trouble to reply to my letter.

In her reply, the outgoing Prime Minister says that she appreciated the support that Jean-Claude Juncker and I showed to her team, and our determination to find a solution. She also praises the serious and proactive work of the task force on behalf of her colleagues, mentioning Sabine and Stéphanie in particular.

Mrs May says that this constructive relationship has enabled us to negotiate what she believes to be a good deal. She regrets, as I do, that she has not been able to obtain the support of the British Parliament for the text.

Looking ahead, she recognizes that it will be up to her successor to find a solution that respects the referendum result. She emphasizes the need to build a future relationship that will allow us to continue to work in partnership to defend our common interests and values and, crucially, to preserve the fruits of the peace process in Northern Ireland.

In the late afternoon I receive a final message from Theresa May's team. I had been careful, in my letter to the outgoing Prime Minister, to mention Olly Robbins and her deputy Kay Withers personally and to thank them. In an email to me, Olly writes: 'You didn't have to, but we appreciated it and shared it with our small team in the Cabinet Office. I hope you know that the feeling is mutual.'

Thursday, 25 July 2019: Boris Johnson at Number 10…

Yesterday Boris Johnson was officially appointed Prime Minister by the Queen. Afterwards he gave a combative speech in front of 10 Downing Street in which he reiterated his determination to leave the European Union on 31 October ('no ifs, no buts'), while expressing his confidence in the chances of finding a 'new and better deal' with the EU. According to Mr Johnson, this must be a deal 'without checks at the Irish border', and without 'that undemocratic backstop'…

This morning in the House of Commons, the Prime Minister goes further, stating that the terms of the Withdrawal Agreement are 'unacceptable' and that '[t]he way to the deal goes by way of the abolition of the backstop'. Mr Johnson says he is ready to enter into discussions with the Commission or 'other EU colleagues' only if they 'rethink their current refusal to make any changes to the Withdrawal Agreement'.

While he pledges to protect the rights of EU citizens living in the UK, he also makes the assumption that, in the event of a no deal, the UK would remain entitled to the payments outlined in the financial settlement…

Finally, Mr Johnson insists on the 'opportunities of Brexit', whether it be setting up freeports, making the tax system more favourable to international investments or … adopting GMO-friendly rules!

To implement this programme, the new government is giving pride of place to Brexiteers, from Michael Gove to Dominic Raab to Jacob Rees-Mogg, and including the former director of the Vote Leave campaign, Dominic Cummings, who becomes the Prime Minister's chief adviser.

As regards our negotiations more directly, Steve Barclay remains in post, while Boris Johnson's former adviser, David Frost, becomes the new sherpa for European affairs.

While former Remain supporters are not absent from the government, they have all agreed in writing to the goal of leaving the EU by 31 October, potentially without a deal.

At the end of the afternoon, Jean-Claude Juncker is to speak to the new Prime Minister. This is a somewhat formal ritual. I spend a few moments with him in his office before the meeting. His intention, obviously, is to be courteous – there is no reason not to be – but also to remind Boris Johnson firmly that the current Withdrawal Agreement is the only one possible.

Leaving his office, I take the long corridor from the thirteenth floor to the Secretary-General's office, where I shake hands with Martin Selmayr as he prepares to leave Berlaymont. He announced his resignation on 16 July, realizing that the election of Ursula von der Leyen, a German like himself, makes it impossible for him to continue in his job. His office is cluttered with transparent plastic boxes into which he is piling the memories of so many years of power, rarely shared.

The man has always intrigued me, and for three years we have managed to maintain what, all in all, has been a very effective relationship. I respect the essential bond between him and Jean-Claude Juncker, as well as his pro-European commitment. And he recognizes the personal trust that the President of the Commission has always placed in me. Our last conversation this evening is decidedly cordial.

'What I really want to do is to spend five years in Vienna and meet up with my students again', he says. If you know Martin Selmayr, it's hard to believe this, unless he has some personal reasons to change the course of his professional life. In any case, yesterday the Commission appointed him as head of the EU representation in Vienna, close to his native Bavaria.

It is time for the European Commission to return to a normal, more collegial way of working, with less brutal management and more relaxed, calmer human relations. At the same time, Mr Selmayr must be recognized for having been the one with the audacity to come up with certain

original ideas and new projects, and for having been able to impart new
impetus to this house which, without it, always runs the risk of reverting
to habit, long-held certainties and, on occasion, arrogance.

Thursday, 8 August 2019: Chris Patten

I have often been reminded during my mission of the premonitory
analyses of one of my former British colleagues, Chris Patten. After
having been the last Governor of Hong Kong, he joined the Commission
chaired by Romano Prodi, where he was in charge of external relations,
while I was responsible for regional policy. This morning I reread one of
his speeches, given on 30 January 2004 at Cambridge University, and
eloquently titled: 'The Existential Question – Will Britain Ever "Actually"
Join the European Union?' In this text he questioned the underlying
reasons for British leaders' dislike of Europe – a subject which, in his
view, could not be understood without recourse to psychology, since
Britons' feelings towards Europe are so much a function of their self-
image and their conception of Britain's role in the world.

Mr Patten goes on to make a careful and unapologetic examination of
five reasons why Europe has always been, for British leaders, the source
of a continual 'collective nervous breakdown': the conviction, following
the break-up of the British Empire, that Britain still has a global destiny;
a sense of being 'different and superior', backed up by references to a
largely idealized golden age; anxieties about any infringement of sovereignty and the ability to be 'master of our fate, captain of our soul';
irritation at a Europe that appeals to reason rather than to the heart; and
the certainty that, in the end, no project hatched by the Continentals
– especially the French and Germans – could possibly be any good for
Britain…

He proceeds to brilliantly dissect the premises and the limits of these
beliefs, inviting his audience to look at Britain not for what they would
like it to be, but for what it is: a diplomatic presence that, while certainly
not negligible, is no longer among the world's leading powers; one whose
voice is heard, but whose participation in the war in Iraq showed the
extent to which it is subordinate to the aims of the United States; and
a country that, without realizing it, enjoyed a great deal of influence in
Europe, whether on the Single Market or on enlargement.

In so doing, he invites the British to look at the European project differently; to consider that, while it undoubtedly entailed a sharing of sovereignty, it was proactively in the British national interest. This is one of the points that struck me most about Mr Patten during our discussions: his conviction that defence of the national interest no longer depends exclusively upon the national framework, but also upon the European framework. It's a conviction that I deeply share. I regret that it is so often absent in the discourse of many of my compatriots...

Tuesday, 20 August 2019: A letter from Boris Johnson

Last night we received a four-page letter from Boris Johnson to Donald Tusk. Both the content and the form of this letter caused great surprise, not to say annoyance, in my team and across the European capitals.

Contrary to usual protocol, we were not informed in advance of the content of this letter, despite repeated requests from my staff who had heard that it was to be sent. It seems that the aim of the Prime Minister and his entourage was to surprise us. The least one can say is that this surprise did not arouse any kind of enthusiasm – quite the contrary.

Basically, the British government is simply asking for the backstop to be abolished, without proposing any other operational legal solution that would make it possible to resolve the problem created in Ireland by Brexit. In fact, it goes even further: in one sentence, the Prime Minister himself acknowledges that, in the absence of a backstop, there would be no guarantee that hypothetical alternative arrangements would be in place in time...

An accurate observation, and indeed, this is the reason for having a backstop, which is nothing more than an insurance policy. But Boris Johnson draws no practical conclusions from this, except perhaps a call for mutual goodwill. Both sides should make a unilateral commitment not to implement a hard border in Ireland...

Unacceptable from all points of view, this approach of course elicits an immediate and unanimous response from Europeans, who simply refer to the objective of the backstop, its necessity and its pragmatic nature.

Rarely have the European institutions and the capitals spoken in one voice, as the British press pointed out, visibly surprised that the Europeans responded so quickly.

But it is President Tusk who deserves credit for coming up with the most scathing rebuttal, in a tweet stating that '[t]hose against the backstop and not proposing realistic alternatives in fact support the reinstatement of a border. Even if they do not admit it.'

I certainly share with him the feeling that this letter is in no way a sincere attempt to take up the thread of the negotiations, but instead testifies to a desire to blame EU for their potential failure. I am not sure that this was a particularly smart move, on the eve of the diplomatic sequence that lies ahead…

Tuesday, 27 August 2019: Phone call

Jean-Claude Juncker, who has just undergone surgery, was unable to meet with Boris Johnson at the G20 meeting in Biarritz, but the two leaders talk on the phone this afternoon.

The British Prime Minister clearly has a memo in front of him and he reels it off with hardly a pause.

One senses that he has been invigorated by the Biarritz summit and by his various bilateral talks with Angela Merkel, Emmanuel Macron and Donald Tusk. He believes, or claims to believe, that there is more flexibility on their part than on that of the Commission.

From the outset he says he wants a deal, 'definitively', and that the UK will exit on 31 October. 'We're also preparing for a no deal. I have three priorities: the integrity of the Single Market [!], the economic unity of Ireland, and the sovereignty and integrity of the UK. We can't go back to the British Parliament with the same deal that has been rejected three times. The backstop must be scrapped', he says, citing the paragraphs he wants removed. 'This backstop is not democratic. It's not consistent with the direction we want to go in. And Theresa May wasted too much time negotiating with you on a text where too many options remain open that we don't want, like the Customs Union and links with the Single Market.'

Mr Johnson then sets out some alternative ideas, suggesting that, on agriculture and animal control, he could accept a single framework for Ireland. 'I'd like to see you soon', he tells President Juncker, 'and I'm ready to talk with Michel.'

President Juncker briefly replies that, on the European side, we are ready to examine his proposals and ideas if they are compatible with the

Withdrawal Agreement: 'You have a Parliament in London, that's true', he says to Mr Johnson. 'But we have one in Brussels too, don't forget that.'

From the other end of the line, I distinctly hear: 'Oh God!'. Jean-Claude Juncker scores a point in this otherwise rather familiar dialogue.

Thursday, 29 August 2019: Suspension of UK Parliament

Boris Johnson has just announced the suspension of the UK Parliament from 9 September until the Queen's Speech on 14 October.

This decision will de facto leave only two weeks for British MPs to try to work out an alternative to a no-deal exit, a scenario that is looking increasingly probable. The decision seems largely to be inspired by Dominic Cummings, former director of the Vote Leave campaign and now the Prime Minister's closest adviser, who has repeatedly shown his contempt for the UK Parliament and has little more regard for the European institutions, which he believes it is urgent for the United Kingdom to leave in order to meet the challenges of tomorrow's world alone...

Sunday, 1 September 2019: Michael Gove

Michael Gove, appearing as a guest on BBC political editor Andrew Marr's show, is pressed to answer a seemingly mundane question: if Parliament passes legislation to avert a no deal, will the government comply?

The Minister's answer is less than clear: 'We will see what the legislation says.'

As Labour MP Hilary Benn later summarizes, 'It's a very simple question, so how can there be any doubt about the answer? The government must abide by any legislation that is passed by Parliament.'

Wednesday, 4 September 2019: The Benn Act

Since our first meeting, David Frost has continually promised us concrete proposals for the replacement of the backstop: originally it was coming at the beginning of August, then in mid-August, then on 23 August, then on 28 August, then today... So far, Mr Frost has only given us three general indications.

First, according to him, the objective of Boris Johnson, unlike Theresa May's government, is solely to avoid re-establishing a hard border in Ireland, rather than to preserve North–South cooperation and the 'all-island economy'. In practice, this means that the new government fully accepts that Brexit will lead to a border being reinstated in Ireland, given that between two regulatory and customs jurisdictions there must necessarily be a border. It just wants controls to be carried out elsewhere than on that border.

Second, the British say they are prepared to present us with alternative arrangements for decentralized controls, while recognizing that the issue of sanitary and phytosanitary (SPS) controls will require different measures. We must remain rigorous on this point: the health of European consumers is at stake. Furthermore, accepting half-measures on SPS controls means exposing ourselves to the risk of possible retaliatory measures from our trading partners. And this is not a purely theoretical risk: China took such measures against the EU as a whole following the mad cow disease crisis.

Third, the British recognize that these alternative arrangements are unlikely to be legally workable solutions, unlike our backstop. Yet the purpose of the Withdrawal Agreement is to provide legal certainty; it cannot contain provisions whose implementation remains unclear at the moment of ratification.

Apart from the backstop, David Frost has also mentioned a number of points in the Political Declaration that the British government would like to change. On our future economic partnership, in particular, he wants us to state unambiguously that our objective is a free trade agreement, not a customs union. In light of this, the British would like to revisit the level playing field conditions that we negotiated with Mrs May, with a view to allowing them to diverge further in the future.

This is in line with the ideas of certain Brexiteers who would like to turn the UK into a kind of Singapore on our doorstep, and practise fiscal and social dumping against us as soon as possible.

In this context we must remain vigilant, and continue to prepare ourselves for the no-deal scenario, which will never be the choice of the European Union but which we cannot rule out.

Thursday, 5 September 2019: Jo Johnson

A harsh blow for Boris Johnson: his own brother, Jo Johnson, Minister for Universities and Science, has resigned from the government.

A Remainer who is in favour of a second referendum, Jo Johnson explains his decision in a tweet: 'It's been an honour to represent Orpington for 9 years & to serve as a minister under three PMs. In recent weeks I've been torn between family loyalty and the national interest – it's an unresolvable tension & time for others to take on my roles as MP & Minister.'

Neither this resignation, nor the fact that the House of Commons yesterday passed the Benn Act, which would oblige the Prime Minister to ask the EU for a further postponement until 31 January 2020 if no agreement is reached by 19 October, seem to have led Boris Johnson to deviate from his line.

This afternoon, the Prime Minister said that he would rather 'die in a ditch' than ask the EU to postpone Brexit, before once again calling for an election in October.

Sunday, 8 September 2019: Olly Robbins

Olly Robbins joins Goldman Sachs. No comment.

I have a great deal of respect and sympathy for this senior civil servant, who may have been frustrated and bitter, but who undoubtedly still had much to contribute to public service in the UK.

Monday, 9 September 2019: Boris Johnson in Dublin

For the first time in his capacity as Prime Minister, Boris Johnson is in Dublin today to meet Leo Varadkar. And not a moment too soon.

Although their joint statement speaks of a 'positive and constructive' meeting allowing for a better understanding of positions on both sides, speaking before the press the Taoiseach does not mince his words:

> The story of Brexit does not end if the United Kingdom leaves on 31st October or even January 31st – there is no such thing as a clean break. [...] Rather, we just enter a new phase.

If there is no deal, I believe that's possible, it will cause severe disruption for British and Irish people alike. We will have to get back to the negotiating table quite quickly. When we do, the first and only items on the agenda will be citizens' rights, the financial settlement and the Irish border. All the issues we had resolved in the Withdrawal Agreement we made with your predecessor. An agreement made in good faith by twenty-eight governments.

If there is a deal – and that is (also) possible – we will enter talks on a future relationship agreement between the EU and UK. It's going to be tough dealing with issues ranging from tariffs, to fishing rights, product standards and state aid. It will then have to be ratified by thirty-one parliaments.

Negotiating FTAs with the EU and US and securing their ratification in less than three years is going to be a herculean task for you. We want to be your friend and ally, your Athena, in doing so and I think the manner in which you leave the European Union will determine that.

I am ready to listen to any constructive ways in which we can achieve our agreed goals and resolve the current impasse. But what we will not do is agree to the replacement of a legal guarantee with a promise. Our businesses need long-term certainty.

The people of this island, North and South, need to know that their livelihoods, their security and their sense of identity will not be put at risk as a consequence of a hard Brexit.

When placed alongside the Taoiseach, who speaks so lucidly and with great poise, Boris Johnson seems a little withdrawn and maladroit in his remarks. It is clear that this is a forced visit, delayed as long as he could manage it, to this country that is the closest to the UK in so many ways.

Leo Varadkar reminds him of this with emotion as he recalls the long and perilous crossing of the Atlantic in the middle of the Second World War by Winston Churchill and the British Chief of Staff Lord Alanbrooke, and their relief and excitement at the sight of the Irish coast. He concludes:

I fear the vista when you flew in this morning was not quite as spectacular or as exciting. But you are nevertheless coming at a crucial time in the history of relations between our two countries. We may sometimes differ, but we are bonded by our shared past and our shared kinship. And I think we have a shared dream, too: one of peace, freedom and prosperity.

Tuesday, 10 September 2019: The curse of Brexit

In *Le Point* Emmanuel Berretta publishes an article titled 'The Great Brexit Burnouts', in which he suggests that, from David Cameron (the 'original culprit') to Theresa May ('a martyr despite herself to a never-ending Brexit') and perhaps one day Boris Johnson, Brexit is like a machine that crushes one British politician after another.

Its latest victim is John Bercow, the Speaker of the House of Commons, known for his mastery of parliamentary procedure and tactics, his talent at presiding over parliamentary debates with his resounding cries of '*Order!*', and his multicoloured ties.

This afternoon, the Speaker announced that he would like to make a personal statement:

> At the 2017 election, I promised my wife and children that it would be my last. This is a pledge that I intend to keep.
>
> If the House votes tonight for an early general election, my tenure as Speaker and MP will end when this Parliament ends. If the House does not so vote, I have concluded that the least disruptive and most democratic course of action would be for me to stand down at the close of business on Thursday, October 31.
>
> Throughout my time as speaker, I have sought to increase the relative authority of this legislature for which I will make absolutely no apology to anyone, anywhere, at any time.

Mr Bercow, who has always been careful to divide parliamentary time fairly between MPs, including those who do not always take centre stage, added: 'To deploy a perhaps dangerous phrase: I have also sought to be the backbenchers' backstop.'

British parliamentary debates will certainly be all the poorer for the loss of Mr Bercow's voice, colourful ties and, above all, his great competence in the role.

Thursday, 12 September 2019: New Parliament, new Commission

Before joining the seminar organized by Ursula von der Leyen with the new Commissioners at Genval, I take up an invitation this morning to attend the Conference of the Presidents of the European Parliament's political groups.

I make no secret of the fact that at this stage we have little reason for optimism, but say that we remain open and available to work with the British, if they can provide answers to the questions and problems created by Brexit in Ireland.

Philippe Lamberts, quick-witted as ever, quizzes me on a sensitive point: 'Has Boris Johnson made a move to return to the first backstop proposal which only concerned Northern Ireland?'

I choose to respond cautiously, because a few feet away from me is Diane Dodds, one of the leaders of the DUP, who sits in the European Parliament as a non-attached member. When she speaks a little later, I am struck by her own caution on the substantive issues. She no longer rejects any Northern Ireland solution in general terms, as she had done up until now, but insists only on the requirement for a 'consent' procedure, and on the requirement that both communities in Northern Ireland, Unionist and Republican, have a veto over any solution.

Friday, 13 September 2019: Team meeting

At 8 o'clock this morning I meet the President-elect's new Head of Cabinet, Bjoern Seibert, who has long been Ursula von der Leyen's right-hand man at the Ministry of Defence in Berlin.

This tall young man is direct in his dealings. He remembers the work we did together on European defence, together with Ursula von der Leyen, back in 2015.

I want our conversation to put an end to the uncertainty, and even anxiety, of my team. Stéphanie told me a few days ago that she had been asked to head up the cabinet of the French Commissioner-designate Sylvie Goulard. A logical and quite legitimate move given her energy and capability, but this departure, coming so soon after that of Sabine, and recently of François Arbault, another pillar of the task force, risks exacerbating these anxieties. I need to reassure my team and put things into perspective for everyone, while at the same time ensuring the continuity of the negotiations during a sensitive phase.

Bjoern Seibert understands what is at stake. Rather than decentralizing the negotiations to the level of the Directorates-General, we agreed that the task force responsible for coordinating the future negotiations with the United Kingdom should be maintained under my authority for the coming year, in direct contact with the President and her cabinet, of course. I agree to integrate the small team from the General Secretariat which had worked on the preparations for no deal.

Sunday, 15 September 2019: The Hulk

In an interview with the *Daily Mail*, Boris Johnson optimistically reports that 'huge progress' has been made towards a Brexit deal.

Confirming his desire to leave the Union on 31 October, the Prime Minister invokes the comic-book character Hulk: 'The madder Hulk gets, the stronger Hulk gets. Hulk always escaped, no matter how tightly bound in he seemed to be – and that is the case for this country.'

The comparison has its limits: no one has tied down the United Kingdom, which has always been an influential member of the Union since it joined in 1973. Nor is there anything stopping the UK from leaving the Union, except perhaps the difficulty the British seem to find in agreeing amongst themselves…

Monday, 16 September 2019: Lunch in Luxembourg

I drive to Luxembourg and meet Stéphanie Riso, whom I expressly asked to be present along with Clara Martínez Alberola for this working lunch, to which Jean-Claude Juncker has invited Boris Johnson.

The city centre of Luxembourg is charming, and very sunny today. Everything is on a human scale, and one can very quickly get from the Grand Duke's Palace to the Parliament or the Prime Minister's residence.

At the appointed hour, Boris Johnson arrives by car in front of the restaurant where a hundred journalists and photographers are waiting for the handshake. This is the first time he has met the President of the European Commission since 24 July when he first arrived at 10 Downing Street, but it seems they have older memories in common.

From the outset, Mr Johnson appears as he wants to be: tough, moving like a bulldozer, clearly trying to force his way through. But there is something genuine and mischievous in his eyes and in the expression on his face. All in all, a rather likeable character.

Obviously, Mr Johnson wants to show that he is actively negotiating with us. In fact, he has stated in public that there has been significant progress in the negotiations on the basis of his ideas, and even that we are close to an agreement, which does not correspond to the reality of the situation.

He takes the time to reiterate what is already in the documents we have received. He does not want the backstop. He wants a consent process for Northern Ireland. He wants to build a strong relationship with the European Union, but based on a basic free trade agreement.

For Northern Ireland, he makes a move towards a single island-wide control system for live animals and sanitary and phytosanitary products. He also takes up a famous statement made by Northern Ireland's Unionist leader, the Reverend Ian Paisley, acknowledging that 'our citizens may be British but our cows are Irish'. At which point I cut in with: 'Your cows are not Irish, they are European', to which he replies, 'Good point!'

Jean-Claude Juncker, in turn, reminds him why the abolition of the backstop pure and simple is impossible, but adds that we are prepared to replace it with another solution provided it is operational and fulfils the same objectives of peace in Ireland, the absence of a hard border, and obviously the protection of the internal market.

The conversation then gets into the details. Stéphanie Riso explains in full to the British Prime Minister why we need customs information on the quality and quantity of products entering Northern Ireland. Only with such an information system can sanitary and phytosanitary controls be effective. My impression is that during the course of this explanation the Prime Minister begins to understand a series of technical and legal problems that have not been explained to him very clearly by his own team. I can see that his main problem is the trade and customs sovereignty of the United Kingdom, in which he obviously includes Northern Ireland. He promises to send us more detailed written material shortly, as we have been asking him to do for several days.

In closing, Mr Johnson tells us, very frankly, 'I want a deal, I need a deal.' He now knows the conditions: no hard border in the middle of the island of Ireland and no veto for a single Northern Irish party. The Prime Minister then goes out to join the BBC journalists, while I go to Prime Minister Xavier Bettel's office for a brief meeting. He himself is due to receive Boris Johnson, who is visiting his capital, a few minutes later. As he escorts me into the main courtyard of his residence we pass the same hundred or so journalists, but also, a little further on, two hundred anti-Brexit demonstrators loudly anticipating the arrival of the British Prime Minister.

Mr Bettel tells me that he is annoyed because Boris Johnson's staff have asked at the last minute for the press briefing to be relocated to an inside location away from the protesters. 'There are too many journalists', he tells me, 'and everything is set up in the courtyard. I can't change it all at the last minute.'

A little later, after their brief meeting, Mr Johnson simply chooses not to hold the press conference with the Prime Minister, and immediately gets into his car. And so Mr Bettel decides to speak alone, standing next to a second, unoccupied lectern. Images of this press conference travel round the UK and are interpreted immediately by journalists and tabloids alike as an attempt to humiliate the British Prime Minister.

The true story, minor as it is, is different, and simpler – but it all goes to prove that there is continuing sensitivity and passion around Brexit that cannot be ignored.

Wednesday, 18 September 2019: Plenary in Strasbourg

There are many new faces in the great hemicycle of the European Parliament in Strasbourg today. Sixty percent of the MEPs here have been elected for the first time, and I have decided to take the time to inform them of our work by meeting their political groups, visiting their committees, or writing to them.

I find myself standing beside Jean-Claude Juncker, still a little shaken by his recent operation but upright as ever despite being in pain.

He asks me to speak after him. I use the occasion to say a few words about the two key issues in our current discussions with the British: Ireland and Northern Ireland, and the future relationship.

On the backstop, I point out that our insistence is pragmatic, not ideological. Behind the word 'backstop' there lie very concrete guarantees, which we need, and which all citizens on the island of Ireland need – for the sake of peace and stability, for the sake of everyday life and economic relations on the island. And of course, for the health of the consumers of the twenty-seven, the safety of products and the protection of national budgets, which requires controls on the outer edges of our internal market.

The other key issue over which the British government is seeking to renege on the commitments made by Theresa May is the 'level playing field' that must accompany any ambitious future relationship between ourselves and the UK. Behind this technical expression lie human, social and territorial realities. Any ambitious economic partnership with a large country so close to us, and which does half its trade with us, will require a set of common ground rules.

Things are clear enough: the level of ambition of a future free trade agreement will depend upon the guarantees we have put down on paper in regard to social, environmental, competition and state aid issues.

On these questions and others, we remain willing to hear out any British proposal, provided that it brings progress.

Friday, 20 September 2019: Steve Barclay

In a speech in Madrid yesterday Steve Barclay once again rejected the backstop, saying that he saw no need for a legally workable solution in the Withdrawal Agreement since the UK will retain the rights and obligations of a member state until the end of 2020, as part of the transition period agreed with Theresa May.

Mr Barclay called on the EU to be flexible and to compromise, even going so far as to invoke General de Gaulle:

> Great political leaders have always respected the need to take risk. Indeed It was General de Gaulle, who said 'a true statesman is one who is willing to take risks'. Yet a refusal by the Commission to accept any risk would be a failure of statecraft. And put at risk the future relationship of the UK and the EU because of a lack of flexibility, creativity and indeed pragmatism. Leadership requires more than remaining within a safety net.

This morning, Mr Barclay is in Brussels, and I open our meeting with four framing remarks.

First, following our lunch on Monday, our position is extremely clear. The onus is on the UK to make legal and operational proposals that are compatible with the Withdrawal Agreement and that therefore respect the objectives of the backstop. The Commission is available at any time to examine any such proposals rigorously and objectively. However, we are not prepared to pretend to negotiate.

Second, on the alternatives to the backstop mentioned by Mr Barclay in Madrid, it is true that we are committed to doing our utmost, after the ratification of the Withdrawal Agreement and by December 2020, to conclude a subsequent agreement on alternative arrangements that could replace the backstop in whole or in part. But it is precisely because we are not sure, despite all of our respective efforts, that we can achieve this result – which we have not achieved thus far in three years of work! – that we need the backstop, which is nothing more nor less than an insurance policy, to be included in the Withdrawal Agreement. In other words, we are absolutely not prepared to accept the removal of the backstop in favour of nothing more than alternative, non-operational arrangements.

Third, I tell Mr Barclay that I was particularly sensitive to his citing of General de Gaulle, having been a member of the Gaullist party since my teens. However, I tell him that I do not accept his use of it here, because the risks we are talking about are too serious for us to take refuge in posturing. We are talking about preserving the peace and stability of the island of Ireland and the integrity of the internal market. The Union will never agree to jeopardize these objectives; they are part of who we are. Statesmanship means doing everything possible to ensure that such objectives are not placed at risk.

I push the point home: 'There are two things that may be important for you to know about General de Gaulle. The first is that, in 1958, the General implemented the Treaty of Rome when he became President of the French Republic, despite all his misgivings – and that he was very much attached to the Common Market. The second is that General de Gaulle loved Ireland, and had personal and family ties to the island...'

Finally, I reaffirm that an agreement is possible, but that it can only take place in a respectful and constructive spirit. We will not accept threats. And we will not accept any attack on the European Commission, which, I remind him once again, is negotiating on behalf of and with the full confidence of the twenty-seven member states.

Today is also a day of transition for our team. In a tweet I confirm the departure of Stéphanie Riso, who is now working alongside Sylvie Goulard, and has thus left our team very suddenly.

My concern is to ensure the continuity of our work and our relationship with the British, and I am fortunate to have a series of strong and capable unit heads and managers to support me in this. All of them know that this is a crucial moment and that everyone is on the job. But we also need a team leader to face the British negotiator, David Frost.

I therefore call on Paulina Dejmek Hack to take on this mission alongside me. She has been on the Commission President's team for five years and has been responsible for following the Brexit dossier from day one. Jean-Claude Juncker has agreed to make her available to the task force as a matter of urgency – we will settle administrative matters later.

Paulina is an extraordinarily energetic and capable young woman – as well as being a sportswoman who is used to running marathons. Through her parents she is both Swedish and Czech! I know her well because she worked for five years in my office as Commissioner for the Internal Market and Financial Services. At that time, along with Bertrand Dumont, she was in charge of implementing the financial regulation roadmap set out by the G20 at the height of the 2008 crisis. We have a long history of working together, and I trust her implicitly.

Tuesday, 24 September 2019: Supreme Court

As part of my ongoing tour of the European capitals, I have been in Berlin since yesterday.

After a meeting with Uwe Corsepius, Angela Merkel's sherpa, I have lunch with Peter Altmaier in the large dining room of the Bundesministerium für Wirtschaft und Energie, where the great Ludwig Erhard once sat. Peter has been an 'old friend' in Europe for twenty-five years and is very close to the Chancellor. He always takes the time to explain German policy and its impact on European policy to me, which, however, has not always worked to my advantage… My impression has generally been that he and the Chancellor do not enjoy open conflict, but this does not prevent them from acting with a firm hand. Today's lunch is lively and jovial, and the Minister has a few words and anecdotes for my advisers Stefan Fuehring, Georg and Matthieu, whom he even confuses with one of his former comrades at the Commission. Matthew is easily twenty years younger, but it matters little; Peter is at the top of his game.

And it is at this point that Uwe Corsepius, whom we have just left, calls Georg with the shocking news that in a unanimous decision, the UK Supreme Court has ruled that Boris Johnson's suspension of Parliament is illegal.

This is no time for hasty reactions, but the significance of this reversal in London is clear.

The reading of the judgment by Lady Hale, Chief Justice of the Supreme Court, is illuminating. In particular, the Court found that

> the decision to advise Her Majesty to prorogue Parliament was unlawful because it had the effect of frustrating or preventing the ability of Parliament to carry out its constitutional functions without reasonable justification.
>
> This means that the Order in Council to which it led was also unlawful, void and of no effect and should be quashed. This means that when the Royal Commissioners walked into the House of Lords it was as if they walked in with a blank sheet of paper. The prorogation was also void and of no effect. Parliament has not been prorogued.

Boris Johnson intended to dispense with parliamentary debate at this critical stage of the Brexit process. That was too much, too fast. In London, the game is not over yet.

Thursday, 26 September 2019: Jacques Chirac

At midday, Jacques Chirac's death is announced. The media goes crazy and I receive many requests from journalists looking for a reaction.

Alone in my office, I take the time for a slightly nostalgic pause. So many memories come flooding back, of good and bad times spent with Chirac.

I had never been a 'Chiracian' until June 1995 when, to my surprise, Alain Juppé asked me, in the name of the new President of the Republic Jacques Chirac, to remain in the government and become Minister Delegate for European Affairs. I had supported Édouard Balladur in the presidential campaign. I was his Minister for the Environment, he trusted me and was a member of my party.

I remember a few weeks later being received at the Élysée Palace by the new president and telling him how astonished I was: 'For ten years you mistrusted me for no reason, because I had a more European and more Jacobin line than yours; now you have a real reason not to trust me and you are appointing me as minister.' His answer came immediately, and was an eminently practical one: 'I need you, I need a Gaullist and European Minister for European Affairs. And also, back then, you did not betray me.'

My history with Chirac goes back much further, though. As a young parliamentary attaché to Robert Poujade, the first French Minister for the Environment, I had looked on in amazement at a meeting of the Gaullist group during which he launched into a public assassination of our party's candidate, Jacques Chaban-Delmas. Already, over several years of being involved in the young Gaullist movement, I had totally identified with the cause and the commitment of the Gaullist, European and progressive mayor of Bordeaux. And I had fervently put myself forward to participate in his presidential campaign.

A few years later, in 1977, as a young general councillor of Savoie in the Haute-Tarentaise region, I launched myself into the parliamentary campaign to win the seat of the second constituency from the Socialist Party. During the campaign Jacques Chirac methodically visited each of his candidates' constituencies. He came to support me on 22 December, in Albertville – and I really needed it!

This campaign rally is engraved in my memory: it was held in a former church converted into a multipurpose hall. Four hundred people had responded to my invitation. It was a cold day and Jacques Chirac, standing at the lectern, made very indulgent and friendly remarks about me, as was customary for a candidate of his party.

Having invited questions from the audience, he gave the floor to a female citizen in the centre of the room who issued him with a sharp rebuke: 'Mr Chirac, politicians often do the opposite of what they say. You saw fit just now to talk to us about the place of women in society. However, just yesterday in Paris, you passed over one of the rare female deputies in your party in favour of nominating a press baron … for reasons that I prefer not to go into here. Who do you think we are, here in the depths of Savoie? Do you think we don't know what goes on in Paris?'

Chirac rose to the occasion. He had obviously not expected such an aggressive question so early on, in a quiet Savoie valley. But he replied with his usual savoir-faire to this voter that she did not understand what she was talking about. Furious, he returned to sit beside me in the gallery and elbowed me rather roughly: 'Who is that woman?' To which I answered, a little sheepishly: 'That's my mother...'

From that day on, Jacques Chirac no doubt considered me as a rather special elected official. My mother, who meant a great deal to me, was a wonderful woman and a real *grande dame*, heavily involved in civic life. She said to me at the end of that meeting: 'You will never stop me from speaking my mind.'

My relationship with Chirac was one of ups and downs, all connected with Europe.

In 1992, together with five other Gaullist party deputies, including Jacques Chaban-Delmas and Patrick Devedjian, I decided against all the odds to vote in favour of the constitutional reform necessary to enable François Mitterrand's referendum on the Maastricht Treaty, and the creation of the single currency.

I remember the violence of Jacques Chirac's reaction in the group meeting, when he named me directly: 'I've had enough of the egocentric attitude of Michel Barnier and some others.' And yet, a few months later, he himself chose to campaign for a yes vote for the single currency, against a faction of his political party led by Philippe Séguin; thanks to Chirac, the yes vote won by a narrow margin.

After our bitter defeat in 1997 in the ill-timed early legislative elections that he had called, I decided, together with my friends Jean-Pierre Raffarin, Jacques Barrot and Dominique Perben, to help him. The Élysée Palace was often empty during the first months of this cohabitation with the new socialist Prime Minister Lionel Jospin, and evening visitors had become rare. The four of us had imagined the beginnings of a new political consensus between Gaullists, liberals and centrists.

I also remember Jacques Chirac's astonished reaction in 1999 when I told him of my ambition to become a European Commissioner and therefore of my desire to quit the presidency of the General Council of Savoie, which I had held for seventeen years, along with my brand new mandate as a senator: 'You want to become a senior civil servant?' Obviously, in his eyes, a European Commissioner was little more than a prefect on secondment. But in the new relationship that had developed between us since the failure of the legislative elections, he trusted my judgement, and I became one of the two French Commissioners in Romano Prodi's Commission, along with Pascal Lamy.

Three years later, Jacques Chirac was re-elected in very special circumstances, against Jean-Marie Le Pen, and I was at his side on the evening of the election, along with all those who had genuinely supported him. A few days later he appointed Jean-Pierre Raffarin as Prime Minister and we shared some moving and warm moments with him.

On the evening of Mr Raffarin's appointment, I was on my way to meet my family in Brussels when the phone rang. It was Jacques Chirac, calling in person to ask me to accept the position of Minister of National Education. I was in the middle of my time as a Commissioner and, to my knowledge, no European Commissioner had ever returned to his own country to enter domestic politics in the middle of a term of office. I told him simply: 'Jacques, thank you for your confidence in me, but to leave now, when I am beginning to build a network and credibility, would be disrespectful toward the other countries and the European institutions.' He called me back twice the next morning but I held firm, and on this subject he concluded, in a dry tone: 'Very well, you take your chances.' Which did not prevent him, two years later, at the end of my mandate, from appointing me Minister of Foreign Affairs!

Thursday, 3 October 2019: UK proposal

Yesterday Boris Johnson made some new proposals to try to secure a deal before the European Council on 17 October.

He unveiled them at the close of the Conservative Party Congress in Manchester, in a colourful speech where, as usual, he raised a laugh, this time at the expense of John Bercow and Jeremy Corbyn, whom he described as a 'communist cosmonaut'. And, ultimately, at the expense of the British Parliament itself.

This morning I decide to open a 'reading room' for delegates from the member states to read the legal document sent by the British, who expressly requested that it not be published – the opposite of the transparency that we have been practising on the EU side. Last night, in a telephone conversation with Boris Johnson, Jean-Claude Juncker made this clear to him. But since I want to preserve the bond of trust with the governments and their embassies, and so that no one on our side gets the feeling that I am hiding something, I wanted to make sure that the text could be read.

In our own reading of the document we have discovered some 'holes'. The British have amended the Ireland/Northern Ireland Protocol to the Withdrawal Agreement, but in the process they have also deleted a number of paragraphs and recitals from our own text without mentioning it. Let us put this down to haste…

So what is the content of the new proposals?

There are some positive moves, for example the alignment of Northern Ireland with EU rules on goods, supported by a system of controls – yet to be defined – for goods entering Northern Ireland from Britain or from third countries.

But there are three basic problems with the proposals.

First, of the three objectives we set out to satisfy with the backstop, the only one that would be achieved – or half-achieved – is the absence of a hard border, although it's not clear how. The realization of this one objective would potentially come at the expense of the other two, namely the preservation of the European internal market and the economy of the whole island of Ireland.

The second serious point is that the proposed solutions are by no means operational. On the fundamental issue of customs and the system of regulatory controls in Northern Ireland, the British refer to arrangements yet to be worked out. This contrasts sharply with the firm commitment they are asking us to make immediately to rule out all controls at the border between Ireland and Northern Ireland. In our view, these two points are irreconcilable.

Finally, all the proposed solutions are conditional on a positive and unilateral decision being made by the Northern Ireland institutions, both before they come into force and then again every four years. This is simply unacceptable. We will not discuss a solution with such a sword of Damocles hanging over it.

In the short time we have left between now and the European Council in October – about ten days – we therefore need to see some fundamental changes if we are to reach an agreement.

Tuesday, 8 October 2019: Dominic Cummings

The atmosphere is growing tense.

Last night, the *Spectator* published a response sent to one of its journalists, James Forsyth, from 'a contact at 10 Downing Street' whom he had asked about the state of negotiations. In this rather shocking text, the 'contact' in question writes:

> The negotiations will probably end this week. Varadkar doesn't want to negotiate. Varadkar was keen on talking before the Benn Act when he thought that the choice would be 'new deal or no deal'. Since the Benn Act passed he has gone very cold and in the last week the official channels and the backchannels have also gone cold. [...]
>
> If this deal dies in the next few days, then it won't be revived. To marginalize the Brexit Party, we will have to fight the election on the basis of 'no more delays, get Brexit done immediately'.
>
> Those who pushed the Benn Act intended to sabotage a deal and they've probably succeeded. So the main effect of it will probably be to help us win an election by uniting the leave vote and then a no-deal Brexit. History is full of such ironies and tragedies.

It is not very difficult to detect the hand of Dominic Cummings behind these remarks.

The Prime Minister's chief adviser, with his often casual style, is said to have largely inspired not just Boris Johnson's illegal decision to suspend Parliament at this crucial moment in the Brexit negotiations, but also the expulsion from the Conservative Party on 4 September of twenty-one Tory MPs who had voted with Labour MPs the day before. He has also spent more time preparing for a no-deal exit than working on constructive proposals for a deal...

However, this tension within the British cabinet is being felt on the other side of the Channel. In a tweet, President-designate of the European Council Charles Michel gets straight to the point: '@BorisJohnson, what's at stake is not winning some stupid blame game. At stake is the future of Europe and the UK as well as the security and interests of our people. You don't want a deal, you don't want an extension, you don't want to revoke, *quo vadis?*'

Friday, 11 October 2019: A few steps forward

Boris Johnson and Leo Varadkar met again yesterday in Liverpool, in a more positive atmosphere. According to the Irish government, with whom we had set up this meeting, and who reported back to us immediately afterwards, Mr Johnson is now ready to accept the absence of customs controls on the island, even if it means strengthening controls between Great Britain and Northern Ireland. This is essential if we are to make progress.

For his part, Mr Varadkar said that he was ready to work on a mechanism that would strengthen democratic support for our solution.

This morning I have Steve Barclay back here for breakfast, and he confirms these two steps forward made yesterday. I welcome them, but have to put them into context. The need for movement comes primarily because the UK government has reneged on major commitments made by Theresa May. Removing the backstop represents a huge step backwards. The new proposals are therefore far from sufficient.

Coming to an agreement requires that we agree on four fundamental points.

On the consent procedure, first, we cannot accept a mechanism that would make the entry into force of the protocol conditional upon the agreement of the DUP and would then continue to question its existence every four years. As Leo Varadkar said to Boris Johnson yesterday, we are still prepared to work on a mechanism that would strengthen democratic support for our solution.

Second, on customs: we cannot work on the basis of a proposal to create a customs border on the island. We cannot accept any ambiguity on this point. What is at stake is the all-island economy, which is very important to Leo Varadkar, but also to the integrity of the internal market.

Third, we cannot accept a solution in Ireland that has to be developed by the Joint Committee established by the Withdrawal Agreement before it becomes fully operational.

Finally, robust level playing field guarantees are a precondition for a broad and ambitious free trade agreement.

And now I come to the operational aspects: 'In three hours, I am meeting the twenty-seven ambassadors at Coreper. They want to know whether or not you are serious about reaching an agreement. So there are two options: either you tell me that you are ready to accept these four points as a working basis, and my team and I can then prepare to enter into intensive negotiations this weekend, or you do not and I will have to tell the ambassadors that nothing is to be expected between now and next week's European Council, where Brexit may not even be on the agenda.'

Steve Barclay gives me his agreement to work on the basis of these four points. At half past midday, I inform the twenty-seven ambassadors, who authorize me to open an intensive discussion, which the press quickly begin describing as a 'tunnel' – a term I did not use.

Sunday, 13 October 2019: Negotiations

Since yesterday morning, the corridors and meeting rooms of the task force have been packed. The two teams worked late in the evening and then again all day today, but we are far from reaching a conclusion.

So it is that, at 5pm on a Sunday, I am obliged to inform the twenty-seven ambassadors, and later in the evening the members of the European Parliament's Brexit Steering Group, that it seems very unlikely that between now and the European Council we will be able to reach an agreement in the form of legally binding texts to cover all the outstanding points. Unless, of course, the British delegation receives some new political impetus.

The most serious immediate issue for all of us is that of customs procedures and controls. Over the last two days the British delegation, led by David Frost, has not backtracked – at least in principle – on the significant concession made by the Prime Minister and confirmed by Steve Barclay on Friday, namely that there is no longer any question of there being a customs border between the north and south of the island of Ireland.

In our view, all the customs procedures and controls that we need in order to protect the internal market must therefore be put in place around the island. So we have to find a way to reconcile two objectives.

On the one hand, the objective for us Europeans that all customs procedures and checks required by EU law should be carried out in some way on goods entering Northern Ireland, before they arrive on the island.

On the other hand, for the British Prime Minister, the objective that Northern Ireland should remain an integral part of British customs territory, with all the consequences that implies.

Yesterday morning we proposed that discussions should begin again from our original proposal in this negotiation, specific to Northern Ireland, which we are prepared to adjust to reflect the British wish that Northern Ireland remain, *de jure*, within the British customs territory.

This proposal was not accepted, as the British wanted to set out from a new idea closer to Theresa May's March 2018 proposal, namely a system in which a distinction would be made between goods coming into Northern Ireland from Great Britain and for which Northern Ireland would be the final destination, and goods coming into Northern Ireland from Great Britain destined for the European Union.

The fundamental problem with this idea is that it means two customs areas, despite the absence of a customs border between the north and south of the island. It would lead to products with both British and European statuses – sometimes the same products – circulating within Northern Ireland.

As a result, these proposals run the risk of unravelling our customs code in order to introduce new exceptions. They also bring with them a major fraud risk, given the difficulty of controlling the final destination of the goods in question, particularly when they are to be further processed.

I give the example of a shipment of sugar arriving in Northern Ireland via Great Britain through a bilateral agreement with a third country. This sugar is processed into a food product in Northern Ireland that could then be sent to Dublin, where it would enter the Single Market... It is clear from this example that, as far as goods coming into Northern Ireland are concerned, it would be difficult to distinguish whether they will remain in Northern Ireland or are ultimately destined for the internal market.

The same could be said of steel coming from a third country into Northern Ireland, to be incorporated into industrial products there which would then be sent into the internal market.

There is simply no precedent for such an arrangement. But we remain willing to keep working to find legal and practical solutions to the problems raised by the British, provided they accept our concept of a full customs regime upon entrance to the island.

Next, on the sensitive issue of the consent procedure, I confirm to the twenty-seven ambassadors that the British have given up on the idea of granting a unilateral veto to certain political parties in Northern Ireland before the end of the transition.

We are aware that the Taoiseach and Prime Minister Johnson have discussed other ideas apart from this for ensuring that the consent of both communities can be obtained at regular intervals.

But some questions remain unanswered. Would this involve a yes vote to maintain the system or a no vote to discontinue it? Also, what majority would be needed in the Northern Ireland Assembly in order to secure this decision?

I remind the ambassadors that I have no mandate in relation to any of these points, and that therefore the discussion has not been initiated.

Finally, apart from the Protocol on Ireland and Northern Ireland, I report to the ambassadors on our discussions on the Political Declaration setting out the framework for the future relationship.

The British have given us some clarifications, in particular on the dispute settlement mechanism. But at this stage they are holding to their wish to delete specific references, agreed with Theresa May, to a robust level playing field, taking into account our geographical proximity and economic interdependence with the UK. We have strongly reiterated that any reference in the Political Declaration to a free trade agreement – which the British are keen to see – would only be possible if accompanied by these provisions on the level playing field.

In conclusion, I share with the ambassadors our impression that, had the British team really had the will or the mandate to do so, we could have made very substantial progress based on the adaptation of our February 2018 proposal, except on the issue of consent. But this was not the case. Nevertheless, I propose to continue the discussion with the British tomorrow.

Tuesday, 15 October 2019: Vigil at the Berlaymont

After an inconclusive weekend, discussions with the British team resumed yesterday morning and, at the time of writing, are still ongoing with regard to the technical details.

Without any concrete developments to analyse, many journalists around the Berlaymont simply note that it is past midnight and that the lights on the fifth floor are still on. Not for the first time during these negotiations, far from it…

Wednesday, 16 October 2019: A breakthrough on Ireland

The negotiations of recent days and nights have at last borne fruit. Specifically, we have found a solution on the crucial issue of customs procedures and controls in Northern Ireland.

This solution is in line with EU principles. All customs procedures and controls under EU law will apply to goods entering the island of Ireland. These procedures and controls will be subject to the powers of control of EU officials and the jurisdiction of the EU Court of Justice.

In order to reconcile our requirements with Boris Johnson's demands, we have agreed on an exception: goods coming from Great Britain into Northern Ireland, i.e. staying within the British customs territory, and which do not pose a risk of further movement into the Single Market, according to criteria to be defined by the Joint Committee, will not be subject to EU customs duties.

With this solution we avoid risks to the internal market while respecting the fact that Northern Ireland remains part of the UK's customs territory.

We also recognize that, by virtue of being part of the UK's customs territory, Northern Ireland will benefit from the UK's trade arrangements with third countries – provided, again, that Northern Ireland is the final destination of the imported goods.

This means that such goods imported into Northern Ireland will, in principle, be subject to the EU's common external tariff, unless they are goods that present no risk of further movement into the Single Market. In such cases, the goods will be subject not to the common external tariff but to the UK customs tariff, if there is disparity between the two. Goods manufactured in Northern Ireland and exported under these UK trade arrangements will have UK tariffs applied.

On the vexed issue of consent, discussions over the last few days, in Brussels but also in London between the government and the DUP, have also made it possible to reach an agreement that considerably strengthens the democratic accountability of the Irish Protocol.

In practice, four years after the Protocol comes into force, the Northern Ireland Assembly will be able to decide, by a simple majority of those present and voting, whether it should continue to be applied.

If an overall majority is obtained, the Protocol will continue to apply for a further four years, at the end of which a new vote will be held.

Over and above this simple overall majority, if the decision to continue to apply the Protocol receives a cross-community majority, then the Protocol will continue to apply for a longer period of eight years, at the end of which, as before, a new vote will take place.

If there is no majority in favour of continuing to apply the Protocol, it will cease to apply after a cooling-off period of two years, during which time the necessary measures to replace it must be agreed upon.

Finally, we have reached agreement on the issue of the level playing field for our future partnership, a subject upon which Antonio Fernández-Martos and Nicolas von Lingen had to fight to the very end. The British are making a firm commitment to a future relationship that will ensure open and fair competition. The free trade agreement with zero tariffs or quotas will be conditional upon the maintenance of high standards on state aid, competition, social and environmental standards, climate change and fiscal transparency. We also reiterate our commitment to promote the Paris climate agreement.

I return from a meeting with the Brexit Steering Group, where I held a final detailed briefing with Guy Verhofstadt and the other European Parliament leaders. The small team and I eat pizza in my office, and prepare for the final stretch.

A little earlier in the evening, after the British delegation had left, to our surprise David Frost and Tim Barrow came back in, accompanied by a dozen tax experts. Their objective was clear: to obtain, through a lengthy negotiating session, a rewrite of the VAT chapter of the Protocol on Ireland and Northern Ireland. On the pretext of being able to assure the UK that control of tax services remains in British hands, what they actually want is to give Northern Ireland a major tax advantage within the Single Market itself. Not a chance.

Thursday, 17 October 2019: Deal!

A date that has special resonance for me, for it was on 17 October, at 11am, back in 1986, together with Jean-Claude Killy and another fine team, that we won the bid for Albertville and Savoie to host the 1992 Olympic Games.

Once again, the lights in our fifth-floor offices were on most of last night. Having heard out the British, we explained that what they were asking for was impossible. It was no longer the appropriate time to extend the discussion further. But in the end we were able to propose some amendments to the text. Northern Ireland will remain within the UK territory for VAT purposes, and the UK tax authorities will be responsible for enforcing the legislation and for collecting the VAT, the proceeds of which the UK will keep. But in order to avoid a hard border on the island of Ireland and to protect the integrity of the Single Market, EU rules on VAT on goods will continue to apply in Northern Ireland.

This final night demonstrates the importance, at critical moments, of keeping all expertise in play right until the end. Eugenia, Antonio, Stefan, Hannes, Thomas, Philippe, Nina, Nicolas, Georg, Ivo: they were all there scrutinizing the agreement down to the last comma. On behalf of our team, Paulina Dejmek, joined by Richard Szostak from the cabinet of the President of the Commission, asked the British for a final agreement on the text by 6 o'clock this morning. At 8 o'clock, the British are back at it as usual, despite our evident exasperation. David Frost proposes a final amendment to give Northern Ireland the legal capacity to harmonize its VAT rates on a number of consumer products with the VAT exemptions and reduced rates applied by Ireland next door.

He also takes the opportunity to bring up the famous subject of the 'tampon tax', the VAT rate applicable to tampons and sanitary towels, a source of regular controversy between the EU and the UK, which in the past wanted to apply a 0 per cent rate while the minimum rate in force in the European Union is 5 per cent. Ireland, which did not tax these products before joining the EU, has won the right to maintain its 0 per cent rate, and the British are demanding the same for Northern Ireland.

I quite understand the request, which is not entirely in line with European rules but which will avoid distortions on the island of Ireland. And I can't see myself explaining to the European Council that negotiations have failed because of a disagreement on the taxation of these essential hygiene products. So we agree to this one last amendment.

At 9am, Boris Johnson calls Jean-Claude Juncker. Even while expressing his thanks to our teams, the Prime Minister tries yet again to obtain further concessions on VAT. Naturally, President Juncker tells him that it is no longer the time for negotiation. I had told the President before this phone call that the time pressure is on the side of the British Prime Minister, not ours. Courteously but firmly, Juncker sets a final deadline for Mr Johnson, who then has to immediately convene his cabinet. It is clear that we will not go any further. The ambassadors are becoming impatient and demanding to have the legal text of the draft agreement a few hours ahead of the opening of the European Council this afternoon.

All these years, we have done so much waiting for the British! Our team therefore takes it all in its stride and, without waiting for the official green light, has already begun planning the various steps that need to be taken during the day. President Juncker has asked me to hold a press conference if the agreement is confirmed. We are preparing the text for this when I am called back to the President's office for this last decisive phone call from Boris Johnson. The Prime Minister finally confirms his agreement and that of his cabinet. He seems very happy. As does Jean-Claude Juncker – who seems relieved, too.

At one point he hands me the phone and tells Boris Johnson to speak to me directly. I ask him how he sees the process of ratification of the text. 'We will have a meaningful vote this Saturday, and then the votes on the exit bill next Monday and Tuesday,' he replies with great confidence. I am aware, however, that his internal negotiations with the DUP are fraught and that several members of his own Conservative ERG are threatening to drop him. Obviously, the main goal for Mr Johnson today is that there should be no more talk of a prolongation of negotiations. He wants to put maximum pressure on MPs: either you vote for this deal, or we exit without a deal.

President Juncker is committed to helping him on this point, and for my part, I confirm that our briefings will be balanced. There is no reason for either of us to claim victory. This negotiation has gone on too long. We need to end it and open another, far more positive one, about the future of our relationship.

It is time to organize a formal consultation with the members of the College of Commissioners on the legal text and, by 11.30am, the text of the new draft treaty has been sent to the Council and the European Parliament. It will be made public at midday, and it is precisely at midday that I enter the press room.

We have opted for a sober and, as ever, pedagogical tone:

Today we have reached agreement with the UK government on the orderly withdrawal of the UK and the framework for our future relationship.

This agreement is the result of intensive work on the part of both teams of negotiators, the British team and our own, whom I would like to thank personally for their tenacity and professionalism, but also, on the European side, of a continuous dialogue with the twenty-seven member states and the European Parliament, with whom we have really co-constructed this new agreement.

This text provides legal certainty and security where Brexit creates uncertainty, in particular, and above all for citizens, for stakeholders in projects financed by the EU budget, for all persons and companies concerned by other issues of the separation, such as Euratom, the protection of existing intellectual property rights, the protection of geographical indications, and the protection of personal data.

This proposal also incorporates the transition period requested by the UK government, and which will last until the end of 2020 – fourteen months – and possibly one or two more years in the event of a joint UK–EU agreement.

I go on to explain how we managed to satisfy two objectives that were at first sight difficult to reconcile: on the one hand, to include in the Withdrawal Agreement a legally operational solution to avoid a hard border in Ireland, to protect the all-island economy and the integrity of the Single Market, and, on the other hand, to keep Northern Ireland within the British customs territory, which was a key point for Boris Johnson.

I add that, obviously, when discussing Northern Ireland we are talking about the economy, about technical issues, about property, but that for me, for the last three years, my real concern has been the people of Northern Ireland and Ireland. 'What really matters is peace.'

I also want to be clear about the framework for our future relationship:

Boris Johnson's government has chosen a free trade agreement. So any reference to other options, including the option of creating a single customs territory between us, has been removed. What does not change is our geographical proximity and interdependence with the UK economy, and we have agreed to have strong level playing field guarantees to enable an ambitious free trade agreement without tariffs or quotas.

In all, the ambitiousness of our future free trade agreement will be proportional to the level and quality of the economic rules of the game between us.

In conclusion, I say:

On this basis, the assessment that we will present shortly, together with President Juncker, to the European Council is that we now have a fair and reasonable basis for an orderly withdrawal of the United Kingdom and above all for us to begin – as soon as possible, we hope, after 1 November – to work on a new partnership with the United Kingdom.

At the end of this exercise, a number of journalists applaud – which is quite unusual, but perhaps they have had enough of the Brexit drama!

I then meet again with President Juncker, who symbolically welcomes Boris Johnson for a photo call. As usual, the British Prime Minister tries to lighten the atmosphere and create a sense of complicity between us. However, he is clearly campaigning and has been for some time now, his sole objective being to win the upcoming general election in a few weeks.

We then cross the rue de la Loi to join the European Council, which begins late. Once again, the European heads of state or government greet me warmly, and I can sense their relief, even though they all realize that we have not reached the end of the road quite yet.

It is Boris Johnson who opens the discussion on Brexit. He appeals to the emotions by talking about one of his daughters who was born in Brussels, and speaks frankly of 'the two sides of the British heart'. Lucidly, he reminds us that, after this agreement, he will have to win the vote in the House of Commons, after which we will then need to rebuild our relationship. Smiling, he adds: 'I am here for the first time and, I hope, the last.'

Around the table, faces are rather more serious. One prime minister says that 'it all feels like déjà vu'. They all ask Boris Johnson what will happen on Saturday in the House of Commons and whether he will be able to get the deal through. The heads of state and government are obviously fed up with this long negotiation, and I quite understand why. They have become disillusioned, and find it hard to give credence to his speech.

The agreement we reached this morning enables us to turn the page in an orderly and intelligent manner, and I feel that everyone is now keen to do so without delay.

A little later, when Boris Johnson has left the room, Donald Tusk salutes the work of negotiation that has led to this new agreement. The twenty-seven heads of state and government applaud, and I promise to share their accolades with my team.

Donald Tusk immediately gives me the floor to present the agreement, and I remind those present, as I did the journalists at lunchtime, that the trigger for this agreement was the meeting a few days earlier in Liverpool between Boris Johnson and Leo Varadkar. It was there that Boris Johnson moved on two points: first, by accepting that de facto customs procedures would have to be implemented around the island, i.e. at the entry of products into Northern Ireland. And second, by withdrawing the right of veto that he had unwisely granted in his proposals to a single Northern Irish party, the DUP.

I tell them that if all goes well, we will be able to begin the new, major negotiations on the future with the British very soon. But I also have to warn them that these negotiations will be complex, politically sensitive, and constrained by the duration of the transition period.

During the round-table that follows I have the opportunity to answer precisely several questions on the financial commitments, on our new approach to customs, and on the democratic consultation mechanism in Northern Ireland. Donald Tusk then concludes by checking that the twenty-seven are all in agreement to unanimously endorse this new draft agreement. One last time, as he is about to leave office, I note Donald Tusk's contribution to this unity among Europeans. Over the years I have developed a deep respect for this courageous Polish politician, who started out in the Solidarność student movement and who, having served as Prime Minister of his country, came to Brussels and made his mark here.

At this moment I don't know whether British MPs will now finally accept the consequences of the Brexit referendum. But I am sure that, thanks to this agreement, the ball is now firmly in their court and that we have eliminated any further risk of the blame game that the British tried to play against us throughout. If there is another failure, if there is any further delay, any more problems, it will be the responsibility of the British.

Friday, 18 October 2019: Nigel Farage

Nigel Farage addressed members of his Brexit Party meeting in London yesterday.

Unsurprisingly, he criticized our agreement, which he says is a 'reheated version of Mrs May's treaty', an attempt 'to put lipstick on a pig'.

But, contrary to habit, he seems to lay the blame for this on the British negotiators, almost leading him to praise us. He says that I would be 'a damn sight better' than the British negotiators 'have been over the course of the last few years … I wish I could employ him.'

Sorry, but I am not available!

Saturday, 19 October 2019: Eyes on Westminster

A crucial day in London! Boris Johnson intends to have MPs vote on the new agreement. Today is also the deadline under the Benn Act for requesting a further extension until 31 January, should no Withdrawal Agreement be approved.

Just as all signs seemed to suggest that the agreement could obtain a majority, there is a new bolt from the blue: a House of Commons vote, including several MPs who are in favour of the agreement, passes the Letwin amendment which, in order to avoid the risk of a no deal, obliges the Prime Minister to request a postponement of Brexit until after the adoption of the Withdrawal Agreement Bill, i.e. the legislation necessary to implement the agreement.

While stating that he would not negotiate an extension with Brussels, Boris Johnson is nonetheless forced to send Donald Tusk the letter provided for in the Benn Act, requesting an extension until 31 January. However, the Prime Minister takes care not to sign it … and to add a second letter, which is signed and in which, after thanking the members of our team for their 'imagination and diplomacy', he says that 'a further extension would damage the interests of the UK and our EU partners'.

Tuesday, 22 October 2019: Another try

In his letter to Donald Tusk on Saturday, Boris Johnson wrote that he would continue to push for ratification of our agreement by introducing the necessary legislation early this week, saying that he is confident of an orderly exit by 31 October.

And today is indeed a historic day: for the first time since the 2016 referendum, the House of Commons, by supporting the Withdrawal Agreement Bill by 329 votes to 299, has voted in favour of some form of orderly withdrawal from the UK.

The Prime Minister's joy is short-lived, however, as a few minutes later MPs reject by 322 votes to 308 his proposed accelerated timetable, which was necessary in order for the text to be adopted before 31 October. As Speaker John Bercow puts it, the bill is now 'in limbo'.

The Prime Minister then decides to put the process of examining the text on hold, for long enough to discuss with the twenty-seven the request for an extension sent on Saturday, but continues to say that he remains confident about the chances of the ratification of the Withdrawal Agreement: 'One way or another, we will leave the European Union with this agreement.'

Wednesday, 23 October 2019: Extension?

Donald Tusk reacts with a tweet to Boris Johnson's request for an extension:

Following PM @BorisJohnson's decision to pause the process of ratification of the Withdrawal Agreement, and in order to avoid a no-deal #Brexit, I will recommend the EU27 accept the UK request for an extension. For this I will propose a written procedure.

Thursday, 24 October 2019: Thierry Breton

Two weeks after the European Parliament rejected the candidacy of Sylvie Goulard, Emmanuel Macron has proposed Thierry Breton for the post of European Commissioner responsible for the internal market, and also for the digital sector and defence.

Thierry Breton and I have had a friendly relationship since the 1980s. At the time, he was a collaborator of René Monory, working on the creation of the Futuroscope theme park in Poitiers. He had just published two quite successful books, *Softwar – La guerre douce* and *Netwar – La guerre des réseaux*.

I therefore know that, drawing on his experience as a business leader and Minister of the Economy, Finance and Industry, he will be well equipped in the Commission to argue that the European internal market must not be a moveable feast in these negotiations with the British.

In this great reshuffle within the European Commission, my assistant Claire Saelens joins Mr Breton's cabinet. She is replaced by Blanca Huergo Gonzalo, a young, friendly and efficient Spanish assistant.

Friday, 25 October 2019: 31 January!

This morning the ambassadors of the twenty-seven are again discussing an extension request received from the British Prime Minister. The concern of France and others is that such an extension must be justified by a 'good reason'. By this, we have always meant either a general election or a referendum.

Clearly, Boris Johnson, blocked by the notorious Benn Act, has made the choice to force a general election with the support of the SNP and even, despite himself, Labour and the Liberal Democrats. It is clear to all ambassadors that a 'flexible' extension to 31 January is now inevitable.

Monday, 28 October 2019: Letter from the Prime Minister

In a letter to European Council President Donald Tusk, Boris Johnson notes the proposal to extend the Article 50 period until 31 January 2020.

The Prime Minister says that he believes this 'unwanted' (but formally requested) extension of the UK's membership of the European Union is damaging to British democracy and to the relationship between the UK and its European friends. He goes on to confirm his wish for a general election in December 'to ensure the election of a fresh Parliament which is capable of resolving the issue in accordance with our constitutional norms'. There will therefore be a new general election before the year is out.

Wednesday, 6 November 2019: John Bercow

John Bercow, who on 1 November was succeeded in his role as Speaker by his erstwhile deputy Lindsay Hoyle, is no longer bound by a duty of impartiality.

Speaking to the Foreign Press Association, he says that he believes he was 'always fair' to MPs, whether they were Remainers or Brexiteers. When reporters ask him whether Brexit will be positive for the UK's place in the world, Bercow's answer is brief and to the point: 'The honest answer is no', he says, adding: 'I think that Brexit is the biggest foreign policy mistake in the post-war period.'

Saturday, 7 December 2019: British civil servants

In a letter to the *Financial Times* this morning, Sir Jonathan Faull calls for British members of the European Commission to be remembered with respect:

> Effective competition and trade policies, a single market based on common standards and the rule of law, integrated transport policies and world class public administration, to name but a few: many policy areas bear the imprint of political leadership made in the UK and devoted to the wider European interest.

I can testify to the importance of British Commissioners and the role they play, and in particular the role played for the last three years by Jonathan Hill, responsible for financial services, and Julian King, the current Commissioner for Internal Security.

Throughout my European career, I have often chosen to work with British colleagues. In my very first term as European Commissioner, I was joined by Ronnie Hall, who came from Northern Ireland. During the same term I chose another Briton, Graham Meadows, as Director-General for Regional Policy. And then, around the table of the College chaired by Romano Prodi, there were two high-level Britons, the Labour politician Neil Kinnock and, of course, Chris Patten, the last Governor of Hong Kong, whose masterful presentations on the international situation I remember well.

Finally, during my second term as Commissioner it was Cathy Ashton, then High Representative for Foreign Affairs and Security Policy, who, together with Pierre Vimont, an outstanding diplomat, set about building the European diplomatic service from scratch. She also demonstrated its value in the management of two extremely complex issues: Kosovo and Iran's nuclear programme.

At that time, as Commissioner for the Internal Market and Financial Services, I found it a real pleasure to work with David Wright, then Deputy Director-General for Financial Services. And of course it was also my choice to propose Jonathan Faull as Director-General for Internal Market and Financial Services.

I never had any doubt that all of these men and women, senior European officials of British nationality, were loyal to the institution. They were always patriotic and European at the same time, as I myself aim to be. And that is also why Jean-Claude Juncker, very early on, made a commitment to preserve their place in the Commission.

This has not dispelled the concern, and in some cases dismay, of these officials, which has led many among them to seek dual nationality.

Sunday, 8 December 2019: Baby boom

As the UK general election campaign draws to a close, Boris Johnson is never short of new arguments.

In an interview with the *Sunday Times* the Prime Minister predicts a baby boom once Brexit is complete: 'Cupid's darts will fly once we get Brexit done. Romance will bloom across the nation.'

As the French edition of the *Huffington Post* notes, 'Boris Johnson has not given any details or explanation as to why the never-ending Brexit drama would have an impact on the libido of his constituents'...

Wednesday, 11 December 2019: Election eve

On the last day of the election campaign, canvassing in Yorkshire, Boris Johnson is invited in by a couple and shares a steak-and-ale pie with them. I read in *Le Figaro* of the fine metaphor this culinary activity inspires in the PM: 'You saw how easy it is; we put it in, slam it in the oven, take it out and there it is. Get Brexit done!'

In an attempt to clear the air, he also tells the press that there will be no controls on goods between Britain and Northern Ireland – which is not what the Withdrawal Agreement says...

Friday, 13 December 2019: European Council

Unlike the infamous referendum night of 23 June 2016, this morning the verdict of the ballot box is in line with the polls. Boris Johnson has won by a landslide, with 365 seats. The Labour Party led by Jeremy Corbyn has been defeated, obtaining only 203 seats. The Liberal Democrats lost almost half their votes as well as their leader Jo Swinson.

I note two specific results that have potential consequences for the unity of the UK. In Northern Ireland, for the first time, the nationalists of Sinn Féin, along with the SDLP created by John Hume, will have more seats than the DUP. And most importantly, in Scotland, First Minister Nicola Sturgeon, with her great competence and straightforward, down-to-earth manner, won forty-eight of the fifty-nine Scottish seats at Westminster. She immediately confirms that she considers this a mandate to hold a new referendum on Scottish independence.

In Brussels, it is a European Council day. The Council supports the Commission's decision to reappoint me as head of the future negotiations, and outlines the framework for the new mandate I will need to be given in February.

Ursula von der Leyen clearly and precisely enumerates the lessons to be learned from last night's election. Now that the ratification of the Withdrawal Agreement in the UK is certain, we must ready ourselves for the negotiations to come. 'Beware of the time constraints', she advises. 'In eleven months, we won't be able to cover everything.'

A dozen or so heads of state or government then take the floor, both to express their hope that our method of transparency and dialogue will be maintained and to insist on the necessary balance in our economic relations with this great country, soon to be outside the Union and a competitor.

Responding to them one by one, I point out that the agreement signed on 17 October with Boris Johnson has meant that, for the first time in a long time, the election campaign in the UK proceeded with practically none of the usual blame game against Brussels.

Friday, 20 December 2019: Inquest on Article 50

Since the beginning of these lengthy negotiations, I have often wondered exactly who it was that had the idea, at the time of the 2002 Convention on the Future of Europe, to provide for the case of a member state wishing to leave the European Union. In other words, who was behind what in 2009 became Article 50 of the Treaty on European Union?

In recent weeks I have finally taken the time to 'investigate' by interviewing those who, like myself, were involved in working on the Convention.

With the help of Pieter Van Nuffel and Clemens Ladenburger, two excellent lawyers who have since risen through the ranks of the European Commission's legal service, as well as colleagues in the Secretariat-General, I gradually piece together the sequence of events. It is quite clear that the idea came in 2002 from Sir John Kerr, the British Secretary-General of the Convention, in discussions with, among others, Nikolaus Meyer-Landrut, now German Ambassador to France, and Valéry Giscard d'Estaing.

Others who worked on the Convention, such as the Frenchmen Robert Badinter and Alain Lamassoure and the British Peter Hain, also raised this possibility in their respective contributions. Robert Badinter's contribution provides for a period of negotiation between the EU and the outgoing state to define how the withdrawal will proceed, and its possible consequences for the interests of the Union, before going on to stipulate that '[a]ny damage caused to the Union by withdrawal must be borne by the outgoing state'…

Initially reluctant, President Giscard d'Estaing was later persuaded by the argument that this article was necessary in order to silence those Eurosceptics, particularly in the UK, who were constantly propagating the idea that the EU was a prison from which there was no escape.

This proposal was then strongly supported by the members of the Convention during the plenary debate on 5 April 2003, including observers from the Central and Eastern European countries that were about to join the European Union and who saw it as a symbol of freedom for their people.

On reflection, this article was actually quite innovative. As Pieter Van Nuffel notes in a text on our Draft European Constitution,* there was previously 'no clear legal answer to the question of whether or not a member state has the right to leave the Union; at the same time, it was clear to everyone that if a member state had the firm intention to leave the Union, there would be no way to stop it.'

What was to become Article 50 was therefore of great interest to the members of the Convention, who set out its framework and its procedures, in particular as concerns the role of the European Council and of the Commission as negotiator of the Withdrawal Agreement.

The two-year period after which the member state concerned would then leave the Union, even in the absence of an agreement, is, according to Van Nuffel, the 'logical consequence of the principle that the right to withdraw is a matter of free choice for the member state: it cannot be forced to remain in the Union when negotiations have reached an impasse; it cannot be forced to accept the terms proposed by the Union.'

Finally, in his text Van Nuffel focuses on the provision that specifies that the Union must negotiate the withdrawal of a member state 'taking into account the framework of its future relations with the Union'. He envisages different possibilities here, such as maintaining a customs

---

* 'Appartenance à l'Union', in *Genesis and Destiny of the European Constitution*, edited by Giuliano Amato, Hervé Bribosia and Bruno De Witte (Brussels: Bruylant, 2017), 247–84.

union or a free trade area. I am still amazed by the alacrity with which Theresa May ruled out all other options as early as January 2017... As for Valéry Giscard d'Estaing, he told me later, in his characteristic tone, that the idea came from him: 'At the time, there were press campaigns, particularly in the United States, presenting the European Union as a prison. I thought the point was well taken. And I wrote the draft article myself, which was then refined by the Convention's Secretary-General John Kerr. To this day, I still don't understand why it's so complicated to leave the EU. If they want to leave, let them leave!'

It was not the first time I have had to take up the thread of this discussion and explain to President Giscard d'Estaing all the consequences of this departure, for so many citizens worried about their rights, for the European budget and even for the protection of certain Auvergne cheeses!

Monday, 23 December 2019: Citizens' rights

Christmas Eve. Steve Barclay has been trying to reach me for two days and we finally manage to speak. I congratulate him on the Conservative Party result and also ask him how he sees his own future, as Boris Johnson has symbolically announced the abolition of his department! We all know that when you become a minister, you have to prepare yourself immediately for the fact that one day you will be a former minister. He tells me straightforwardly that he will spend January ensuring that the treaty is properly ratified by the House of Commons and the House of Lords, and will thereafter remain at the disposal of the Prime Minister as part of the post-Brexit reshuffle of the UK government.

During this brief conversation, I talk to him again about the need for a proper implementation of the Withdrawal Agreement with regard to citizens' rights, which will be a top priority for the European Parliament, the Commission and the member states alike over the coming months.

In particular, the Commission will be monitoring the functioning of the UK authority responsible for dealing quickly and impartially with complaints from EU citizens, and also the conditions for granting settled status, especially to the most vulnerable.

Mr Barclay's response is reassuring: the EU (Withdrawal Agreement) Bill passed on the second reading in the House of Commons on 20

December establishes an independent monitoring authority and grants it full powers to monitor the implementation of the Withdrawal Agreement's provisions on citizens' rights. EU citizens are also granted a 'grace period' which gives them plenty of time to apply for UK residency under the EU settlement scheme. According to Mr Barclay, of the 2.6 million applications received from EU citizens, only five have been rejected, on the grounds of criminal conviction.

In conclusion, Mr Barclay believes that it is important to continue to discuss the implementation of the Withdrawal Agreement for all citizens that are affected by it: 'Many of the issues you raise in your letter will also affect British citizens in the EU, and I note that some member states have yet to work out the details of what the British will have to do to protect their rights.' Indeed, this is a subject that will be followed closely on both sides!

2020

Wednesday, 1 January 2020: Happy New Year!

This morning, taking to Twitter to wish all my followers – and of course everyone else – a Happy New Year, I choose to post a poetic image of my home village of Saint-Martin-de-Belleville in Savoie. The photo was taken by my son-in-law Augustin, and presents a perfect illustration of the contrasting landscape of our current relationship with the UK. The beautiful village is depicted in the morning mist, the bell tower of its baroque church only just visible, pointing up towards blue sky.

I accompany the photo with this message:

> Happy New Year from my home in #Savoie! 2020 will be challenging: we Europeans need to build on our unity & work together to achieve our goals & defend EU interests in the world. We want to build a new, strong & fair partnership w/UK our close friend & ally. Best wishes to all!

Monday, 6 January 2020: Full house!

Very early this Monday morning, I meet in the office with Clara Martínez Alberola, who is joining the team as my deputy. I have had this choice in mind for several weeks. For a long time, Clara was deputy head of Jean-Claude Juncker's cabinet, and then became Head of Cabinet upon Martin Selmayr's departure. A very experienced Spanish lawyer, she has a natural authority and never loses her composure – a definite asset in our often lengthy and trying days of negotiation. Despite her sometimes rather stern appearance, I know she will be an attentive, humane and much appreciated team leader. In the Juncker team she worked with Paulina Dejmek Hack, and the two of them will support and complement one another.

Ours is a solid team that I can rely on, and it is now highly experienced in negotiation. Several pillars of the first task force have chosen to stay. Antonio Fernández-Martos, former Spanish Director-General for Trade, will lead the trade negotiations, with his deputy Nicolas von Lingen for the level playing field issues and the expert Mariano Fernandez-Salas on services. Stefan Fuehring, with his hard work and attention to detail, will cover regulatory and transport issues. Marie Simonsen, a Danish lawyer who drafted the agreement on citizens' rights, will be responsible for governance. Luca Rossi, Italian, also a talented lawyer, will deal with police and judicial cooperation. Philippe Bertrand will continue to oversee budgetary issues in relation to the UK's participation in EU programmes.

I have also asked Stefaan De Rynck to take charge of preparation among the member states for the consequences of Brexit, whether or not we obtain an agreement on the future relationship. Finally, the great legal expertise of Hannes Kraemer will be very useful for the drafting of the agreement we hope to reach. Dan Ferrie's expertise as spokesperson will be equally useful in terms of communication, in tandem with Matthieu. Lastly, I have asked Georg to take charge of the negotiation strategy along with Clara and myself. He has chosen Ivo, also a veteran of the first negotiation, to assist him. Together they will write the weekly strategy briefing that I send to the President.

Wednesday, 8 January 2020: Return to 10 Downing Street

Ursula von der Leyen and Boris Johnson have chosen to meet at the beginning of this year at 10 Downing Street, and I accompany the Commission President to London.

They do not know one another, and Ursula von der Leyen is making a gesture of goodwill by travelling to London in person for this initial meeting. I know how reluctant the Johnson team is when it comes to anything to do with Brussels and its bureaucracy. I find it curious, however, that the British Prime Minister has not made any effort to organize lunch, as Theresa May did for Jean-Claude Juncker.

The meeting is to take place for just one hour in the afternoon. There will be a simple photo opportunity but no press briefing or even a joint statement. In short, the bare minimum.

Ursula von der Leyen, who wants to speak about Brexit and its aftermath, has chosen to give a lecture at her former university, the London School of Economics. There, she is greeted by many friends and even some family. She has chosen a fine title for her speech: 'Old Friends, New Beginnings'. That describes our state of mind well.

At the beginning of her speech, she admits that during her student years she spent more time in the bars of Soho and the record shops of Camden than in the university library. After speaking of her personal connection to the United Kingdom, she delivers a clear message, warning the British people that not everything can be done within eleven months, the deadline Boris Johnson has chosen to set for the negotiations, and that we will have to choose what to prioritize. She continues:

> As we embark on this new partnership with the United Kingdom, the European Union must also continue to forge its own path in today's world. One consequence of the Brexit vote has been to strengthen the unity and the faith in Europe as a project for the common good. The truth is that Brexit has highlighted the value of being together in today's ever more unsettled world.

There is time for questions afterwards, and one is on the specific subject of the trade agreements that the British will have to renegotiate on their own behalf after leaving the EU. Spontaneously, the President asks me to respond. Encouraged by the audience, I go and sit on the side of the podium where there is a microphone. All of this presents the image of a good rapport between us, and of an open and responsive European Commission.

A little later we go on to 10 Downing Street, where Boris Johnson greets Ursula von der Leyen on the doorstep. The Prime Minister also greets me cordially before I join them inside. The conversation on Brexit lasts for around forty minutes.

As always, Boris Johnson is direct, perhaps a little too much so. He is filled with the confidence of a man who has just won an election. 'No more Brexit! *Finito!* People want us to move on.' After this jarring introduction, the politician who fought his election on 'getting Brexit done' adds: 'It will be a difficult discussion, but we're approaching it with a positive mindset. We want to achieve what's set out in the Conservative Party manifesto. We're not going to go back to the Chequers plan.'

I am not surprised by his determination. The British want to diverge from European regulations. The Chequers plan, which he no longer wants to hear spoken of, was based on the idea that the UK would keep one foot in and one foot out of the Single Market. And that we would have fairly similar regulations and perhaps even a customs union. Now we are being warned that the new government will be demanding a simple free trade agreement, like the one we have with Canada.

The Prime Minister adds: 'We understand what you're saying about dumping, but I don't see a problem. We will continue to trade, we want maximum access. Often the EU standards are lower than ours, as is the case for pig farming in Denmark. Today we are aligned. Our products are among the best in the world.'

During his lengthy tirade he enumerates the British red lines, in particular on fisheries: 'We are going to regain control of our waters, control immigration and refuse any incursion by the EU Court of Justice.'

Once this speech is over, Ursula von der Leyen, very calmly, confirms that we must work together in the future because we are friends, and because we have common values and goals. 'We will do our best, but it is your decision to leave the Union and the Single Market, to place a distance between us. There can be no free movement of goods or services if there is no free movement of people. Time is very short.'

With his customary aplomb, Mr Johnson replies that 'we can get to an agreement. It's just a question of political will.'

It is then my turn to intervene in the discussion, firstly to thank the Prime Minister and his team for the positive cooperation that led to an agreement on orderly withdrawal on 17 October. 'In this room we are politicians, not super-technocrats. What we are talking about is translating political will into the legal text of a treaty. For us, the level playing field is a major issue. We are not concerned about the quality of British products that may enter the Single Market, because our standards and regulations must be respected for all imports, but about the way in which British products are produced. The state aid issue is key for us too.'

This meeting is cordial enough, and offers no surprises. Obviously, Boris Johnson wants to have done with Brexit as soon as possible. And I sense that he will never ask for an extension of the transition. He can't afford for there to be two or three years in his five-year term during which his government would be obliged to continue applying EU regulations.

Thursday, 9 January 2020: Stockholm

My first visit this year is to Stockholm, a beautiful cold but sunny city in the heart of Sweden, a country that has traditionally been very close to the UK, and which is worried about the impact of Brexit.

This morning the hall at the European Commission Representation Office is packed for a presentation on our future relationship with the UK.

I am very much aware of the friendly relationship between Sweden and the UK. The first formal Anglo-Swedish alliance dates back some 365 years, when Queen Christina of Sweden signed a commercial treaty with the Commonwealth of England. At the time, the British Ambassador to Sweden, Bulstrode Whitelocke, said that Sweden and England were a perfect match as nations, 'at a perfect distance and situation [...] neither so near as to cause jealousies; nor yet so far off, but that they may give [each other] timely assistance'. Over the years this friendship has grown, both bilaterally and within the EU where Sweden and the UK have had shared views on many matters including trade, EU enlargement, innovation and the digital Single Market.

Here more than anywhere else, I want above all to reassure the audience that the Withdrawal Agreement we have reached with the UK will protect the fundamental interests of the EU and those of Sweden. It also grants us eleven months of continuity during which we will do our utmost to prepare for our future relationship: 'It will never be the EU that fails on common ambition', I say. 'We will strive for a partnership that goes well beyond trade and is unprecedented in scope, covering everything from services to fisheries, climate action, energy, transport, space, security and defence.'

Of course, we will not be able to achieve all this in less than a year, and I take this opportunity to emphasize three priorities for 2020.

First, we must build up a new capacity that enables us to work together, both bilaterally and in global fora. Only by joining forces can we tackle major challenges such as climate change, the promotion of multilateralism and finding peaceful solutions in the Middle East.

Second, we need to build a very close security relationship. There can be no compromise on our mutual security. Even if we will no longer be able to cooperate with the UK as we do between member states, we must be able to count on each other.

Third, we need to build an economic partnership based on a level playing field. Competition is positive, and the European Union is not afraid of it. But we cannot compete on social and environmental standards, because that can only lead to a race to the bottom that would put workers, consumers and the planet on the losing side. So we will insist on an economic partnership with zero tariffs, zero quotas, but also zero dumping.

At the end of my speech I am touched by the attentiveness of the Head of Representation, Katarina Areskoug, who gives me a candle to blow out. I had warned the audience in advance: 'I am happy to take your questions, but be nice – it's my birthday.'

Friday, 10 January 2020: Who to disappoint?

In his column in *Le Monde* on 8 January ('Brexit: Who will Boris Johnson betray?'), Éric Albert highlights the dilemma that the British Prime Minister will have to overcome in the weeks to come.

Either he must confirm the hard Brexit approach favoured by some of his advisers, in particular Dominic Cummings, at the risk of disappointing his new voters in the disadvantaged regions of the north of England, who will be among the first to suffer the economic consequences of a 'clean break' with the EU. Or he must opt for an ambitious deal that limits the negative economic consequences of Brexit, but at the risk of alienating some of the most hard-line Brexiteers who have supported him from the start.

The choice he makes will determine the dynamics of the negotiations that are to begin in just a few weeks' time...

Monday, 27 January 2020: Dublin to Belfast

Back to Dublin. I get a good feeling from this city, and from Ireland in general.

I start the morning with Leo Varadkar. Speaking in his office, I emphasize how we must remain vigilant in ensuring that the Withdrawal

Agreement is properly implemented. Ireland, which has been consistently supported by the other twenty-six member states for the past three years, must show the same solidarity in the forthcoming negotiations, particularly on the issue of the level playing field.

After a very useful meeting with all the Irish economic leaders, we set off for Belfast. It's a journey of an hour and a half between the two cities and of course we cross an invisible border along the way. When we arrive, I make a point of signing the register of condolences at Belfast City Hall in memory of Séamus Mallon, a courageous man who was a colleague of nationalist leader John Hume, and one of the architects of the Good Friday (Belfast) Agreement.

We then climb Stormont Hill, where the Northern Irish Parliament sits and where the new executive, now finally reconstituted after three years of uncertainty, works. The First Minister Arlene Foster is not there. That is her choice. Her deputy Michelle O'Neill, a member of Sinn Féin, offers me a warm welcome. Alongside her, if I might put it this way, is Diane Dodds, the new Home Secretary for Northern Ireland and an ardent DUP activist, representing the First Minister. Throughout our meeting the two of take them great care, for photos and when seated around the table, to position themselves either side of me, one on the left, the other on the right, so as not to appear side by side. I hope that, nonetheless, they will be able to make joint decisions.

Unsurprisingly, Diane Dodds collars me on the implementation of the agreement, which formally provides for checks and controls on products entering Belfast, at the port or airport through which they come in. She refers adeptly to the need to avoid 'barriers'. I tell her that our intention is indeed not to erect barriers, but to control products or animals, in the same way that sanitary and phytosanitary controls have always been applied in Belfast on some products and animals arriving from Great Britain. All in all, the welcome they offer me is very cordial.

Immediately afterwards I go to Queen's University, where an audience of three hundred people awaits me, among them the principal political and economic leaders of Northern Ireland, but also, sitting in the front row, the former Taoiseach of Ireland and one of the signatories of the Good Friday (Belfast) Agreement, Bertie Ahern.

My team and I have drafted a text for this speech that is respectful of the UK but clear and firm as to the principles of Brexit and its consequences, particularly for Northern Ireland, likely to be the hardest-hit part of the UK.

At the end of the speech, an initial salvo comes from journalists who suggest that I am at odds with Boris Johnson over these famous checks and controls between Great Britain and Northern Ireland. There is obviously a difference between the British Prime Minister and ourselves, but the treaty is the treaty, and there is no ambiguity on this subject. Three times over I repeat that there will be controls on goods entering Northern Ireland and therefore the Single Market. Then near the end, a student asks me, quite emotionally: 'What can you say, Mr Barnier, to young Irish people today, on the eve of Brexit?' Spontaneously, I reply: 'Speak out, use your voting power, get involved. No one can stop you from being European.'

Wednesday, 29 January 2020: A temporary farewell

At the European Parliament in Brussels, today we mark the conclusion of three years of work.

Along with the vote on the Withdrawal Agreement, it is also – forty-eight hours before Brexit – the last day of the session for the seventy-three British MEPs. For them, as for us, it is an emotional moment. At the top of the Chamber, members of the Brexiteer group are triumphant, surrounding Nigel Farage and proudly waving the British flag.

And then there are all the others, Labour, Liberal Democrats, Greens and two Conservatives, who have remained in the EPP. Today is their last stand, and many of them speak with great dignity and in some cases high emotion. I have been invited to conclude this plenary session, following Ursula von der Leyen and standing alongside her. The vote is about to take place, and I salute the quality of the work of the many British MPs who have contributed to the construction of the European project over the past forty-seven years, without of course being able to name them all. But I make sure to pay particular tribute to Andrew Duff and Richard Corbett, with whom I worked on the Convention on the Future of Europe. Subsequently, as European Commissioner, I worked very closely with three parliamentary committee chairmen, Malcolm Harbour and then Vicky Ford for the internal market, and Sharon Bowles for financial services.

Finally, I set out three points to mark the occasion, at the very end of my speech.

First, I say, as has been the case throughout this negotiation, in the coming year our task will be to deal with the consequences of Brexit. But I also recommend that we take time to listen to the popular sentiment that was expressed in the British referendum, and which is being heard also in many of our own regions. We must take time to learn the lessons of Brexit.

Second, I recall the question raised by Chris Patten, a former European Commissioner, at the end of a conference in Dublin: 'Can defence of the national interest be only national?' We could ask the question in another way: 'Shouldn't we be European as well as patriotic?' I am convinced that we can and must be patriotic and European at the same time, and that the European dimension only lends greater strength to our patriotism.

Third, at the moment of this new departure, I conclude by sincerely wishing the best for the United Kingdom.

And then, at last, the electronic vote finally puts the seal on this long negotiation. The result is clear: 621 votes for, 49 against, and 13 abstentions. I note with some amusement that the Brexiteers, led by Farage, ultimately voted to ratify the agreement even though they have criticized it endlessly over the past three years.

Immediately after the vote, one might have expected the European anthem and *God Save the Queen* to be played in the Chamber. But rather than it being a solemn moment, what follows is emotion. Almost all members of the European Parliament rise to sing *Auld Lang Syne* and, irrespective of country and political group, we all join hands.

Friday, 31 January 2020: An emotional day

This is the day! So long awaited and hoped for by some, so feared by others. A historic day in a sense, as it is the first time that a member state has left the EU – and hopefully the last. I have mixed feelings this morning. Sadness, obviously. Brexit is a failure for the European Union. It is also a failure for the UK and for us. I still don't understand what the point of it is, even from the perspective of the British national interest. But the messages of sadness are growing in number, and whatever my personal feelings, I choose not to join the chorus of lamentation.

I limit myself to one tweet: 'An emotional day. Unity. Transparency. Respect. Our work continues', accompanied by four symbolic photographs.

First, a photo of the three new presidents of the European institutions, Ursula von der Leyen, Charles Michel and David Sassoli, who chose to come together this morning to express both their regret at the departure of the British and their hopes for a strong and respectful future relationship.

Second, the press conference on 19 March 2018 when, standing alongside David Davis, I presented candidly the state of play of the negotiations on the draft treaty, with the articles already agreed highlighted in green behind us.

Then the brief dialogue with a group of schoolchildren at Derry/Londonderry Town Hall on 1 May 2018.

And, finally, my visit to the City of London on 5 February 2018, where an electronic news ticker on a building behind me displays a phrase that still holds true: 'EU tells Britain: Time has come to make a Brexit choice.'

Later on in the afternoon, Emmanuel Macron asks me to meet him. The timing is no coincidence. Immediately after our meeting ends he will make a brief statement to be broadcast on all television channels. In this broadcast, in serious and solemn tones, he emphasizes the lessons that Europe must learn from Brexit.

During our conversation, to me he seems tired – understandably so. A great many concerns are piling up, with the never-ending debate on pensions and other controversies that could have been avoided. Nonetheless, he takes the time to listen, to question, to set out France's position. It goes without saying that France wants to continue in its cooperation with the UK, but it does not want to see the unravelling of the Single Market or the rise of unfair competition. President Macron asks for explanations from Paulina on financial services and from Georg on the impact of the negotiations between the United States and the United Kingdom. He also focuses on the fisheries question, with which I am very familiar.

Tonight I receive many touching messages, but I am also struck by the expression in both London and Brussels of so much sadness, anger and nostalgia.

Of all the messages, perhaps the most moving and dignified is that of two Second World War veterans, Stephen Goodall, 98, and Sid Daw, 95, whose reflections appear in a video projected onto the cliffs of Dover for anyone who wants to hear their words in the Netherlands, Germany, France or Belgium: 'I feel really depressed at the idea that we are leaving Europe', says Goodall, 'because it has meant so much to me. I like to be called European. And the feeling that one has of comradeship as one goes around Europe is really quite something.' At the end of their message, we see the stars of the European flag gradually fade away until only one remains: 'This is our star, look after it for us.'

Again, my feelings are mixed. By making this deal with Boris Johnson, we make Brexit possible. But it is orderly, as much as a divorce can be. Even though the break-up is happening, there is no drama tonight, and I feel that my team has done its job.

I just wonder what would have happened had we not made that deal on 17 October. Boris Johnson would still have gone to the country. He would have won the election after another anti-European campaign against those 'Brussels technocrats' who just don't get it. And then either Brexit would have happened today without a deal, causing real turbulence and crisis. Or else, under pressure from certain governments and economic circles, we would have patched together an imperfect agreement, sacrificing some of the Union's interests in order to avoid a no deal.

All in all, then, since Brexit had become inevitable, it is better that it happens as it is happening now. Without any chaos, but just a great deal of sadness.

A SECOND NEGOTIATION

2020

Monday, 3 February 2020: New negotiations, new mandate

This Monday following a rather sad weekend, the first for the European Union without the United Kingdom, I am a guest on the morning show on France Inter. After answering questions from Nicolas Demorand and Léa Salamé, a listener, Pierre, asks me: 'For three years we've been told "we're negotiating, we're negotiating, we're negotiating". And now that's it, it's done, we can sign the divorce papers – and now we're told "we're going to negotiate". I must say I'm a bit confused: what have you been negotiating over those three years, and what's left to negotiate?'

A good question, which shows that the need for this second negotiation is not self-evident! I answer it by explaining that, when the British told us that they wanted to divorce, the first priority was to deal with all the questions of legal insecurity that a divorce creates. But once you are divorced, you then have to rebuild everything: what kind of relationship do you want to have with the other party? This is the purpose of the new negotiation.

For this new negotiation, the European Commission, and within it our negotiating team, required a new mandate from the twenty-seven member states, with the support of the European Parliament.

And we needed this mandate quickly. According to the Withdrawal Agreement, the transition period ends on 31 December 2020 unless both parties agree before 30 June 2020 to extend it by one or two years. During this transition period, nothing changes for citizens and businesses because the UK, although having left the EU institutions, remains in the internal market and the Customs Union.

Whatever happens, we know that the new negotiation will be a race against time. And that the British will certainly try to make it go at their chosen pace, and will even accuse us of dragging our feet.

That is why, over the past few weeks, I have asked my teams to prepare a complete draft legal text of the final agreement, which we can put on the table when the time comes. Under the leadership of Clara and Paulina, the task force worked throughout January, often working nights, to get ahead of the game.

This is also why the European Commission is adopting, without delay, the draft negotiating directives on the future relationship, which the twenty-seven member states will have to vote on.

There are no surprises in this draft mandate, which I am presenting to the press this morning, as it is in line with two essential documents. First, the guidelines set by the European Council on 29 April 2017 and, second, the Political Declaration on the framework for our future relationship, agreed with Boris Johnson's government on 17 October 2019 and approved by the European Council.

Our aim is to conclude an ambitious partnership with the UK. But let us be clear, the most ambitious partnership was the one we had before!

We must now face the consequences of the UK's decision: leaving the EU is a done deal. And leaving the Single Market and the Customs Union will likewise be done, if I understand Boris Johnson correctly, on 31 December next year. The UK will then no longer be bound by the free movement of persons. It will leave our common ecosystem of regulations, standards, rights and supervision. And it will no longer enjoy the rights and economic benefits of being a member state.

This is the framework within which we must act and negotiate the best possible relationship. We propose to work on three distinct chapters.

First chapter: a very ambitious economic partnership. No tariffs or quotas on any goods entering our Single Market of 450 million people. An ambitious free trade agreement also on services, digital commerce, intellectual property issues and access to our respective public procurement markets.

But this will be an agreement with two conditions. First, competition must be open and fair. In the Political Declaration, we agreed with Boris Johnson to avoid 'unjustified competitive advantages'. We must now find ways to ensure fair competition – a 'level playing field' – in the long term. For this we need mechanisms to maintain the high standards we share today, whether in social, environmental, climate, tax or state aid matters.

The second condition we are setting concerns fishing. We know that this is our Achilles heel. By leaving the EU and the Common Fisheries Policy, the British are regaining sovereignty over their territorial waters and their exclusive economic zone. For we Europeans, several thousand jobs are affected. There is no reason why European fishermen should be sacrificed to Brexit. We will therefore demand continued access to British waters if the British want to access our markets, to which they export almost two-thirds of their fish products.

Any free trade agreement will therefore have to include conditions on fair competition and this agreement on fisheries. Beyond this, we propose to cooperate in other areas such as transport and energy, and EU programmes such as Erasmus and the research and innovation programme Horizon Europe. Finally, there is the difficult question of movement of persons, which some – Farage and others – see as being one of the reasons for the Leave vote. We want to be ambitious on this score, in line with the hopes of so many people – young people in particular.

The second chapter concerns internal security. At the beginning of February there was another knife attack in the London Borough of Streatham. In my press briefing, I reaffirmed European solidarity with the victims and with the British authorities. This solidarity cannot and will not be bargained over.

The fight against terrorism, and that against organized crime and cybercrime, require close cooperation between the European Union and the United Kingdom. The same cooperation is needed on the external front against groups that seek to destabilize our democracies.

In such a dangerous world, it would be wrong to give up the ability to exchange fingerprints, DNA data or licence plate numbers for the purpose of investigations – or the ability to extradite criminals. We will therefore need to rebuild a legal and operational framework. This is not easy, since as well as leaving our agencies, such as Europol and Eurojust, the UK is not part of the Schengen area, and will now be a third country.

We set three further conditions. The UK must commit itself to the European Convention on Human Rights, a sensitive issue for some Brexiteers. The British government must guarantee adequate standards of data protection. Any cooperation will also have to be subject to an effective dispute resolution mechanism, and to the EU Court of Justice where EU law is involved.

Finally, in our mandate we propose continuing cooperation on foreign policy, defence and development aid. To us, as well as to Josep Borrell, the EU's High Representative for Foreign Affairs and Security Policy, this seems an obvious choice. We have a common interest in maintaining a close political dialogue on the major crises of this world, whether global challenges such as climate change, or 'new terrains' such as networks, the Arctic or space. And we also have to be able to act together via external operations or sanctions.

Finally, the ambitious partnership we envisage will require a robust institutional framework to ensure its proper implementation by both parties over time.

As well as mechanisms for political dialogue and consultation, we need a toolbox of effective 'dispute resolution' mechanisms and means for their enforcement. This governance framework must cover all areas of economic and security cooperation.

If certain obligations are not respected or are even violated by one party, the other party must be able to react quickly and effectively, including via autonomous measures.

Monday, 10 February 2020: A winning method

In the car on the way to Luxembourg, where the General Affairs Council is held for three months of every year, Clara and I review my presentation of the mandate to the ministers of the twenty-seven.

I know that the discussion will not just be about the substance, but also about the method by which it can be successfully achieved in time.

This is a discussion that we have also had internally. On the thirteenth floor of the Berlaymont there was an eagerness to identify the highest priorities for the next nine months, and to focus on issues where the end of the transition period will have the strongest negative impact and where contingency measures are not possible: questions regarding customs tariffs, fisheries, the level playing field and governance.

The idea is commendable, but I know it won't work. No specific issue that is important to any one member state can be left out, whether it's aviation for Finland and Spain, road transport for Poland or Slovakia, free movement of persons for Romania or Bulgaria or cultural goods for Greece.

My proposal to the ministers is therefore to make progress on all subjects in parallel. Specifically, we are looking to open a dozen thematic negotiating tables with the United Kingdom.

Leaving the ministers, we set off for Strasbourg to join the plenary session of the European Parliament. This is an opportunity to publicly announce the method and attitude that I will continue to adopt towards the British: patience, respect and firmness. From day one, I have chosen to display no emotion or passion in these negotiations. The British tabloids would love that. I am not about to change my approach now.

Making a success of this second negotiation will be a team effort. An effort within the European Commission, with President Ursula von der Leyen and each of the twenty-six Commissioners, their cabinets and their departments; in particular with the Trade Commissioner Phil Hogan, who now has Sabine Weyand as Director-General. An effort within the European Council, with its President Charles Michel and each member state – the key here is the Council's working group on trade relations with the UK, led by Didier Seeuws. And, of course, an effort with the members of the European Parliament, its president David Sassoli, and in connection with the coordination group for the UK chaired by David McAllister. I am their negotiator and will continue to act as such, in the service of all the EU's institutions and the unity of Europeans.

I will also be seeking to enter into dialogue with national parliaments in each of the twenty-seven EU countries, and to listen to stakeholders – trade unions, businesses, associations and nongovernmental organizations. And as before, these negotiations cannot be kept secret.

Monday, 17 February 2020: A philosophical gap

David Frost, the Prime Minister's European adviser and now the UK's Chief Negotiator, returns to Brussels. The man chosen to lead the British teams is courteous, if not particularly forthcoming, and definitely loyal to Boris Johnson. He arrives with another such loyalist, the British Ambassador to the EU Tim Barrow, whom we now know well, and

Oliver Lewis, an MP who I don't know but who I understand is close to Dominic Cummings and has been working on the no-deal scenario. In any case, he proudly wears the Union Jack on his lapel.

I welcome David Frost in his new role, and make my concern very clear from the outset:

> If we are to succeed within the very tight timeframe that you have set for this negotiation, then we need to pay attention to all the points where there is a risk of failure. The first is compliance or noncompliance with the Political Declaration on the framework for our future relationship that we agreed with Boris Johnson on 17 October. The further away you move from that Political Declaration, the more difficult things will be.
>
> The second is the issue of the level playing field: any broad, open, zero-tariff and zero-quota free trade agreement with the UK will be accompanied by a framework of common rules of play. This is to eliminate the risk of unjustified competitive advantages. Again, we agreed with Boris Johnson that we would make our best efforts to do this.
>
> The third risk lies in the implementation of the Withdrawal Agreement ratified by the House of Commons and the European Parliament. The proper implementation of this treaty, particularly in Ireland and Northern Ireland, is closely linked to the successful completion of our new negotiations. And I will be reporting very regularly to the Council and Parliament on the preparation of this implementation.

After an initial exchange of very British pleasantries, the first bombshell hits: as if it is no big deal, David Frost mentions that Boris Johnson's government do not feel themselves to be bound by the Political Declaration, which it signed on 17 October, barely four months ago. 'We can accept some elements but not all. There is', he tells me, 'a philosophical gap between us about the so-called level playing field' – as if it were a question of philosophy!

What follows is no less explosive. Mr Frost tells us that he does not intend to negotiate on defence and foreign policy issues. 'We have the tools of traditional diplomacy, bilateral agreements and ad hoc cooperation for that.'

The stage is set. No doubt this is all largely tactical, a way to put us in a position where they can make whatever demands they see fit. I reply to him: 'You know my mandate. Obviously, if you don't want to talk about foreign policy and defence, that's your choice, we won't talk about it. I can't force you.'

Such administrative arrangements may well prove useful, however, if ever the UK wants to participate with the EU in an external operation, to cooperate with the European Defence Agency, to use Galileo services or to join us in the fight against cyberattacks.

I then have to exit the meeting, leaving Clara and Paulina to continue the discussion on the agenda, the subjects of the negotiation, and the timetable, which will also be difficult. David Frost follows me into the corridor; he wants to let me know that he will be speaking at the Free University of Brussels this evening. The fact had not escaped me! I congratulate him for taking this initiative and participating in the public debate, and tell him that I intend to do the same thing when I go to the UK. As if he feels the need to justify himself, he then adds, 'This talk is really about my personal journey.'

In the evening, in his talk, entitled 'Reflection on the Revolutions in Europe' – an audacious (to say the least) reference to a 1790 book, *Reflections on the French Revolution*, by philosopher and politician Edmund Burke – David Frost seeks to explain why he, who had supported a first great revolution, that of the construction of Europe, had come to support a second revolution, in favour of the resurgence of the nation-state and national decision-making.

He paints the picture of an abstract and distant Europe, which was originally a 'partnership agreement in a trade' but has since come to be 'looked on with reverence', a shift refused by the British, who have always had radically different objectives, as they have shown by refusing Schengen, by their opt-out on justice and home affairs and by their 'ambivalent attitude towards the Lisbon Treaty'.

Mr Frost then turns to the economy:

It's clear that many in Britain more or less unenthusiastically went along with the EU for mainly economic rather than political reasons. It is this group who now fear the economic consequences of leaving. Indeed for many it seems to be a simple fact, rather than a prediction, that Brexit is going to do economic harm. They include, it seems, Michel Barnier, who said in Belfast that Brexit was 'always a matter of damage limitation'. I believe this is wrong and I will explain why.

He goes on to challenge the economic studies carried out in recent years by the UK government and the Bank of England, which he alleges exaggerate the impact of non-tariff barriers and the cost of customs procedures, misunderstand the relationship between trade and productivity, and underestimate the positive effects of Brexit, such as 'expanded trade with the rest of the world or regulatory change'.

A few curiosities crop up in this eloquent and well-constructed speech.

On the issue of the level playing field, Mr Frost refers to Boris Johnson's commitment, a few weeks ago, that the UK would 'not accept any diminution in [...] standards': 'It is perfectly possible', says Mr Frost, 'to have high standards, and indeed similar or better standards to those prevailing in the EU, without our laws and regulations necessarily doing exactly the same thing.' He takes as an example 'the ability to support our own agriculture to promote environmental goods relevant to our own countryside, and to produce crops that reflect our own climate, rather than being forced to work with rules designed for growing conditions in central France.' As a former Minister of Agriculture, I find it hard to see how the EU could possibly force British farmers to produce on the model of their colleagues in the Massif Central...

Going even further, to demonstrate the absurdity of our demands for a level playing field, Mr Frost imagines what the EU would say if the UK, with its higher standards, demanded that it dynamically harmonize its rules with those decided in Westminster. This thought experiment has its limits, though: after all, it is not the European Union that is leaving the United Kingdom...

The talk ends with a reference to General de Gaulle, of whom Mr Frost claims to be, like myself, a great admirer, and whom he sees as 'the man who believed in a Europe of nations'. I am touched by the reference. But de Gaulle is also the man who, upon returning to power in 1958, did not oppose the Treaty of Rome, and anchored France firmly within the European construction.

Wednesday, 19 February 2020: Slide wars

In his speech at the Free University, David Frost clearly explained the UK government's strategy in the negotiations on trade. It wants 'the Canada-Free Trade Agreement-type relationship which the EU has so often said is on offer – even if the EU itself now seems to be experiencing some doubts about that unfortunately.'

Echoing this statement, the UK government press office, put up to it, from what I hear, by Dominic Cummings, does us the honour of posting on Twitter our famous 'staircase' slide, which they then try to use against us:

> In 2017, the EU showed in its own slides that a Canada-style free trade deal was the only relationship available to the UK. Now they say that offer is not on the table after all. @MichelBarnier what has changed?

In reality, nothing at all has changed! And our 'staircase' shows very well that it is possible for a third country to have a more ambitious relationship with the Union than a free trade agreement, for example by being in the internal market like Norway, or in the Customs Union like Turkey.

It is the UK, with its red lines (regulatory autonomy, no substantial financial contribution to the EU budget, end of the free movement of persons, no jurisdiction for the EU Court of Justice, independent trade policy) that has closed these doors one by one. So it is the UK that has opted for the kind of free trade agreement that the Union has concluded with South Korea, Canada and Japan.

But as UK leaders know very well, and as we have always made quite clear, these different free trade agreements are not identical. There is no 'one size fits all'. Our agreement with Canada, CETA, is not like our agreement with Korea. Obviously, we have to adapt the deal according to individual partners.

And when it comes to the UK, there are many particularities to consider. Our geographical proximity, for one: we are five thousand kilometres from Canada, while on the island of Ireland we are zero kilometres from the UK. And then the intensity of our trade: €516 billion with the UK in 2018 as compared to €54 billion with Canada.

In fact, this sortie by the British came just at the right moment. Because for some weeks now we have been preparing for this little joust. We knew that the battle of ideas would have to be won with a 'visual'. Same thing again, then: as with the staircase, a mini internal competition was launched, this time won by Rachel Smit, who has joined our communications team after working at the Commission's internal think-tank.

Her slide objectively illustrates the geographical and economic proximity of the United Kingdom, which is incomparable with the situation of any other partner country of the European Union. This is why our agreement cannot be the same as others, and why we will insist to the very end on a credible level playing field.

In a context of feverish excitement in London, this graph is interpreted as a response to 10 Downing Street. Nick Gutteridge, the *Sun*'s Brussels correspondent, goes so far as to declare that the *Slide Wars* have begun!

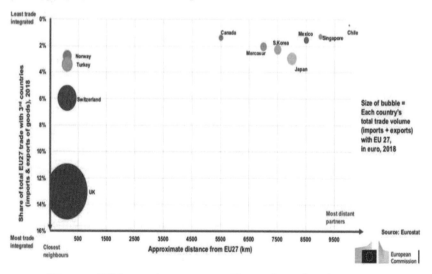

Diagram: EU free trade agreements: Geography and trade intensity
Source: Eurostat

In any case, most observers are not fooled by this somewhat childish dispute sparked by Dominic Cummings. Gavin Barwell, former chief of staff to Theresa May, who knows what he is talking about, writes in a tweet: 'Nothing has changed. The EU has always said an FTA with the UK would need greater level playing field provisions than CETA because of the UK's geographic proximity and the interdependence of the two economies.' He then refers to paragraph 77 of the Political Declaration agreed by Boris Johnson's government: 'Given the Union and the United Kingdom's geographic proximity and economic interdependence, the future relationship must ensure open and fair competition, encompassing robust commitments to ensure a level playing field.'

Wednesday, 26 February 2020: The UK is not Canada

As if we needed reminding, the negotiation will also be played out in public debate. For weeks now we have been preparing the terms in which to present our 'philosophical' framework. They will be set out in a speech to students of the five European campuses of ESCP, the university from which I graduated, who are gathered today in the hemicycle of the European Parliament in Brussels.

It's time to drive the point home. Drafting the text, Rachel and Matthieu propose that we go on the offensive.

> We are no longer in the 1970s, when the main purpose of trade agreements was to take down tariff walls.
>
> A modern trade agenda is about more than boosting economic exchanges and commercial opportunities.
>
> Modern trade is sustainable trade.
>
> It is about ensuring high standards, from social or environmental issues to health and safety.
>
> This is even more true with a very close partner like the UK, with whom we should develop a common ambition.
>
> As a member of the EU, the UK was central in reshaping the EU's trade policy, turning it into a tool to lift millions out of poverty, and to promote sustainability and fairness around the world.
>
> How would we explain it if our future partnership with the UK did not now follow this same philosophy?

How credible would we be going into the next COP26 meeting, in Glasgow, if our future agreement allows businesses to cut corners on environmental and social rights for the sake of gaining market shares?

Of course, we have heard Prime Minister Johnson's assurances that the UK would never engage in a race to the bottom; that it would not seek to undermine European standards; that the UK would in fact maintain higher standards than the EU.

And we are ready to believe this.

In fact, I do not believe that the UK will become some sort of 'Singapore on Thames'.

But that means it should not be a problem for the UK to agree on a number of ground rules.

Monday, 2 March 2020: Curtain up

It is with the serenity of a well prepared and united team that we approach the first round of negotiations.

A new ritual is inaugurated: after intensive consultations with the member states and the European Parliament, each week begins with a preparatory meeting between the members of the task force and our correspondents in each of the twenty-two Commission Directorates-General involved in the negotiations, and the European External Action Service.

In total this amounts to around a hundred people, all of whom I ask to leave their mobile phones at the door and to respect strict rules of confidentiality. For each of the eleven negotiating tables, we review our positions and the difficulties we are likely to encounter, and we refine our strategy for the week. I also assure them that they are all instrumental to the discussions, that their role is important and that I have confidence in them.

David Frost arrives at the Berlaymont in the afternoon. During our first conversation he is friendly and his thinking is structured, even if behind the polite and friendly tone there are some very hard negotiating positions.

The curtain then rises on the negotiations. Forty-four negotiators, twenty-two on each side, meet in the large Schuman Room on the first floor.

In the face of worrying news of the spread of a new virus, Covid-19, we take care not to shake hands and to keep as much of a distance as possible. David Frost and I have a quick photo taken for posterity at the back of the room before a few words of introduction.

Table by table, the members of the task force and their correspondents in the Commission's Directorates-General explain very clearly and competently the EU's positions and our expectations for this first round. The British go through the same exercise. The tone is courteous and quite solemn. On the British side, I notice that each negotiator tries to include certain key words in their technical presentation: 'sovereign state', 'independence', 'take back control'. A way for the UK to try and show its determination, as if anybody had any doubts on that score…

After this initial meeting on Monday, the actual negotiation can begin. Marco Abate, Urška Grahek and the team of assistants have done a great job of establishing a functional framework for this negotiation. The SQUARE building on the Mont des Arts in the heart of Brussels is the venue for this first session. Its rooms are bright and well equipped. One floor for the British, one floor for the European Union, a common floor for sharing coffee and buffets. In total, some fifteen rooms are reserved for the various negotiation tables.

Wednesday, 4 March 2020: More questions than answers

This first round is first and foremost an exercise in listening, respecting one another and comparing positions. From one negotiating table to the next we see some points in common, but also some fundamental disagreements – overall, more divergences than there are convergences.

One thing has been confirmed: the British are not accepting as a starting point the Political Declaration negotiated and signed by Boris Johnson himself only a few months ago. I am scheduled to meet David Frost for coffee in SQUARE this Wednesday. In a negotiation, informal, direct exchanges and the trust they build count as much as plenary sessions. I arrive at this meeting with Clara, Paulina and Georg. On the British side, in addition to David Frost, his main deputies Tim Barrow, Oliver Lewis and Lindsay Appleby are there.

I ask him: 'David, in the very short time we have, how can you expect to move forward by taking steps backwards?' He simply replies that our starting positions are different, which is quite normal. And also that we don't share the same reading of the Political Declaration.

Thursday, 5 March 2020: 'Like Jesuits'

In concluding this round of negotiations, I emphasize the importance of respect for any pledges given here and of the proper implementation of the Withdrawal Agreement. Without this there will be no basis of trust between us for a future partnership. David Frost responds in kind and confirms the British commitment on this score. I thank him for that, even if we remain concerned about the implementation of the Protocol on Ireland and Northern Ireland.

My second point is on the free trade agreement, which must be the main pillar of our economic partnership. No doubt there is a common ambition, but I emphasize that for us there is a precondition: a level playing field with a robust implementation mechanism. A balanced agreement on fisheries must also be a part of this economic partnership. All of this goes together as a package.

My third point concerns the overall governance of our agreement. The UK wants a 'suite of agreements'. But in the Political Declaration we committed ourselves to seeking a single framework for governance. For us this is fundamental for the credibility and effectiveness of our future partnership.

Finally, I come to security. I note that the UK does not wish to negotiate at this stage on foreign policy and defence, but I emphasize that 'the table remains open'. On internal security, I stress the need for common guarantees on fundamental rights and data protection, and also dispute settlement mechanisms in line with the EU legal order – in other words, the EU Court of Justice, which is the only body that can interpret EU law in this area.

'Even if you do not share these guarantees', I say to the British negotiators, 'I note that you aim to participate in several European systems: PNR for air passenger security and Prüm for DNA data exchange, citing your geographical proximity and the level of our exchanges. So, in these areas, distance matters!'

David Frost takes his turn to speak, beginning by listing what he sees as our areas of convergence: trade in goods, services, aviation, nuclear and EU programmes – 'in short, all the areas where there are precedents'.

Echoing my diagnosis, he adds, however, that 'I am not as pessimistic as you', while nonetheless listing certain challenges: the 'so-called' (*sic*) level playing field, fisheries and governance. 'The aim of Brexit is change, and in all these areas the Union is offering continuity.' With no apparent sense of contradicting himself, he then declares himself surprised that, when it comes to internal security, the UK cannot remain connected to the EU's information systems relating to Schengen (SIS II) and criminal records (ECRIS)…

On the economic front, he then expresses the British desire for a simple free trade agreement accompanied by a small number of sectoral agreements, before concluding by mentioning the forthcoming negotiations with the United States: 'In some areas, such as cumulation of rules of origin, we think it is possible to be more ambitious with the Americans than with you.'

On this last point, I reply that I have read their negotiating mandate with the United States with great interest: 'I wish you luck!'

In the round-table discussion that follows, I notice that in each of the British speeches the word 'ambition' is used, just as in our first plenary session on Monday each of the British speakers took care to recall the requirement for 'independence'.

The session ends with a warning from me against the temptation to cherry-pick: 'You want the standard arrangements of a third country when these arrangements suit you, but on judicial cooperation, Europol, Eurojust, Prüm, SIS II, and on services, particularly financial services, you are asking us for an agreement without any preconditions. I simply observe that your ambition is sometimes rather selective.'

Throughout the week the British remained structured, coordinated, opportunistic, all singing 'from the same hymn sheet'. We expected nothing less.

At the beginning of this first round, David Frost told me of his concern that we remain very careful in our external communications: 'In relation to the press, we must conduct ourselves like Jesuits.' Naturally, I agreed that we should ask negotiators on both sides during each round to avoid any 'small talk' or informal briefings, which are always somewhat partial and never very productive. But at the end of each round I expect to report to the press, and therefore to the public, on the progress of the discussions.

And so this Thursday, after the closing plenary session, I am pleased to be back with the journalists in the European Commission's main press room. It's a useful exercise in order to record the progress made – on some of our objectives and some specific points, for example cooperation on civil nuclear matters and the participation of the United Kingdom in certain EU programmes – but above all to warn of the remaining differences. I mention four points of divergence: the level playing field, judicial and police cooperation in criminal matters, the governance of our future agreement and, finally, fisheries.

I end by publicly citing the two keys to the success of these negotiations: first, not reneging on commitments made, and, second, showing mutual respect. During this round, the UK has insisted a great deal on its independence. No one disputes this independence! And for our part, we ask the UK to respect our independence too. Just as the UK wants to set its own conditions for opening its market, the EU sets its own conditions for opening its goods and services markets. The real question is, how do we deal with our respective independences?

In asking this question I have in mind several editorials, including the one by Wolfgang Münchau in the *Financial Times* on 11 March: 'The UK's threat to walk out of EU trade talks is real.'* I believe that some of Boris Johnson's team have such a strategy in mind, a strategy of 'total liberation', of unconditional independence. This is Dominic Cummings's line, although it is obviously contrary to British economic interests in the short and medium terms.

The debate under way in the UK involves a conflict between economic realism and political ideology. And as Wolfgang Münchau rightly says, '[s]uccess or failure will depend on what the UK does with its new freedom'.

I believe – and I say this to the journalists present – that as independent entities, our common challenge is to agree on ground rules that allow us to cooperate. And also on high standards, at a comparable level, over

* https://www.ft.com/content/c49c986e-5a42-11ea-a528-dd0f971febbc.

the long term, to protect our citizens, our consumers, our workers and our planet.

I conclude with a message of hope: if we work in mutual respect, without going back on any commitments made, then I think an agreement is possible, even if it is difficult to achieve.

Sunday, 8 March 2020: Light of day

After a few days of internal debate, we decide to publish the full legal text of an agreement with the UK on Wednesday. Reasons both for and against were cited. For: to take the initiative by proposing a text around which discussions can be structured – and to avoid allowing the British to take the lead. Against: we run the risk of the British rejecting our positions out of hand, proposing a competing text and thus getting into a deadlock.

Marie Simonsen, head of our legal unit, has done some great work with her deputies Liana Bratusca and Felix Ronkes Agerbeek to push the text across the finish line, together with the other colleagues in the task force, legal services, and all the Directorates-General of the Commission.

A real team effort, this involved nothing less than translating the principles and the content of our mandate into legal terms and into the format of a final agreement right now – more than eight hundred pages in total. This team spent the weekend at the office, and this morning I come to thank them and encourage them by bringing them *pastéis de nata*.

Next week the Commissioners and their cabinets will be invited to read this document, which we will then submit to the member states. The text can then be developed further. It is also a negotiating tool in itself, and I know that the British will try to contradict it or trivialize it. But at least it will prove that an ambitious and comprehensive treaty is feasible even within a limited time frame, if there is a will on both sides.

Friday, 20 March 2020: Patient zero?

Over the last two weeks, news about the Covid-19 pandemic has become increasingly worrying. In Brussels, as elsewhere in Europe, teleworking has become widespread, and there are reports that schools will not reopen after the winter holidays. Members of my team, like other Commission officials, have started taking their laptops home at the end of the day in case they can no longer come into the office.

Last Friday, 13 March, I gathered the whole task force together to get ourselves ready for the Commission's new working rules. I then left as planned to take a few days off with my family at our house in Sologne. That evening, a member of my team informed me that he was not feeling well and that his symptoms corresponded to those of the coronavirus. As a precaution he had stayed home since Tuesday, 10 March and had informed his colleagues. On Sunday I also felt feverish and, in order not to endanger my team, decided not to return to Brussels. I consulted a doctor, who prescribed a PCR test.

The result was quick: the day before yesterday, at the end of the day, I tested positive for Covid-19.

I want to be honest and inform all those I have met in the past few days – to say things simply, with the same responsibility I take for the negotiations. My eldest son, Nicolas, who is also passionate about politics, even if he has his own ideas, has some good advice. It is he who suggests that I tell this truth in a short video posted on my Twitter account. I add a word of solidarity and support to all the many families already affected by this virus, in some cases very seriously. And a word of recognition and respect for all medical staff, who are doing a wonderful job, as I can testify.

In my library I find a book I wrote a few years ago on the ecological emergency, entitled *Chacun pour tous* (*Each for All*). This is precisely the watchword that we have to respect today: each of us, every citizen, has a role to play for the sake of all of us, if we are to win this collective battle, this war against the virus. Everyone at home, each for all. For the collective good of all, each of us must make a personal commitment to solidarity, unity and benevolence. With this, I believe we will be able to emerge from this crisis stronger than ever.

Today it is David Frost who experiences Covid-19 symptoms and has to self-isolate. We haven't seen each other for over two weeks, but that hasn't stopped some British tabloids from linking Covid to our negotiations. And when, a few days later, the Prime Minister himself is hit by the virus, the *Mail on Sunday* will go so far as to run the headline 'Did Barnier infect BoJo?', suggesting that 'the EU negotiator could be the "patient zero" who brought virus to No 10'. The British tabloids definitely still have more than enough cynicism to go around!

Monday, 30 March 2020: Second major project for 2020

For a fortnight, distanced within the house, I felt highly fatigued and, on the eighth and ninth days, had such violent coughing fits that I wasn't sure where this illness was taking me. But finally the symptoms are receding, and I am grateful to my wife Isabelle for her help and support.

In this lockdown period the vast majority of our team is staying at home, but the distance does not prevent us from working. Like everyone else, we are getting used to videoconferencing as the new norm.

Today, for example, marks the first meeting of the Joint Committee stipulated in the Withdrawal Agreement as a means to ensure its proper implementation. This Committee is made up of representatives of the United Kingdom, headed by Minister of State Michael Gove, and of the European Union, under the aegis of Vice-President Maroš Šefčovič. A former diplomat and Slovak presidential candidate, Mr Šefčovič has taken up the torch for the implementation of the Withdrawal Agreement. It's no easy task, but he has the energy and strength to succeed.

On citizens' rights, the UK has confirmed its commitment to EU citizens, who can register as legally resident in the country and thus benefit from the rights guaranteed by the Withdrawal Agreement. For our part, we will work with the member states to ensure that British citizens living in the EU enjoy the same rights.

In Ireland and Northern Ireland, the British must put in place the customs, regulatory and phytosanitary procedures for all products arriving from a third country or from Great Britain at Northern Ireland ports and airports. None of this can be left to chance. It requires personnel to carry out the controls and it requires infrastructure. It is not a question of renegotiating the Withdrawal Agreement but of making it operational in practice on 31 December.

Monday, 20 April 2020: Virtual rounds

The second round, scheduled for the week of 18 March, had to be cancelled. The third round, supposed to take place during the week of 6

April, also had to be cancelled owing to the health conditions. Not only were the two negotiators affected, but several members of our teams were as well. Nonetheless, throughout these weeks we have maintained contact at a distance.

But time is short. In order to resume formal exchanges we have announced a week of virtual negotiations starting today. In the midst of a crisis that is hitting Europe hard – particularly the UK, which has not yet followed Italy, Spain, France and Belgium in imposing a strict lockdown – it is clear that the Brexit negotiations are no longer at the top of the political agenda. Cécile Ducourtieux, the respected London correspondent of *Le Monde*, even dubs the negotiations 'surreal'.*

Paradoxical perhaps, in the midst of such a crisis, but certainly not surreal. On the contrary, we have a duty to be realistic in the face of two deadlines that are fixed in law. First of all, 30 June, the date upon which we, together with the British, must decide whether or not the transition period will be extended, and with it the negotiations. And then of course 31 December, the day set for economic Brexit, following the political Brexit of 31 January. On that day, will the UK leave the Single Market and Customs Union with a deal or without one? Do we want to risk compounding the health crisis with another economic shock caused by a no deal? There is nothing 'surreal' about asking this question.

We are therefore initiating an unprecedented new schedule, with a round of negotiations consisting of forty virtual meetings. Thanks to our team of assistants, the remote negotiations go as smoothly as possible, even if the quality of the discussions suffers somewhat.

David Frost confirms to me that Boris Johnson has to refuse any extension of the transition period, and that the UK will therefore leave the Single Market and Customs Union on 31 December 2020, eight months from now.

We take note of this choice, and I simply recommend to David Frost that he thinks carefully before the high-level conference where the decision will have to be made formally. Because before the end of June, the President of the Commission and probably the Presidents of the

---

* https://www.lemonde.fr/international/article/2020/04/20/brexit-reprise-surrealiste-des-negociations-entre-londres-et-bruxelles_6037228_3210.html.

European Council and the European Parliament will have to be apprised of the state of negotiations with Boris Johnson.

In the days that follow, despite our proposal for a comprehensive legal text, the discussions do not go beyond the stage of clarifications. I report on this very limited progress at a press conference of a kind I have not experienced before: the large press room of the European Commission is empty apart from two cameras and a screen through which the journalists, at home, ask their questions. Despite this very impersonal atmosphere, I am happy to see the Brussels correspondents again, looking alert and asking precise questions. I choose to conclude this press briefing on an optimistic note:

> I have been open about the serious difficulties that lie ahead.
>
> I still believe that we can surmount them in the coming months with political will, realism and mutual respect.
>
> And I would add that the current sanitary, economic and social crisis adds to the duty that we have – Europeans and Brits – to build, in the coming months, an ambitious partnership between us.

Monday, 27 April 2020: A time for reflection

An optimistic note for the journalists, but in reality I am concerned. Time is passing, and a kind of trench warfare is taking hold. Over the weekend I spoke to Clara and we decided to hold a strategic meeting with those in charge of the different negotiating tables.

How can we overcome such pointless opposition? How can we approach the high-level meeting, which is not only the deadline for deciding on a possible extension of the transition period, but also marks an inevitable mid-term political assessment of the negotiations? What will the British attitude and strategy be as they prepare for this deadline with a view to concluding negotiations in the autumn?

Clara paints us a picture of the next few rounds – a tight schedule but no major breakthroughs in sight. The British did set a deadline of June in their mandate at the beginning of the year: if no results were in sight by then, they said, they would be prepared to leave the table. But Covid has shaken things up. In her regular, sometimes daily contact with David Frost, Clara senses very little initiative or will to get things moving.

Paulina reports the same noncommittal attitude among the member states. The priority is elsewhere. The high-level meeting will almost certainly be a non-event. But maybe, Ivo says, the British are trying to use this deadline – and the confirmation of the non-extension of the transition period – to make the twenty-seven nervous.

In reality there are two possible trajectories for this negotiation. A rational outcome, with positions gradually coming together through the will and the efforts of both parties. Or the more chaotic scenario of a war of nerves, with the permanent threat of a no deal being lifted only at the very last moment. But, as Georg suggests in a briefing that he has prepared for the occasion, neither can we rule out a 'madman strategy'. Behind the scenes, Dominic Cummings is steering the negotiations in London. The British government could try to get their way with surprises, unpredictability and threats.

For our part, we must remain calm, confident and solid. We must show that we are true to our principles while seeking solutions to unblock the discussions. Antonio and Nicolas, who are leading two of the most difficult tables, on trade and the level playing field, suggest a method for the high-level conference: set targets for June and milestones for each round between now and then. We all agree. This gives us a roadmap. It is our responsibility to find a rational way of proceeding.

Tuesday, 5 May 2020: Fair play is not for sale!

Movement on the UK side: Michael Gove says that the UK might be willing to abandon the 'zero-tariff, zero-quota' objective in order to avoid a level playing field.

This proposal would mean the reinstatement of tariffs and quotas that have not existed for decades, an anachronism that the EU does not want to see. It would also require detailed – and extremely sensitive – negotiations on each tariff line. As we have seen recently with Japan and Canada, this can take years.

Above all, even if certain tariffs were to be kept in place, the EU would continue to demand strong guarantees of a level playing field. For the EU, fair competition, essential to protect consumers, must lie at the heart of any new trade agreement. We will not trade away our European values for the benefit of the British economy. Economic and commercial fair play is not for sale!

Even today, the ambassadors I meet at the Coreper meeting clearly restate that, without a level playing field, and without an agreement on fisheries, there will be no agreement on our economic and trade partnership.

And these conditions of fair competition will even have to be specified further in certain domains, for example for road transport by detailing the working conditions of drivers.

The whole paradox of this discussion is that the UK government is telling us that it would be happy with a Canada-type agreement, while at the same time asking us to maintain the benefits of the internal market in countless different areas: service providers, electricity interconnection, auditing firms, lawyers, financial services.

To this day there is still a complete lack of understanding in the UK of the objective – and in some cases mechanical – consequences of the UK's choice to leave the Single Market and the Customs Union.

To make progress in this negotiation, the UK will need to be more realistic, will have to overcome this misunderstanding and, perhaps, change its strategy.

As they say in English, you can't have it both ways. The German idiom gives an even more striking image: '*Man kann nicht auf zwei Hochzeiten gleichzeitig tanzen*': 'You can't dance at two weddings at the same time!'

Friday, 15 May 2020: Disappointing exchanges

Third round. At each of the tables, our negotiators are expressing our expectations for June and trying to find a path with the British to achieve them.

Our discussions are stimulated by new draft texts sent by the UK, but I regret that the British do not wish to make these texts public, which prevents us from communicating their contents to the member states and the European Parliament.

These texts provide useful clarifications on a number of subjects such as trade in goods, transport and the UK's participation in future EU programmes. But there is still no progress on the most difficult issues, and in particular that of the level playing field.

As for fisheries, which we are finally starting to discuss this week, our positions are very far apart. The UK is demanding that it regain 'sovereignty over its waters', and the ability to control access through annual decisions. It extends this sovereignty to the fish in its waters, and wants to impose the principle of 'zonal attachment' in the allocation of fishing quotas. But, as everyone knows, pelagic fish are highly migratory, born in one sea and swimming and maturing in another. As I explained to David Frost, 'trying to count fish at home makes no sense'. We have a responsibility to manage these resources – one hundred different species – together. We have also been unable to make progress on the single governance framework and we are disappointed by the UK's lack of ambition in other areas that are not so symbolic, such as the fight against money laundering and the respective roles to be played by the European Parliament, the UK Parliament and civil society in the implementation of our future relationship.

Finally, on police and judicial cooperation on criminal matters, the UK refuses to commit to guarantees to protect fundamental rights and individual freedoms under the European Convention for the Protection of Human Rights. It insists on lowering current standards and deviating from agreed data-protection mechanisms. It would even have the EU ignore its own law on PNR data. Obviously an impossible demand.

Reciprocity in the exchange of data between UK authorities and member states is also an important question. The European Parliament is very vigilant on this, particularly with regard to the exchange of biometric data, which is governed by the Prüm programme.

At my press conference at the end of the round, I decided to respond publicly to Michael Gove and his suggestion of reintroducing tariffs in order to dispense with the level playing field: 'Such a negotiation, which would take much longer, would therefore only be possible with an extension of the transition period. Is this what we are to understand from Mr Gove's statement?'

Friday, 29 May 2020: Theodore!

Progress or not, the negotiations must be explained. Just as I met with the European Trade Union Confederation (ETUC), this morning I am meeting with the employers' association Business Europe, capably headed up by Markus Beyrer.

In the middle of my presentation I receive a text message announcing the birth of our grandson Theodore, son of my daughter Laetitia and her husband Augustin. I share my great joy at the news spontaneously with the hundred or so participants, who applaud, giving this meeting a warmer atmosphere than the negotiations.

Friday, 5 June 2020: Bis repetita

The scenario of a remote, antiseptic negotiation leading to no real tangible results is repeated in our fourth round.

On all points, and on the level playing field in particular, the British negotiators continue to ignore the Political Declaration, negotiated and approved by Boris Johnson and then voted for by the British Parliament just six months ago.

For example, in paragraph 77 of this declaration, Boris Johnson committed himself to 'uphold[ing] the common high standards applicable in the Union and the United Kingdom at the end of the transition period in the areas of state aid, competition, social and employment standards, environment, climate change and relevant tax matters'. Four rounds of negotiations later, this remains a distant prospect!

Not to mention fisheries, where we are committed on both sides to making our 'best efforts' to conclude and ratify a new agreement before 1 July 2020…

Friday, 12 June 2020: One-way borders?

An announcement by the British government: the United Kingdom will not impose systematic checks on lorries entering its territory through the port of Dover or the Channel Tunnel at the end of the year. The government will opt for lighter controls, 'probably not very different from what exists today'.

According to Denis MacShane, this is a reversal of the British government's supposed desire to 'take back control'. Tony Blair's former minister says it is also 'a sign that the hard Brexit camp in government may not be as hard as previously thought'.

Others do not see it that way. I note the analysis of the BBC's Katya Adler, who simply sees it as a reality that the UK government is forced to accept: they will not be ready. So the government therefore does not want to risk disrupting supplies of food and other goods into the UK.

The stakes are high. Lidl alone brings in 1,300 trucks from the EU to its shops every day. But this solution is inherently flawed, firstly because it does not rule out controls on UK exports such as fresh foods or those delivered in real time. On the other hand, it is not clear how the UK could sustainably tolerate a porous border.

Denis MacShane alludes to this, saying that in these uncontrolled lorries there could be not just food and other goods, but also illegal migrants. This, he says, may explain why the British insist on addressing the issue of unaccompanied minors in our agreement, although this was not mentioned in the Political Declaration.

Monday, 15 June 2020: High-level meeting

Finally the moment arrives for the political progress report. The Commission President is in the audiovisual studio in the basement of the Berlaymont. I stay in my office on the fifth floor. We are connected, and on the four-way screen there appear Boris Johnson and the three presidents of the European institutions, David Sassoli, Ursula von der Leyen and Charles Michel. The introductory remarks are rather conventional. No surprises there. But then suddenly Boris Johnson's voice rings out: 'Where is Michel?' 'I'm here,' replies the President of the European Council, Charles Michel. 'No, the other Michel!' replies Johnson. '*I'm here!*' I say, in English. Isabelle Misrachi turns on my camera, finally making my presence known...

On the timetable, the die is cast: Mr Johnson confirms that he will not ask for an extension of the transition period. The UK will therefore leave the Single Market and the Customs Union on 31 December, and we have little more than four useable months to find an agreement. Then the Prime Minister gives us three red lines: no role for the EU Court of Justice in the UK; the right for his country to decide its own laws without constraints; and a fisheries deal that adds up to a real difference. 'We need to double the value of what we fish in our waters', he exclaims, adding: 'We need to speed up, instruct our teams to intensify these negotiations. We need to put a tiger in the tank, Ursula!'

And so an 'intensification' of the negotiations is agreed upon. David Sassoli, with whom we carefully prepared the conference, adds his grain of salt, reminding Prime Minister Johnson of his Latin: '*Pacta sunt servanda*, Boris.* We need you to honour your commitments on the level playing field.' Charles Michel, not to be outdone, calls on his schoolboy memories of English lessons: 'Yes, Boris, we are ready to put a tiger in the tank, but not to buy a pig in a poke!'

Quite an inspired day…

Monday, 29 June 2020: 'A missive from a free country'

At the beginning of this summer I received a rather curious letter from Mark Francois, chairman of the famous European Research Group (ERG), a group of committed Brexiteers who were prominent at various moments during the withdrawal negotiations, notably when they advocated a purely technological solution to the Northern Ireland border issue.

In this letter dated 26 June and headlined 'A missive from a free country', Mark Francois introduces me to the ERG as if I had been born yesterday: '[I]t is possible that you may have heard of us'…

In the letter Mr Francois goes on to express his concern about the EU's demands for a 'so-called "Level Playing Field"', which he says 'seems like little more than a demand that the UK continues to follow EU laws and judgements, even though we have now formally left the European Union'. On fisheries, Mr Francois refers to the 'extremely damaging Common Fisheries Policy, … anathema to us and to many of our countrymen'. Finally, '[i]n the spirit of honesty among friends', Mr Francois lets me know that 'there can be no way that the European Court of Justice (ECJ) can be allowed have any role in the UK's national life after the end of this year'.

In my reply I point out that, as a former parliamentarian myself, I am always interested in the views of British parliamentarians, and that in

---

* 'Pacts must be respected.'

recent years I have met British politicians of all stripes, including ERG members.

I then attempt to clear up any misunderstanding:

> While nobody has been able to demonstrate to me the added value of leaving the most integrated economic and free trade area in the world, I have always respected the UK's decision to withdraw from the EU. In this spirit, the EU negotiated the Withdrawal Agreement with your government. In this same spirit, we approach the ongoing negotiations with your great – and indeed free – country, which will remain a close neighbour, friend and ally of the European Union.

Finally, I respond to all the points that Mr Francois raises, with reference to the terms of the Political Declaration voted for by the House of Commons, including Mr Francois himself.

Tuesday, 30 June 2020: Reunions

This week talks resume in physical form with a round in Brussels, followed by two weeks of technical discussions in London, and then back to Brussels again.

I am rather relieved to be resuming this face-to-face work, which makes communication easier and saves time. We're going to need it!

We continue with our strategy of constructive engagement. Boris Johnson has set out his three red lines. We cannot take everything at face value, but we will seek to take them on board as far as possible. I decide to offer an opening on the issue of the EU Court of Justice. This is not an ideological position for the Union, but a constitutional principle. The Court must remain the ultimate arbiter of European law. If the British refuse it, then we are prepared to reduce the scope of our cooperation so that our law and our court will have no need to intervene.

But if we make a gesture towards the UK, we also expect a commitment from them in return. I therefore repeat to David Frost that there will be no economic partnership without robust guarantees of a level playing field, a balanced, sustainable and long-term solution for fisheries, and a single institutional framework including effective dispute settlement mechanisms. The day ends with a telephone conversation with Micheál

Martin, the new Irish Taoiseach, who is already fully aware of the issues at stake in this negotiation. We agree to stay in close contact so as to follow both the negotiations and the situation in Ireland and Northern Ireland.

Tuesday, 7 July 2020: London calling

I head for the Gare du Midi to catch my train to London where a few of us are to have dinner with David Frost at 10 Downing Street after a meeting with Boris Johnson. In the car, my phone rings. It's Angela Merkel, who wants to give me a detailed report on the phone conversation she just had with Boris Johnson. 'I made our positions clear, and said that we were all behind you.' Just a few words, but messages that count. The British may have thought that we would start to waver under the pressure of their inflexibility, national interests and the passing of time. Going to London with a strong message of unity from the twenty-seven is of inestimable value to me.

Only a small delegation is going, but there is a taste of freedom to the trip after months of lockdown. Marco and his team will explore the possibility of further rounds of negotiations in London later this month.

Clara, Paulina, Georg and I arrive at Downing Street. David Frost first welcomes us to Margaret Thatcher's study, where we sit around the large oak table used for the G8 summit in Lough Erne, Northern Ireland, in 2013.

The British, hosting for the first time, engage in a lively but constructive discussion on the level playing field. Oliver Lewis, deputy to David Frost and Dominic Cummings, points to 'philosophical differences' that we need to overcome. For him, sovereignty is the first principle. The UK will not be able to commit to non-regression of standards, especially environmental standards, if it means tying the hands of its Parliament in the future. We try to take his arguments on board. Paulina explains that we are not imposing anything on the British, since to date we have had common standards, and that non-regression is a standard concept in free trade agreements.

Then Boris Johnson bursts into the room, followed by Mark Sedwill, the Cabinet Secretary. A few hearty handshakes, a quip or two – 'You managed to cross the Channel, then?' – before David Frost suggests a face-to-face meeting in the Prime Minister's office.

'So, if I read the papers correctly, it was you who gave us Covid?' says Boris Johnson with a smile. To which I reply, 'Maybe it's the other way around…'

I know I have to choose my topic carefully, as we cannot talk about everything. So I start the conversation on state aid. 'We can have totally open markets, but not if you dump or compete unfairly against us. We like British-made cars, but we won't like your subsidies any more than you will like ours. How can we cooperate openly if we don't know about your new national system of state aid control?'

'Good point! Let's work on that!' he replies.

Friday, 17 July 2020: Political sovereignty

The past ten days have been devoted to a sequence of meetings in London and Brussels. The 'philosophical gaps' observed at 10 Downing Street are reflected subject by subject, table by table.

The *Financial Times* supplies a lucid analysis of the situation in its editorial today:

> In truth, Brexit was never an economic issue for those who championed the cause. It was about political sovereignty. As such it will deliver for those who wanted a new immigration system controlled by the British government. It may even – though this is far less certain – deliver for the fishing communities that were promised a new settlement outside the Common Fisheries Policy. But while these political gains, for those who see them as such, may be realised, the government has so far failed to come even close to demonstrating how Brexit will bolster the nation's economy.*

Thursday, 23 July 2020: Watching live at the pub

In this last week of July it is the turn of the whole task force to leave for London, along with the representatives of the Commission Directorates-General negotiating with us.

* 'Reality punctures Britain's Brexit balloon', *Financial Times*, 17 July 2020.

Isabelle Misrachi, Julie François and Giovanna Di Ruberti from our team have done an impressive job of organizing the event. At a time when Covid-19 is still very much in evidence across the Channel, we have the Eurostar almost entirely to ourselves, and the very friendly staff at the Conrad Hotel, in close proximity to the UK government centre where the negotiations are taking place, say they are delighted to welcome us.

It's a convenient and comfortable place, if perhaps a little dark in the basement meeting rooms. British MPs have established habits here, especially in the nearby pub, where there is not only a gallery of portraits of former prime ministers but also a bell that is rung to let MPs know when debate is resuming in the House.

In the middle of the health crisis, the atmosphere is of course quiet, and we quickly get used to this place where we will be spending a lot of time from now on.

The actual discussions take place five minutes' walk from the hotel, in the conference centre of BEIS, the UK Department for Business, Energy and Industrial Strategy. Here too we are housed in a basement, albeit a large and well-lit one.

Unfortunately, this change of setting has no noticeable effect on the substance of the negotiations. We continue to engage sincerely and constructively in the discussion, to seek solutions within the red lines set out by Boris Johnson. But we do not feel that the UK is committed to respecting our own principles and interests in return.

The round ends, however, with a small glimmer of hope. Welcoming us to dinner at 1 Carlton Gardens, David Frost is keen to show me the statue of General de Gaulle that stands in front of the offices he occupied on behalf of the Free French during the war. I appreciate this gesture, and so the conversation begins on a point of common interest, which is not a bad start.

And tonight Mr Frost is a little more conciliatory, even on fisheries,: 'We must have full sovereignty over access to our waters, but we understand your concern: we cannot keep putting up the shutters.' We get a foot in the door. 'No shutters, no annual guillotine', says Georg.

As I have chosen to do after every round, I give a detailed account of the discussions in a press conference. This is a first on British soil, and for me it's an important exercise. Last night at the hotel I reviewed the text carefully with Matthieu and the small team, over a studious but, as always, convivial dinner. Stéphanie Fromm, who joined us from the Commission's Spokesperson's Service, is working hard organizing the event at the European Commission's London delegation. The building, which served as the headquarters of the Conservative Party under Margaret Thatcher, does not have the technical facilities of the Commission's press room. But nothing is impossible for Stéphanie and Dan when it comes to communicating with the press. In the end, Dan reads the journalists' questions from the lectern, and I answer them live. Several members of the team watch the press conference from the pub next door, thanks to a live BBC broadcast. The first time this has happened to me, and probably the last!

I choose to end the press conference on a positive note:

I want to reaffirm the EU's willingness to reach an ambitious partnership agreement in all areas including, even later on, in external security and defence. This is also the wish of Presidents Ursula von der Leyen and Charles Michel, the European Parliament and the twenty-seven heads of state or government.

I continue to believe that Prime Minister Boris Johnson and the UK government want to find an agreement with the EU.

Because it is in our common interest to cooperate and to address the many and serious challenges of today: climate change and biodiversity, health and security, research and innovation, democracy and fundamental rights, the fight against poverty and financial stability.

If I may borrow a famous line from Saint-Exupéry, negotiation is not just to look or to speak at one another. It is to look together in the same direction.

Saturday, 1 August 2020: London wants to reflect

Following the intense discussions in July, the British have asked that the first two weeks of August be used as a 'period of reflection', which in fact allows the teams on both sides to take a few days off, even though we should already be preparing for the seventh round, scheduled to take place in Brussels on 17 August.

We have some hopes that the British will use this period to shift their positions, as we did when working on Boris Johnson's three red lines. We even wonder whether it could mean moving a few more steps forward. If circumstances warrant, we could go a step further towards them to reach an agreement on the access to waters regime, which would clear one of the two major fisheries obstacles. Stefan Fuehring and his teammate Viktória Varga-Lencsés are therefore considering this. But there are doubts as to the sincerity of the British negotiators. We cannot rule out that their objective is still to draw us out while keeping their own options open until the last minute.

Thursday, 6 August 2020: Inevitable changes

We are also taking advantage of the summer months to explain the changes to citizens, companies and government administrations. We want to alert them to the changes that will come into effect on 1 January 2021, whatever happens. Because from that date we will have two separate markets, with all the inevitable consequences that implies.

For example, rules of origin will come into force to ensure that products imported into the EU from the UK are genuinely British products (or at least have sufficient British inputs). There will inevitably be new customs formalities, if only to check that these rules of origin are being properly applied.

All imports of goods, whether toys, medical devices or food products, and all services provided in the Union, will have to comply with our rules on health, safety and other public policy standards. So there will also be regulatory controls on goods entering the Union.

And of course there will no longer be harmonization or mutual recognition of regulations. This means, for example, that British financial services providers will lose the 'passport' that formerly allowed them to offer their services throughout the EU while being based in the City of London. Several British banks are already informing EU customers that they will have to close their accounts by 31 December.

At the beginning of July we detailed all these changes for citizens, businesses and administrations in a Commission publication called *Getting Ready for Changes*.* We have also updated the hundred or so notices that, for each sector of activity, detail the actions to be taken to

* https://eur-lex.europa.eu/legal-content/EN/TXT/PDF/?uri= CELEX:52020DC0324.

prepare for the end of the transition. Finally, I am pleased to say that the heads of state or government of the twenty-seven member states, in the historic agreement of 21 July on the recovery plan and the EU budget for the next seven years, have decided to create a special fund of €5 billion, the 'Brexit Adjustment Reserve', to help the economic sectors and territories most heavily affected by Brexit.

Over the summer I chose to relay this explanation through a series of tweets in each of the twenty-four languages of the Union.

The British response was swift. Two hours after my first tweet in English, they also took to Twitter to put out their own preparedness document, stating that the end of the transition period on 1 January will allow UK businesses and the UK economy to benefit from new trade deals…

But for the moment, rather than 'new opportunities', the press is reporting on new complications for UK businesses.

For example, according to an official document presented by Michael Gove, British businesses will have to fill in 215 million additional customs declarations at an estimated annual cost of £7 billion. As some commentators point out, the days when Brexiteers promised fantastic savings from Brexit now seem like a distant memory…

One consequence of these new customs controls is a risk of massive traffic jams in the south of the UK.

The UK government is even planning to have two thousand lorries park on a slip road on the M20 motorway in advance of their arrival at the ports of Dover and Folkestone. A further two thousand spaces are planned at Ashford in Kent. These measures help to show what Brexit really means.

Friday, 21 August 2020: Illusions dispelled

On Monday, nearly two hundred negotiators from both sides called an end to their holidays – in fact, some had hardly taken any – to prepare for the resumption of negotiations. As if to encourage us, David Frost tweeted last week: 'Our assessment is that agreement can be reached in September and we will work to achieve this if we can.' But at our dinner on Tuesday evening, Mr Frost warned me not to expect anything from this round. The requested 'pause for reflection' has not delivered on its promises.

I therefore tell the teams that we need to hold as firm a line as possible, with strict respect for parallelism. If the British do not commit themselves on governance, the level playing field and fisheries, then there is no reason for us to give them any satisfaction on energy or transport.

This makes it all the more necessary to prepare for the risk of a no deal, which would have far more dramatic consequences than the inevitable changes of Brexit.

At the time of the negotiations on the withdrawal of the United Kingdom, we had already devised 'contingency measures' that would allow us to mitigate the most serious consequences of a possible British exit without an agreement. This time the situation is a little different. We can rely on the Withdrawal Agreement, which remains in place and settles many issues. Since 1 February 2020, the transition period has also given companies and administrations the time they need to prepare for all scenarios. Finally, some measures that the Union adopted in 2019 will remain in force or will become applicable at the end of the transition period. For example, the United Kingdom will be listed among the third countries whose citizens are exempt from visa requirements for short stays in the EU.

The contingency measures we would need in the event of a no deal would therefore be far more limited than those imagined at the end of 2019, but we must focus on the most serious effects of a no deal – those that no amount of preparation can avoid, in domains where no international agreement offers a satisfactory 'safety net'. This is the case in aviation, where negotiating bilateral agreements between the UK and each member state would fragment the Single European Sky.

For a limited period, during which time a specific agreement will be worked out with the United Kingdom, we therefore propose to guarantee minimal air connectivity by allowing British airlines to fly over EU territory, to make technical stops and to carry passengers and freight between the UK and one EU airport. But they will not be able to drop off or pick up passengers at any other EU airport. So a flight arriving in Madrid from London would then have to return to the UK, and would not be allowed to stop in Paris to drop off or pick up passengers. Naturally, these contingency measures will be conditional upon reciprocal measures by the UK for European airlines.

I ask my team, in particular Noura Rouissi and Guido Dolara, to prepare these contingency measures now – for air connectivity, but also for air safety and road transport – even if it is too early to make them public.

Wednesday, 2 September 2020: Meeting at Chequers

Since the resumption of negotiations in April, the rounds have come and gone. Following the frustrating round in mid-August, we returned to London yesterday as a smaller select committee.

I feel the need to hold a strategic review with members of the inner team. I gather Clara, Paulina, Antonio, Stefan, Georg, Marie, Nicolas and Luca in the small room called 'Chequers' in the hotel basement. Each of them speaks in turn, but their reports on what we have achieved are similar: not much. Clara and Paulina both remind us that we must be realistic. The British are not afraid of a no deal, and we must be ready for it. Antonio and Stefan qualify this: the British want us to *believe* that they are not afraid of a no deal. On one point we all agree: the British have opted against working towards a rational and constructive agreement.

Georg uses a striking image: we are in a game of 'chicken' – two drivers are heading towards each other on a collision course, and one has to swerve to avoid a crash. Of a total of one thousand metres of negotiation, as of 1 September we have travelled only six hundred metres. We have to keep our cool. Agreement may very well not be reached until December…

We don't agree on the timetable. Marie reminds us of the deadlines for ratification and feels that a conclusion must be reached well before December. I think that we can go until November at the latest. But yes, the British are playing for time and exhaustion. We must therefore be prepared for a war of nerves, and prepare the member states for that too.

From the very beginning, our intuitions are confirmed. In a one-on-one meeting, David Frost warns me that the time for substantial steps forward has not come. I tell him that we have great reserves of calm and serenity on our side!

And so we prepare ourselves to make the most of a new round of negotiations next week, which we know will be unsuccessful.

Monday, 7 September 2020: A warning shot

Yesterday the *Financial Times* ran the headline: 'UK plan to undermine Withdrawal Treaty puts Brexit talks at risk. Internal market bill to override parts of N Ireland protocol as Johnson says sides should move on if no deal by Oct 15.' The announcement that the Withdrawal Agreement might be called into question comes as a shock. Taken by surprise by what is undoubtedly a leak, the British go on the attack. In a statement on 'the final phase of our negotiations with the EU', Boris Johnson turns up the heat:

> If we can't agree by [15 October], then I do not see that there will be a free trade agreement between us, and we should both accept that and move on.
>
> We will then have a trade arrangement with the European Union like Australia's. I want to be absolutely clear that, as we have said right from the start, that would be a good outcome for the UK. As a government we are preparing, at our borders and at our ports, to be ready for it. We will have full control over our laws, our rules and our fishing waters. We will have the freedom to do trade deals with every country in the world. And we will prosper mightily as a result.

The Prime Minister is adopting the timetable we had envisaged, talking about the need for an agreement before 15 October, which would leave plenty of time for ratification before the end of the year.

But above all I am surprised to hear the Prime Minister present as a 'good outcome' what would actually be the failure of our negotiations. What he calls the 'Australian model' is nothing other than a no deal! It would mean going back several decades, and would see us trading with each other under the rules and tariffs of the World Trade Organization…

With this statement the Prime Minister is probably trying to show that the United Kingdom has nothing to lose in this negotiation, and is attempting to persuade the EU to give up its principles:

> There is still an agreement to be had. We will continue to work hard in September to achieve it. It is one based on our reasonable proposal for a standard free trade agreement like the one the EU has agreed with Canada and so many others. Even at this late stage, if the EU are ready to rethink their

current positions and agree this I will be delighted. But we cannot and will not compromise on the fundamentals of what it means to be an independent country to get it.

A great start to a week of negotiations!

Tuesday, 8 September 2020: Political filibustering

The second bombshell was not long in coming. The very next day after Mr Johnson's statement, we obtain a copy of the Internal Market Bill which, in effect, reverses certain points of the Withdrawal Agreement, in particular the Protocol on Ireland and Northern Ireland. It allows the British government, in the absence of an agreement on the future relationship, to unilaterally decide to modify or even not to apply certain rules on state aid and the movement of goods between Great Britain and Northern Ireland.

This plan is even more serious than the leaks suggested. If passed, it would upset the delicate balance struck just a year ago with Boris Johnson himself to ensure that there is no physical border on the island of Ireland, to protect all dimensions of the Good Friday (Belfast) Agreement, and to preserve the EU's internal market. We would no longer have any way of ensuring that goods entering Northern Ireland comply with EU rules. And once in Northern Ireland those goods would be able to move freely throughout the island of Ireland and into the rest of the EU.

Since the Withdrawal Agreement has come into force, this would be a breach of international law, coming from a country that, for centuries, has built its reputation on the trustworthiness of its signature. In the House of Commons, Brandon Lewis, UK Secretary of State for Northern Ireland, even acknowledges that it would indeed be a breach of international law, but 'in a very specific and limited way'...

The truth is that by acting in this way, the British government is doing nothing less than political filibustering. At this moment, I feel that the threat is a betrayal of their word. It seems they will stop at nothing. Perhaps most seriously for me personally, I do not feel that the team currently in 10 Downing Street is equal to the challenges of Brexit and what is at stake in it, nor to the responsibility they bear for having brought Brexit upon themselves. I simply don't trust them anymore. And we need trust to make a deal on our future relationship.

Wednesday, 9 September 2020: Holding the line

Such is the mood this week in London. Clara and Paulina told David Frost of our profound misgivings about the conduct of the British government at a chilly dinner in London last night. Maroš Šefčovič did the same in a phone call with Michael Gove.

I myself am taking the Eurostar to London this morning after a day of consultations in the Berlaymont with member states and the European Parliament. We could have suspended the negotiations immediately on the grounds that one does not negotiate under threat. But suspending the negotiations ourselves on these serious grounds, as the British presumably wanted us to do, would have placed the responsibility for a likely failure on us. We do not wish to give in to this provocation. Together with the President of the Commission, Ursula von der Leyen, we have therefore decided to avoid a breakdown of negotiations but to maintain a firm line. The President expressed this in a tweet:

> Very concerned about announcements from the British government on its intentions to breach the Withdrawal Agreement. This would break international law and undermines trust. *Pacta sunt servanda* = the foundation of prosperous future relations.

We are putting the British government on notice. Neither the European Parliament nor the Council will approve any treaty on our future relationship under threat of a breach of the Withdrawal Agreement.

Meeting urgently in London at our request, the joint committee responsible for implementing the agreement allows Maroš Šefčovič to dot the i's and cross the t's. He reminds Michael Gove of the objectives of the Protocol on Ireland and Northern Ireland, which is legally binding whether or not we have an agreement on our future relationship. He insists: 'Peace on the island of Ireland should never be used as a bargaining tool', and calls on the UK to remove the contentious proposals from its bill.

Thursday, 10 September 2020: 'Throwing a dead cat on the table'

Paradoxically, after these large-scale British offensives, the closing meeting of this week's round is quite constructive. British negotiators are listening, and drop hints that they are looking for solutions: 'We are committed to this process', David Frost tells me, 'and we are working towards an agreement.' Still the same tactic of blowing hot and cold and playing for time. None of this is very impressive.

The more open attitude, at least on the surface, is pursued to varying degrees at the different negotiating tables. On trade in goods and services, for instance, Mr Frost notes that we want a more detailed discussion, and that we are asking for a balance: 'On the whole, I agree with what you are saying.' The same for customs ('We need to find an internal balance'), geographical indications ('It's possible to move forward, we need a legal text, there is a way'), and even public procurement. On this last point, Mr Frost begins by saying that 'a dedicated chapter would simply not be in the UK's interest'. I reply very decisively: 'This is an area in which work needs to start now if we are to move forward on goods and services as a whole.' To which Mr Frost replies: 'I hear what you are saying and I take it seriously. We are sticking to our position, but we will think about it.'

What could explain this change in tone? One of two things: either David Frost is putting on a façade of goodwill by showing a constructive attitude in order to try and compensate for the disastrous atmosphere created this week. Or the British really do want to negotiate, and have simply sought this week to create disruptions along the way to make an impression on us and give themselves extra leverage in the negotiations, even if they mean to abandon it later. In short, the 'madman strategy', as an article in the *Irish Times* puts it.

There is no doubt also a domestic political dimension to this. A text published in 2013 by Boris Johnson seems prescient in some ways:

Let us suppose you are losing an argument. The facts are overwhelmingly against you, and the more people focus on the reality the worse it is for you and your case.

Your best bet in these circumstances is to perform a manoeuvre that a great campaigner describes as 'throwing a dead cat on the table, mate'.

That is because there is one thing that is absolutely certain about throwing a dead cat on the dining-room table – and I don't mean that people will be outraged, alarmed, disgusted.

That is true, but irrelevant. The key point, says my Australian friend, is that everyone will shout 'Jeez, mate, there's a dead cat on the table!'; in other words they will be talking about the dead cat, the thing you want them to talk about, and they will not be talking about the issue that has been causing you so much grief.*

Seen in light of this theory, the threat to violate the Withdrawal Agreement may be a way to divert attention from the difficulties Boris Johnson is having domestically in managing the health crisis. And also from the British refusal to find reasonable solutions, in particular on state aid – a refusal that is all the more unjustifiable given that, at the same time, the UK is signing a trade agreement with Japan committing it to a far stricter control of state aid than it is prepared to accept from us…

As in October 2019, I am convinced that Boris Johnson, who is a pragmatic politician, will want to reach an agreement with us because he will need it.

Sunday, 13 September 2020 : 'Food blockade' in the Irish Sea

At the end of last week, the British chose to launch a third offensive, seizing on a seemingly technical issue: the inclusion of the United Kingdom among third countries that can import agrifood products into the European Union. They presented this standard procedure as a threat from us, claiming that we are trying to ban the movement of agrifood products from Britain to Northern Ireland.

This accusation, first taken up by some journalists, was then briefed in London by British officials and gained increasing traction, culminating in the Prime Minister's own words in an article published by the *Telegraph*, where he accuses the EU of nothing less than threatening the UK with a food 'blockade' in the Irish Sea that would destroy the 'economic and territorial integrity of the United Kingdom'!

* Boris Johnson, 'This cap on bankers' bonuses is like a dead cat', *Telegraph*, 3 March 2013.

This is the pretext the Prime Minister has found to try to justify the violation of the Withdrawal Agreement. But the reality is quite different. As I explain it in two tweets:

> Protocol on IE/NI is not a threat to the integrity of the UK. We agreed this delicate compromise with @BorisJohnson & his gov in order to protect peace & stability on island of Ireland. We could not have been clearer about the consequences of #Brexit

> Sticking to facts is also essential. A case in point: the EU is not refusing to list the UK as a third country for food imports (SPS [sanitary and phytosanitary regulations]). To be listed, we need to know in full what a country's rules are, incl. for imports. The same objective process applies to all listed countries.

David Frost feels compelled to respond in a series of seven tweets, in which he accuses us of bad faith. '[T]he EU knows perfectly well all the details of our food standards rules because we are operating EU rules.' True enough! But what we need to know is not the current situation, but exactly what rules the UK will adopt at the end of the transition period on 1 January 2021. I choose not to answer, so as to avoid one-upmanship.

What is certain is that the British bill has created a great deal of outrage, including in the UK. In a joint op-ed published in the *Sunday Times*, two former prime ministers from opposing parties, John Major and Tony Blair, call it 'irresponsible, wrong in principle and dangerous in practice', going so far as to claim that it would call into question 'the very integrity of our nation'. Along with Gordon Brown, David Cameron and Theresa May, this means that all living former prime ministers have now declared themselves against the bill. Added to which, former Attorney General Geoffrey Cox, who when in post opposed the Withdrawal Agreement, believes that the bill puts at risk 'the standing and reputation of Britain in the world'.

Monday, 14 September 2020: Revolver

Opening the House of Commons debate on the Internal Market Bill, the Prime Minister again accuses the EU of wanting to impose a food blockade in the Irish Sea. Boris Johnson goes so far as to say that 'the

EU has not taken that particular revolver off the table' and that 'these threats [...] reveal the spirit in which some of our friends are currently minded to conduct these negotiations'. He goes on to cite article 4 of the Protocol whereby 'Northern Ireland is part of the customs territory of the United Kingdom.' and insists: 'We cannot have a situation where the boundaries of our country could be dictated by a foreign power or international organization. No British Prime Minister, no Government, and no Parliament could ever accept such an imposition.'

Sic.

Wednesday, 16 September 2020: Washington

Dominic Raab, former British negotiator and now Foreign Secretary, has been in Washington since yesterday for free trade negotiations between the UK and the US. In a much-analysed press conference alongside US Secretary of State Mike Pompeo, he sought to reassure Americans about the Internal Market Bill by blaming the European Union:

[T]he threat to the Good Friday Agreement as it is reflected in the Northern Ireland Protocol comes from the EU's politicisation of the issue [...] The UK action here is defensive in relation to what the EU is doing, it is precautionary [...] and it is proportionate.

What we cannot have – and this is contrary to the Northern Ireland Protocol [*sic*] and a risk to the Good Friday agreement – is the EU seeking to erect a regulatory border down the Irish Sea between Northern Ireland and Britain.

Many US parliamentarians and politicians have a longstanding, almost emotional connection with Ireland. And they are not fooled. They know that the EU simply wants to implement the Withdrawal Agreement that we negotiated with Dominic Raab.

Over the past few days I have had several exchanges with Simon Coveney, Ireland's Foreign Minister. Always perceptive, methodical and well-informed, he has assured me that in Washington the British government's messages are meeting with some strong reactions.

This is confirmed by Richard Neal, a Democrat Congressman from Massachusetts and president of the Friends of Ireland organization, who called me today. He is very familiar with the context of the negotiations. I spoke with him before when we were trying to avoid the return of a physical border on the island of Ireland.

Shortly afterwards, Democratic presidential candidate Joe Biden sums the situation up well in a tweet:

> We can't allow the Good Friday Agreement that brought peace to Northern Ireland to become a casualty of Brexit. Any trade deal between the U.S. and U.K. must be contingent upon respect for the Agreement and preventing the return of a hard border. Period.

Wednesday, 16 September 2020: In the words of Margaret Thatcher

Meanwhile, on our side of the Atlantic today is an important day: the President of the European Commission, Ursula von der Leyen, is delivering her first State of the Union address. There is no shortage of challenges: the response to the health, economic and social crises, of course, with the implementation of the recovery plan, new ambitious climate objectives, the migration issue, digital initiatives, the role of the EU in the world confronted by Russia and tensions in the Eastern Mediterranean, and its relationship with the United States.

On Brexit, the President chooses to continue to keep the hand of friendship extended, while being very firm:

> We need new beginnings with old friends […]. But with every day that passes the chances of a timely agreement *do* start to fade.
>
> Negotiations are always difficult. We are used to that.
>
> And the Commission has the best and most experienced negotiator, Michel Barnier, to navigate us through.
>
> But talks have not progressed as we would have wished. And that leaves us very little time.
>
> That agreement took three years to negotiate and we worked relentlessly on it. Line by line, word by word.
>
> And together we succeeded.
>
> […] This agreement has been ratified by this House and the House of Commons.

It cannot be unilaterally changed, disregarded or dis-applied. This a matter of law, trust and good faith.

To hammer the point home, President von der Leyen recalls the words of Margaret Thatcher herself: 'Britain does not break Treaties. It would be bad for Britain, bad for relations with the rest of the world, and bad for any future Treaty on trade.' She concludes: 'This was true then, and it is true now. Trust is the foundation of any strong partnership.'

This sets up the line we will take in the discussions over the coming weeks. If the British are constructive, then we will reciprocate. But we shall remain on our guard. One example among many is that of geographical indications, which protect quality agricultural products, Greek feta cheese as much as Scotch whisky or Beaufort cheese from Savoie. The existing 3,000 indications are protected by the Withdrawal Agreement. The British negotiators want to reopen this point and give themselves more freedom in their future trade negotiations, especially with the United States. Of course, this could make it easier for us to agree on the protection of future indications.

But now we are forewarned, and therefore very cautious. I ask our team to take a firm line. We will tell the British people that the way in which their government has provoked the European Union and attacked the Withdrawal Agreement makes us reluctant to reopen any discussion on its content.

Thursday, 17 September 2020: Picking up the pieces

The members of our task force continue discussions in spite of everything. Today I speak frankly to David Frost: 'I cannot help noticing that the unnecessary polemics and provocations have not stopped. On the contrary, they have been stepped up by your Prime Minister and Secretary of State Dominic Raab. This is not our style of negotiation. Nor will we negotiate under threats or false accusations. We are engaged in this process in good faith, in a calm, serious, constructive and transparent manner, as dictated by our mandate and the Political Declaration agreed between us. Every word counts. The European Union is not threatening the territorial integrity of the United Kingdom, let alone threatening an "allied blockade". What is creating problems in Ireland and Northern Ireland is Brexit.'

'It's not Brexit that's creating a problem in Ireland,' says Mr Frost, 'it's more complicated than that. Northern Ireland is part of our country. These issues go back centuries.'

I reply that I know a great deal about Irish history: 'I care very much for the country and its people.'

After this somewhat tense exchange, we take stock of the state of negotiations. On the question of state aid, after quite a constructive start to the discussion, the British negotiators tell us that they are only prepared to consider general and non-constraining 'high-level principles'. Quite obviously this is out of the question!

And when we talk about the implementation of these rules, the British state their refusal to enter any agreement with the EU that will prejudge what their own regime of state aid will be. 'Our agreement', Mr Frost tells me, 'has to inhabit a delicate space that points in a certain direction while leaving room for choices to be made by the British Parliament.'

But we need effective implementation of future commitments. The UK still refuses to find solutions that take into account the EU's red lines, even though we have made significant efforts to take account of theirs.

Friday, 18 September 2020: Tentative progress

In the discussions of the past few days there have nevertheless been a few modest steps forward – in defining what would constitute a regression in relation to existing social or environmental standards, for instance. A little progress was also made on fisheries: our positions may remain far apart, but we now agree on the list of 109 fish stocks upon which we will establish the sharing of quotas. The list has come a little late, but it is something! Discussions on trade in goods and services have also been constructive. But I repeat to David Frost that we must now make parallel progress on all issues. This will remain our demand right to the end.

During this week I note two more positive 'micro-signs' coming from London. Westminster's opposition to the Internal Market Bill continues unabated. And on Wednesday Boris Johnson made a concession to moderate Conservative MPs: the possibility of derogating from the

Protocol on Ireland and Northern Ireland would only be activated with the agreement of the House of Commons. This 'parliamentary lock' reduces the risk somewhat, especially as the government would have to prove that the EU is 'engaged in a material breach of its duties of good faith, thereby undermining the fundamental purpose of the Protocol'.

The bill remains on the table, nonetheless. A few days later, Theresa May, who knows the subject well, criticized it again, pointing out that it is of no use since the Withdrawal Agreement already provides for the settlement of any disputes by arbitrators. According to the former Prime Minister, the violation of international law that it implies is 'reckless and irresponsible'. The effect of all this will be that some communities in Northern Ireland will have less trust in the British government, which could pose a risk to the integrity of the UK.

The second sign this week was that, after responding to Labour MP Hilary Benn that he did not believe the EU was negotiating in good faith, Boris Johnson added: 'It's always possible I'm mistaken.' Some commentators read this as the Prime Minister giving himself a way out to ultimately reach a deal with us. But the hope is slight.

Tuesday, 22 September 2020: Mega traffic jam

A few days before the ninth round, I review the situation before the ministers of the twenty-seven at the General Affairs Council. During the round-table discussion I am once again struck by the unity of the twenty-seven. All the ministers express their support for the Commission and for our strategy.

This unity is our greatest asset in relation to the British, who are beginning to adopt a more constructive attitude. Perhaps this change in tone reflects the mood in London, where many are calling for a deal with the EU. For example, a report by the London School of Economics and the think-tank UK in a Changing Europe predicts that the shock of a no deal would have a long-term economic cost (8 per cent of GDP) two to three times that of Covid-19, as estimated by the Bank of England.* On another note, in a post by Oscar Guinea on the European Centre for International Political Economy (ECIPE) blog, I read that the UK buys

* https://ukandeu.ac.uk/the-uk-economy-brexit-vs-covid-19.

more than 604 products exclusively from the EU, while the EU buys only one exclusively from the UK: a specific type of timber.*

Finally, one hundred days before the UK is due to exit from the Single Market and Customs Union, Michael Gove presents to the House of Commons what he calls the 'reasonable worst-case scenario' at the end of the transition period. Under this scenario, only 30–60 per cent of trucks arriving at Dover would be prepared for the new formalities. This could create congestion, with seven thousand lorries stuck in Kent and waiting times of up to two days. To avoid this, lorries will have to obtain a 'Kent Access Permit' – which some commentators are interpreting as a new Brexit-related internal border!

Wednesday, 23 September 2020: 'Landing zones'

On the eve of our ninth round, David Frost is optimistic. 'The UK wants a deal', he tells me at a meeting in London. 'I can see landing zones on all issues.' He also tells me that he is concerned about the passage of time and the developing health crisis. The European Council scheduled for 24–25 September has just been postponed until next week, as its President, Charles Michel, is in isolation after having been in contact with a case of Covid-19. David Frost fears that this situation may be repeated, jeopardizing the European Council meeting on 15 October. He mentions the British threat to leave the negotiations if no agreement is reached by then, but without much conviction.

Today I leave London for Paris, where I meet the President of the Republic for a long conversation that will allow us to discuss many subjects in the negotiations rigorously and in detail. Like the other EU heads of state or government, Emmanuel Macron has expressed a certain weariness in the face of the latest initiatives and declarations of the United Kingdom, and in particular the proposals contained in the Internal Market Bill that jeopardize the Protocol on Ireland and Northern Ireland. His message was forcefully relayed by Clément Beaune, his former European adviser who became Minister for European Affairs in the Jean Castex government. A capable young senior civil servant driven by political

* https://ecipe.org/blog/deal-with-no-deal-eu-uk/.

ambition, Mr Beaune expresses himself clearly, and unhesitatingly asserts his European convictions.

Talking to the President, I obtain further confirmation that the effect of the British bill has been to infuriate the twenty-seven and reunite them strongly around the Union's shared positions. This afternoon the French President displayed no disquiet at the possibility of a no deal, and no inclination to compromise on the essential interests of the Union, in particular the level playing field, a subject upon which, he tells me, France and Germany share the same position. Nor, obviously, on fisheries.

Friday, 25 September 2020: No diving with open hatches!

On the eve of a new formal round, I bring together the Directors-General of the European Commission who have been with me since the very beginning of these negotiations.

The UK's tactics are clear. At the end of this ninth round, the British want to drag us into a continuous negotiation, a 'tunnel' that we would only get out of the day before the European Council of 15 October, even though too many serious issues, particularly those that are priorities for us, remain open. By doing this they hope to secure new concessions and put pressure on the heads of state or government at the European Council to obtain even more.

Describing this strategy to my team and to the Commission's Directorates-General, I use the image of a submarine going into a dive without having closed all the hatches. Danger! The negotiations are not ready to dive yet. And the members of the European Council have always refused to be manipulated in these negotiations.

With only a few days to go before the European Council, and without a parallel effort from the British on our priorities, there is no question of hurrying, of allowing ourselves to be rushed, and still less of working on legal texts concerning matters of British interest only.

Friday, 2 October 2020: Light at the end of the tunnel?

This week saw the start of the ninth round of negotiations upon which many, in particular the British press, are pinning their hopes. And it must be said that work at the eleven negotiating tables is proceeding in a constructive and respectful spirit.

We have confirmed points of convergence, notably on certain aspects of trade in goods, services and investments, civil nuclear cooperation and participation in EU programmes. We have also seen new positive developments on subjects such as air safety, the coordination of social security, and respect for fundamental rights and individual freedoms, which is a precondition for police and judicial cooperation in criminal matters.

On the other hand, there is still no real progress on the protection of personal data, the fight against climate change or carbon pricing. Above all, there remain serious divergences on subjects that are essential for the EU. In a press release I emphasize once again that any economic partnership agreement requires three conditions. Solid and long-term guarantees of open and fair competition, which can be given while respecting the regulatory autonomy and sovereignty of both parties. Effective governance, on the basis of a comprehensive agreement and robust dispute settlement mechanisms – this requirement is obviously only reinforced by the threats of the Internal Market Bill. And finally, a stable and fair fisheries agreement that allows the UK to develop its fishing economy, while ensuring the sustainability of resources and protecting the activity of European fishermen.

At the end of this week's round, we observe that the conditions for a negotiation 'tunnel' have not been met. You can only enter such a tunnel if you can see some light at the end of it – i.e., possible 'landing zones' on each of the subjects under discussion.

During one of the long debriefing sessions that I hold with my team every evening during the round, one European expert has this to say: 'Even if there is light at the end of the tunnel, let's make sure it's not the headlights of a train coming full speed in the opposite direction on the same track!'

This week, the debate in the UK on the consequences of leaving the Single Market has also intensified. With only three months to go, it's about time!

For example, in a letter to the British car industry revealed by the BBC and the *Financial Times*, David Frost admits that the EU is not going to give preferential treatment to UK car and truck exporters.

The EU, explains Mr Frost, refuses to count vehicle parts manufactured in third countries with which the UK and the EU have free trade agreements, such as Japan or Turkey, as 'local' UK inputs.

This is the essential point about rules of origin, and all non-tariff barriers. A vehicle or any other good will have to incorporate a fair proportion of UK inputs in order to be exported to the EU without tariffs or quotas. In our view, there is no question of going beyond bilateral cumulation, whereby each of the two partners, the UK and the EU, can treat parts from the other as local inputs. To go further with the UK would be against our interests. It would force us to give the same treatment to other third countries, under the 'most favoured nation clause' in our free trade agreements.

In the media, the leaking of this letter from David Frost to 10 Downing Street is interpreted as a sign that things are shifting. Some see it as a sign that Boris Johnson's government is preparing the business community and public opinion for the concessions that will be necessary in order to reach an agreement. Other more sceptical voices see it as a British offensive designed to shift the responsibility for the failure of negotiations onto the EU…

Saturday, 3 October 2020: The 'revenge' of Scottish fishermen

Ursula von der Leyen and Boris Johnson have agreed to talk on the phone. The President of the Commission asks me to attend the meeting, for which, as always, she has carefully prepared. Boris Johnson clearly has only one aim: to raise the stakes on fisheries. From the outset he paints a very black picture of the situation of British fishermen, and Scottish fishermen in particular, of the sacrifices they made when their country joined the Union in 1973, of the revenge they are due…

A more than questionable line of attack. At the time the UK joined the EU, everything beyond twelve nautical miles from the coastline was considered as 'high seas', international waters in which other countries' vessels could fish freely. It was well after the UK joined that the international legal regime introduced an 'exclusive economic zone' stretching to two hundred nautical miles from the coast. The waters beyond twelve nautical miles have therefore never been exclusively British, they have always been either international or EU waters. With the UK's exit from the Common Fisheries Policy, EU fishermen, for the first time, will not have free access to these waters. This is why the Belgian government and Flanders have unearthed a privilege dating back to 1666 and signed by King Charles II of England, which gives fifty fishing boats from Bruges the right to fish in British waters in perpetuity…

During our conversation, Ursula von der Leyen chooses not to counter Boris Johnson's arguments on fisheries, despite the preparations we have made. Of course, when he talks about sacrifice, Boris Johnson does not mention the opportunities that the Single Market offered for British fisheries products. Or the results of the Common Fisheries Policy, which greatly facilitated the recovery of fish stocks in British waters. Thanks to the Common Fisheries Policy and the joint effort of all the countries involved, biomass in the northeast Atlantic increased by 50 per cent between 2003 and 2018. Not to mention that, in this negotiation, British fishermen will come out better than European fishermen anyway. On the other hand, the President does try to bring the discussion around to other subjects, in particular the level playing field and governance. But each time, the Prime Minister evades the point by referring it to the negotiators. On several occasions, she also lays great emphasis on respecting the commitments made in the Withdrawal Agreement concerning Ireland and Northern Ireland, and therefore the necessity of retracting the proposals of the Internal Market Bill.

Here too, Boris Johnson does not really bother to answer. He knows of course that he is going to have to sort this out if he wants a deal on the future relationship. And he also knows that his relationship with a potential Biden administration in the US is at stake.

Mr Johnson does however dwell on the date of 15 October. 'I need to know by then whether an agreement is possible', he says. To which the President replies that this British deadline is not our deadline. We are prepared to work through October, and even beyond.

At the end of this conversation, which, surprisingly, is interrupted three times by technical issues, both agree to intensify negotiations. But this acceleration does not mean the same thing to us as it does to the British. A few minutes later, David Frost submits to Clara an agenda for the coming week on all issues. This does not suit us. We want to accelerate, focus and intensify negotiations first of all on the issues where there is divergence. But in any case, there is no longer any question of a tunnel or of a continuous negotiation. The conditions are not in place to finalize any agreement when so many important or essential points for the Union remain open or blocked.

Sunday, 4 October 2020: Countering Boris

This Sunday, our small team is at work as usual, reflecting on the outcome of the President's meeting with the British Prime Minister and on the messages to be conveyed in Berlin tomorrow.

It is clear that we must counter Boris Johnson's offensive on fisheries by insisting strongly on how this connects to the wider economic partnership. There can be no access to markets without access to waters for European fishermen. Georg suggests that he work out the figures with the technical teams to show what access to our markets is worth to the British, sector by sector, in relation to the 650 million euros' worth of fish that Europeans catch in British waters.

I arrive in Berlin in the evening, this time with a reduced delegation because of the Covid situation. The airports are empty. This is the first flight both Paulina and I have taken since the beginning of the corona-virus crisis in March. Precautions linked to the health situation are very strict everywhere, and we had to take a test, which was negative, before arriving in Germany.

Monday, 5 October 2020: The Chancellor and Brexit

In the middle of a series of meetings with German Foreign Minister Heiko Maas and then with the most prominent bosses in the German economy, members of the BDI and the BDA, Angela Merkel makes an appointment to meet me at the Chancellery.

Ms Merkel is very friendly and attentive, as always. For an hour she takes time out, around a very large round table, to listen, to understand the details of the negotiations, to ask precise questions on the sticking points, and in particular on the level playing field, which she is worried about – quite rightly so!

If the UK gets 'zero-tariff, zero-quota' access to our market of 450 million citizens and consumers, it must not be allowed to distort competition by granting excessive state aid, to its car manufacturers, for example. It must also commit to not backsliding on our air pollution standards, our CO_2 emission targets, or our rules on safety at work or tax evasion.

We then discuss the next steps and the prospects for a deal. 'Boris Johnson is facing internal pressure to reach a deal quickly', I tell the Chancellor. 'He has set himself a deadline of 15 October. That deadline is not ours. We can go to 1 November, or even 15 November, which would still be compatible with ratification by the Council and the European Parliament.'

'That's why we must remain very calm, firm and determined on our core demands. My analysis remains that Boris Johnson ultimately wants a deal, and that this will not happen until the end of October or the beginning of November, perhaps by way of a last minute, take-it-or-leave-it offer from the EU.'

I can sense that the Chancellor wants to reach a reasonable agreement with the United Kingdom but that she is still very concerned about fair competition. She also knows that Europeans must remain united on all issues, especially fisheries, even if the latter is of less interest to Germany than it is to the Netherlands, France or Denmark. I also have a meeting with Ms Merkel's sherpa, Uwe Corsepius. We discuss in detail the problems we have with the level playing field, governance and fisheries, which the British want to leave until the end of the negotiations. Mr Corsepius immediately understands the political problem that a bad fisheries agreement would pose for the countries concerned. It is clear that calls have been taking place, especially between Paris and Berlin. He suggests that, if we were to end up with an annual access regime to British waters, we should have to impose a similar regime for electricity interconnection between the UK and the wider EU energy market.

As I pass through the gates of the Bundeskanzleramt, I think to myself that I will always retain a profound respect for Angela Merkel as a great German and European leader. Essentially, she has continued the European legacy of Helmut Kohl, considering European integration to be in the fundamental interests of Germany. Myself, I have always thought that France is stronger when it is European, and that it must avoid the arrogance of wanting a French Europe.

Tuesday, 13 October 2020: No 'tiger in the tank'

Curiously enough, while in the press British government sources insist on the 15 October deadline set by the Prime Minister, the British negotiators, with whom we have been meeting in London and then in Brussels since last week, do not really seem willing to put a 'tiger in the tank', to use Boris Johnson's expression.

The atmosphere is certainly more constructive. We are making further progress on extradition cooperation, road transport and social security coordination. But even on these issues there are still conditions yet to be met. As an example, any agreement on the movement of persons – on mutual visa facilitation or the coordination of social security, for instance – will require respect for equal treatment of, and non-discrimination between, citizens of EU member states.

On a range of other issues, such as customs, sanitary and phytosanitary standards, geographical indications and public procurement, the EU has made proposals to which the UK has been slow to respond.

Finally, important questions remain on the three major sticking points in this negotiation, and in particular on fisheries. At the beginning of October, I once again took the time to call the fisheries ministers of the eleven member states most concerned with the matter, for between thirty and forty-five minutes each. They all told me of their great concern and stressed that there can be no global agreement without a stable, fair and sustainable agreement on fisheries.

One of our regular discussions with David Frost provides an opportunity to lead the counterattack, following Boris Johnson's offensive: 'The gap is not closing, it is widening. There are two conditions for a fisheries agreement, and therefore for an overall agreement: access to waters without an annual "guillotine", and a stable distribution of quotas – I can't say it any more clearly.'

We have proposed very significant increases in UK quotas on priority stocks for the UK, including cod (+25 per cent), haddock (+100 per cent), sole (+135 per cent), hake (+200 per cent) and sand eels (+400 per cent). We therefore agree to increase the British 'slice of the cake', but not to let them have 'the whole cake'. What they are asking for would exclude European fishermen from areas where they have been fishing for hundreds of years.

I repeat to David Frost: 'The ideas you have in mind at the moment are totally unacceptable. I can say this all the more clearly because I have discussed them personally with several heads of state and with all the fisheries ministers concerned this week. They simply don't understand how you can make such suggestions.'

I proceed to demonstrate, with the help of figures carefully prepared by my staff, how and why our fisheries proposal fits into the overall agreement: 'The electrical interconnection with the Continent that we are offering you has an economic value to you of between €700 million and €2 billion per year. This is far more than the value of all the fish that Europeans catch in your waters... There is no reason why you should get access to our electricity market and at the same time deny our fishermen access to your waters...'

'Tariff-free access to our market under a free trade agreement is also quite valuable, to put it mildly, compared to what we are asking for on fisheries. For your road haulage exports alone, the free trade agreement, by avoiding customs tariffs, is worth a billion a year compared to a no deal, not to mention cars, chemicals and plastics where your exports amount to tens of billions a year.'

'The free trade agreement is also worth a billion a year for your dairy exports as compared to a no deal. For prepared foods, 500 million. For beef and lamb, between 300 and 400 million.'

It's not long until the European Council. I tell David Frost of my intention to inform the heads of state or government precisely and factually. 'And this comparison of figures between fishing and the rest, between the fishing activity you are denying us and what you are asking for, is precisely what I will have to explain to them. To be perfectly honest, it is precisely this that some leaders have asked me to explain...'

My little presentation has a definite effect. The Commission's strength in these negotiations is the expertise it can mobilize. From our team, Nicolas Kuen, João Pereira, Mariano Fernandez-Salas and Arnaud Rohmer worked with Georg and Ivo to put figures to our argument. Nothing was left to chance.

Coming up to the European Council, then, we are taking the lead. But the British continue to stick to their guns. During another videoconference between Boris Johnson, Ursula von der Leyen and Charles

Michel, the Prime Minister declares himself disappointed at the state of the negotiations. 'My friend David Frost tells me that if this continues, we are heading for a no deal.' On the other end of the line, Ursula von der Leyen and Charles Michel remain very calm: 'If it's a no deal, then that's your choice. On our side, we are ready to continue working towards an agreement.' Boris Johnson seems to realize that his threats are not having the desired effect, and takes two steps back. 'We will continue', he says.

Thursday, 15 October 2020: Rendezvous with the 'top leaders'

Today is an important day: for the first time in a year, the European Council has Brexit on its agenda, and I have been invited, along with Ursula von der Leyen, to give an update on the negotiations. As I wait in the anteroom during the traditional discussion between the heads of state or government and the President of the European Parliament, David Sassoli, I see the President of the Commission rush out of the room and shut herself into one of the offices reserved for the Commission. A few minutes later, a tense Stéphanie Riso informs me privately that the President will have to leave the meeting because her secretary has tested positive for Covid-19.

I therefore enter the European Council room alone. All the heads of state or government demonstrate their unity and confidence in the work of our team by immediately adopting their conclusions on the negotiations. In their text, the European Council begins by noting, with concern, that 'progress on the key issues of interest to the Union is still not sufficient for an agreement to be reached.'

It goes on to reaffirm 'the Union's determination to have as close as possible a partnership with the United Kingdom [...] while respecting the previously agreed European Council guidelines [...] as regards the level playing field, governance and fisheries.' The heads of state and government invite me to continue negotiations in the coming weeks, and also call upon the UK to 'do everything necessary to make an agreement possible'.

Finally, the European Council recalls that the Withdrawal Agreement and its protocols must be implemented in full and on time. It calls upon member states, the Union institutions and all stakeholders to 'step up their work on preparedness and readiness at all levels and for all outcomes, including that of no agreement, and invites the Commission, in particular, to give timely consideration to unilateral and time-limited contingency measures that are in the EU's interest'.

In my initial intervention, I want to show that we are determined. 'Of course', I say to the heads of state or government, 'we cannot rule out a no-deal scenario. But I still believe that a deal is possible. The European Union wants a deal. A good deal. And not at any price.'

'Whether on fisheries or on other economic issues, there is no reason to be daunted', I say, insisting on the need to put things in perspective and to show, on each of the subjects, that there is room for manoeuvre to protect our fundamental interests. For example, on rules of origin, we must be careful not to allow the UK to become an 'assembly hub' on our doorstep, incorporating aluminium, steel and other inputs from third countries and then bringing them into the Single Market without tariffs or quotas. That is why we have insisted on sufficiently strict general rules of origin. But, on the other hand, we are ready to find specific solutions for certain products, which are of real economic interest to the UK and to ourselves. I end on a more personal note, which allows me to look to broader horizons:

> For the last four years I have always kept a close eye on three focal points in these negotiations: peace in Ireland; the integrity of the internal market and the interests of each of your countries; and obviously, in the medium and long term, the need for a strong and lasting partnership with this great country, the United Kingdom, to better face together a number of global challenges such as climate change, terrorism and poverty.

After my speech, some fifteen heads of state or government take the floor. What strikes me most is their demand for a genuine agreement on the rules of the economic game with the British. They are all concerned that the regulatory freedom the British gain with Brexit should not be turned into a tool for dumping.

I also note a great deal of unity on fishing, including from countries that are landlocked but want to show their solidarity.

Several of them mention the threat that Boris Johnson regularly brandishes of leaving the negotiating table. We all know that tomorrow he might do the same thing again. The line that will be taken will continue to be to remain calm and leave the door open.

After two and a half hours of debate, a press conference begins in which Charles Michel has asked me to participate. This is an opportunity for me to reiterate that we are absolutely determined to reach a fair deal with the United Kingdom, and to do everything we can, but not at any price. In this short press briefing I repeat three times that we are ready to negotiate intensively in the few remaining weeks, if necessary including weekends.

Things are quite clear. And yet, in a startling tweet right in the middle of a press conference where I am saying the exact opposite, David Frost declares himself '[d]isappointed by the #EUCO conclusions on UK/EU negotiations. Surprised EU is no longer committed to working "intensively" to reach a future partnership as agreed with @vonderleyen on 3 October. Also surprised by suggestion that to get an agreement all future moves must come from UK. It's an unusual approach to conducting a negotiation.'

What is the meaning of these inopportune statements? Most likely the British government is looking for a pretext. Throughout the last few weeks Boris Johnson has been raising the stakes by presenting 15 October as the final deadline for negotiations, but without removing any of the remaining obstacles to a successful conclusion... The Prime Minister probably does not want to compromise himself by agreeing to intensify negotiations the day after the European Council. This would be an admission that the self-imposed deadline was meaningless. Mr Johnson is therefore seeking to justify a decision to continue negotiations by blaming it on new elements entering the picture.

Friday, 16 October 2020: British political cinema

In a strongly worded statement, the Prime Minister confirms this interpretation:

[G]iven that [the EU] have refused to negotiate seriously for much of the last few months, and given that this summit appears explicitly to rule out a Canada-style deal, I have concluded that we should get ready for January 1 with arrangements that are more like Australia's based on simple principles of global free trade.

Boris Johnson, Michael Gove and David Frost are taking it in turns to call for intense negotiations on the basis of a comprehensive legal text and a 'fundamental change of approach by the European Union'. So, as our team prepares for intensive negotiations from Monday 19 October, David Frost tells me that the conditions are not right for us to come to London...

As for Michael Gove, speaking in the British Parliament he states that the EU's refusal to intensify the negotiations has 'in effect, ended the trade negotiations' – before being alerted to one of my tweets in which I confirm that the EU remains available to intensify discussions in London this week on all subjects, on the basis of legal texts. Still speaking in front of British MPs, Mr Gove then backtracks and claims that my statements are a 'reflection of the strength and resolution' that Boris Johnson showed when he threatened to leave the negotiating table...

Later in the day I have a videoconference with David Frost, in which I include Stéphanie Riso from the President's office. David Frost is in a room in Downing Street with his two deputies Matthew Taylor and Oliver Lewis. With no vehemence, but in a rather theatrical manner, he opens proceedings with an indictment: 'We agreed to seek a deal by mid-October. You did not play the game. The EU was unfair to us at the European Council. The conclusions call upon the UK to change its positions. You are trying to teach us a lesson, with a threat of a no deal. This is unacceptable. Especially as it is a request on behalf of only a few member states.'

Clara, Paulina, Georg and Stéphanie gaze at one another in disbelief. It's almost childish. I answer calmly: 'David, the European Union has always expressed its positions clearly and will continue to do so. You know what they are, they are not going to change. If that shocks you, then there is not much else to say.' I almost add: 'If the European Union spent its time taking umbrage at everything that is said and talked about in London...' – but I restrain myself.

'You heard what the Prime Minister said', he reiterates. 'If you want these negotiations to continue, the Union must fundamentally change its approach, in form and substance. One, we need to move straight to consolidation of a legal text. Otherwise, there is no hope of finishing in time. Two, the Union must state that it is ready to change its approach on the substance as well.'

Spontaneously, I say: 'No problem, David, on the legal text. We have always been ready for that. As you know, as early as March, we put a complete legal text on the table. Our position is simply that, if we have to work on a legal text, then it should be done across all tables. As for your second point, I don't understand what you are trying to achieve. This is the position of the European Council. You must respect it when the Union defines its positions, as we respect you when you define yours.'

The discussion ends here. But we agree to talk again on Monday. To tell the truth, this little episode seems quite ridiculous to me. Over the past weeks and months, we have had more than enough reasons to lose patience and to introduce drama into the negotiations in reaction to this or that British statement or attitude. But once again – and to the end – we will control ourselves and keep our nerve.

Saturday, 17 October 2020: Quo vadis?

The British have left the negotiating table – or, to be precise, they don't want us to come back to London. So the crisis that we have repeatedly anticipated has finally arrived. *Quo vadis*?

This morning I talk with Clara, Paulina and Georg. Opinions differ as to what is going on in London. Clara, as direct, realistic and succinct as ever: 'I think this is the final chapter. As we said, the higher they go, the harder it is for them to climb down. And now they are going very high indeed…'

Georg takes the opposite view: 'Chin up! We always knew it would end in some kind of crisis. Now we've got to it, we should do what we've always said we would do: be the adults in the room, calm, united, ready for any scenario. Give ourselves the time we need. Tactically, the purpose of their crisis is to present no deal as a credible outcome. They will most likely return to the table. What matters to us is that it happens on our terms, and that our positions remain intact.'

It seems that David Frost underestimated the dynamics of the European Council, and misled his Prime Minister by telling him that the heads of state would be more flexible than the task force. So now, in order to save face, he is creating a drama.

Paulina adds: 'The European Council conclusions are a pretext. I agree: as with the Internal Market Bill, it's up to us to be the adults. The British internal debate will play out eventually. As for Australia, nobody believes that.'

Stefaan gives his view: 'It's hard to interpret. Now we're back with Canada, just days after David Frost told the House of Lords that the UK was ready for more. Their posturing, taking the high ground, may well become self-fulfilling. We have an interest in de-escalating the situation.'

Clara concludes: 'In any case, we have one last round left, a "take-it-or-leave-it" offer closer to the final deadline.'

All these opinions are valid and useful. It is by sharing them that we can find the right way forward. On Monday we will have another video-conference meeting with David Frost. He will let us know what's going on. Meanwhile, we shall do as we said: we shall remain calm and work on behalf of the unity of the twenty-seven. Boris Johnson and David Frost have taken the conclusions of the European Council, rather than the task force, as their target. That is to our advantage.

Monday and Tuesday, 19 and 20 October 2020: Two days, two calls

On Monday we had our second call with David Frost since negotiations were interrupted. Speaking from the same room again, he revisits our exchange and repeats his conditions: 'We agree to start working on legal texts but the basic problem remains the same. We now need an authoritative voice to say that the Union's position has changed. We can't just leave it at the conclusions of the European Council. The EU must respect our sovereignty and our rights as a third country.'

Stéphanie Riso answers: 'An authoritative voice? What is that supposed to mean?' she protests. I also repeat my argument from Friday – adding that we have always respected Brexit, the choices of the British government, but that we have the right to define our own positions on the future of our partnership: 'Yes, we respect the sovereignty of the United Kingdom, but contradicting the conclusions of the European Council is obviously impossible.'

We leave it at that, with another meeting set for Friday.

We stay for a while in room S5 of the Berlaymont. Georg gives his analysis: 'It's not serious. They're looking for an excuse to climb down, a ladder. It's up to you to judge whether or not this blockage should continue, but the solution seems to be within reach. It will probably just take a few words in your debate in the European Parliament about respecting British sovereignty, as you have already said so often.'

The next day, a third call to David Frost, who again says that the conditions for us to come to London have not been met. The British government needs a statement from us affirming our respect for British sovereignty.

I reply: 'That's what I have been saying in almost all my speeches for the last three years! You only have to check them. I will take this same line tomorrow in the European Parliament.'

It's up to the British to judge whether or not this is enough to 'set the political scene' for the resumption of negotiations. What is clear is that every day we miss comes at a price. Once we resume negotiations, they really need to be ready to move forward.

Wednesday, 21 October 2020: Let's hear it...

Finally, the plenary session of the European Parliament gives me the opportunity to clarify things in the way the British are waiting for, if that's what is needed.

I repeat that the European Union wants an agreement. An agreement that is mutually beneficial, that respects the autonomy – the sovereignty – of each party, and that reflects a balanced compromise. But not at any price.

In order to reach this agreement, we will remain calm, constructive, respectful, but also firm and determined in defending our principles and interests. We will seek the necessary compromises, on both sides, until the last possible moment. Our door will always remain open. We are ready to intensify discussions on all issues on the basis of legal texts.

The principles of the European Union were clearly stated from the moment the United Kingdom chose to leave the Union over four years ago. And, as I emphasize, these principles are of course compatible with respect for British sovereignty, a legitimate concern of Boris Johnson's government. What is at stake today in these negotiations is not the sovereignty of either party, but the proper organization of our future relationship after the divorce, which is now a foregone conclusion.

The speech, which could not have come as a surprise to MEPs given that it contained nothing new, has an instant effect on the other side of the Channel. 'We have studied carefully the statement by Michel Barnier to the European Parliament this morning', says a spokesperson for 10 Downing Street. 'As the EU's Chief Negotiator, his words are authoritative.' Very pleased to hear that my authority to speak on the subject is recognized...

All in all, the spokesman gives my speech a thumbs up. The British government says it is 'ready to welcome the EU team to London to resume negotiations later this week'. As David Frost says, without a hint of a smile, 'the basis for negotiations has been restored'.

All of that just to get here! Frankly, we could have done without this psychodrama orchestrated by London, which has cost us days of negotiations. But it was probably necessary in order to create a smoke screen so that the British could finally agree to negotiate on the substance of the most difficult issues. The *Daily Express* runs with the headline 'EU agrees to respect our sovereignty', as if this had not been our intention up to this point... No one mentions the 15 October deadline set by the Prime Minister, who thus manages to save face.

One thing is clear to me: by agreeing to resume negotiations following this episode, the British government is showing us that it wants a deal.

We therefore immediately come to an agreement with David Frost on the organizational principles for what is to come. From tomorrow, intensive discussions will take place every day, including weekends, at all eleven negotiating tables. These negotiations will be conducted on the basis of legal texts presented by both parties. On the European side, we don't have any ego about being the authors. What matters is that the best text is chosen for each subject.

A small joint secretariat, consisting of legal experts from both sides, will have the task of keeping a consolidated text up to date. Discussions should focus on the most sensitive issues, with regular meetings at Chief Negotiator level to resolve any sticking points.

Thursday, 22 October 2020: The final stretch?

Before taking the 2.52pm Eurostar together, the only one of the day during this lockdown period, I gather my team again to ensure that everyone is on the same wavelength. Without dwelling on the drama of the last few days, I remind our negotiators that we are leaving for London on the basis of an extremely clear position taken by the European Council. The Union's position has not changed, either on the level playing field or on fisheries. If the British want a trade agreement without tariffs or quotas, they must accept an agreement on fishing.

I also agree that each negotiating table leader should send his or her British counterpart one or more legal texts, taking care to highlight the concessions we propose to make, such as abandoning our demand for dynamic alignment of the UK with the Union's state aid rules – but also making sure to retain some leverage for the end of the negotiations, for example on the role of the EU Court of Justice, which we are prepared to reduce.

Clara and I recommend that members of our delegation go over and above the necessary precautions to deal with the health risk. We don't have much time left and we can't afford to have our whole team quarantined. We will therefore work in separate brigades that will only meet when strictly necessary, and of course will wear masks at all times.

Finally, I want to make sure that we all have a shared perspective: we are on the final stretch of a historic mission here. As the heads of state and government have reminded us, this mission is not only about the future of our bilateral relationship with the United Kingdom, but also about the future of the European Union itself. We must keep this objective in mind, stand firm, and live up to our responsibility.

As I disembark from the Eurostar at St Pancras station, a crowd of journalists, photographers and cameramen are waiting for me and surround my car, until the police politely ask them to clear the way. 'I think it's very important to be back at the table', I tell them in English. 'Every day counts. The European Union and the United Kingdom share a huge common responsibility.'

The whole team gets back to its usual routine at the Conrad Hotel. After a day of work at the eleven tables, the British offer us a '1 + 5' dinner at Lancaster House. They put on a great spread and bring out some good French wines from the cellar.

We agree on the schedule for the next few days. To avoid our teams having to travel too often, I propose that we stay until next Wednesday, including the weekend, and that they then come to Brussels, staying there for All Saints' weekend.

The dinner is obviously not a working session, but it must be made use of, and I ask David Frost specifically about two points: 'If you want an agreement like we do, when is the right time to conclude it? Does that timing depend, for you, on the US election on 3 November?' The British Chief Negotiator is adamant, clearly protesting too much: 'The US election has no bearing upon this negotiation.'

Many analysts believe, however, that Boris Johnson himself will be tempted to wait for the verdict from the American ballot box before deciding whether to make a deal with us. Rightly or wrongly, the re-election of Donald Trump would be a relief for him. He has often demonstrated his partiality for the American president. On the contrary, Joe Biden will be keen to re-establish a more balanced relationship with the European Union, which he will no doubt consider to be the principal partner of the US. And, above all, Mr Biden will be very vigilant in ensuring that the Good Friday (Belfast) Agreement, threatened by the British Internal Market Bill, is respected.

That is the subject of my second question to David Frost: the bill is being discussed in the House of Lords, which has already rejected it once. It will come back on 12 November and then return to the House of Commons. Could this legislative timetable have anything to do with the timing of our agreement? The British know that any agreement on our future relationship will only be ratified in the European Parliament if the contentious proposals are removed from this legislation.

David Frost is equally categorical on this, again rather too much so: 'It's completely unrelated.' And he sees fit to add that the British government will present its Budget Bill in mid-November and that it will include a third provision challenging the Protocol on Ireland and Northern Ireland, this time on VAT. I note this point and reply curtly: 'You know your responsibilities on this issue, and you will have to assume them.'

Apart from this exchange with Mr Frost, I also explain to the British team what happened at the European Council, and ask them about the situation in the UK. The answers are disarming. According to my interlocutors, Boris Johnson's latest speech has reassured everyone. Everyone is now quite happy with the prospect of a no deal. The private sector is ready for it. Adviser Oliver Lewis adds: 'All the MPs I have met are now very informed and very calm.' In short, *tout va très bien, madame la marquise!* 'Brexit is no longer at the top of the agenda', adds David Frost. What do they take us for?

I reply in a very serious tone that we are very impressed by this new situation, that we congratulate them, but that on the European side we are not quite so sanguine. Is this what the British call 'wishful thinking'? Is the Prime Minister being led to believe that, deal or no deal, everything will be fine, or at least no worse? We know very well that a no deal would be a very serious matter for the European Union, and even more so for the United Kingdom.

As the cheese course comes around, I deliberately put a dampener on things by speaking the truth about this first day in London between our teams. On each of the eleven tables, we put down texts. Immediately, the British set in motion a two-speed negotiation, pushing for legal discussion on all the subjects that interest them, such as goods and services, and going back on certain past agreements, for example on sanitary and phytosanitary controls, which cannot be the object of any discrimination between EU member states. They tried to find leverage wherever they could across all the negotiating tables, and refused any commitment on key issues for the European Union. No progress was made on the level playing field or on governance, even less so on fisheries.

'Your negotiating technique today has been a masquerade', I say to the British negotiators. 'You're trying to play with us. I'm not going to accept this attitude for very long. If you want an agreement, you will have to move on the important issues for us.'

David Frost feigns astonishment at such a stern judgement. I suggest that we talk about it again tomorrow morning at 8.30 when we do the table-by-table examination, and I get up from the table.

Monday, 26 October 2020: Creativity required

Over the weekend I made a brief return trip to Brussels, where I took the opportunity to brief the President's office. Over the last few days Ursula von der Leyen has met with the French Prime Minister, Jean Castex, and the Dutch Prime Minister, Mark Rutte. Both reaffirmed their determination on one essential point: if the British want an agreement, they will need to propose a credible framework for a level playing field.

Upon my return to London today, the situation had not changed: after five days of intense discussions, it was still a two-speed negotiation. I tell David Frost that the negotiations cannot continue like this for very long. If the talks are not concluded by the beginning of next week, early November, I will have to report to the Council and the European Parliament, and publicly give reasons for the lack of progress.

In order to move forward, I therefore propose to David Frost that we devote Wednesday, our last day in London this week, to a series of in-depth discussions at Chief Negotiator level on three key topics: fisheries, the governance of our future agreement, and trade in goods and services. I indicate that we are prepared to be creative, but that this creativity cannot be a one-way street.

Tuesday, 27 October 2020: Herring and blue whiting

On fisheries, there are two main sticking points: the issue of access to waters and the issue of quotas.

On access to waters, the British have not given up on their idea of an 'annual guillotine'. They still propose to wait for the outcome of the annual negotiations on total fishing opportunities, and then determine each party's quotas and grant access to waters.

To break the deadlock, we propose to link access to waters not to an annual negotiation on total fishing opportunities, but to the level of fishing considered sustainable by scientists. As long as this scientifically sustainable level of fishing is not exceeded, access to waters would be maintained.

On the thorny issue of quotas, we have already proposed to increase quotas on twenty-eight stocks identified by the UK as priorities. It's a significant offer, which we are ready to rework, in particular by including pelagic stocks such as mackerel, herring and blue whiting.

But I want to be clear: in terms of magnitude, none of the heads of state or government concerned will be able to go to their fishing ports – to Boulogne-sur-Mer, Zeebrugge, Killybegs, Thyborøn – and convincingly justify a huge reduction in fishing opportunities. '15 to 18 per cent maximum. This is a simple, unavoidable political reality, which I believe can be explained to your Prime Minister. So we have to find ways to work around that.'

I therefore propose to David Frost a 'toolbox' that could help us find pragmatic solutions, for example by introducing a 'surplus' mechanism. Indeed, thanks to our common fisheries policy, we have seen an increase in certain stocks. On these stocks, for a limited period, we could allow the future increase in total annual fishing possibilities to be distributed in favour of the UK over the EU.

Finally, we can of course work on a transition period, provided that there is a clear position on the distribution of allowances at the end of this period.

'In any case', I say to Mr Frost, 'there will be a net benefit to you and a loss to us on fisheries, but the loss must be justifiable and explainable. No European leader could justify opening our markets to British companies and closing British waters to our fishermen. And it is those leaders who will have the final say on the deal, unanimously.'

In responding, Mr Frost is calm and courteous as usual, but not very constructive: 'Your toolkit is useful', he tells me, 'but you have to understand that you can't get access to water without a big change in the existing quotas.'

Friday, 30 October 2020: A misunderstanding

After a rare day without negotiations, we take up the discussions again, this time in Brussels. Covid restrictions are tightening, with a second wave sweeping across much of Europe. The British, who had planned to stay for a week, may have to leave for London sooner than expected. All the more reason to speed up the discussions!

However, after two intensive days at the European Commission's Albert-Borschette Centre, little progress has been made. As one of our

team members put it, it's as if the British were beginning a year's negotiations, not a week's...

In the middle of this week in Brussels, the British asked to meet
Stéphanie Riso, who as deputy-head of Ursula von der Leyen's cabinet
continues to follow the negotiations closely. The next day, reviewing the
discussions chapter by chapter, I realized that a serious misunderstanding
had arisen from this meeting. As they have been trying to do for the
past four years, the British think that they have opened a second line of
negotiation.

I have invited David Frost to lunch today in the dining-room on the
thirteenth floor of the Berlaymont. Nothing fancy. It is quite natural
to return the many invitations received in London and to try to renew
contact in a more informal way.

But David Frost and Tim Barrow are slow to arrive. The few members
of David Frost's team who are there, Oliver Lewis and Matthew Taylor,
are delighted with Clara's tour of the thirteenth floor and the College of
Commissioners' room. But still no David Frost. We wait for forty-five
minutes before he arrives.

The lunch starts badly, without any explanations for the delay. As far
as substantial matters go, David Frost, in a rather arrogant tone, gives
me to understand that all the important subjects of negotiation will
henceforth be dealt with at the level of the President of the European
Commission and the British Prime Minister. This method clearly runs
contrary to my mission and my responsibility. It is also not the most
effective method, since it is unimaginable that all of these issues could be
tackled at the level of Ursula von der Leyen and Boris Johnson without
first ensuring that they have been clarified and fully developed.

I reply to David Frost that, indeed, there are a number of disagreements which, on my side, will have to be taken up for final arbitration
at the level of the President of the Commission and, I would add, that
of the President of the European Council, who has given me a mandate.

I can see that this last point causes some confusion on the British
side, particularly for Tim Barrow, who obviously had not considered
including the European Council in this parallel line of negotiation.

This afternoon, I apprise Stéphanie Riso of the situation: 'I don't
know what was said in your office, but the negotiation is going off the
rails.' She very quickly understands that I will not accept these methods.

She promises me that she will make it clear to the British that there has been a misunderstanding between them, and that from now on she will involve Clara or Paulina in all her meetings with the British.

And in fact, the next day the whole thing is over with. David Frost suggests that I should do as much arbitration as possible at the level of our negotiating teams, primarily between our deputies, Clara and Paulina on our side, Tim Barrow and Lindsay Appleby on his, and, where necessary, at our level. Only a few points, the most sensitive ones, may be submitted at the last minute to the President of the Commission and the British Prime Minister. And I still think that the European Council and its members, as well as the European Parliament, should be involved in this final compromise.

Tuesday, 3 November 2020: Governance

In recent days, two important steps forward have been made in the negotiations: first, on a number of key principles of our agreement. For example, both parties have committed to the Paris climate agreement. Second, we now have stable texts on the institutional framework for our agreement.

The stumbling block is that at this stage we do not know to which areas this framework will apply. The British are insisting on separate agreements on fisheries, internal security cooperation, information security and civil nuclear energy to run alongside the main text. For our part, we want at least a coherent economic package. And there is no question of isolating fisheries from this package. If the British were ever to decide to withdraw from the fisheries agreement, all of our economic relations would be called into question.

Finally, if the British insist on building this 'final governance package' without giving any role to the EU Court of Justice, we need a clear dispute settlement mechanism and the possibility of cross-suspension in case of noncompliance with the agreement.

Following the same logic, a link must be established with the Withdrawal Agreement: in case of violation of the Withdrawal Agreement by one party, the other party must be able to take measures to suspend any future agreement.

Sunday, 8 November 2020: And the winner is…

After two days of videoconference meetings we return to the Eurostar terminal at Brussels Midi station on a Sunday evening for another group departure for London. With the required social distancing, even in its pared-down form the team occupies three carriages of the train. It's a pleasant moment, allowing everyone to relax a little before the long days of negotiations that lie ahead. Yesterday, after a long wait for the final results, the world learned that Joe Biden had been elected in the United States. The BBC is repeatedly playing a clip of the president-elect walking past journalists. One of them calls out to him: 'Mr President, a question for the BBC.' And Joe Biden replies with a smile: 'The BBC? I'm Irish!' In the aftermath of this long campaign, much of the commentary on British television is about what will become of the famous 'special relationship' between the UK and the US.

It is clear that Boris Johnson engaged too much with Donald Trump, sometimes heavy-handedly. Similarly, Donald Trump advertised his support for Brexit all too often, even appearing alongside Nigel Farage. All of this will leave its mark. The US and the UK will always have a special relationship, which is something other Europeans need to under-stand. But I doubt that Joe Biden will have a special relationship with Boris Johnson.

What is certain is that this election means that the government in London has lost the leverage it wanted to generate in our negotiations by holding Ireland hostage. It is now certain that the famous Internal Market Bill will have to be dumped at some point.

Will this new situation encourage Boris Johnson to reach a deal with us? I have long thought so, even though I don't believe that a deal is quite as imminent as some media outlets claim. Yesterday, Mr Johnson and President von der Leyen spoke again, and it was clear that there are still differences, which make this agreement unlikely as yet.

Monday, 9 November 2020: Mr Churchill's competition

This morning I repeat Ursula von der Leyen's message during a bilateral discussion with David Frost: 'We are prepared to redouble our efforts to find an agreement, and we believe that an agreement is possible this week. But for that to happen, we need to see a real commitment from you to find solutions on the European red lines.'

'I also think that a deal is possible this week', says David Frost, 'even if it will be difficult.'

'In that case, David, we will take more time.'

I can see that the British, who know that our ratification procedures are more complex than theirs, now want to blame the time pressure on us. My aim is to show them that we are not willing to come to an agreement at any cost.

As my assistant Barthélemy reminds me, this Monday, 9 November, is a special day. It is fifty years since the French learned in the early hours of the morning that General de Gaulle had died. I was nineteen at the time and my involvement some years earlier in the young Gaullist movement remains one of the things I am most proud of.

Thanks to the friendly intervention of Catherine Colonna, the French Ambassador in London, the doors of 4 Carlton Gardens are opened for us at 1pm. It was in this building, on the second floor, that General de Gaulle set up the modest offices of the Free French a few months after his arrival in London.

It is with great emotion that we visit these rooms, which, unfortunately, have not been preserved in their original state, except for a large clock that was in the meeting room at the time. On the way back down the stairs, I remember a photograph taken at this very spot, of young French people waiting on the stairs to be registered.

Beyond the controversy and turbulence of Brexit, there remains the immediate solidarity of the British with this general who came to represent France. In a tweet I cite this passage from the General's war memoirs, which Barthélemy searched out for me:

Already in the afternoon of June 17, I outlined my intentions to Mr Winston Churchill. Washed up from a vast shipwreck upon the shores of England, what could I have done without his help? He gave it to me at once [...].

Wednesday, 11 November 2020: New ideas

Another discussion on fisheries. Once again, I tell David Frost that the European Union would be prepared to reduce its fishing opportunities in British waters by 15, perhaps even 18 per cent. The British, on the other hand, are asking for a reduction of … 80 per cent. 'We can't find a permanent solution on the current basis of our discussion', Mr Frost tells me.

Behind this thought I think there is the idea of a review clause, or even a sunset clause, which would automatically terminate our agreement at the end of a predefined period.

I simply tell Mr Frost that any time limit on our fisheries agreements will mean the same limit being applied to our entire economic agreement. 'I understand', he replies soberly.

On the level playing field, it's a real cold shower. The British are blocking everything, both on the reciprocal control of state aid and on non-regression in relation to current common norms and standards. But application of these rules of economic fair play is a fundamental condition that has been set by the EU for more than four years – a condition in which each of the twenty-seven member countries of the Union has a direct interest, which explains their unwavering unity on the subject.

But the British are hiding behind their new-found sovereignty to refuse any serious commitment. It is clear that their idea is to use this regulatory autonomy, acquired with Brexit, as a dumping tool against us.

I know at this moment that if they do not budge, there will be no agreement. In fact, they are making a twofold mistake: by blocking negotiation on this issue, the subject of fisheries, which directly concerns eight countries out of twenty-seven, will no longer be isolated at the very end of the negotiation. But even more than this, they are mistaken in thinking that the twenty-seven member states will be interested in a trade agreement in the absence of these common rules.

I tell David Frost that if it persists, this disagreement will lead to a no deal. I add that it would be easy for us to explain that the British do not want economic fair play, that they are seeking to create opportunities for dumping, and that, in these conditions, we will not open up the Single Market without tariffs and quotas on British products.

I then ask David Frost nine precise questions. His answers are more amicable, but still very vague. I suggest that, if he wants to give this negotiation one last chance to succeed, we intensify meetings at our level, staying in London until Friday and then meeting again in Brussels on

Sunday. Without hesitation he accepts this new timetable, which to me is a sign that he wants a deal.

Mr Frost also tells me in passing that, on the question of state aid, his government would be amenable to a two-year phasing-in period during which the new regulations would not apply and the British would be able to help their companies without any controls from us. According to David Frost, this would be the time needed to deal with the exceptional situation of Covid-19 through massive public investment. It is probably also a question of preparing for the next general election, when Boris Johnson will have to answer to the people. This request brings with it the risk that some British companies will be massively supported by public funds and will compete with our own companies before the new state aid regime comes into force. But the proposal has at least the merit of being clearly formulated.

On this day, 11 November, at precisely 11am, along with all Britons we join David Frost's team in observing a two-minute silence in memory of the millions of soldiers who have died in battle since 1914. Among them were many young Britons who lost their lives to liberate Europe. Today, those 'civil wars' between Europeans seem a long way off. This, also, is part of the success story of the European Union.

Saturday, 14 November 2020: A risky bet

David Frost and his team return to Brussels tomorrow. Up on the thirteenth floor, we review the situation with the President. Faced with yesterday's impasse and with time running out, how should we respond? I present the President with the state of play. On the level playing field, fisheries and governance, deadlock. 'And the other issues?', she asks.

'We can see landing zones on the other major areas of negotiation. But we need to keep our cards close to our chest for the final stage. On transport, we have not yet told the British how far we can go in terms of access to our markets: cabotage for lorries, the "fifth freedom" for aviation. Similarly, on services, we have not yet put our entire offer on the table. They are extremely demanding. Finally, on goods, there is still the question of rules of origin, a key issue for them. They want to know exactly which UK-produced goods will enter our market tariff-free.'

The President replies: 'Stéphanie thinks we should put it all on the table now.'

There are clearly pros and cons. I can see the point of creating a sudden shock. In any negotiation, someone has to 'jump first'. On the other hand, there is a risk that the British will pocket our concessions without giving us anything in return. That has been their attitude since the beginning of these negotiations. I also believe that it is not our offers at the negotiating table that will unblock the process, but the political context in London that will determine if and when agreement is reached.

But I allow myself to be convinced that this risk is worth taking. In a negotiation, one should never have regrets. Deal or no deal, we can show what steps we have taken towards the UK.

Clara and I leave the President's office with hopes of a new dynamic. By putting definite offers on all the negotiating tables, if the British play ball we may be able to conclude next weekend.

Friday, 20 November 2020: Quarantine

On Sunday it was the turn of the British to take the Eurostar. The deadline of the end of October, which we had set ourselves to allow time for ratification, has long passed. David Frost continues to greet each of my thoughts with 'Very useful, Michel!' But every time he tells us that it is not yet the right moment, that we need to consult his Prime Minister, or that he needs more time.

Yesterday I felt like we were a long way off. In the event, our strategy didn't work. The British pocketed all the concessions we made without giving us anything in exchange. We'll have to go back to the old-fashioned method of resistance. David Frost tells us that he needs further consultations in London. Hopes of a swift conclusion are fading.

It is at precisely this moment that a member of my delegation, sitting next to me, receives a call on her mobile phone, goes out of the room to answer it, comes back a few seconds later and picks up her papers, telling us: 'I tested positive for Covid-19.'

Once again, Covid has hit the negotiations. We have to stop, talk to the whole team, and urgently organize a test for everyone, including the British. But the physical negotiations will definitely be interrupted, at least for a week, in order to respect the quarantine rules currently in force in Belgium.

Wednesday, 25 November 2020: Confined at home

This week is inevitably chaotic, in every way. In isolation at home, we try as best we can to negotiate via screens. Personally, I find it tiring to spend the day reading legal texts and discussing them in front of a screen with the British, my close negotiating team and, every evening, all my colleagues from the Directorates-General.

I have often had the feeling in recent months that the British were playing for time. This virtual negotiation week gives them a real, indisputable excuse to further drag out the negotiations. We must respond in kind. No more movement on our positions.

Saturday, 28 November 2020: European students in the UK

After another negative test for the whole team, we headed back to London yesterday. Despite the fatigue and tension, all team members are at their posts during this last week of virtual negotiations.

In London, where we are back in our hotel probably for the last time, the atmosphere is extremely focused. In a message to all negotiators, I emphasize the need to remain confident and united, and to maintain good coordination between the task force, led by Clara and Paulina, the Directorates-General, and Stéphanie Riso, our daily link with the President. One team, united.

Once again we experience ups and downs. Each of the negotiating tables is moving forward. Luca Rossi and his team, responsible for security, external relations, climate and energy issues in the task force, close the chapter on judicial and police cooperation with their counterparts.

But the next morning, as we seek to reach conclusions on cooperation on social security, the British demand that EU students who come to the UK pay extra for their healthcare. There is no possible reason for this except deliberate discrimination against foreign students as compared to British students. We are making this a matter of principle. The British are trying to bargain for the opening of the European market to their service companies. At my side, Stéphanie Riso threatens them: 'If you don't settle this student issue, the whole social cooperation chapter will fall with it.' A solution is found after two more days.

Monday, 30 November 2020: End of the road

The day begins with the issue of road transport. We reach an agreement with David Frost on the rights and obligations of operators. The UK accepts fair competition rules specific to this sector, including drivers' working hours. Our agreement provides for reciprocal market access, but with British trucks limited to two further operations on the Continent. Later in the day, the chapters on EU programmes and nuclear safety cooperation are also concluded.

Wednesday, 2 December 2020: Hot and cold

On Monday, a vote in the House of Commons on measures to tackle Covid-19 revealed the first serious cracks in Boris Johnson's majority, with fifty-six Tory MPs voting against the government. It's a warning: these are the most radical MPs, hard-line Brexiteers. Boris Johnson knows very well what it means because, for a year and a half, it was he who led this kind of charge against Theresa May and finally brought her down.

What should our analysis of this vote be? Boris Johnson may want to speed up the negotiations and conclude them, and thus 'deliver' Brexit, stealing a march on his right-wing MPs. But, on the other hand, he may pander to the right wing and try to appease it by rallying it against any kind of agreement with the EU.

When we arrive on Wednesday, David Frost tells us for the first time that he has 'a mandate to conclude'. The words resonate in the large room we are occupying in order to maintain social distancing.

So has Boris Johnson chosen the first option? There is a sense of relief in our team, and a feeling that European time and British time could finally fall into step by the end of this week. The negotiation is regaining the necessary momentum to close the remaining chapters.

But progress is difficult on the level playing field, we are still going around in circles on fisheries, and the British are still stuck on governance

– though all the economic issues are moving forward, as they obviously want them to.

By blowing hot and cold, the British may be trying to get us to empty our pockets while refusing to move on our priorities. I am aware of this possible strategy. However, all the legal work on each of the subjects of this 1,200-page treaty is necessary anyway, and we are not giving up anything that it is against the interests of the European Union to give up.

Saturday, 5 December 2020: A final blockade?

On Friday, David Frost and I realized that we weren't finished yet. It's not that they are leaving the table, nor that we are. It's just that the differences are still too great on the three main sticking points. Besides which, the UK continues to make demands on issues that fall outside our mandate on rules of origin and financial services, including a commitment from the EU to allow cross-border financial transactions by UK-based asset managers.

This morning we leave London with a deadlock. The fatigue of these ten days, of negotiations in London, including long evenings, is hitting the team hard. There is also a certain weariness born of the feeling that the outcome of all the efforts we might make in these negotiations actually depends on the vicissitudes of British politics, which are largely beyond our control. Several of my close associates tell me that they think that no agreement will be possible, and that we will probably have to go along with a no deal in order to get people to focus and find solutions.

Nevertheless, contacts with Boris Johnson have intensified, which is a sign. On our return from London, he and Ursula von der Leyen spoke. They themselves also saw that we had reached a deadlock, but asked us to resume discussions the next day.

Monday, 7 December 2020: A war of nerves

We are entering a crucial week on the European side, as the European Council meets to come to an agreement on the budget for the next seven years and on the €750 billion recovery plan. Obviously, the twenty-seven, Charles Michel, Angela Merkel and the German Presidency want to focus on issues other than Brexit over these two days, and that's fine.

On the negotiating side, the British are playing hardball. In another telephone conversation, Boris Johnson and Ursula von der Leyen delve a little deeper into the details. The Prime Minister comments in a fatalistic tone: 'We tried, but the differences are too great. Now we have to think about what we can do to protect the citizens, the poor people who will suffer from a no deal. Why not take the pieces of the agreement that are already in place and implement them right away, on energy, transport, social security, safety?'

We know that this is a strategy that has been pursued by some in London from the outset: negotiating separate agreements only on those issues of interest to the UK.

Boris Johnson mentions rather heavy-handedly that he wants to have a meeting with Emmanuel Macron to discuss fisheries, and with Angela Merkel to discuss the level playing field. These are two Community remits that must be dealt with by the European Commission, and President von der Leyen told him so. A few hours later, we learned that both the French President and the German Chancellor had refused to accept Boris Johnson's calls, in order to preserve a single negotiating line.

The Prime Minister, it seems to me, is beginning to realize the consequences of a no deal. I'm sure he wants to avoid it, but at the same time he remains dependent on the seventy most extreme Tory MPs. Nevertheless, he says that he is open to a face-to-face meeting with Ursula von der Leyen, who immediately invites him to Brussels. I can hear his hesitation. He has bad memories of Theresa May's successive visits to the European Commission's headquarters, from which she came away empty-handed. But finally he accepts, and an appointment is made for dinner on Wednesday evening.

Wednesday, 9 December 2020: The return of Boris Johnson

Before this dinner, the British offer a sign of goodwill. Together with Maroš Šefčovič, my team has been looking for and finding technical solutions for the proper implementation of the Withdrawal Agreement in Northern Ireland. This work, on the issues of sanitary and phytosanitary controls, VAT, state aid and risky products, has borne fruit. The British government has finally agreed to end the crisis triggered by its Internal Market Bill, as Michael Gove has accepted a practical solution to ensure that controls and trade in Northern Ireland are carried out in accordance with EU law. Just in time, the UK government announces the withdrawal of the bill's contentious proposals. A lot of wasted time and controversy only to end up simply honouring their own signature and applying what had already been decided upon and ratified.

This evening, as he boards the plane to Brussels, Boris Johnson tweets: 'A good deal is still there to be done. But whether we agree trading arrangements resembling those of Australia or Canada, the United Kingdom will prosper mightily as an independent nation.'

The meeting at Berlaymont is a bit like the one in Luxembourg with Jean-Claude Juncker back in September 2019. In both cases, I get the impression that Boris Johnson has not taken the time to go into the details himself with his team before meeting the President of the European Commission. Ursula von der Leyen is well prepared. She calls me at 4pm to check an important point about fishing quotas.

Before coming to the table, President von der Leyen and Prime Minister Johnson have a long one-to-one. A three-hour discussion then begins, allowing each of them to explain their points of contention and to lay out what margins of flexibility are available. On several occasions, on the fisheries issue, Boris Johnson barks: 'I want to be extremely generous with the fishermen. I can be flexible. But I need to show real change in three years' time at the latest, at election time. We need to regain our sovereignty, unconditionally, as soon as possible.' I reply: 'No one is disputing your sovereignty over your waters. For fishing, if we have an agreement, you will win and we will lose out. It's easier to explain one way than the other. But if we lose too much, it becomes unjustifiable and inexplicable. How can you explain that the only people to lose their jobs immediately because of Brexit will be European fishermen?'

We move on to the level playing field, where his main demand, once again, is sovereignty. 'I cannot accept the framework that you are imposing on us on state aid. I am prepared to be generous on fish. We have thought about equivalence on the level playing field. We could move in your direction, but we don't want to agree to any incentive mechanisms under another name.'

Mr Johnson is trying again to get separate agreements on issues that are already negotiated. The President replies that it is not possible to make a piecemeal agreement. Mr Johnson insists: 'We could even, in the event of disagreement, show a willingness to cooperate with a treaty on foreign policy and defence.' There is general astonishment on our side, since less than a year ago it was the UK that brutally opposed any discussion on this subject. I point out to him: 'But Boris, it was you who refused to open a chapter on defence, cooperation and foreign policy in the negotiations.' And he replies: 'How me? Who gave this instruction?', looking at his collaborators. The stage-management continues.

This evening, however, does not bring a breakdown of negotiations. President von der Leyen still wants to be constructive: 'We must ask our teams to continue working on these major issues. There may still be solutions. I would like you to come back on Sunday to make a final assessment.' Boris Johnson does not commit himself to returning, but makes it conditional on the outcome of the last few days of discussions.

Frankly, like Clara and Stéphanie Riso, who are at this dinner, I am tired of this constant back and forth and endless discussion of the same subjects. If there is a way forward, I am willing to take it in the next few days, but it is a very narrow path indeed.

Thursday, 10 December 2020: Gauging the real effects of a no deal

The day after this dinner, the Commission publishes the set of targeted emergency measures that we have envisaged to prepare for the no-deal scenario. These measures are limited, temporary, subject to reciprocity and can in no way replicate the benefits of the Single Market. They do, however, avoid the most radical disruptions on 1 January by ensuring basic road and air connectivity between the EU and the UK and by granting EU and UK vessels reciprocal access to each other's waters.

Sunday, 13 December 2020: A 'political agreement'…

What followed the Brussels dinner proved very disappointing. Despite a new round of discussions with David Frost, we are once more at a virtual standstill. As at the end of October, David Frost refuses to engage in dialogue on several substantial points – in particular, the maintaining of a level playing field over time. And on fisheries, the British are even taking serious steps backwards. A 'political agreement' has been reached,

Mr Frost tells me several times, justifying himself and thus avoiding giving any answer on the substance.

We have once again to clarify that there is only one line of negotiation. At my side, in a meeting with David Frost and Tim Barrow, Stéphanie Riso sends the message clearly: 'The scope of this global agreement has been known from the beginning. Fisheries is a part of it. You cannot hide behind traditional fisheries agreements. We are in a totally new context, in this negotiation with a country that is leaving the European Union. This agreement will only be concluded with a correct level playing field and an acceptable agreement on fisheries.'

Today, in a discussion with Boris Johnson, Ursula von der Leyen for the first time sets a deadline for the negotiations. In view of the demands of the Council and the European Parliament, everything must be completed by next Wednesday. For an agreement of such importance, working in a hurry at the last moment is obviously not good practice from the point of view of respecting interinstitutional cooperation and democratic exigencies. But this negotiating timetable is the choice of the British, not ours. David McAllister, head of the European Parliament's coordination group, among the many ministers and MEPs I regularly brief on the negotiations, assures me of the European Parliament's continued support. His name may not suggest it, but David is German. He is the energetic and capable chairman of the Parliament's Foreign Affairs Committee, and has a perfect grasp of German and European politics. The trust between us is based on four years of transparency.

Wednesday, 16 December 2020: 'A matter of a few mackerel'

The British negotiators are still in Brussels, but it is taking them longer and longer to take a position or to react to our demands, and time is passing.

Today Boris Johnson chooses to crank up the arrogance: 'Michel Barnier has proposed seven years of transition and 22 per cent on fishing quotas. We can't accept this. Sovereignty cannot be regained after seven years. You cannot deliver on your mandate. And if this continues, we will come back to equivalence in regard to the level playing field.'

The British have undoubtedly taken a step towards us by accepting that a distortion of competition through massive state aid or deregulation justifies the other side's responding in order to protect itself. This is what we call rebalancing. But since then they have been trying to put constraints and deadlines on this 'belt-and-braces' mechanism so that, in reality, the mechanism will not work.

'We need a fresh wind in this negotiation', continues Johnson. 'The member states must give us more flexibility. If they don't, we'll be moving towards an Australian model.' Australia is definitely the reference of choice here. The Australian Prime Minister Scott Morrison, meanwhile, has just said that the Australian model amounts to zero...

Ursula von der Leyen does not want to be the one to close the door. She knows that the blame game can work against us. Whatever happens, the Commission will remain available for dialogue and negotiation with the British until 31 December and beyond. But today she has a better understanding of what I have often told her, sometimes without being understood by her cabinet.

The last few days have seen intense exchanges with the sherpas of the main countries with an interest in the fisheries issue. On Tuesday, I myself alerted them to the state of the negotiations – so as to avoid any surprises. Trust, which lies at the heart of the Union's position, is based on taking into account the interests of all member states.

The fisheries issue is one of the conditions for economic agreement, just like the rules of fair competition. It is not a secondary issue, nor is it 'a matter of a few mackerel' as I once heard someone say. It concerns men and women who work hard and in dangerous conditions – courageous communities that provide a living for entire territories along the coast. As I will say publicly this Friday before the European Parliament plenary session: 'It would be neither fair nor acceptable for European fishermen to have only transitional rights in UK waters, which would one day simply evaporate, while everything else in the deal – especially for UK companies – remains stable.'

Saturday, 19 December 2020: A proposal on fisheries

The whole team is back in the office. Thanks to our assistants, housekeeping follows and everyone has a packed lunch and dinner with a salad. Scant consolation for a seventh consecutive weekend stolen from our families.

I appreciate the efforts, and often sacrifices, made by each and every team member. I hope that those who read this Diary will not see the negotiation as a series of meetings held just at my level with my British counterparts and European officials. That would not be fair, nor would it be true. In between these official moments there were endless days of discussion, negotiation and tension, directed with great tenacity and patience by Clara and Paulina, and before them by Sabine Weyand and Stéphanie Riso, along with the members of the task force.

Today we have a series of conversations with the European capitals, and the stumbling block now is clearly fishing, which the British have always wanted to isolate and leave until the end of the negotiations.

Yesterday I took the risk of putting a new proposal on the table. A six-year transition with guaranteed access for European fishermen, after which there would be an annual negotiation with compensation for the EU if the level of access changed. On the issue of quotas, European fishermen would give back to the British 25 per cent of its fishing quotas in UK waters – i.e., €162 million out of every 650. Current access rights of our vessels to UK waters between six and twelve nautical miles from the coast would be broadly preserved.

Emmanuel Macron and the Danish Prime Minister Mette Frederiksen express their surprise at this proposal, which they consider excessive. In my view, this is the final proposal. I know it is at the limits of what is acceptable. I think that European fishermen will understand it, as long as these quotas remain stable thereafter, and providing that, after these six years, we keep in hand the capacity to react or retaliate to any excessive shutting down of access by the British.

I therefore introduce a 'mirror clause' to this offer in the energy chapter, under our own sovereignty. Electricity interconnectivity and cooperation in the North Sea represent an annual gain for the British of between €700 million and several billion euros, a figure that should be set against the €650 million from our fishing activity in British waters. The mirror clause therefore allows for a transition period of six years, and, beyond that, an annual discussion with the British on whether to maintain or discontinue electricity interconnectivity. At 7.34pm I text David Frost:

> Dear David, 27 hours have passed since we last met, at a critical time of negotiation, on the key issue of fisheries, and 24 hours since we sent you

a text reflecting the EU offer. We are still awaiting a formal response from you.

Finally, at 9.30pm, the President asks me to her office to be with her as she receives an envelope. In fact, she already knows what it contains; it is the British response to our proposal on fisheries. 'I don't have a good feeling about this,' she tells me, alongside her Head of Cabinet Bjoern Seibert, before opening the envelope.

The British proposal is unacceptable. It amounts to the destruction of half the European fleets that fish in British waters. Better a no deal, in this case. A bad deal would be definitive for European fishermen, whereas a no deal would not be. Ursula von der Leyen knows that the proposal will not be acceptable, especially to the Danes, Dutch, Irish, Belgians and French.

She then proposes another scenario, which would consist of adopting for two years the entire economic package that has already been finalized, asking the British for the status quo on fisheries, and in two years' time, letting it all go if there is no agreement on fisheries. I tell her that this idea undoubtedly has the advantage of preserving the achievements of our work and avoiding an immediate crisis, but that it has the serious disadvantage of depriving investors of medium- and long-term predictability. Above all, it would put the pressure back on the coastal states alone in two years' time, but without their any longer having the leverage of the global negotiations. Emmanuel Macron, whom she consults on this idea, will hear nothing of it, and I can understand why. It is now clear that we cannot go much further than the proposal I made on Friday.

President von der Leyen also mentions the idea of organizing a videoconference with the twenty-seven to inform them of the situation. I understand the interest in consulting the heads of state or government, but there is also a real risk of isolating the leaders of the coastal countries. 'For four years', I say, 'we have built the unity of the twenty-seven through dialogue, transparency and equal attention for each country, whatever its size. And we have also built solidarity between the twenty-seven. We have found solutions to protect the interests of each of them. Cyprus when it came to British military bases, Spain when it came to Gibraltar, Finland when it came to air services, and of course Ireland when it came to peace and the Good Friday (Belfast) Agreement. Today, between five and eight countries have a major interest in reaching a good agreement on fishing. We must show the same solidarity with them.' The President replies that she is aware of this, and that it is the right line to take.

Sunday, 20 December 2020: Chaos in the UK

At 3pm I go up to the eleventh floor with Georg to meet the British trio, David Frost, Tim Barrow and Lindsay Appleby. Stéphanie Riso joins us. I confirm to them that the European offer on the duration of the transition and on the quota shares is the last one that will be able to achieve unanimity among the twenty-seven European leaders. For the first time in a long time, I have the feeling that Mr Frost is listening to me on this subject.

In the meantime, the situation in London has become very serious in economic, health and social terms. The emergence of an even more contagious variant of Covid-19 has forced Boris Johnson, in a sudden turnaround, to introduce new restrictions which, for many Britons, amount to 'cancelling Christmas'.

EU countries one by one close their borders to the British, including France, which decides to close the Channel Tunnel completely for twenty-four hours pending a coordinated European response. A huge queue of lorries forms in Kent, and many drivers are forced to spend days and nights in precarious conditions, not knowing whether they will be able to get home to their families for Christmas.

This is not a good situation for anyone, but it obviously creates a very serious problem for Boris Johnson. Rationally, the British Prime Minister should not risk adding a no deal to the health crisis.

On the contrary, Mr Johnson needs some good news to warm up the atmosphere of this particular Christmas. And this, undoubtedly, is what is driving the British to continue negotiations, while seeking to make them last longer so as to obtain last-minute concessions. I know the tactic well. It was the same one used by George Osborne, then Chancellor of the Exchequer, on financial regulation, for which I was responsible as European Commissioner from 2009 to 2014. The British delegation would wait until a hard-fought agreement was reached, around two or three in the morning, only to announce that they had just one last detail to sort out – concerning a point that often turned out to be far more than a mere detail.

In the process, all the deadlines have been missed, including the one set by the main groups in the European Parliament, which indicated that their assembly would not be able to examine an agreement if the negotiations lasted beyond Sunday, 20 December. And here we are! If there is an agreement, the Commission will therefore have to propose its application to the member states, pending confirmation of this agreement by a vote in the European Parliament, probably in the early months of 2021.

Monday, 21 December 2020: Rumours of an agreement

A long day of waiting and uncertainty. The rumour mill is in full swing. We are said to be very close to an agreement on fisheries. The EU, we are told, is going to accept a 35 per cent reduction in fishing opportunities in British waters and a five-year transition period. Of course, there is no way this is the case. Most likely the British are trying to shift the negotiations by just putting it out there as established fact.

On the other hand, it is true that the number of subjects still under discussion has been considerably reduced. On the level playing field, thanks to the skill and tenacity of Nicolas von Lingen, Teresa Vecchi and many others, we are almost there. There are just two important points left to resolve in order to preserve the effectiveness and credibility of our approach to state aid: guarantees for the recovery of illegal state aid and binding principles in the energy sector.

We must also remain vigilant on certain British demands, particularly on financial services, where the British want free access to our market for their portfolio managers.

Finally, there is no question of the British participating fractionally in certain EU programmes, nor of their treating EU citizens differently depending on their nationality.

Tuesday, 22 December 2020: Final discussions on the thirteenth floor

With three days to go before Christmas, and in advance of the final moment of truth as to whether it will be deal or no deal, the tension over the most fraught issues is palpable.

Clara has had a meeting with the British Ambassador to the EU Tim Barrow, who, throughout the negotiations, has sought to find solutions where they were difficult to discover. On the level playing field, we are on the way to winning them over. There are only a handful of British demands still open, which appear to be technical but are of considerable importance: financial services, a subject upon which we can at best make a declaration committing ourselves to a regulatory dialogue with the UK; the rules of origin for a few specific products such as electric cars, for which the British are requesting a six-year transition period; and finally, the potential for rebates on customs duties, which the UK wants to be implemented in freeports.

Of course, there is also the question of fisheries, discussions upon which are concentrated in the cabinet of the President; she and her cabinet know my position and the red lines of the member states concerned.

And it is now only at the level of the President of the Commission and the British Prime Minister that these last knots can be untied.

Throughout these negotiations I have kept Ursula von der Leyen regularly informed of our progress. Today I give her a final update on the situation.

'Given the historical and political dimensions of this negotiation', I tell President von der Leyen at the end of my report, 'I have always thought it proper and necessary that its final conclusion should take place directly at your level as President, with Prime Minister Boris Johnson.'

Wednesday, 23 December 2020: Final act

We await this conclusion all day long on 23 December. The signals are good. And, at around 3pm, Boris Johnson and Ursula von der Leyen agree on the phone that an agreement has been reached in principle. 'I think I have good news!', the President tells me.

My team holds its breath because it knows that the devil is in the details – in this case, in the legal text and the fishing quota figures. A long discussion ensues, pushing back the announcement of the agreement hour by hour, with the Commission spokesman finally predicting it will be made at midnight – before advising vigilant journalists to go and get a few hours' rest and set the alarm clock for early the next morning.

I get home around 2am. The inner members of my team stay in the office all night, despite their exhaustion, dissecting the latest legal text that the British have put on the table on fisheries and which has reached us from the thirteenth floor. A text full of traps, false compromises and backtracking. Such a negotiation cannot be concluded without help from the experts! I am grateful here for the support of the Commissioner responsible for fisheries, Virginijus Sinkevičius, and to my colleagues in the Directorate-General for Fisheries Stijn Billiet and Joost Paardekooper, who defend the European positions with great tenacity.

Thursday, 24 December 2020: 'A day of relief, tinged with sadness'

I am back at Berlaymont at 7.30am on Christmas Eve. I needn't have bothered!

Discussions are ongoing. The teams are on the verge of exhaustion, which perhaps explains some of the tensions that are emerging.

Over the preceding hours, Ursula von der Leyen has, as I recommended, made sure to check in personally with the most affected member states about the red lines on fisheries. In this way, by maintaining a very firm position on fisheries, she manages to bring about the final compromise with Boris Johnson on the Union's positions.

A few moments later, I meet David Frost in a large room in Berlaymont. He takes his seat on the right of the President. I am on his left, to witness the agreement with Boris Johnson who joins by videoconference from London.

After nine months of negotiations, this is the last time that I see David Frost, and our final exchange is cold and professional. He knows that I know that up until the last moment he was still trying to bypass me by opening a parallel line of negotiation with President von der Leyen's office. And he knows that he did not succeed in doing so.

Finally, at around 3.30pm, I accompany the President to the press room to announce the agreement.

At this moment, I regret that the journalists who have been so patient throughout this negotiation are not before us in person, but connected via screens. To tell the truth, my feelings are mixed. I am relieved but tired. Proud of the work done by our team, but a little surprised at the way this historic page is being turned, in this way and at this moment.

After Ursula von der Leyen's speech, I open by referring back to the phrase repeated so many times in front of these journalists during the negotiations on the Withdrawal Agreement: 'The clock is no longer ticking.'

I recall the three objectives I have always kept in mind during these three years: preserving peace and stability on the island of Ireland, protecting citizens and the Single Market, and building a new partnership with our neighbour, friend and ally, the United Kingdom.

I admit that my feelings are conflicted: 'Today is a day of relief, but tinged with some sadness, as we compare what came before with what lies ahead.' The UK has chosen to leave the European Union and the Single Market. To give up the rights and benefits of a member state. Our agreement does not replicate those rights and benefits. So despite this agreement, there will be real changes on 1 January for many citizens and businesses. This is the consequence of Brexit. But we have also built a new partnership for the future, around four pillars.

First, an ambitious and fair free trade agreement, without tariffs or quotas. And at the heart of this agreement, a set of new economic rules, the level playing field, which for the European Union inaugurates a new generation of free trade agreements.

Second, an economic and social partnership that is unprecedented in its scope, since it covers air and road transport, energy, the fight against climate change and, of course, fisheries.

The compromise finally reached between Boris Johnson and Ursula von der Leyen consists of a transition period of five and a half years, accompanied by a reduction in fishing quotas in British waters of around 25 per cent. It is a reasonable solution that provides a global basis for reciprocal access to waters and resources. It will require an effort from European fishermen, but I believe that this effort is acceptable, especially as the EU will help the sector via the new Brexit Adjustment Reserve.

Our partnership also includes cooperation in research and innovation, nuclear safety and space, within the framework of existing EU programmes. In this domain, our agreement also contains a clause of non-discrimination between European citizens, which applies equally to visas, services and social security coordination. I have just two regrets about this societal cooperation. That the British government has chosen not to participate in the Erasmus exchange programme, and that the agreement's ambition in terms of free movement of citizens falls short of the historical links between us. Again, this is the choice of the British government.

The third pillar of our agreement is the security of citizens. We have always said that our security – the security of our citizens – is not something to be bargained with. The fight against terrorism and crime requires close cooperation between the EU and the UK. Our work together will be based on two prerequisites: respect for the protection of fundamental rights and respect for personal data. I only regret that the British government did not want to negotiate an agreement on foreign policy, defence and development at this stage.

Finally, the last pillar concerns the governance of this agreement, which will be based on political dialogue and consultation, binding dispute settlement mechanisms, credible implementation in both of our legal systems, and swift and effective remedies and sanctions, including unilateral ones, where necessary.

This is the proposed agreement that we are presenting to the twenty-seven member states and to the European Parliament.

'There should be no surprises', I say, 'since, as with the Withdrawal Agreement, we have constructed this agreement together, step by step, through transparency, respect and dialogue.'

Throughout these four and a half years, the strength of the European Union has been the unity and solidarity between all member states and with the European Parliament.

It has been an honour for me to be a part of this unity among Europeans.

2021

Sunday, 21 February 2021: Paris

Two months have passed since the 'historic' day of 24 December. On that day, the conclusion of the agreement, coming too late in the afternoon, did not allow me to join my wife Isabelle and my family in central France.

Throughout these incessant trips back and forth between Brussels, London and the capitals of Europe, I was always able to rely on Isabelle, who was attentive, always spontaneous, and gave invariably good advice, and also on the unfailing solidarity of my children Nicolas, Laetitia and Benjamin, and their spouses. This meant far more to me than I was ever able to tell them.

I spent that Christmas alone, then. I had become accustomed to this solitude, the 'sweet absence of looks',* during these four years of travel, meetings, public debates and negotiations. Tonight, all of a sudden, the tension fell away.

Strangely, my primary feeling is not satisfaction at a mission accomplished, even less so nostalgia for that extraordinary experience. I have always been wary of nostalgia. I remember in the final moments of the closing ceremony of the Olympic Games, on 23 February 1992, after ten years of effort and sixteen days of magic, Jean-Claude Killy's words: 'Okay, Michel, let's wrap it up!' No nostalgia then, but certainly a great many memories. In particular, memories of the time I shared with a formidable team, which will soon be dissolved but which embodied so well the 'collective morale' that I believe is necessary in public life.

This evening I am thinking first of all of the road that remains to be travelled. The ratification of our agreement by the European Parliament,

---

* Milan Kundera, *Immortality*.

of course, and the explanatory work that goes with it, but also and above all the implementation of our two treaties.

We spent so much time discussing every detail, on fair competition rules, on fisheries, and before that on Ireland and Northern Ireland. But for me, the proper, objective and accurate implementation of these agreements is as important as their negotiation. Any government that acts correctly must attach as much importance to the follow-through as to the announcement. Such attention is neither easy nor, unfortunately, very common.

For tomorrow and for history, there are three things to remain vigilant on in order to ensure that things go well between the UK and Europe.

The first is peace in Ireland, which has been so fragile for twenty years and remains at the mercy of the slightest spark. This is why it was absolutely necessary for the European Commission to quickly correct the mistake it made on 29 January. With the aim of controlling the export of vaccines, a text that had been hurriedly drafted provided for the activation of Article 16 of the Protocol on Ireland and Northern Ireland which, in exceptional circumstances, allows safeguarding measures to be taken – in this case putting controls in place between Ireland and Northern Ireland. This stood in direct contradiction to our efforts and the responsible attitude we had taken over four and a half years precisely so as to avoid the return of a hard border in the middle of the island of Ireland – often in the face of British provocations. And these provocations continue, unfortunately! I am sincerely convinced that the best guarantee of peace and stability lies in the objective implementation of the Protocol, with each of the two parties respecting its signature. In short, the United Kingdom will have to face up to the consequences of Brexit on the island of Ireland as elsewhere.

The second point to be vigilant on is defence of the Single Market. In the UK, musicians, salmon exporters, lorry drivers and service providers have been the first to recognize the serious nature of the regulatory barriers that are a mechanical consequence of Brexit. In an attempt to erase these consequences of Brexit, the British government will seek to re-enter through the windows of the Single Market which it closed the door on itself. We must therefore remain alert to any new form of cherry-picking.

And it won't be long before the UK government seeks to use its new legislative and regulatory autonomy to start constructing competitive advantage sector by sector. Already some ministers are talking about changing working hours, increasing the use of pesticides, or relaxing prudential rules in financial services. Then, familiar questions will arise. Will this competition remain free and fair? Will regulatory competition remain under control or will it become a tool for social, economic and fiscal dumping against Europe? Our trade and cooperation agreement provides us with the tools to react.

Finally, there is a third area of vigilance, more for us on the European side than for the British. We will have to be vigilant to avoid a return to habit, certainty and arrogance in Brussels. As a European Commissioner and then as Chief Negotiator, I have occasionally met senior officials who, with their technical knowledge, look down on politicians, whom they see as easily manipulated, often incompetent and inevitably just passing through, whereas they consider themselves to be in control over the long term. But I have also often worked with European officials who are open, curious and motivated, who are experts in their subject, and who speak three or four foreign languages without ever showing off their knowledge. Each will know who they are. In each of our countries, we must beware of always blaming Brussels for our own weaknesses. As I have written before, there are lessons to be learned from Brexit. There are reasons to listen to the popular feeling that was expressed then and is still being expressed in so many parts of Europe. And to respond to it. This requires time, and a great deal of respect and political courage.

Finally, to those of you who have had the perseverance to read this long Diary to the end, I want to say that I have always seen this extraordinary negotiation from a double perspective.

First of all, the perspective of a history that has often seen the United Kingdom standing in solidarity with Europeans, and in particular with my own country. It is also the history of a great people who have given to Europe and to the world many new possibilities and ingenious inventions, who have opened up new cultural horizons and produced great statesmen and women. At the end of this Diary, I simply wish the best to the British people.

Second, the perspective of the future. A future in which the challenges and risks – pandemics, terrorism, climate change, financial instability – will be so numerous and serious that, well beyond Brexit, we will have new reasons to cooperate.

Acknowledgements

Throughout the negotiation process, I was fortunate to be able to count on an exceptional team, skilfully led by Sabine Weyand and Stéphanie Riso, and later by Clara Martínez Alberola and Paulina Dejmek Hack.

I would like to thank them warmly, and also Marco Abate, Isabelle Alen, Merle Allikvee, François Arbault, Martin Åström, Tristan Aureau, Peter Barany, Adolfo Barberá del Rosal, Ligia Bartkiewicz, Anne Charlotte Becker, Philippe Bertrand, Alexandra Brannigan, Liana Bratusca, Jelena Brejeva, Lieven Brouwers, Raluca-Elena Càlin, Sandra Cavallo, Dorthe Christensen, Sonia Collaco, Randolph De Battista, Stefaan De Rynck, Fabio Della Piazza, Véronique Depovere, Giovanna Di Ruberti, Liliia Dimitrova, Guido Dolara, Elena Dulguerova, Eugenia Dumitriu-Segnana, Antonio Fernández-Martos, Mariano Fernandez-Salas, Maxime Ferrand, Daniel Ferrie, Julie François, Ramunas Freigofas, Stephanie Fromm, Stefan Fuehring, Norbert Gacki, Nicolas Galudec, Urška Grahek, Frédéric Guiot, Matthieu Hébert, Blanca Huergo Gonzalo, Jos Hupperetz, Ivaylo Iaydjiev, Magdalena Jagiełło, Adalbert Jahnz, Tuuli Kainulainen, Jeanne Kindermann, Hannes Kraemer, Christian Krappitz, Arne Kubitza, Nicolas Kuen, Guillaume de La Brosse, Bertrand Lapalus, Justyna Lasik, Thomas Liefländer, Nicolas von Lingen, Martina Lodrant, Sylvie Maudhuit, Michal Meduna, Anne-Laure Mengin, Anouk Mertens de Wilmars, Isabelle Micallef, Emmanuelle Minne, Isabelle Misrachi, Ward Möhlmann, Aurora Mordonu, Jayne Morris, Nathalie Ndjali Ya Longo, Nina Obermaier, Tadhg O'Briain, Silvana Patat, João Pereira, Nicola Pesaresi, Barthélemy Piche, Sonia Plecita Ridzikova, Félix Poirier, Georg Riekeles, Maximiliano Rodríguez Sánchez, Arnaud Rohmer, Felix Ronkes Agerbeek, Luca Rossi, Noura Rouissi, Fabrizio Sacchetti, Claire Saelens, Joel dos Santos Domingo, Uku Särekanno, Maud Scelo, Sebastian Schneider, Marie Simonsen, Nina Sirbiladze, Rachel Smit, Peter Sørensen, Deša Srsen, Anatoly Subocs, Julie Timon, Bence Tóth, Sabine Tuerck, Daniel Vancampenhout, Maria Luisa Van de Westelaken,

Viktória Varga-Lencsés, Teresa Vecchi, António Vicente, Yolanda Villar Ruberte.

This team fluctuated as the negotiations progressed. Some brought in their expertise for a few months, others remained steadfast pillars. All have done the European civil service proud.

I would also like to thank all the men and women of the European Commission's Directorates-General, whom I cannot mention individually, but who have all been recognizable faces and strong voices on all the subjects of these negotiations, from trade to fisheries, via the budget, transport and energy. Not forgetting the thirty interpreters who were on rotation during these four years. Thanks to their precise and efficient work, everyone was able to express themselves in English as well as in French, while retaining the advantage of speaking in their mother tongue.

The team of translators also did an extraordinary job in ensuring that these two treaties were rapidly made available in the twenty-four languages of the European Union. Well beyond the European Commission, this joint project was also supported by many talented and determined colleagues in the European Parliament, the Council, the European External Action Service, and in each member state.

I would like to thank them all.

Glossary

Association Agreement – An agreement between the European Union and a third country creating a framework for cooperation between them, possibly including the development of political, commercial, social, cultural and security links. The legal basis for the conclusion of such an agreement is Article 217 of the Treaty on the Functioning of the European Union.

Backstop – A solution of last resort negotiated with Theresa May's government and set out in the first version of the Protocol on Ireland and Northern Ireland attached to the Withdrawal Agreement, aiming to ensure that there will be no physical border between Ireland and Northern Ireland. The Protocol also commits the UK not to regress on the rights set out in the 1998 Good Friday (Belfast) Agreement, and to protect North–South cooperation.

Brexit Steering Group – Created by and placed under the aegis of the Conference of Presidents within the European Parliament, the Brexit Steering Group was responsible for coordinating and preparing the European Parliament's deliberations and resolutions on the UK's withdrawal. Chaired by Guy Verhofstadt from 2016 to 2019, it comprised six members, each representing a political group in the European Parliament.

Chequers – The UK Prime Minister's holiday residence in Ellesborough. It was here that Prime Minister Theresa May convened her government on 6 July 2018, prior to the publication on 12 July 2018 of the White Paper on the UK's future relationship with the European Union. In this document, the British government called for, among other things, the establishment of a single market for goods only, which it said would have allowed frictionless trade to continue between the European Union and the United Kingdom, while allowing the latter to regain autonomy over its trade policy and the ability to diverge in its regulation of services.

Customs union – The substitution of a single customs territory for two or more customs territories, resulting in the elimination of tariffs and restrictive trade regulations for substantially all trade in products originating in the constituent territories of the union, and in the application by each member of the union of substantially the same tariffs and restrictive regulations for trade with territories outside the union.

DUP (Democratic Unionist Party) – The Democratic Unionist Party is a British political party in Northern Ireland, led from 2015 to 2021 by Arlene Foster. Founded in 1971, it supports socially conservative policies (against abortion and gay marriage in particular), advocates keeping Northern Ireland within the United Kingdom, and has traditionally taken a hard line on this issue, which led it to campaign against the Good Friday (Belfast) Agreement in 1998.

European Council – The European Council brings together the leaders of the European Union's member countries to decide on the EU's political priorities. As such, it represents the highest level of political cooperation between the member states of the Union. It is one of the seven official institutions of the European Union and takes the form of summits, usually held every three months, bringing together all the heads of state or government. It is headed by a permanent president.

Europol – Headquartered in The Hague (Netherlands), Europol is an agency supporting the member states of the European Union in their fight against serious international crime and terrorism.

Financial passport – The European passport allows certain lenders as well as mortgage credit intermediaries and insurance and reinsurance intermediaries to also operate in another member state of the European Economic Area so long as they are licensed or registered with the competent authority in their home member state. There are two types of European passport: one for the freedom to provide services, the other for the freedom of establishment (branches).

Free Trade Agreement – An agreement between two or more customs territories with a view to eliminating tariffs and other restrictive trade regulations on the principal trade in products originating within the territories of the parties.

Good Friday Agreement – Also known as the 'Belfast Agreement', the Good Friday Agreement, signed on 10 April 1998 by UK Prime Minister Tony Blair, Irish Taoiseach Bertie Ahern and the main political forces in Northern Ireland both nationalist and Unionist, brought an end to the troubles that had torn Northern Ireland apart for thirty years.

Level playing field – A framework for fair competition. One of the conditions set by the European Union, given its geographical proximity and economic interconnectedness with the UK, for allowing the UK access to the Single Market without tariffs or quotas.

Single Market – The European Union's internal market is a single market in which, since its creation in 1993, goods, services, capital and people move freely and in which European citizens can live, work, study or do business freely.

Taoiseach – Head of Government of Ireland. This title is equivalent to that of Prime Minister in other member states.

Transition – Transitional period provided for in Articles 126 to 132 of the Withdrawal Agreement, during which the United Kingdom continues to have access to the European Union's Single Market and continues to benefit from Community policies while applying all standards applicable to the member states of the Union, but without being represented within the institutions of the Union (Council, Commission, Parliament, Court of Justice, etc.) or participating in its decision-making mechanisms.

UKIP (UK Independence Party) – Founded in 1993, the UK Independence Party is a British political party. It is a nationalist party that holds anti-immigration positions and advocated the withdrawal of the UK from the European Union.

Chronology

25 March 1957 – Signature of the Treaty of Rome establishing the European Economic Community (EEC) and the treaty establishing the European Atomic Energy Community (Euratom) by six founding countries: France, the Federal Republic of Germany, Belgium, the Netherlands, Luxembourg and Italy.

14 January 1963 – First French veto of the UK's application to join the EEC. In a press conference, General de Gaulle mentions the incompatibility between Continental and island economic interests.

29 September 1967 – The Commission of the European Communities proposes to open accession negotiations with the UK, Ireland, Denmark and Norway immediately.

27 November 1967 – General de Gaulle opposes the entry of the UK for a second time, arguing that the UK's accession to the European Communities would require a radical prior transformation of Britain, both politically and economically.

10 July 1969 – The new President of the French Republic, Georges Pompidou, refers to the new priorities of the EEC with the three words 'completion, deepening and enlargement', paving the way for the first enlargement of the EEC.

7 July 1971 – In the UK, Edward Heath's government publishes *The United Kingdom and the European Communities*, a white paper in which it examines point by point the potential advantages of the country's joining the EEC.

28 October 1971 – In the UK, the House of Commons votes in favour of joining the EEC.

23 April 1972 – In France, a referendum is held on the accession of the United Kingdom, Ireland, Denmark and Norway to the European Communities. The 'Yes' side wins with over 68 per cent of the vote.

1 January 1973 – The United Kingdom, Ireland and Denmark join the EEC. In the end, Norway opts out.

9–12 June 1979 – First election of the European Parliament by universal suffrage. French national Simone Veil becomes its President.

1 January 1981 – Second enlargement. Greece joins the EEC.

25 and 26 June 1984 – Compromise reached in Fontainebleau between the ten heads of state or government on the Communities' budget, after a period of tension with the UK, which felt it was contributing too much. 'I want my money back', Margaret Thatcher said at the time. Since then, the UK has received a rebate on its contribution to the Community budget.

1 January 1986 – Third enlargement: Spain and Portugal join the EEC.

7 February 1992 – The Maastricht Treaty is signed and enters into force on 1 November 1993. It creates the European Union and lays the foundations for the single currency, without the UK or Denmark, which obtain an opt-out clause.

1 January 1995 – Fourth enlargement: Austria, Sweden and Finland join the EU.

2 October 1997 – Signature of the Treaty of Amsterdam, which comes into force on 1 May 1999. Among other things, it establishes an 'area of freedom, security and justice', from which the UK obtains a new opt-out.

1 January 1999 – Creation of the euro, a single currency to which the UK does not belong.

26 February 2001 – Signature of the Treaty of Nice, the aim of which is to reform EU institutions so that the European Union can continue to function effectively after the enlargement involving ten new states planned for 2004.

1 May 2004 – Fifth enlargement: Cyprus, the Czech Republic, Estonia, Hungary, Latvia, Lithuania, Malta, Poland, Slovakia and Slovenia join the EU.

29 May 2005 – The 'No' vote wins in the French referendum on the Treaty establishing a Constitution for Europe. The treaty is then also rejected by a referendum in the Netherlands on 1 June 2005.

1 January 2007 – Sixth enlargement: Bulgaria and Romania join the EU.

13 December 2007 – Signature of the Treaty of Lisbon, which enters into force on 1 December 2009. Article 50 of the Treaty provides for the possibility of a member state leaving the European Union.

11 May 2010 – David Cameron becomes Prime Minister of the UK.

23 January 2013 – In a speech, David Cameron supports a referendum on the UK's membership of the EU. The promise to hold such a referendum is included in the Conservative Party's 2015 general election manifesto.

1 July 2013 – Seventh enlargement: Croatia joins the EU.

1 November 2014 – Jean-Claude Juncker becomes the twelfth President of the European Commission. The following month, Donald Tusk succeeds Herman Van Rompuy as President of the European Council.

23 June 2016 – UK referendum result: 'Leave' wins with 52 per cent of the vote.

13 July 2016 – Theresa May becomes Prime Minister of the UK.

29 March 2017 – The UK gives formal notification of its intention to leave the EU, on the basis of Article 50 of the Treaty on European Union.

29 April 2017 – The European Council adopts its principles and guidelines for the negotiations.

8 June 2017 – In an early general election, the Conservative Party loses its majority in the House of Commons and has to make a deal with the DUP, Northern Ireland's Unionist party.

19 June 2017 – First round of negotiations with the UK on its withdrawal from the EU.

8 December 2017 – The twenty-seven heads of state or government of the European Union consider that sufficient progress has been made in the withdrawal negotiations, opening the way for discussions on the framework of the future relationship.

23 March 2018 – The European Council adopts its guidelines on the framework for the future relationship with the UK after Brexit.

14 November 2018 – Agreement reached with Theresa May on the Withdrawal Agreement and on a Political Declaration setting out the framework for the future relationship.

25 November 2018 – The twenty-seven EU heads of state or government approve the Withdrawal Agreement, which includes the Protocol on Ireland and Northern Ireland, as well as the Political Declaration on the future relationship.

24 July 2019 – Boris Johnson succeeds Theresa May as UK Prime Minister. He calls for the renegotiation of the Ireland and Northern Ireland Protocol.

17 October 2019 – Agreement reached with Boris Johnson on the revised Withdrawal Agreement and Political Declaration. The twenty-seven EU heads of state or government approve both texts.

1 December 2019 – Ursula von der Leyen becomes President of the European Commission. Charles Michel becomes President of the European Council.

1 February 2020 – The UK leaves the EU. Beginning of the transition period during which the rights and obligations of the EU continue to apply to the UK, even though it no longer participates in EU decision-making.

25 February 2020 – The Council adopts the negotiating mandate for the future partnership between the EU and the UK.

2 March 2020 – Launch of formal negotiations on the future partnership between the EU and the UK.

24 December 2020 – EU and UK negotiators agree the Trade and Cooperation Agreement.

1 January 2021 – End of the transition period. The UK leaves the Single Market and Customs Union. The new Trade and Cooperation Agreement applies provisionally, while awaiting ratification by the European Parliament.

Abbreviations

BDA	*Bundesvereinigung der Deutschen Arbeitgeberverbände*, German Confederation of Employers' Associations
BDI	*Bundesverband der Deutschen Industrie*, Federation of German Industries
BEIS	UK Department for Business, Energy and Industrial Strategy
CDU	*Christlich Demokratische Union*, Christian Democratic Union (German political party)
CETA	Comprehensive Economic and Trade Agreement, free trade agreement between the EU and Canada
Coreper	*Comité des représentants permanents*, Committee of Permanent Representatives (EU institution that prepares the agenda for European Council meetings)
COSAC	Conference of Parliamentary Committees for Union Affairs
DIT	UK Department for International Trade
DUP	Democratic Unionist Party (Northern Irish political party)
EBA	European Banking Authority (a regulatory agency of the EU)
ECB	European Central Bank
ECJ	European Court of Justice
ECRIS	European Criminal Records Information System
ECSC	European Coal and Steel Community
EIOPA	European Insurance and Occupational Pensions Authority
EPP	European People's Party (centre-right political party and prominent group in the European Parliament)
ERG	European Research Group (UK research support group of Eurosceptic UK Conservative MPs)
ESCP	*École supérieure de commerce de Paris* (business school with campuses throughout Europe)

ESMA	European Securities and Markets Authority
ETUC	European Trade Union Confederation
Euratom	European Atomic Energy Community
Eurofi	Non-profit organization based in Paris that aims to promote dialogue on the financial industry and financial regulation
FPÖ	*Freiheitliche Partei Österreichs*, Freedom Party of Austria
FTA	free trade agreement
GDR	German Democratic Republic
GNSS	Global Navigation Satellite System
IMF	International Monetary Fund
IOC	International Olympic Committee
MSB	mid-sized business
ÖVP	*Österreichische Volkspartei*, Austrian People's Party
PNR	Passenger Name Record (data provided by air passengers and held by air carriers)
PRS	Public Regulated Service (robust encrypted navigation service for governmental authorized users and sensitive applications, part of the EU's Galileo programme)
REACH	Registration, Evaluation, Authorisation and Restriction of Chemicals (an EU regulation intended to protect chemical risks to human and environmental health)
RPF	*Rassemblement du Peuple Français*, Rally of the French People (French political party founded by Charles de Gaulle in 1947)
SDLP	Social Democratic and Labour Party (Irish social democratic and nationalist political party)
SIS II	Second generation Schengen Information System (a security information system for information exchange on border control, customs and law enforcement)
SME	small to medium-sized enterprise
SPD	*Sozialdemokratische Partei Deutschlands*, Social Democratic Party of Germany
SPÖ	*Sozialdemokratische Partei Österreichs*, Social Democratic Party of Austria
SPS	Sanitary and phytosanitary (refers to measures to protect humans, animals and plants from disease, pests or contaminants)

UCITS   Undertakings for the Collective Investment in Transferable Securities (regulatory framework for the sale of mutual funds across the European territory)

UJP   *Union des jeunes pour le progrès*, Union of Youth for Progress (French pro-Gaullist national youth movement)

UUP   Ulster Unionist Party (Northern Irish conservative and Unionist political party)

Index